LAWYER

From accidents, contracts, and divorce

ON

to lawsuits, real estate and wills –

CALL

a complete guide to more than 130 legal problems

STEVEN MITCHELL SACK
Attorney at Law

PRENTICE HALL

Library of Congress Cataloging-in-Publication Data

Sack, Steven Mitchell
    Lawyer on Call   /   Steven Mitchell Sack. — [Rev. ed.]
        p.   cm.
    Rev. ed. of: The Lifetime Family Legal Guide. c1999.

    ISBN 0-13-042431-5 (ppc)
    1. Law—United States—Popular works.   I. Sack, Steven Mitchell—The Lifetime Family Legal Guide.
    II. Title.
    KF387.S226   1999
    349.73—dc21

                                                                98-29482
                                                                   CIP

This publication is designed to provide accurate and authoritative information in regard to the subject matter covered. It is sold with the understanding that the publisher is not engaged in rendering legal, accounting, or other professional service. If legal advice or other expert assistance is required, the services of a
competent professional person should be sought.

*—From the Declaration of Principles jointly adopted by a Committee of the American Bar Association
and a Committee of Publishers and Associations.*

Printed in the United States of America

10 9 8 7 6 5 4 3 2 1

ISBN 0-13-042431-5 (ppc)

This book was originally published as: *The New Lifetime Legal Guide and the New Lifetime Family Legal Guide*

Copyright © 1996 and 1998 by Steven Mitchell Sack.

This edition was especially created for Book-of-the-Month Club.
All rights reserved.

Legal review of the text was performed by Peter Janovsky,
an attorney at the firm of Zeichner Ellman & Krause.

The editors wish to thank Peter Lohman for his technical contributions.

Printed in the United States of America

PRENTICE HALL
Paramus, NJ 07652

http://www.phdirect.com

To Joan,

with all my love

To Andrew and David,

for future dreams

ACKNOWLEDGMENTS

I would like to thank the following individuals for assisting me in the preparation of this book.

First, I express my gratitude to my literary agent, Alexander Hoyt, for his capable efforts and talents.

I also wish to thank Leslie M. Pockell, my editor at Book-of-the-Month Club. Les guided me in the writing style of this book. I am grateful to have worked with him during the conceptualization, drafting, and production of the text and forms. Les shared my interest in providing the American public with valuable, no-nonsense legal advice, and his vision was compelling.

Faith Hanson's work is greatly appreciated for her capable assistance in editing the book.

In addition, I offer my warmest appreciation to friend and fellow attorney Stanley M. Spiegler, who taught me more about the practice of law than he could ever realize. I also acknowledge the friendship and expertise of Shirley and Larry Alexander, who helped me develop and hone my legal writing skills.

Thanks are given to my brother and law partner Jonathan Scott Sack, Esq., for his love and interest in my work. Of course, personal gratitude is extended to Joan and Sidney Pollack for their constant encouragement and to my wife, Gwen, who provides the nourishment and family support to enable me to work such long hours "stress free" and uninterrupted during my writing activities.

I also acknowledge Dr. Subhi Gulati, who literally saved my life; my mother, Judith; my sons, Andrew and David; and my extended family and friends for their constant love and encouragement.

Finally, as always, I wish to express my appreciation and gratitude to my father, Bernard, whose insights and dreams helped make this book a reality.

In response to the very positive feedback from readers of the first edition, I have here added more than seventy new documents—sample demand letters you can write to protect your rights, agreements an attorney can prepare for you, examples of legal documents you may be required to sign, and checklists to help guide your thinking when coping with such major events as losing your job or getting divorced. These documents supplement and enlarge on many of the topics covered in the original text.

I have also updated the text in areas, such as Domestic Help, Malpractice, Medicaid, and Patients' Rights, where new legislation or other developments have changed the legal landscape.

Most of the new documents are to be found in the Appendix, and cross-references to them appear at appropriate points throughout the text. In the Table of Contents you will find a list of *all the documents* in the book, whether they are part of the main text or the Appendix.

To make these documents as useful as possible to readers, all of them are contained on the floppy disk that accompanies this book. You may use these forms freely as models when composing your own demand letters, checklists, and memos.

I urge you to read the "How to Use This Book" section that follows, and I am confident that you will find valuable guidance throughout this book for whatever legal problems you may face.

This book was written to save you money and aggravation.

Like most Americans, you probably know very little about the way the law affects your life. As a practicing lawyer, I see the mistakes people make, particularly in employment, business, and family matters. They make hasty, uninformed decisions such as signing agreements without understanding the fine print.

Many problems can be avoided if you know what to do. One of the most frustrating aspects of practicing law is telling a client she waited too long before taking action, or that a case could have been worth a great deal of money if the right moves had been made. In fact, millions of dollars are lost each year by people who have valid claims, but who fail to take appropriate action.

The public shares a popular misconception that lawyers only represent people who are in trouble. This isn't so. Lawyers have been providing knowledgeable clients with information on how to stay out of trouble ever since the profession began. That is what preventive law is all about. Just as business people keep lawyers on retainer to obtain ongoing advice, you, too, will now have this information.

That is the purpose behind *Lawyer on Call.* Since it is essential to know how to protect your family, job, money, and home, this book is intended to serve as a visit to a lawyer's office, where you will find valuable information, advice, and counsel.

I learned this even before I was admitted to practice law. My grandmother fell in a supermarket and broke her hip. She told bystanders she was okay because she was embarrassed to ask for help. Despite her injuries, she managed to hobble out of the store and cross the street to her apartment before collapsing in her bed. At the trial, the store owner's lawyer argued that her hip could have been broken any time she was not in the store. My grandmother had little choice but to accept a settlement possibly ten times smaller than she might have obtained had she requested an ambulance take her directly to a hospital.

That is the kind of aggravation I want you to avoid.

The following pages contain practical, useful strategies for virtually all the legal decisions you will make throughout your life. Whatever your background, education, and experience, this information will help detect problems before they occur, and make you aware of the legal consequences of your acts. If litigation becomes necessary, your chances of success and value of a claim will increase substantially because you will recognize potential exploitation and know what to do about it.

These guidelines were written to give you a lawyer's wisdom and experience when you need it, whatever your concern or problem. For example, in addition to knowing the key terms to discuss during employment negotiations, you will learn the proper steps to take if you resign or are fired from your job. I've included strategies to protect yourself when arrested, suing in small-claims court, forming a partnership, or hiring a lawyer, stockbroker, real estate agent, or home-improvement contractor.

In the area of family law, what would you do if you were named as a defendant in a palimony lawsuit, a divorce action, or a child-custody case? Chances are one day you may be embroiled in a similar proceeding. How would you go about protecting your assets from an ex-lover seeking revenge? What information would help you properly negotiate a separation or prenuptial agreement?

The following pages contain hundreds of legal strategies pertaining to the acts that affect your life. Armed with this information, you will become aware of the right steps to take to protect your rights, assets, property, and loved ones while anticipating and avoiding legal hassles before they occur.

To make the book as useful as possible and help you find a topic of interest quickly, the subjects are presented in alphabetical order. Significant effort was expended to make the text easy to read, often in a checklist format, with suggestions of questions to ask to protect your rights. Where appropriate, I have included sample letters you can send to protect your rights. I have also included many agreements to illustrate how lawyers prepare documents evidencing a particular matter. These are the actual documents used in a lawyer's practice, and are quite valuable. The book also contains lists of important agencies that can help you implement many of my suggestions and guidelines. The glossary will help you understand the meaning of important legal terms and concepts.

This is the all-encompassing legal guide I've dreamed about writing. As the author of eleven other legal books for the American public dealing with specialized subjects, I have come to the conclusion that most people, unlike my business clients, do not have access to practical, valuable legal strategies at a low cost. The desire to provide such information for the people who most need this prompted me to write *Lawyer on Call.*

This book was not meant to replace a lawyer, but it will help you understand if your problem requires a lawyer's assistance. If you currently have a lawyer, the information will help you work with your lawyer more effectively and enable you to make more intelligent choices. For most subjects I also suggest numerous courses of action to take before consulting a lawyer; such advice may prove invaluable to your lawyer once you have retained one.

You will discover that most of my suggestions can be followed without the help of a lawyer to obtain satisfaction on your own. For example, you will learn what to do when you or a family member is involved in an auto accident. These steps can minimize civil and criminal exposure and increase the value of personal injury and property claims. If you want to stop collection agency harassment, protect your credit, or collect benefits at an unemployment compensation hearing, for example, material in this book will show you how.

I have provided you with all the practical information my clients receive, at a fraction of the cost. Keep this guide in an accessible place. Refer to it before a matter arises. For example, read the applicable sections before negotiating the terms of an apartment lease, separation, or shareholder's agreement. Examine and use the valuable sample forms, agreements, and letters to gain valuable insights into protecting or strengthening your position. It's that simple.

The benefits of applying this information can be significant, as the following story demonstrates.

A client recently heard me discuss the subject of employee rights on a national television show. He came to my New York City law office for a consultation. He told me that he had recently been fired from his job, and based on something he heard me say, believed he had been treated unfairly. After investigating the facts, I determined the man had been fired illegally and was owed a substantial amount of commissions and post-termination benefits from his former company. I contacted the firm and almost immediately was offered a lump-sum settlement of $46,000. I later learned that the man initially did not think he had a case and was prepared to go away meekly after being fired. Fortunately, he saw me on television; that made all the difference.

The experience of this individual is not unique. Knowledge is power, and that is the concept behind *Lawyer on Call*. Knowing your rights in all phases of your life will enhance them, and protect you, your family, and your friends.

STEVEN MITCHELL SACK, ESQ.
New York City

LIST OF FORMS

The following is a list, arranged by topic, of all the forms and documents that are contained in this book and its accompanying CD-ROM. *(Note: An asterisk indicates that a document is to be found in the Appendix of the book.)*

The law protects everyone from various forms of abuse. This section identifies common forms of abuse and discusses what to do if you, a child, or someone you know is victimized.

CHILD ABUSE

Like other forms of domestic violence, child abuse is usually not reported, yet more than one million cases are reported to state and local authorities each year. When someone is engaging in child abuse or neglect, the first step is to seek the assistance of a child-protection agency such as the National Center on Child Abuse and Neglect in Washington, D.C., or the Children's Aid Society in New York City. Contact the agency and describe the situation. A representative will determine if the case falls within the definition of child abuse and whether to commence an investigation. Once an investigation has been conducted, the agency either will label the case as "unfounded" or will verify the abuse and find assistance, including day care for the child and counseling for the abusive parent(s). Often the family is placed under home supervision. This allows the family to stay together while a social worker makes regular visits to determine if the child is being adequately cared for.

Anyone in contact with an abused child can apply to the local family court for an order directing temporary removal of the child from the home, and all fifty states have mandatory child-abuse reporting laws. These require health-care professionals, teachers, social workers, and law-enforcement officers to report child abuse to the appropriate child-protection agency in their county; fines and penalties are imposed for individuals who do not comply.

State laws governing child abuse and neglect vary as to specifics, but all are targeted toward identifying a general pattern of parental conduct that is abusive or neglectful. The signs that most family court judges look at include:
- Infliction of physical injury by nonaccidental means
- A substantial risk of injury or death
- Excessive corporal punishment
- Disfigurement or impairment
- Lack of proper supervision and guardianship
- Failure to provide adequate food, clothing, shelter, and medical care
- Abandonment

Parents often counter these charges with a variety of defenses; for example, they may claim:
- Legitimate parental action, such as discipline
- Financial difficulties

- Religious prohibitions against medical treatment in cases of neglect
- Temporary insanity due to stress, or wrongful behavior due to an adverse reaction to a drug prescription

If a judge finds severe child abuse or neglect, the court may recommend criminal prosecution of the abusive parent as well as permanent separation of the child from the family. When termination of parental rights is an issue, the court carefully examines all the evidence at a fact-finding hearing. Some judges seek a permanent solution for child abuse and neglect through adoption. Steps are taken in this area after it has been determined that the parents' rights in raising the child should be permanently severed.

If your child is suffering because of abuse from your spouse, consult with a lawyer to explore the possibility of obtaining sole custody of the child (or children) via divorce or custody proceedings. Refer to the sections "Divorce" and "Child Custody" for more details if applicable. Finally, when warranted, contact a child-advocacy organization, such as the Children's Aid Society, for further information. Additional types of aid, such as welfare assistance, food stamps, Medicaid, day care, and marriage counseling, are available, and such agencies often direct people in these areas.

SPOUSE ABUSE

Until recently, battering was considered a private family matter rather than a crime. Now, pressure from a changing society has caused officials' perceptions and the law to change. More women are seeking legal protection and criminal prosecution, and are suing husbands directly for their injuries. The following strategies are helpful in this area.

Act quickly and decisively. Most wives submit to abusive husbands because of social pressures or their own idealistic expectations. Others cannot afford to leave their marriages for economic reasons. However, a failure to act may only prolong the misery and produce increasingly violent attacks. Seek help from friends, religious organizations, victims' services agencies, crisis intervention centers, marriage counselors, and battered women's shelters. If a situation is serious, it may be necessary to leave home and stay overnight in a battered women's emergency shelter. Some cities maintain shelter programs through their department of social services.

Battered women's shelters may be unable to accommodate every woman who needs assistance even if immediate help is required, and a legal problem may arise from the lack of confidentiality of records. Information indicating a stay at a shelter can be subpoenaed unless such records are protected from being disclosed by state law. Frequently, a traumatized victim may tell a therapist at the shelter, "I feel guilty," "I think maybe I asked for it," or "I want to get revenge." Defense lawyers representing husbands are learning how to use such statements in subsequent litigation.

Save evidence. Take color photographs of injuries as soon as possible to prove the extent of the abuse. Have the pictures signed and dated by a witness or the person who took them.

Seek immediate medical attention after a beating. Ask the doctor or nurse to document the injuries in a written report. Be sure the name of the person causing the injury is mentioned in the report. A doctor's visit can help prove that injuries were caused by the beating, and the medical records can be used in court to prove a case. Other evidence, including torn or bloody clothing, pictures documenting damage to a house or car, and the testimony of witnesses, should also be saved for future use.

Do not take the law into your own hands. In many states, to prevail with a self-defense claim, a battered spouse who fights back must prove a reasonable apprehension of imminent danger and great bodily harm. Some lawyers use evidence of past beatings and threats to prove reasonable apprehension. Others argue that it is a reasonable response for a woman of slight build to use a lethal weapon (e.g., a gun or knife) when a man attacks her with his fists. However, women who fight back often face criminal charges.

Call the police if you want the attacker arrested or need protection to leave the home. This is your right whether or not you are married to the attacker. In some states, if the police refuse to arrest the attacker, a woman can make the arrest herself; the police must then assist by taking the accused to the police station and filling out the arrest form. If the police refuse to help, write down their names and badge numbers. Report them to their commanding officer or to the civilian complaint review board. In some states, you can also go to the police station to sign a complaint and request that the attacker be arrested. Contact the district attorney's office if you were seriously hurt and required hospital care and the police would not make an arrest.

Seek legal assistance immediately. Spousal abuse is now considered a crime in most states, and district attorneys can prosecute husbands even when wives change the minds about pressing charges. Conviction rates are high, so consider the following objectives:

▶ Do you want to save your marriage or punish your abusive spouse?
▶ Does your spouse pose a continuing danger of physical injury to you and the children?
▶ Does your spouse need psychological help?
▶ Can the problem be solved through the legal system without spending a fortune?

Without a lawyer, you can go to a family or domestic-relations court and get counseling for yourself and your spouse. Before doing so, it is a good idea to

FORM 1. **Sample Cease and Desist Letter Sent by Spouse**

                                                        Date

Name of Spouse
Address

Dear Name of Spouse:
     I am writing you this letter to document a series of physical beatings I received from you during the month of (specify).
     Such conduct has caused me to suffer severe humiliation and embarrassment, emotional distress, and physical discomfort from lacerations and other visible bruises. I have taken photographs of my injuries as proof of your acts.
     Please treat this as my final demand for you to cease and desist perpetrating any conduct of a threatening nature upon me. This includes verbal threats, abusive language, and physical contact. In the event this request is ignored, be assured I will call the police and seek a temporary order of protection in the family court. This order may, among other things, prohibit you from remaining in our marital residence. I have consulted an attorney who will file criminal charges as well as a civil lawsuit grounded in assault and battery, not to mention a request for the police to arrest you.
     Hopefully, all of this will not be necessary. I suggest you hire an attorney to contact my lawyer within the next several days in the amicable attempt to resolve our marital difficulties and avoid expensive and protracted legal intervention.

                                                Very truly yours,
                                                Name of Spouse

cc: Name of Your Attorney

▷ Send certified mail, return receipt requested.
▷ *Author's note:* A similar version of this letter can be sent by your attorney if you prefer.

send your spouse a "cease and desist" letter to help prove your case. (See the example of this kind of letter above). It may also be possible to have the judge issue a directive (an order) that requires your spouse either to leave the house and stay away from you and the children (called a restraining order) or pay support and your attorney fees. The problem with orders, however, is that if a spouse is determined to disregard them, the only alternative may be to have the spouse arrested. This may not accomplish the anticipated results and place further stress on your children.

    With the services of a lawyer, you can obtain all the objectives stated above and also:

- ▶ Obtain a decree of divorce, separation, or annulment of the marriage
- ▶ Obtain a decree for a share of the marital assets (e.g., furniture, family car, and cash in bank accounts), maintenance (i.e., alimony), and/or child support once the divorce is finalized

> Obtain a criminal conviction for assault, battery, and/or harassment in criminal court

Once you decide to take legal action, the first step to consider taking against your abusive spouse is to obtain a temporary order of protection from the family court in the county where you reside. This measure will give immediate relief but is not a final solution to the problem. The order may maintain the peace while an attempt is made to iron out family difficulties and keep your violent spouse away from you or the children at your home, school, or business for a specified period of time (which varies from state to state). In many states the order can be renewed if you demonstrate need. The advantage of a temporary order is that your spouse can be arrested if the terms are violated. In most cases, the police will make the arrest. Temporary orders are not expensive and can be obtained by paying a small (e.g., $4) filing fee.

If the marriage is not worth saving, a temporary order of protection can be used as a means of proving grounds in a divorce or separation action, as well as in a civil lawsuit based on assault or battery. A violation of the temporary order can also provide an immediate right to proceed in criminal court to obtain permanent protection.

Contact the police for procedural information. They can tell you how to obtain an order (e.g., what court to go to, how to file, and so on). Speak to a knowledgeable clerk when you go to family or criminal court for further information.

Limiting visitation periods for your spouse is a common feature of temporary orders of protection, so tailor this when appropriate. For example, if you perceive a threat to the children or fear they may become victims of child snatching, insist on a plan that will give you as much control over visitation as possible. Establish other conditions for your spouse to follow. For example, the order can require him or her to seek medical treatment for a drug problem. Speak to a lawyer's referral service or lawyer for an explanation of all your options. Although you can obtain a temporary order of protection on your own, it is wise to hire a lawyer for assistance in this area if you can afford one.

If the problem is particularly severe, consider filing criminal charges in criminal court rather than going to a family court. In many states, people cannot use both courts to litigate the same issue, so know what you want to accomplish. If you want to help your spouse, commencing an action in family court is probably the better and less intimidating way. Although many criminal court judges incorporate nonpunitive orders (e.g., a requirement to seek psychiatric treatment), these may be given in conjunction with jail sentences and fines. Family court judges, however, rarely order imprisonment (although they can remove the case to criminal court if they believe that the spouse is dangerous and more violence is likely to ensue). In most states, removal of a case from criminal court to family court cannot be done without the victim's consent, and the potential may exist for your spouse to pressure you into dropping criminal charges. However, prosecutors are investigating and proceeding with criminal cases of spouse abuse more often nowadays and have leverage to bring what were once considered harmless "family spats" into court.

Do not be intimidated by your abusive spouse. Be candid with the police, the district attorney assigned to the case, and your lawyer. Most cities have established domestic-violence prosecution units to investigate and prosecute criminal cases and offer counseling and referral services. Warning letters are sometimes sent on behalf of victims who choose not to press criminal charges; prosecution then follows if the violence does not end.

A judge in criminal court has the power to:

▶ Set criminal charges against an abusive spouse, ex-spouse, or lover
▶ Release an abusive spouse without bail on the promise to return to court for a hearing
▶ Release an abusive spouse with bail
▶ Issue a temporary order of protection for a victim spouse and children
▶ Adjourn the case on a spouse's promise not to hurt or threaten anyone
▶ Sentence an abusive spouse to probation pending medical or psychiatric evaluation
▶ Convict an abusive spouse of a crime

It is possible to obtain a temporary order of protection before a spouse is arrested. The order may even accompany an arrest warrant. A temporary order of protection can also be requested at the arraignment, even if the spouse has fled and the hearing is being held in his or her absence. After a conviction, a criminal judge may issue an order of protection for as long as the court determines is necessary for your protection and that of family or household members.

Be prepared when bringing criminal charges. For example, sworn affidavits from witnesses such as friends, relatives, and neighbors who saw the beatings or observed lacerations and bruises; medical reports describing the number of visits and injuries received; and a copy of the police report that documents the violent incident(s) can greatly improve a case's chances of success. Collect these items before visiting a lawyer or prosecutor. Request an award of permanent physical and legal custody of the children, child support, damages as a result of the abuse, including reimbursement for medical expenses, loss of earnings or support, attorney's fees, court costs, and all other out-of-pocket losses resulting from the injuries, where applicable.

MARITAL RAPE

More than 85 percent of all marital rape cases include some form of physical violence. Do not wait for your husband to repeat his actions. Avoid allowing social, economic, or emotional pressures to cause you to delay taking corrective action. The failure to act may raise doubts about your credibility and give your husband the impression that his conduct is accepted. The following strategies should be considered.

Communicate the problem. No one can assist if you remain silent. One excellent source of assistance is a rape crisis center located in your community (consult the local telephone listings). Call a rape crisis center immediately if you are attacked. Most centers maintain twenty-four-hour hotlines. Staff members can accompany you to the hospital or police station and assist in preparing examination forms and police reports. Ask a counselor if you have a legal cause to file criminal charges and how to go about doing this. A positive answer may serve as a starting point for legal action.

Explore all legal options. State law varies considerably with respect to marital rape. In many states marital rape is considered a crime. Other states impose certain conditions before making it a crime (e.g., the rape must be

LOSS	EVIDENCE
Injury-induced pain	Authorized drug prescriptions, medical reports; affidavits from nurses and attendants, color photographs of injuries; testimony of medical experts, therapists, psychiatrists, friends, and relatives
Pain and suffering	Same as above
Shock, mental anguish, anxiety, embarrassment, humiliation	Same as above
Depression, neurosis, psychosis	Same as above
Reduced sexual pleasure	Authorized drug prescriptions; medical and psychiatric reports; testimony of medical experts, therapists, and psychiatrists
Medical and drug expenses	Canceled checks, receipts, unpaid bills
Inpatient and/or outpatient hospital care	Canceled checks, receipts, unpaid bills
Reduced earnings from work	Wage statements, affidavits from employer and fellow employees, recent tax returns
Reduced profits from business	Books and records of your business, affidavits from partners and employees, recent tax returns
Court costs, filing fees, witness fees, stenographic fees, legal fees	Canceled checks, receipts, unpaid bills

accompanied by severe physical violence). An experienced matrimonial or criminal lawyer can provide a thorough explanation of all options. Schedule an interview with a lawyer if this is appropriate.

Consider obtaining a divorce or separation. Rape can be used to prove grounds for divorce or a separation. A legal separation may provide time to attempt to resolve difficulties and save the marriage. If a husband, for example, consents to therapy and the therapy is successful, the partners may be reconciled. Consult the section "Separation" for more information if appropriate.

Consider suing for personal injuries. If you live in a state where lawsuits by one spouse against another are permitted, it may be possible to sue a husband for damages resulting from a rape. A lawyer specializing in matrimonial or personal injury law can advise if it is worthwhile to commence a civil lawsuit to recover damages for physical, psychological, and emotional injuries as well as other losses attributable to the rape or assault. The following table lists the kinds of losses victims may be able to recover as well as the required evidence.

Consider filing criminal charges if you live in a state where marital rape is a crime. However, many cases are unsuccessful. In some states, certain conditions, such as fear of resistance or imminent danger, must be proved to make criminal charges stick. Some of the major problems include:

- Proving there was a lack of consent
- Overcoming the jury's predisposition to doubt there was a rape
- Proving there was no other motive behind pressing charges
- Lack of witnesses and corroborated testimony
- Failing to submit other kinds of proof

Many women fail to obtain prompt medical attention and/or take color photographs of their injuries after a rape. This should always be done to strengthen a claim. A visit to a doctor or hospital can document the seriousness of your injuries and corroborate your story. Medical tests can be performed to prove the existence of semen in your body, thereby proving that a sexual act occurred. The test can also determine when the act occurred, if given within twenty-four hours.

Standard defenses used in marital rape cases include:

- The victim was intoxicated
- The rape was victim precipitated
- There is lack of evidence of assault or battery

Although many rape cases are unsuccessful, you can prevail by doing your homework and being represented by competent counsel.

Many people have legitimate personal injury claims but fail to take proper steps to recover damages. Some decide not to contact a lawyer because they think that an accident was their fault. Others fail to seek immediate medical treatment and are unable to prove that the accident caused the injury. Still other people do not know the true value of their case. They foolishly accept a small settlement, sign a release, and are precluded from recovering additional money. You can avoid mistakes such as these. It is also important to act properly if you are involved in an accident and someone else is injured.

In situations where no-fault laws (see later in this section) do not apply, an injured person seeking redress must prove that an accident was caused by the negligence of another. This is eventually decided by a judge or jury in a civil court trial. Once this is proved, the injured person is entitled to receive money as compensation for his or her losses. Losses include out-of-pocket expenses, including court costs; past and future estimated medical fees and hospital bills; and lost wages. Money can also be awarded for pain and suffering, inconvenience, disfigurement, and loss of companionship.

Most automobile owners, business establishments, innkeepers, and homeowners maintain insurance policies to protect themselves in the event of accidents. This obligates insurance companies to negotiate settlements, pay money to the specified maximum in the policy, and defend any claims brought against the negligent policy owner. The typical personal injury lawsuit is settled before the trial stage in private negotiations between the injured party's lawyers and the insurance company adjusters or before a jury renders its verdict.

Insurance adjusters play a powerful role in the settlement process. Their job is to secure releases and settle claims at the minimum cost. Often they prefer to settle claims rather than go to trial. This is where proper planning by the injured party pays off.

HOW TO PROCEED AFTER AN ACCIDENT

The following strategies can help substantiate claims and produce larger settlements for injuries.

Ask for help. Avoid trying to get up when you are seriously injured. If necessary, request an ambulance to take you to the hospital. If you get up and leave the scene, the defendant may assert that your injuries could have been caused or aggravated at any time.

See a doctor immediately. Ask the doctor to document your injuries in a written report. A doctor's visit can help prove that the accident caused an injury or worsened an earlier injury. The longer the time between the date of the accident and the date the doctor sees you, the more difficult it sometimes is to prove that the accident caused your injury. Ask the doctor if additional visits are necessary and whether you should be referred to a specialist. Obey the doctor's instructions regarding physical activities, particularly those observed by others. Avoid participating in strenuous physical activities if you are not supposed to, so you don't aggravate an injury or give the insurance company evidence to assert a defense.

Avoid discussing or minimizing injuries. Statements such as "It's all right," "I'm okay," or "Nothing to worry about" can reduce the value of a claim. Weeks later, and although an injury may be worse, the insurance adjuster may learn about these remarks and offer less money in settlement.

Take color photographs. Do this immediately after any accident to prove the extent of your injuries. Untouched pictures are admissible evidence in court. Long after bruises, cuts, or broken bones have healed, the pictures will still demonstrate the injuries at their worst and provide evidence of pain and suffering.

Speak to a lawyer immediately. Although most lawyers charge a contingency fee (e.g., a percentage, sometimes up to 40 percent of all money collected), larger settlement offers are typically made to claimants represented by lawyers, and the fee may be worth it. Adjusters know that settlements for valid claims must be paid to avoid protracted and expensive trials. Unrepresented claimants sometimes make incriminating statements and are ignorant about the kinds of damages to which they are entitled. Always hire a competent attorney well versed in personal injury law. Consult the section "Attorneys" for more information on this subject.

If a lawyer won't take your case, you can notify the other party yourself by sending an initial demand letter by certified mail, return receipt requested, similar to the one on page 11. This will begin the process of documenting the claim while formally notifying the other party of the accident. It is possible that you will receive a favorable response and be able to settle the matter amicably out of court.

Document all medical expenses and actual damages. Proper substantiation of the damages will greatly increase the amount of money offered in settlement or after a jury verdict. The table on page 12 lists compensable items and shows how to prove them.

Resist settling claims early. As a general rule, avoid accepting settlements within a month of the accident. The reason is that you need time for proper diagnosis of the extent of all injuries, to determine whether prolonged medical treatment is necessary, and to calculate the effects of the accident (e.g., lost business).

Take precautions. Insurers sometimes hire detectives to investigate the condition of an injured claimant. Alert people who may be questioned. Ask them not to discuss your injuries or the cause of the accident with anyone.

Prepare a daily diary. Include dates and times of all medical treatment, hospital visits, prescription purchases, who you saw, what was said, and how

FORM 2. **Accident Claim Notice**

Your Name
Address
Telephone number
Date

Name of Individual, Owner, or Officer
Name of Company (if applicable)
Address

Dear (Name),

Please be advised that on (specify date and time) at (location), the following accident occurred to me (describe, such as a slip-and-fall accident at a restaurant) which I believe you (or your agents) caused and/or were responsible for.

Either you, your representative, or your insurance carrier should contact me immediately so that we may attempt to resolve a number of issues in an amicable fashion and avoid expensive and protracted litigation.

Thank you for your cooperation and prompt attention to this matter.

From the hours of 9 a.m. to 5 p.m., weekdays, I can be reached at: (specify your daytime telephone number).

Very truly yours,
(your name)

▷ Send certified mail, return receipt requested.

you felt. The diary may help document a claim and refresh your recollection if you are required to testify at a trial.

Don't consent freely to a medical examination. Insurance companies have the right to examine you when a claim is filed. Doctors hired by insurance companies are paid to ask questions and find medical reasons to minimize the claim. One favorite tactic is to diagnose the injury as being caused by a prior condition rather than the accident. Avoid agreeing to a physical examination unless your lawyer is present.

HOW TO PROVE NEGLIGENCE

In addition to proving injuries, it is necessary to show that the other party acted improperly (i.e., negligently) in order to prevail. The following strategies demonstrate ways to prove negligence and reduce exposure from lawsuits in several common situations.

Shopping-related accidents. Storekeepers owe a legal duty to their customers. The law requires them to keep their stores in a reasonably safe condition and warn customers of dangers on the premises that are not obvious. Besides

ITEM	PROOF
1. Loss of regular wages, tips, overtime	Income tax returns, employment and payroll records, letters and affidavits from employers, fellow employees
2. Loss of a job as a result of the accident	Affidavit or testimony from ex-employer, fellow employees
3. Loss of fringe benefits, commissions, promotions	Same as 1 above
4. Loss of profits or income from one's business	Same as 1 above
5. Loss of future earning capacity; special skills	Professional degrees, medical records, affidavits, testimony from expert witnesses
6. Expenses of a job search	Transportation receipts, interview records, affidavits, testimony of interviewers, telephone records
7. Medical and drug expenses	Canceled checks, receipts, unpaid bills
8. Inpatient or outpatient hospital care	Same as 7 above
9. Nursing care, special diet, prosthetic devices	Same as 7 above
10. Treatment for injury-induced pain	Authorized drug prescriptions, medical reports, detailed diary prepared by claimant, affidavits from nurses and attendants, color photographs, testimony from expert witnesses
11. Pain and suffering	Same as 10 above
12. Shock, mental anguish, anxiety, embarrassment, humiliation	Same as 10 above
13. Depression, neurosis, psychosis	Same as 10 above
14. Loss of sexual pleasure ("loss of consortium")	Same as 10 above
15. Court costs, filing fees, witness fees, stenographic fees	Canceled checks, receipts, unpaid bills
16. Transportation costs for medical treatment	Same as 15 above

Note: This list is not meant to be all-inclusive but rather a good summary of the kinds of damages that are compensable and how to prove them. The law provides reimbursement for all these expenses if they can be proved. Careful documentation of appropriate expenses helps build a strong case.

customers, liability extends only to other persons to whom this legal duty is owed, such as children, friends who accompany customers, and people who pass through the store with permission. If someone enters a store merely to use a public facility, such as a telephone or toilet, the question of whether the proprietor owes a legal duty to this individual is not clear-cut. The fact that an injury occurs does not automatically mean that compensation will be awarded. In all negligence cases, the following elements must generally be proved to be successful:

> That you suffered an injury on property under the store's supervision and control (e.g., in the store or outside on store-owned or -managed property)
> That you were owed a legal duty of care and that the owner and/or his employees failed to act properly
> That the failure to act properly was a direct cause of the injury
> That your own conduct did not cause the accident

For example, people slip and fall over large objects (e.g., boxes) and small items (e.g., food or chewing gum) or because of slippery floor surfaces. Unless a person was distracted by a promotional display, he has a better chance of recovering damages after slipping on a small item because people are usually considered responsible for noticing larger objects and walking around them.

To win a slip-and-fall case in court, you must prove that you were injured in an area under the store's control (e.g., that you slipped on a banana peel in the store) and that the condition causing the accident existed for a sufficient period of time. A sufficient period of time must pass in order to make storekeepers and their employees negligent for (1) failing to remove an object from the floor and/or (2) failing to discover its presence and warn customers about it. This is determined by a judge or jury if the case is tried in court. The longer it is proved the condition existed, or a witness can testify that he saw a store employee cause the condition, the better your chances of prevailing. To help prove negligence in slip-and-fall accidents:

> Document the cause of the accident.
> Inspect the area where the accident occurred.
> Examine the conditions closely.
> Look for signs of age if you slipped on an item.
> Report the accident to the storekeeper to document your claim.
> Listen to what is said in response; volunteered statements may be used as admissions of liability.
> Gather names and addresses of witnesses who saw the accident; speak to them to determine if they remember where and what you slipped on.

ACCIDENTS INVOLVING FAULTY PRODUCTS

People can recover damages when they are injured by a defective or faulty product. This is called product liability. Generally, an injured party can sue and

WHAT MUST BE PROVED	HOW TO PROVE IT
The existence and severity of an injury	Written medical reports, hospital records, testimony of witnesses
That the product caused the accident and injuries	Testimony, expert witnesses
That the product was defective by manufacture or design, or that the product was unreasonably dangerous, had inadequate safety features, or improper warnings were given	Examination of the product, testimony of expert witnesses, similar accidents to other users
That the user maintained the product properly, followed instructions, and used the product in the manner intended	Testimony, expert witnesses

recover from any seller in the distribution chain. Thus, the manufacturer, distributor, and even the retailer are potentially liable for product-caused injuries. It is not necessary to have actually purchased the product in order to sue; non-purchasers are protected when they are foreseeable users (e.g., one roommate injured by the other roommate's faulty hair dryer). The chart below generally describes what must be proved for a product liability case to be successful.

Damages are recoverable under several legal principles in product liability cases, including misrepresentation, negligence, strict liability, and breach of warranty. There are fine distinctions among these categories. If you are injured by a defective product, contact a lawyer immediately.

HOW TO HANDLE AN AUTO ACCIDENT

Most people are involved in at least one serious automobile accident during their lifetime. Even if you suffer no personal injury or property damage, an auto accident can expose you to civil and criminal liability, suspension or revocation of your license, and serious financial loss. The following strategies should be followed if possible.

Stop the car and stay calm. It is against the law to leave the scene of an accident. Pull over and get out of the vehicle (if you safely can) as quickly as possible. If you drive away, go back to the scene immediately.

Don't obstruct traffic. Use reflectors and flares at night so that drivers will not hit you or other cars. People in minor accidents often cause additional accidents, and are sued for huge sums of money. Take all precautions to avoid additional accidents.

Help injured passengers. The law requires people to assist the injured. This means calling for help to obtain the police, a doctor, or an ambulance. It does not mean actively helping injured people (e.g., removing them from their cars or applying tourniquets) unless you are a trained medical professional and the injured person is in a dangerous location. If you render medical assistance and your actions cause or worsen injuries, you may be liable for assault and/or negligence despite your good intentions.

Call the police if you think you were not at fault. Police departments respond to even minor property accidents. Ask that an accident report be prepared. Accident reports help prove claims because they document the position of vehicles and other details, including weather and road conditions.

Don't apologize or admit the accident was your fault. If the other driver screams that you caused the accident, ignore him. Merely give your name, address, and telephone number. Show your driver's license, registration, and insurance card. Ask for the same information in return. Record the make, model, year, plate number, and vehicle identification number. Check the other driver's insurance card, and write down the name of the insurer, policy number, and expiration date. If insurance coverage has expired, copy the information on the card anyway, and ask if the driver is currently insured.

Avoid revealing prior traffic infractions when showing your license to the other motorist. These records are on the backs of licenses in some states.

Be careful when talking to police officers. Never volunteer unnecessary information. Answer all questions honestly. If you are asked a question you do not wish to answer, simply say, "I don't know." A police officer cannot force you to say anything.

Speak to passengers and other witnesses. Write down the names, addresses, phone numbers, and statements made by witnesses so you can contact them if necessary. If you are involved in an accident with a commercial driver or company employee, speak to him and his passengers. Employees frequently pin liability on their company. A comment such as "I told the boss twice this month there was something wrong with the steering wheel" can be used as an admission of liability.

Inspect the accident site. Note traffic controls and stop signs; the position and length of skid marks; damage to trees, dividers, and other items; the point of impact and damage to autos (sometimes helpful in determining fault); and the exact spot where the cars stopped.

Understand no-fault laws. Currently, thirteen states (Colorado, Florida, Hawaii, Kansas, Kentucky, Massachusetts, Michigan, Minnesota, New Jersey, New York, North Dakota, Pennsylvania, and Utah) have adopted some form of no-fault insurance. Under a pure no-fault system, motorists buy insurance, known as "first party" coverage, that covers their losses if they are involved in accidents. Determining accountability for accidents is irrelevant under no-fault because car accident claims are resolved through an administrative process instead of the courts.

Theoretically, no-fault is designed to ensure prompt payment for injuries arising from an accident. This includes compensation for medical bills, lost wages, and the cost of hiring replacement labor to run a business or home. Payment is made by the injured party's insurance company or the insurer of the car in which the injured party was riding, regardless of fault. Pedestrians are paid by the insurance company of the owner of the car that hit them. Motorcycle riders are often not covered under no-fault, and generally people are not entitled to benefits when injured while driving intoxicated, committing a felony, racing, or operating a stolen vehicle.

No-fault laws vary on a state-by-state basis. Generally, they limit the amount of recoverable damages. Damages for death, pain and suffering, property damage, and certain noncash expenses may not be reimbursable. Some no-fault states allow you to commence a private lawsuit to collect damages when your medical expenses have met or exceeded the law's dollar threshold, but may reduce awards if you did not wear a seat belt. In other no-fault states, you must first file claims with insurers for medical expenses, but can then file legal claims in court against drivers who caused the accidents for other injuries, including gross disfigurement. Some other states allow motorists the option of no-fault or the tort system, but the consequences are often tricky. Thus, always consult a lawyer to determine the best course of action.

ACCIDENTS AT HOME

To reduce exposure to personal injury lawsuits arising from an accident on your premises:

Examine your homeowner's insurance policy. Do you have general liability coverage? If the minimum coverage is less than $50,000, talk to an insurance agent and review the policy. Additional coverage is inexpensive and essential, because if you own a house and other assets, you are a prime target for a lawsuit.

Hire workers who carry workers' compensation. Many states require independent contractors to carry workers' compensation and public liability insurance for protection in the event the worker injures himself or someone else on your premises. If anyone works in your home on a regular basis, you may be required to carry workers' compensation coverage. Insurance companies frequently claim they are not required to defend and pay damages on behalf of homeowners who employ individuals on a steady basis. Review your policy and speak to an insurance agent to clarify this if applicable.

Warn workers, guests, and employees of hidden defects. Homeowners have a legal duty to keep their home in reasonably safe condition and warn guests of potential hazards. Failure to do so could cause liability in a lawsuit for negligence. The same is true for tenants, although the duty to maintain a safe premises generally extends only to the apartment and not to common areas (e.g., hallways). Homeowners are not liable for injuries caused by dangerous conditions impossible to detect.

Never admit liability. Do not incriminate yourself if someone is injured on your property by acknowledging that the accident was your fault or that you were aware of a dangerous condition that caused the accident.

Protect guests from dangerous pets. Homeowners are required to exercise control over dangerous pets. If your dog has bitten someone in the past, or has a reputation of being vicious, you will be liable if the dog bites a guest, because warning a social guest or business invitee of the presence of a dangerous pet may not be legally sufficient.

Protect children from dangerous, attractive nuisances. If an object on your property (e.g., a swimming pool or a bush whose berries are poisonous) causes injury, you may be liable even if the child is a trespasser. The law requires homeowners to take extra precautions in protecting children from their own curiosity.

ON-THE-JOB ACCIDENTS

Employers have a legal duty to warn employees of dangers and provide a safe place to work. However, in most situations, because of workers' compensation, you cannot sue an employer for negligence if you are injured on the job. Payment is made by the employer's insurance company. The only questions to be settled are whether the injury was caused by a job-related accident and the amount of compensation to be paid. State law spells out the amount of compensation allowable for each type of injury. Injured employees are generally reimbursed for costs of medical treatment, partial lost wages (e.g., 60 percent of gross weekly salary), temporary disability to meet living expenses, and permanent disability. Partial disability may also be awarded if you return to work but cannot work full-time.

Whenever you are involved in a job-related accident:
▶ Document the accident.
▶ Gather witnesses immediately.
▶ Report the accident to a supervisor, shop steward, or boss.
▶ Seek prompt medical attention.
▶ Ask a boss for a detailed explanation of workers' compensation rights.
▶ File a timely claim.

The law requires an employer to notify the insurance carrier and direct you to the appropriate insurance company representative or claims officer once the accident is reported. You cannot be fired, demoted, or retaliated against for filing a workers' compensation claim. Call the nearest Workers' Compensation Board Office if you have any questions. An assistant will tell you how to file a claim or make an appeal. You are not obligated to accept the amount offered by your employer's insurance company. If the insurer refuses to pay or cuts off payments before you are able to go back to work, you can file an appeal and schedule a hearing before the Workers' Compensation Board.

Although you can represent yourself at a Workers Compensation Board hearing, it's best to have a skilled lawyer present. The lawyer's fee is set by most workers' compensation statutes: typically, 20 percent of the money received and nothing if you lose. An assistant at a local Workers' Compensation Board will advise you of applicable fee regulations. Never pay the lawyer more than he or she is entitled to by law.

If you are injured while going to or from work, or suffer an injury caused by stressful conditions on the job, you may still be entitled to workers' compensation and other benefits, including nonoccupational disability insurance from the employer, food stamps, and social security benefits.

If you are an independent contractor, you can file a separate lawsuit, since employers do not maintain workers' compensation on your behalf. Examples of independent contractors include sales agents, owners of small businesses, and other self-employed persons. There is no precise legal definition that explains what constitutes independent contractor status. When courts or Workers' Compensation Boards attempt to determine if a person is an employee or independent contractor, they analyze the facts of each case. Significant factors include whether the individual controls his own work schedule, operates his own place of business, is not required to report to an employer on a daily basis, pays his own withholding and social security taxes, and whether the parties have an employment contract that states that the worker is an independent contractor. For more information, consult the section "Independent Contractors."

COMMON CARRIER ACCIDENTS

Common carriers (e.g., cruise ships, airplanes, trains, and taxis) owe paying passengers a high degree of care, and the law requires them to use extraordinary vigilance and skill in transporting passengers safely. Thus, it is often easier to prove that a carrier and its employees acted negligently than is the case with other kinds of businesses. Speak to a competent lawyer if you are injured while on or by a common carrier.

Never be intimidated if language on the back of a ticket seems to exculpate the carrier from liability. People mistakenly believe they are precluded from recovering damages after buying a ticket that says for example: "The carrier assumes no liability for property loss, death, or physical injuries arising from the acts of its employees." Common carriers insert this language to deter people from investigating their rights. Such clauses may have no legal effect because the obligation to transport passengers safely is so important that carriers cannot disclaim liability. Thus, if the ticket says you must commence a lawsuit within one year, or notify the carrier of your claim within six

TO ALL TO WHOM THESE PRESENTS SHALL COME OR MAY CONCERN, KNOW THAT

(Name of Person) residing at (specify address), as RELEASOR, in consideration of (specify $, or write: the sum of Ten Dollars and other good and valuable consideration), received from (specify person or company and address), as RELEASEE, receipt whereof is hereby acknowledged, releases and discharges the RELEASEE, RELEASEE'S heirs, executors, administrators, successors, and assigns from all actions, causes of action, suits, debts, dues, sums of money, accounts, reckonings, bonds, bills, specialties, covenants, contracts, controversies, agreements, promises, variances, trespasses, damages, judgments, extents, executions, claims, and demands whatsoever, in law, admiralty, or equity, which against the RELEASEE, the RELEASOR, RELEASOR'S successors and assigns ever had, now have, or hereafter can, shall or may have, for, upon, or by reason of any matter, cause, or omission whatsoever.

Whenever the text hereof requires, the use of singular number shall include the appropriate plural number as the text of the within instrument may require.

This RELEASE may not be changed orally.

IN WITNESS WHEREOF, the RELEASOR has caused this RELEASE to be executed and duly witnessed in the presence of (specify name of witness).

_____
Signature of RELEASOR

_____
Signature of Witness

STATE OF (specify), COUNTY OF (specify)
On (specify date), before me personally came (name of RELEASOR), to me known, who, by me duly sworn, did depose and say that deponent resides at (specify RELEASOR'S address), and who executed the foregoing RELEASE in my presence; and that deponent signed deponent's name by like order.

_____
Signature of Notary

months of the accident, such a clause may be unenforceable. Just to be safe, consult a lawyer.

FINAL COMMENTS

Be sure the individual, government agency, or business has sufficient assets to satisfy any judgment before deciding to sue for injuries. Ask your lawyer to contact a credit reporting agency or banking institution to learn more about the location and identity of real property and other assets before suing a small business or individual.

Speak to a lawyer before accepting a settlement and signing a release (see the example of a release above). A competent lawyer may be able to predict how much an accident case is worth. Select a lawyer with a good reputation who spends a significant amount of time handling personal injury matters. Calculate the total cost of the lawsuit before deciding to sue. Sign a retainer agreement with your lawyer that spells out how fees are to be computed and paid. For more information about how to hire a lawyer properly, consult the section "Attorneys."

ADOPTION

Adoption is a court procedure by which one or more persons enter into a legal parental relationship with another, establishing legal obligations of child support for food, clothing, education, inheritance, and custody rights. Although each state has its own particular adoption laws and standards, the laws have undergone great changes in recent years to accommodate the needs of all the parties involved—that is, the adopting parents, the natural parents, the child or other adopted person (sometimes an adult or a lover), private investigators, lawyers, and judges. Whereas the more traditional agency adoptions arranged by licensed charities and publicly funded social service agencies, or county adoptions conducted by state agencies, were once the norm, now independent adoptions, arranged privately between natural mothers and adoptive parents and requiring court approval, have become more common.

To adopt a child, you must be intimately familiar with state law. A good first step is to contact an adoption agency administered by a local religious, charitable, or community organization or public agency. Information about these types of agencies is available through a local department of social services or the state welfare department. It is also helpful to talk to other adoptive parents, who can provide information about procedural requirements and insights.

Be candid with an agency representative when discussing your needs. Seek answers to questions about eligibility standards and other legal requirements such as:

- ▶ What is the waiting period before a child can be received?
- ▶ What is the process to become an adoptive parent?
- ▶ How much will the adoption cost in placement fees and expenses?
- ▶ What legal steps are required to make the adoption final?
- ▶ What rights does the child have to look for his or her natural parents when the child grows up?

HOW TO PROCEED WITH AN ADOPTION

The following strategies will facilitate the adoption process.

Contact a lawyer who practices primarily in the area of family law for an initial consultation. The lawyer can help you better prepare for the interview with the adoption agency. Ask the lawyer about your state's eligibility requirements and for an explanation of the various petitions and legal documents that must be filed in court to consummate the process. (See the examples of an adoption petition and an agreement with an adoption agency on pages 22 and 24. Note that the contents of these documents will vary from state to state and will depend on the facts of the case.) The lawyer you speak to for initial advice may not be the same lawyer who specializes in finding babies for clients. Contact a local bar association, a legal referral service, or the American Academy of Adoption Attorneys for names of lawyers who have expertise in these matters. Consult the yellow pages under "adoption," since many lawyers now advertise.

Know the eligibility requirements. Many states impose age and life-style requirements. Some judges are reluctant to grant adoptions to elderly couples or grandparents for reasons of age. Others are unwilling to grant adoptions to unmarried or homosexual couples. However, such decisions may be successfully appealed where circumstances dictate it is in the best interest of the child. Although not common, a few states allow visitation by grandparents when a grandchild is adopted by a stepparent, particularly when the biological parent is deceased.

Residency requirement problems may be encountered if the child you want to adopt lives in another state. You must either bring the child to your state or institute adoption proceedings in the state where the child resides. If the child resides in a temporary foster home in another state, it is necessary to obtain consent from the person or organization having legal custody before bringing him or her into your state. If problems develop, the only option may be to proceed in the state where the child resides, but some states require people to reside in that state for a minimum period of time before being allowed to adopt.

Consider a private adoption. Most states now allow adoption through private agencies, but there are limits on the fees that can be charged by natural parents, surrogate mothers, and lawyers. Typically, an attorney specializing in private adoption placement must be registered with the state as an adoption agency and must provide the same counseling service for prospective adopting parents that a public adoption agency provides. Beyond the cost of payments needed to complete an adoption, an attorney is prohibited from accepting a fee for placing a child. Legitimate costs include:

- ▶ Placing advertisements in newspapers throughout the country
- ▶ Reasonable legal fees for advice and services, such as drafting required documents and representation in court
- ▶ Reimbursement for filing fees and incidental court costs
- ▶ The natural mother's medical costs if a parental adoption agreement was made with her, plus her travel and living expenses (e.g., food, maternity clothes, gas, electric and water payments, telephone bills, housing expenses, and lost wages) before giving birth if needed

Some companies issue insurance for out-of-pocket expenses that are paid

FORM 4. **Sample Petition to Adopt**

In the Matter of the Adoption by (Name of Parents) of a minor having the first name of (specify) whose last name is contained in the schedule annexed to the Petition herein.

To the Surrogate of the County of (specify):

The petition of (name of parents) respectfully shows:

1. That your petitioners are of full age, married, and living together as husband and wife, citizens of the United States of America and reside at (address).

2. That (name of adoptee) has resided with and has been in the care and custody of your petitioners since (specify date), and until the filing of this petition, that said infant was placed with your petitioners by (name of agency), an authorized adoption agency, so that (name of adoptee) would reside and might have a good home and become the adopted child of the petitioners.

3. That (specify name), the mother of said infant, is deceased and that (specify name), her late husband and the father of said infant, has married again and lives with his wife and two grown children at (specify address).

4. That your petitioners are informed and believe that the father of said infant is without sufficient pecuniary means to pay for the support and provide a proper home for said infant; that said father has been properly notified of the pending adoption and has expressed his desire to allow the adoption to proceed; that your petitioners have become greatly attached to said infant since she has resided with your petitioners; that the petitioners have tried for almost ten years to have a biological child of their own and have been unsuccessful, and petitioners are desirous of adopting and treating said infant as their own and are able and willing to provide for her proper support and education during her minority and to provide a proper home for her.

5. That the petitioners have a joint income of (specify $); that (specify husband) works as a (specify) and that (specify mother) works as (specify); that petitioners have lived at (specify address) in a home they have owned for more than (specify years).

6. That the said infant has no income or property, now or in expectancy, and has no guardian of her person or property; that there is no other person other than those herein-before mentioned in this proceeding who are interested in this proceeding or in said infant, and that no previous application has been made for this order now hereby sought.

7. That no previous application has been made for the adoption of said minor.

8. That, on information and belief, there will be annexed to this petition a schedule verified by a duly constituted official of an authorized adoption agency as required by (specify applicable state law).

WHEREFORE, your petitioners pray that the Surrogate of the County of (specify) will entertain the proceeding for the adoption of said child by your petitioners as prescribed by state law, and after said proceedings, that an order may be granted, filed and recorded in accordance with such law, allowing and confirming said adoption and directing that the said child (specify name), shall henceforth be regarded and treated in all respects as your petitioners' own lawful child with the name of (specify) and with all the rights and privileges conferred by law; and your petitioners pray for such other relief as to this court may seem just and proper in the premises.

Dated: the _____ day of _____, _____

_____
Signature of Petitioners

Verification and Signature of Notary

when an adoption fails to take place. Speak to an adviser about such optional insurance. Inquire if your state has enacted insurance legislation requiring that if an adoptive parent's insurance policy has maternity benefits, this insurance must also cover the birth mother's medical expenses. If such coverage exists, provide the insurance company with the name of the birth mother and expected due date. Confirm the existence of possible or expected coverage in writing. After the birth, communicate again with the insurance company by telephone and in writing to provide essential details for payment.

Know what expenses are not allowed under state law, to avoid nullification of the adoption. Criminal sanctions can be imposed where evidence of direct payment for the child is shown. Each state has laws covering the types of items for which the adoptive parents may pay, but no state allows the birth parent to be paid for the child. Take all necessary precautions in private adoptions to demonstrate that the natural mother placed the child willingly and after careful consideration of her needs and desires. Also be sure that:

> The child's natural father has been given legally adequate notice to prevent a challenge on the grounds of due process
> No payments can be claimed to have gone to "pay for" the child
> Sworn affidavits are prepared and presented to the court to demonstrate that all expenses, fees, compensation, and other remuneration were neither unreasonable nor improper

Attorneys play a different role in private adoptions than in agency adoptions. The role is that of facilitator between the birth parents and the adoptive parents. Typically, the lawyer finds the parties, puts them together (possibly arranging for them to meet before the birth), and handles all financial aspects of the adoption. The lawyer makes an investigation similar to the one an adoption agency would make to ensure that the prospective adoptive parents are well suited to care for the child.

Private adoption attorneys are not allowed to practice in some states. Working with a lawyer who doesn't have much experience or skill will increase costs and the risk that an adoption may be annulled, so investigate the background and qualifications of the lawyer you are considering hiring. Ask for references from past clients. Talk to family and surrogate court personnel to find out the names of competent attorneys they would recommend. Check out the lawyer's and agency's credentials with a county social service agency and the Better Business Bureau to determine whether the lawyer has a reputation for charging huge fees, not returning deposits, or making promises that are not kept. If you are overcharged or the lawyer is engaging in irregular practices, contact the nearest district attorney's office immediately. Always receive a signed retainer agreement that itemizes all charges and services to be rendered (with timetables if possible) for maximum protection.

FORM 5. **Sample Adoption Agreement with Agency**

AGREEMENT, made on (specify date), by and between (specify name of potential parents) and (specify agency), a charitable corporation duly organized under the laws of the state of (specify), located at (specify address).

WHEREAS, the undersigned institution was informed by the department of public welfare on (specify date) that (specify name) a minor child was born on (specify date) and was abandoned by its father prior to its birth; and that its mother being unable to take care for it, was committed to the department of public welfare on (specify date).

WHEREAS, the said child was placed with (name of agency) for placement with adoptive parents for adoption; and

WHEREAS, said child is by reason of the religious faith of her mother, of the (specify) religious faith, and the adopting parents are also of said faith; and

WHEREAS, said parents desire to adopt the child pursuant to (specify state law), and agree to treat said child as their own lawful child, and to extend to such child all the benefits, privileges, and rights contemplated by state statutes; and

WHEREAS, the agency approves of and consents to the said contemplated adoption of said child;

Now, in consideration of the premises, the said parties hereby mutually covenant, agree, and consent as follows:

FIRST, THEY, the said adoptive parents, hereby covenant and agree to adopt and treat the said child as their own lawful child and rear it in the (specify) religious faith, and further agree that the adoptive parents and said child shall sustain toward each other the legal relation of parents and child, and that they shall severally have all the rights and be subject to all the duties of such relation.

SECOND, the agency hereby consents to said adoption.

THIRD, the parties hereto agree that the name of said child shall be changed to and said child shall hereafter by known by the name of (specify).

IN WITNESS WHEREOF, (name of parents) have severally set their hands and seals, and the agency has caused this instrument to be signed and sealed by its corporate name by (specify), duly authorized in writing by its directors to sign the corporate name thereof, and its seal was thereunto affixed the day and year above written.

In the presence of: _____   Signatures: _____

Verification and signature of Notary

Consider the legal implications of an adoption. The following are various legal rights and responsibilities that arise with a complete adoption:

CHANGE OF NAME. Request that the name change be made a part of the final adoption decree and be sure to include this request in the petition for adoption that is filed with the court.

INHERITANCE. State law varies as to what may and may not be inherited by and from an adopted person. Typically, a child loses all rights involving the natural parents, including the right to support and the right to inherit from a biological parent who dies without a will. Some states bar adoptive parents from inheriting, sharing, or receiving property inherited by the adoptee from his or her natural parents.

SEALED RECORDS. Usually a court order must be obtained to open the file, and this may be granted only for a good reason such as a medical emergency (learning the true identity for an organ donor match).

Consider the concept of an open adoption, which allows the adoptee to have ongoing contact with certain blood relatives. This is occasionally provided for in an agreement with older children; the proposed agreement is introduced at the adoption proceedings, and the judge carefully scrutinizes the document and weighs all the factors to determine whether this should be granted. The Sample Agreement of Open Adoption on page 322 in the Appendix illustrates this concept.

Understand other kinds of specialized adoptions. To preserve a child's heritage, some states impose restrictions when you adopt a child of different racial, religious, or ethnic background. Be prepared to prove a willingness to develop the child's consciousness of his or her native culture if you desire to adopt such a child.

When seeking to adopt a child in another country, it is advantageous to locate an adoption agency that specializes in placing children by region. The amount of red tape people endure to secure an adoption varies from country to country, so inquire about:

FEES. These should include all charges from the first consultation with an international agency. Ask how much it will cost in total fees to consummate a foreign adoption. Get a binding written estimate that itemizes all costs, expenses, and fees that may arise.

RISK OF DISEASE. Most children adopted from foreign countries come from impoverished homes. Inquire about the risk of disease before proceeding.

VISITING THE COUNTRY OF ORIGIN. You may want to investigate economic, hygienic, and other conditions before going through with any adoption.

PREADOPTION REQUIREMENTS. International adoptions are made either by bringing the child into the United States or by going to the child's country and completing the adoption there. The requirements are typically the same as for a domestic adoption: filing the adoption petition, obtaining favorable consents, submitting to a home investigation, appearing before the court, and obtaining a final order of adoption. However, you must also deal with the U.S. Immigration and Naturalization Service in order to secure the adopted child's entry into this country. Make an appointment at the nearest INS office to learn further details.

SPECIAL-NEEDS CHILDREN. In the United States, there is presently no shortage of adoptable children with physical or emotional handicaps, and some states provide an economic incentive for the adoption of a special-needs child by offering subsidy payments to the adopting family.

ADULTS. Adoption is not limited to children. Some states provide for the adoption of adults as well as minors. Speak to a lawyer for more details if applicable.

STRATEGIES TO IMPROVE ADOPTION SUCCESS

One of the most important phases of an adoption involves obtaining the consent of the various parties connected with the adoption. Those parties are:

The natural parent(s), unless parental rights have been terminated because of abuse, neglect, incompetence, or some other reason

The child, if old enough under state law, or the adult adoptee

The child's guardian, next of kin, or the adoption agency having legal custody of the child if there are no natural parents

Specific requirements as to the content and form of the consent vary from state to state, and all proper steps must be taken to secure consent and prove notice. Failure to obtain the proper consents in the proper manner can hinder efforts to consummate the adoption or can lead to the loss of the child at a later date. Thus, seek assurances that there was no fraud, duress, or undue influence behind the execution of the instrument of surrender negotiated between the natural parent(s) and the agency.

Unfortunately, there is always a chance that the natural parent will change her mind and seek the return of the child. Each state has its own rules regarding whether this is permitted. Thus, understand your state's treatment of revocation of consent. In some states, the natural parent has the absolute right to revoke consent prior to a final adoption decree by the court. In other states, a parent's surrender of a child is deemed irrevocable except in case of fraud or duress. Other states allow the court to exercise its discretion to decide whether approval of the natural parent's revocation of consent is in the best interest of the child. Discuss this possibility with your lawyer before you embark on the adoption process to understand all your rights and the potential risks.

Be sure to notify the natural father of the pending adoption, if he can be located. If the natural father has been given notice of the pending adoption but fails to come forward, the natural mother's consent alone should suffice, so inquire whether the natural father was given adequate notice. Examine all copies of certified letters, telegrams, faxes, and other documents sent to the father's last known address or place of employment.

Be prepared to submit to a court-ordered investigation. Every state requires an official investigation of the adopting parents before approving a final order of adoption. This is required even if an adoption agency has conducted its own home study. The court will order an investigation after receiving the petition for adoption, agreement for adoption, and various consents. The purpose of the investigation is to verify the truth and accuracy of the assertions contained in the petition, as well as the physical and mental health, marital and family history, and income and property owned by the adopting parents and adopted child. Inquiry will also be made as to whether either adopting parent has ever been abusive to or neglectful of their other children.

A written report detailing the findings of the investigation will then be submitted to the court. Recommendations regarding the fitness of the adopting parents may also be required. Sometimes a hearing is conducted whereby the judge will evaluate the investigative report and house visits and confer with the adopting parents and the child if he or she is old enough. If the report is favorable and the court is satisfied with the suitability of the adopting parents in regard to their financial security, marriage stability, treatment of natural children, stable job history, no history of child abuse or neglect, interest, and reasons for the adoption, the order can be either final or temporary and subject to further review. In some states, if a temporary decree is issued, the court can exercise the option of annulling the adoption if the arrangement doesn't work out. However, once a final order is issued, the adoption cannot be undone, except under unusually serious circumstances.

ADULTERY   *See Divorce*

AFFIRMATIVE ACTION   *See Civil Rights; Employment*

AGE DISCRIMINATION   *See Employment*

AGENTS   *See Independent Contractors*

AIDS   *See Employment*

ALIMONY   *Also see: Divorce; Prenuptial Agreements*

Alimony is money paid by one ex-spouse to the other for support under the terms of a settlement agreement following a divorce or pursuant to a court order. It is also referred to as maintenance or spouse support. A husband (and in some cases, a wife) is liable for the support of his spouse. This is to be distinguished from child support, which is discussed in the section "Child Support." Depending on various factors, alimony can be made payable on a temporary or permanent basis during the life of the other party. It is determined by a judge after considering the circumstances of the case, the reasonable needs of the parties, the spouse's ability to pay, and other factors. The amount and duration of alimony are generally determined according to the following guidelines:

▸ The income and property of each spouse, including marital property distributed in the action

FORM 7. **Pertinent Alimony Clauses to Consider Including
in a Separation Agreement**

1. RESPONSIBILITY FOR DEBTS: Both parties represent, warrant, and covenant that they have not hereto, nor will they hereafter, incur or contract any debt, charge, obligation or liability whatsoever for which the other party, his or her legal representatives, property, or estate is or may become liable, except as otherwise specifically set forth in this Agreement. Both parties agree to indemnify and hold the other party harmless of all loss, expenses, including reasonable attorneys' fees, and damages, in connection with or arising out of a breach by the other of his or her foregoing representation, warranty, and covenant.

2. SUPPORT AND MAINTENANCE OF THE WIFE: The Husband shall pay to the Wife for her support and maintenance, the sum of (specify $) per week, due in advance on Saturday of each week. Said payments shall continue for a period of (specify) years from the execution date of this Agreement; however, all payments shall cease prior to the end of said ___ year period in the event the Wife remarries, or in the event the Wife cohabits with another man. Remarriage of the Wife as used in this Agreement shall be deemed a remarriage of the Wife regardless of whether such marriage shall be void or voidable or terminated by divorce, annulment, or otherwise. Cohabiting shall mean living with another man for a minimum consecutive period of at least (specify) days, or (specify) nonconsecutive days within any three-month period.

All payments by the Husband to the Wife under this Article shall be made by check or money order and forwarded to the Wife at her residence or at such other place as she shall designate in writing to the Husband. The parties hereby acknowledge that the aforesaid payments made by the Husband to the Wife as support and maintenance shall constitute taxable income to the Wife and be a tax-deductible expense to the Husband, and the sums specified herein have been computed with such tax consequences in mind and in consideration of the relative tax burdens and benefits upon the parties based upon the respective incomes of the parties.

OR: The Wife acknowledges that she is in good health and is capable of earning an adequate salary of at least (specify $) as a (specify job function) and that she has sufficient means of her own support from her share of the joint property distributed between the parties including (specify, such as transfer of the husband's share of marital premises, other property, or assets). Accordingly, she waives and renounces (specify) all and any claims against the

- ▸ The duration of the marriage
- ▸ The age and health of both parties
- ▸ The present and future capacity to be self-supporting of the person to receive alimony
- ▸ The presence of children of the marriage in the respective homes of the parties
- ▸ The standard of living established during the marriage where practical and relevant
- ▸ The tax consequences to each party
- ▸ Previous contributions of the party seeking support to the career or

Husband for support and maintenance exceeding those amounts specified in this Agreement, and for any other property, either joint or separate, owned by or due to the Husband, and agrees that she will not at any time demand or apply therefore for said additional support, maintenance, or property, and will hold the Husband harmless therefrom.

3. LIFE INSURANCE: The Husband's life is insured by (specify company, address, policy number) in the face amount of (specify $) of which the Wife has heretofore been sole beneficiary. The Husband agrees that he will provide and maintain, at his own expense, said life insurance policy insuring his life for the benefit of the Wife, until the youngest child of the parties is emancipated or reaches the age of 21, whichever comes sooner. The Husband shall not pledge, hypothecate, or encumber the policy by loan or otherwise during such period. Each year he shall forward written proof to the Wife that said policy remains in full force and effect. Any dividends payable under said policy shall belong exclusively to (specify). (Note: If to the Husband, the clause could read, "who shall have the option of accepting payment thereof or applying same in reduction of premiums.")

4. TAXATION: Regardless of their marital status, the parties shall file separate tax returns from this day forward. Each party agrees to cooperate fully with the other in the event of any audit or examination by a taxing authority of any previous joint tax return filed by the parties. Each party agrees to furnish to the party being examined or his or her designees, promptly and without charge, such papers, records, documents, and information as may be reasonably appropriate in connection with such audit or examination. In the event an audit indicates that additional money, interest, and penalties are due, the party who is primarily responsible for said deficiency shall be responsible to pay all such sums, and shall indemnify and hold the other party harmless from same.

5. DIVISION OF PROPERTY: The parties acknowledge that all items of personal property, fixtures, furnishings, and real property wherever they may exist, as enumerated more fully on Schedule A attached to this Agreement and made a party hereof, have previously been divided to the satisfaction of both the Husband and the Wife upon the signing of this Agreement. Accordingly, neither party will make any claim against the other in the future with respect to any of the aforesaid stipulated property.

▷ *Author's note:* The above clauses merely illustrate a few of the important concepts to be addressed in a comprehensive separation agreement. Speak to your lawyer for advice and guidance where applicable.

career potential of the other party and value of previous services rendered as a spouse, parent, wage earner, and homemaker
▸ The wasteful dissipation (i.e., gambling) of family assets by either spouse
▸ Other factors a judge finds to be just and proper

In most states, alimony is usually paid only for a brief period of time (perhaps no more than five years) after the divorce. This is because the emphasis has shifted to giving nonworking spouses a larger share of marital assets in one lump-sum payment and then terminating any continued involvement between the parties. In some states, alimony is awarded only until a recipient has become self-supporting (this is called "rehabilitative maintenance"). Although alimony awards are increasingly no-fault oriented, marital misconduct is a bar to alimony in some states, and others consider fault grounds such as adultery and cruel and inhuman treatment as relevant factors. Several states provide for modification or termination of alimony on proof that the spouse receiving such payments is cohabiting with an individual other than the former spouse.

When parties are considering implementing a prenuptial agreement governing the disposition of matters in the event of a divorce, some states prohibit such agreements from eliminating alimony upon divorce. Check the law in your state on this point where applicable.

When negotiating a separation agreement, list child support separately and understand the tax ramifications. While alimony payments are taxable income for the receiving spouse and tax deductible for the paying spouse, payments received or made for child support are neither taxable nor deductible. Utility bills, medical expenses paid on behalf of an ex-spouse, and life insurance premiums for policies in which an ex-spouse is the sole and irrevocable beneficiary can be considered part of the total alimony payments and deductible by the payer. Often, divorce lawyers representing husbands will recommend larger alimony payments provided the payments are tax deductible. To maximize tax savings and structure a divorce settlement properly in this area, speak to a lawyer, accountant, or other professional adviser.

In some cases, the circumstances of the parties will change drastically after the divorce and it will become necessary to modify the previous agreement or court order concerning alimony. If the parties agree without court intervention, this is called a stipulated modification and no judicial intervention is required. However, if one person reneges on the modified agreement, court approval will be required to accept and enforce a modification.

Parties sometimes seek to modify alimony agreements in such cases as:

▸ A need for periodic cost-of-living adjustments to reflect the impact of inflation
▸ Changed circumstances, such as the loss of employment or poor health of either of the parties
▸ Unforeseen financial emergencies
▸ Cessation upon the remarriage of the recipient spouse or extensive cohabitation with another

If the parties cannot agree between themselves on the modification of alimony, a motion is typically made in court and a judge will decide whether to grant the application for increasing or decreasing alimony payments. Because such motions are often made, it is important for a lawyer to carefully consider and anticipate potential changed circumstances before the divorce settlement (i.e., during negotiations) to minimize conflict and unnecessary expense after the divorce. (The clauses contained in the sample document on pages 28–29 describe some possible events and should be incorporated into a separation agreement when appropriate.) Consult the Alimony Questionnaire on page 323 in the Appendix to help determine your support needs.

ANNULMENT   *Also see: Divorce; Marriage*

A marriage can be legally annulled on the basis of certain facts that must be proven. If a marriage is annulled, it is considered void (i.e., it never happened in the eyes of the law). This is important to some people because an annulment does not carry the stigma of divorce. In some religious circles, it is easier to remarry after obtaining an annulment than after getting a divorce.

To be legally married, a man and a woman must be legally capable of entering into a valid marriage. (Note: Marriages between members of the same sex are not legally recognized in this country.) This means, for example, that if the marriage cannot be consummated sexually (one of the parties is incurably incapable of having sexual intercourse); if one or both parties to the marriage are minors and no parental consent is given; or if one party deliberately concealed important information from the other before the wedding, the marriage can be annulled by direction of the court.

An annulment can be obtained based on the following:

▶ Concealment of a major problem or fact, such as being a convicted felon, having minor children from a previous marriage, having a serious drug or alcohol addiction problem, or possessing a sexually transmittable disease such as herpes or AIDS

▶ Misrepresentation of a major fact, such as failing to state you are still married to someone else, or are not of sufficient age to marry

▶ Inability or unwillingness to have children

Most annulments are obtained on the basis of fraud. In such a case the annulment is granted because one party concealed facts that, if known, would have caused the other to cancel the wedding. Depending on the length of the marriage and other factors, it may be wise to consider obtaining an annulment rather than a divorce. Speak to a lawyer about this if you have been married only for a short period of time and it is applicable in your case.

ANTENUPTIAL AGREEMENTS
See Prenuptial Agreements

The vast majority of lawsuits never go to trial; they are either discontinued or settled. However, every case that is tried has a loser, and the losing party must decide whether or not to appeal the unfavorable decision.

An appeal is a request that a higher court review the decision of a lower court. In those states that have an intermediate appellate court, the losing party challenging a trial court decision first brings the appeal to the intermediate court. In the federal court system, the losing party brings the appeal to the court of appeals in the appropriate circuit. For serious criminal cases (i.e., felonies), the right to an appeal is mandatory. In civil cases, an appeals court may have the discretion not to consider the appeal in certain circumstances. After the appeal is decided by an intermediate appellate court, the case can be further reviewed by the highest state appeals court (although some state cases are reviewed by the U.S. Supreme Court). In the federal system, after the appeal is decided by the U.S. Court of Appeals, the Supreme Court of the United States has the power and discretion to review and rule on the history of the case and the most recent appeal.

Appeals judges read the transcript of the trial together with legal documents called briefs to determine if the trial judge or jury erred in their decision. Typically, the intermediate appellate court will concern itself with issues of law as opposed to facts. It is rare that the appellate court will overturn a jury's factual decision. Rather, a verdict can be reversed if the wrong law was applied, incorrect jury instructions were given by the judge, or significant legal mistakes occurred, such as important evidence being mistakenly excluded by a judge from the trial.

Less than 20 percent of all criminal cases and 30 percent of all civil cases are reversed on appeal. Most decisions do not get reversed, but if a person or business has spent several years and thousands of dollars pursuing or defending a valid claim, the additional money spent on an appeal can be worth it, particularly if the delay caused by the appeals process works to an appellant's advantage.

Speak to a lawyer immediately if you receive an unfavorable trial verdict. There is a limited period of time (often thirty days) in which to file a notice that you intend to appeal. This must be done without delay to preserve your rights. To evaluate the chances of a successful appeal, it is necessary to carefully reconstruct (in an objective fashion) the reason the case was lost. Consider whether to hire a specialist in appeals matters. Although your current attorney is familiar with the case, there are distinct advantages to hiring an attorney who makes a living writing briefs and arguing oral appeals (it is an art), and a new attorney is more likely to discover mistakes made by the original attorney. Be certain you know how much the appeal will cost. Always sign a retainer agreement (similar to the simple example of one shown on page 33) that clearly spells out attorney fees, costs, and disbursements.

FORM 9. **Sample Retainer Agreement with Attorney for Appeal**

Date

Name of Client
Address

Dear (Name of client),

This letter confirms that you have retained me as your attorney to represent you in the prosecution of an appeal of a judgment granted against you by Justice (specify name) on (specify date) in the (specify trial court) and entered on (specify date) in the office of the Clerk. The appeal will be taken to (specify court).

You have agreed to pay to me promptly a flat fee of (specify $) for all legal services to be rendered in this matter. This fee shall be paid as follows: (specify how much up front and how much later upon the happening of certain events). In addition to my fee, you also agree to pay for all costs and disbursements upon my request. Disbursements include, but are not limited to, the cost of the transcript of the trial (which the court reporter has estimated at about $X,XXX), the cost of the appellate printer to print the record on appeal and the briefs we submit, and to cover the costs for serving the papers on appeal. All of these costs and disbursements are estimated to be approximately (specify $) but the actual disbursements may vary from the estimates, which are only approximate.

I promise to keep you informed of all developments as they occur and to send you copies of all incoming and outgoing correspondence immediately after it is generated/received.

I will personally handle the drafting of your brief and the arguing of any motions or the appeal in court if necessary.

I look forward to working with you on this matter. Kindly indicate your understanding and acceptance of the above terms by signing this letter below where indicated.

Very truly yours,
Name of Attorney

I, (name of client), have read and understand the above letter, have received a copy, and accept all of its terms:

_____
Name of Client

Remember that no matter which lawyer handles the appeal, it is generally costly, time-consuming, and frequently does not produce anticipated results.

APPRAISALS

Appraisals are used to determine the proper amount of insurance needed to cover a purchase or loss, determine the reasonable fair market value of an item donated to charity, or compute appreciation of antiques and family heirlooms when distributing assets or figuring estate taxes. Appraisals are also commonly obtained for private sales, such as for determining the fair market value of marital property upon divorce.

Choose an appraiser who is an accredited member of the American Society of Appraisers (ASA) or the Appraisers Association of America (AAA). Select an individual with a degree in the specialty that most closely relates to the object to be appraised. Estate appraisals, for example, are divided into such specialties as commercial, residential, and income properties, which are further divided into urban and rural properties. It is always preferable to hire a full-time appraiser with specific experience in the kind of property to be appraised.

Be sure you inquire about fees and costs when hiring an appraiser. Confirm business, museum, and insurance company references. Ask how the appraiser arrives at a value for an object. Is this determined from a relevant publication or current price index? Most important, ask to see a sample report and ask if the appraiser will document and support the appraisal at a trial if necessary. Is there an extra fee for this?

Tell the appraiser your specific needs, the item(s) to be appraised, and the purpose of the appraisal. Make all objectives clear so that you receive a proper and usable report. Appraisers must preserve the confidentiality of the subject matter, be objective, not charge excessive fees, and prepare clear, concise, and correct reports. It is unethical for appraisers to accept assignments and appraise items that they have an interest in buying.

Do not agree to a fee based on the value of an item, because this may tempt an appraiser to overvalue the item. Fees are usually determined by the type and purpose of the appraisal, the degree of difficulty, and the type of item appraised. Speak to several appraisers, and do not necessarily hire the one charging the lowest fee. Most good experts charge an hourly fee. Expect to be charged for travel, research, and writing time. For large jobs, like an inventory of an estate, appraisers make a preliminary visit and, for a fee, give an estimate of the entire cost. Get the appraiser to agree to deduct the preliminary visit fee from the entire fee if ultimately hired. Insist on a written contract or letter of agreement describing the arrangement. (See page 35 for examples of appraisal contracts.)

The purpose of an appraisal is to:
- Identify the object(s)
- Describe the object's unique characteristics
- Value the items based on known or comparable objects in the marketplace

You should receive a full description of each piece, including its age, characteristics, physical condition, and, if significant, national origin. The date and purpose of the appraisal and the appraiser's signature must also be present. Do not accept a scribbled, handwritten appraisal with scant listings and inaccurate numbers. A report that states "6 dining room chairs—$1,200" is meaningless.

FORM 10. **Sample Appraisal Contract**

In consideration of an appraiser's fee, (name of appraiser) hereby agrees to evaluate the tangible (specify property) belonging to (specify your name and address) located at (specify place where items are located). The approximate completion date will be (specify).

I have agreed to pay your appraisal fee of (specify $) on receipt of the appraisal. This fee is based on your standard appraisal charges of (specify).

Signed by (name of client) on this _____ day of _____, _____

FORM 11. **Sample Letter of Agreement with Appraiser**

Your Address
Date

Appraiser's Name
Address

Dear (specify name of appraiser),

    This letter sets forth the terms of your services as an appraiser for (describe items to be appraised). This appraisal is sought for the purpose of (state reason for obtaining the appraisal). I agree to pay you (specify $) as a retainer, which sum shall be applied against and deducted from the total fee due of (specify $), which total sum shall be paid on presentment of a certified appraisal report (or set forth the terms of payment as discussed and agreed to with the appraiser).

    You agree that the certified appraisal report that will be provided will accurately comply with all the requirements of the American Society of Appraisers. You further agree to be responsible for all costs incurred by you in connection with your valuation of the (list the item to be appraised). In the event of a false or substantially incorrect appraisal, you shall not disclaim any liability but agree to indemnify me for any direct damages I may incur.

    This letter accurately summarizes all the terms we have discussed and agreed upon. There can be no changes unless stated in writing and signed by both of us. If all of the above meets with your approval, please countersign both copies of this letter and return one to me. Thank you for your cooperation, and I look forward to working with you.

Very truly yours,
Your Signature

ACCEPTED AND AGREED:

_____
Name of Appraiser

If you are exploited, file a complaint with the association of which the appraiser is a member to initiate a grievance procedure before an ethics committee. If a violation is found, the member may be warned, suspended, or expelled. You can also file a complaint with your Better Business Bureau (BBB) or Department of Consumer Affairs or seek redress in court.

Before an appraiser can be held liable for either negligent misrepresentation, intentional misrepresentation, or fraud, you must establish that the statements made were relied upon to your detriment and caused harm (i.e., monetary loss). Gross negligence occurs when an appraisal is intentionally rendered false or made in reckless disregard for the true value of the object.

Some lawsuits against appraisers are for breach of contract. In the case of an under-valuation, the monetary damages awarded is often the difference between the fair market value and the purchase price of the item.

Although as a practical matter it may be difficult, watch out for appraisers who attempt to disclaim their reports by stating that they are not competent in scientific analysis, and thus are not legally responsible for incorrect appraisals, errors, or omissions due to a failure to incorporate such findings into the valuation.

Finally, for complicated or expensive appraisals, consult a lawyer or other professional adviser before hiring any appraiser.

ARBITRATION   *Also see: Mediation*

Arbitration is a formal mechanism for resolving disputes that differs from litigation. Hearings are conducted by arbitrators rather than by judges and are not limited by strict rules of evidence. They can consider all relevant testimony when making an award, including some forms of evidence (e.g., hearsay and questionable copies of documents) that would be excluded in a regular court. Arbitrators have the authority to hear witnesses out of order. Their decision is usually final and unappealable. (Note: Limited circumstances for appeals are mentioned later in this section.)

To obtain an arbitration the law requires both parties to agree to the arbitration process beforehand in writing to prevent claims of unfairness by the losing side. Typically, in an employment contract, lease, loan agreement, or other document, the relevant clause may state some version of the following:

> Any controversy or claim arising out of or relating to this agreement, the parties hereto, or the breach thereof, shall be settled by arbitration in accordance with the rules of the American Arbitration Association and judgment upon the award rendered by the arbitrator(s) may be entered in any court having jurisdiction thereof.

ADVANTAGES OF ARBITRATION

Expense. Substantial savings can be achieved through arbitration. Attorney fees are reduced because the average hearing is shorter than the average trial (typically, less than a day versus several days). Time-consuming and expensive pretrial procedures, including depositions, interrogatories, and motions are usually eliminated. Finally, out-of-pocket expenses are reduced because stenographic fees, transcripts, and other items are not required.

Time. Arbitration hearings and final awards are obtained quickly; cases are usually decided within thirty days, compared to several years in formal litigation.

Privacy. The arbitration hearing is held in a private conference room rather than a courtroom. Unlike a trial, the hearing cannot be attended by the general public.

Expertise of arbitrators. Arbitrators usually have special training in the area of the case. In a textile dispute, for example, arbitrators serving on the panel are probably respected merchants, lawyers, or other professionals with significant experience in the textile industry. Their knowledge of trade customs helps them identify and understand a problem more quickly than a judge or jury.

Increased odds of obtaining an award. Some lawyers believe that arbitrators are more likely than judges to split close cases down the middle. The theory is that arbitrators bend over backward to satisfy both parties to some degree since their rulings are final and binding. This tendency to compromise, if true, benefits claimants with weaker cases.

DISADVANTAGES OF ARBITRATION

Finality. Arbitrators, unlike judges, need not give formal reasons for their decisions. They are not required to maintain a formal record of the proceedings. The arbitrator's decision is binding. This means that an appeal cannot be taken if you lose the case or disagree with the size of the award except in a few extraordinary circumstances where arbitrator misconduct, dishonesty, or bias can be proved.

Arbitrator selection. The parties sometimes agree that each will select its own arbitrator. In such cases it may be assumed that the selected arbitrators are more sympathetic to one side than the other. However, arbitrators are usually selected from a list of neutral names supplied by the American Arbitration Association (AAA). This method all but eliminates bias.

Loss of sympathetic juries. Some knowledgeable lawyers believe that juries tend to empathize more with certain kinds of people, such as fired employees, automobile accident victims, destitute wives, and older individuals. Arbitrators are usually successful lawyers and business people whose philosophical orientation may not lean more toward individuals.

Loss of discovery devices. Some claimants must rely on an adversary's documents and records to prove their case. For example, sales agents, authors, patent holders, and others often depend upon their company's (or licensee's) sales figures and accurate record keeping to determine how much commission and royalties they are owed. The same is true for minority shareholders who seek a proper assessment of a company's profit picture.

These people may find a disadvantage in the arbitration process. Trial lawyers have ample opportunity to view the private books and records of an adversary long before the day of the trial. This is accomplished by pretrial discovery devices, which include interrogatories, depositions, and notices to produce documents for inspection and copying. However, these devices are not readily available to litigants in arbitration. In many instances, records are not available for inspection until the day of the arbitration hearing. This makes it difficult to detect whether they are accurate and complete. And, it is often up to the arbitrator's discretion whether to grant an adjournment for the purposes of reviewing such records. Such requests may be refused.

SUMMARY OF STEPS LEADING TO THE HEARING

Commencing the hearing is a relatively simple matter once arbitration has been selected as the method of resolving a dispute. A party or his lawyer sends a notice called a Demand for Arbitration to the adversary (see page 39 for an example of this notice). Copies of the demand are sent to the AAA, along with the appropriate administrative fee. The AAA is most often selected to arbitrate disputes. It is a public-service nonprofit organization that offers dispute settlement services through its national office in New York City and through dozens of regional offices in major cities throughout the United States. See pages 324–325 in the Appendix for a list of the addresses and telephone numbers of all AAA regional offices.

The notice briefly describes the controversy and specifies the kind of relief sought, including the amount of monetary damages requested. The opposing party then sends a response to the demand, usually within seven days. The response may also assert a counterclaim for damages. Either party can add or change claims in writing until the arbitrator is appointed. Once this occurs, changes and additional claims can be made only with the arbitrator's consent.

After the AAA receives the Demand for Arbitration and the response, an AAA administrator usually supplies the parties with a list of potential arbitrators. The list contains the arbitrator's name, current occupation, place of employment, and appropriate background information. The parties mutually agree to nominees from this list. Potential arbitrators are obligated to notify the AAA immediately of any facts likely to affect their impartiality (e.g., prior dealings with one of the litigants) and disqualify themselves where appropriate. (Note: If the parties do not agree beforehand to the number of arbitrators, the dispute is decided by one arbitrator, unless the AAA determines that three arbitrators are appropriate.)

Once the arbitrator is selected, the AAA administrator schedules a convenient hearing date and location. There is no direct communication between

**American Arbitration Association
Commercial Arbitration Rules
Demand for Arbitration**

Date:_____

TO: (Name)_____
             (of party upon whom the Demand is made)
     (Address) _____
     (City and State) _____ (Zip Code)_____
     (Telephone) _____

Named claimant, a party to an arbitration agreement contained in a written contract, dated _____, providing for arbitration, hereby demands arbitration thereunder. (attach arbitration clause or quote hereunder)

Sample arbitration clause: Any controversy or claim arising out of or relating to this contract, or any breach thereof, shall be settled in accordance with the Rules of the American Arbitration Association, and judgment upon the award may be entered in any court having jurisdiction thereof.

NATURE OF DISPUTE:

CLAIM OR RELIEF SOUGHT: (amount, if any)

TYPE OF BUSINESS:
Claimant_____ Respondent _____
HEARING LOCALE REQUESTED: _____
                          (City and State)

    You are hereby notified that copies of our arbitration agreement and of this demand are being filed with the American Arbitration Association at its _____ Regional Office, with the request that it commence the administration of the arbitration. Under Section 7 of the Commercial Arbitration Rules, you may file an answering statement within seven days after notice from the Administrator.

Signed _____ Title _____
       (May Be Signed by Attorney)

                Name of Claimant _____
Home or Business Address of Claimant _____
                   City and State _____ Zip Code _____
                      Telephone _____

                Name of Attorney _____
            Attorney's Address _____
                   City and State _____ Zip Code _____
                      Telephone _____

▷ *Author's note:* To institute proceedings, send three copies of this Demand with the administrative fee, as provided in Section 48 of the Rules, to the AAA. Send original Demand to Respondent.

the parties and the arbitrator until the hearing date; all requests and inquiries are received by the administrator and relayed to the arbitrator. This avoids the appearance of impropriety. The parties are free to request a prehearing conference to exchange documents and resolve certain issues. Typically, however, the parties, administrators, lawyers, and arbitrator meet face-to-face for the first time at the actual hearing.

THE HEARING

Most hearings are conducted in a conference room at an AAA regional office. A stenographer is present, if requested. (Note: The requesting party generally bears the cost.) The arbitrator introduces the parties and typically asks each side to briefly summarize its version of the dispute and what each intends to prove at the hearing.

The complainant's case is presented first. Witnesses are called to give testimony (usually under oath). After witnesses finish speaking, they are usually cross-examined by the opposing party's lawyer. They may also be questioned by the arbitrator. The complainant introduces all its witnesses, documents, and affidavits until it has finished presenting its side of the case.

The opposing party then introduces its witnesses and documents to defend its case and/or prove damages. After the opposition has concluded its case, both sides are usually requested to make a brief summary of the facts (i.e., what they felt was proved at the hearing). Sometimes the arbitrator may request that legal briefs be submitted that summarize the respective positions of the parties before rendering a final decision.

Arbitrators are generally required to render written decisions within thirty days unless the parties agree to some other time period. The arbitrator can make any award that is equitable. He can order the losing party to pay additional costs, including AAA filing fees and arbitrator fees. Legal fees may be awarded if the arbitration clause so provides. (See page 41 for an example Award of Arbitrator.)

Arbitrators volunteer their time for hearings lasting under two full days; they are paid a reasonable per diem rate (up to $750) for additional hearings. If the parties settle their dispute prior to a decision, they may request that the terms of the settlement be embodied in the consent award.

Arbitrators have no contact with the parties after the hearing is concluded. The parties are notified in writing by the AAA administrator and are sent a copy of the award. The decision in a typical commercial case is brief— usually no formal reasons are given to explain why a particular award was rendered or the basis on which damages were calculated.

It is practically impossible to appeal a losing case. The arbitrator has no power once the case is decided. The matter can be reviewed only by a judge, and judges cannot overturn the award on the grounds of insufficient evidence. The only ways a case can be overturned on review are:

FORM 13. **Award of Arbitrator**

In the Matter of Arbitration between

Smith Supply Company
And
Doe Corporation Inc.   Case No.

I, the undersigned Arbitrator, having been designated in accordance with the Arbitration Agreement entered into by the above named Parties, and dated (specify), and having been duly sworn and having heard the proofs and allegations of the Parties, AWARD as follows:

1. Within ten (10) days from the date of this AWARD, Doe Corporation Inc. ("Doe") shall pay to Smith Supply Company ("Smith"), the sum of Twenty Five Thousand Eighteen Dollars ($25,018.00), plus interest in the amount of Two Thousand Two Hundred Dollars ($2,200.00), for goods sold and delivered.
2. The counterclaim of Doe against Smith is hereby denied in its entirety.
3. The administrative fees of the American Arbitration Association totaling Eleven Hundred Dollars ($1,100.00) shall be borne equally by the Parties. Therefore, Doe shall pay Smith the sum of Five Hundred Fifty Dollars ($550.00) representing one half (50%) of the filing fees previously advanced by Smith to the AAA.
4. Each Party shall pay one half (50%) of the Arbitrator's fee in this arbitration.
5. This AWARD is in full settlement of all claims and counterclaims submitted in this arbitration.

Signature of Arbitrator

Dated: _____

- ▶ For arbitrator dishonesty, partiality, or bias
- ▶ When no valid agreement was entered into that authorized the arbitration process
- ▶ When an issue that the arbitrator was not authorized to decide was ruled upon

Awards are modifiable only if there was a miscalculation of figures, or a mistake was made in the description of the person, property, or thing referred to in the award.

HOW TO INCREASE THE CHANCES OF SUCCESS IN ARBITRATION

Since the arbitrator's award is final and binding, it is essential to prepare and present a case properly the first time around, because you won't get a second chance. The following strategies may help increase the chances of success:

Hire a lawyer. You have the right to appear yourself (pro se), but it's best to have a lawyer represent you at the hearing, particularly if the dispute involves a large amount of money or complicated legal questions. The familiar expression "He who represents himself has a fool for a client" is certainly applicable in arbitrations. Seek the services of an experienced lawyer who is familiar with the intricacies of the arbitration process. Ask your prospective lawyer how many times he has represented clients in arbitration within the past several years. If the answer is "never" or "only a few times," consider looking elsewhere for representation.

Prepare for the hearing. It is important that both you and your lawyer submit evidence to prove the case, so:

▶ Organize the facts—gather and label all documents needed at the hearing so they can be produced in an orderly fashion.

▶ Prepare a checklist of documents and exhibits so nothing will be forgotten during the presentation.

▶ Make copies of all documents for the arbitrator and adversary.

▶ If some of the documents needed are in the possession of the other party, ask they be brought to the hearing or subpoenaed.

▶ Interview witnesses.

▶ Be sure that friendly witnesses will attend and testify; if there is a possibility that additional witnesses may have to appear, alert them to be available on call without delay.

▶ Select witnesses who are believable, who understand the case and the importance of their testimony, and who will not say things at the hearing to surprise you.

▶ Coordinate the witnesses' testimony so your case will seem consistent and credible.

▶ Prepare witnesses for the rigors of cross-examination.

▶ If a translator is required, make arrangements in advance.

▶ Prepare a written summary of what each witness will hopefully prove and refer to it at the hearing.

▶ Anticipate what the opponent will say to defeat your claim and be prepared to refute such evidence.

▶ Practice your story to put you at ease and help organize the facts.

▶ Prepare a list of questions your lawyer should ask the opponent at the hearing.

▶ Dress appropriately by wearing conservative business clothes.

▶ Act professionally and show respect for the arbitrator.

▶ Listen to the arbitrator's questions and instructions; never argue with the arbitrator.

▶ If a question is posed while you are speaking, stop talking immediately.

▶ Answer all questions honestly and directly.

▶ Avoid arguing with your opponent at the hearing; interrupt his presentation only where absolutely necessary.

Finally, most losing parties voluntarily comply with the terms of an unfavorable award. However, if your opponent decides not to pay, you can enforce the judgment in a regular court. Speak to a lawyer for more details if applicable.

ARREST   *Also see: Crimes and Criminal Law*

People are protected against unreasonable searches and seizures by the Fourth Amendment of the U.S. Constitution. With certain exceptions, the police must first obtain a warrant before searching a person or a residence. A judge or magistrate will authorize this only when the police present ample proof (e.g., testimony and other evidence) to establish probable cause that evidence of a crime is present where the search is to be conducted. To be valid, the warrant must clearly describe the location of the evidence and what is to be sought, and the police are ordinarily required to knock and announce their presence before entering a home to execute a search warrant. Only where there is a likelihood of violence or imminent destruction of evidence are the police allowed to enter a residence unannounced or by forced entry.

Generally, the police cannot conduct warrantless automobile searches unless the driver consents, the officer reasonably believes that a search is necessary for his own safety, or the officer has probable cause. If the driver is accused of committing a crime, such as driving under the influence of alcohol or drugs, a warrantless search may be permitted. Since it is difficult to detain someone while a warrant is obtained, the police generally have more latitude in conducting a search, especially where the officer has reasonable suspicion that the vehicle contains incriminating evidence or was used as an instrument to commit a crime. If so, most areas of the auto can be searched, including under and around the driver's seat and the glove compartment. (Note: Recently, the Supreme Court ruled that police generally do *not* need court warrants before searching cars they reasonably believe are carrying illegal drugs. This ruling overturned one state's law requiring warrants unless police could establish that some emergency existed.)

During the search of a home, the police cannot stray into areas outside the warrant to justify a search or arrest unless there exists probable cause or the homeowner consents to a search. Thus, even if you have nothing to hide, never allow the police to search your house or apartment without a warrant and without your lawyer present. A warrant protects you because the police cannot stray into areas outside the scope of the warrant and inspect every item in your home. If you allow the police to search the premises without a warrant, they must stop immediately if you revoke your consent.

After a lawful arrest, a person can be searched without his or her consent. If a person is arrested but not taken into custody, the police can search for weapons and prevent the accused from destroying any evidence. Once the accused is taken into custody, the police can conduct a full search of the accused and the immediate area around him or her. At the police station, the accused can be strip searched if he or she is suspected of carrying any illegal substances.

A person can be arrested when the police have probable cause. Probable cause is established when there are enough facts to lead a reasonable person to conclude that someone is committing or has committed a crime, or there is a fair probability that evidence of a crime will be found. Probable cause requires more than a hunch but less than proof beyond a reasonable doubt. Although individuals can be detained at the police station and not formally arrested for a period of up to forty-eight hours while a warrant is obtained, they cannot be arrested on a mere suspicion. However, a warrant is not required for an arrest when someone commits a crime in an officer's presence or if the officer has probable cause to believe the person committed a crime.

When the police receive a report of a crime, they send officers to the scene as soon as possible. If a person is arrested, he or she will be transported to the police station and booked. People under arrest have many rights, including the right not to be physically abused or assaulted by the police during the arrest and the right to be told why the arrest is being made. The police must also advise accused persons of their Miranda rights before questioning them. Miranda rights provide that "you have the right to remain silent; anything you say can be used against you in court; you have the right to an attorney to represent you; and if you cannot afford one, an attorney will be provided for you at no cost."

The police do not have to advise persons of their Miranda rights when they take them to the station house before being questioned. Thus, keep silent; never volunteer information or make statements during an arrest, while being transported to the police station, or before a lawyer is present.

The following rules are recommended if you, a friend, or a relative is arrested:

- ▶ Maintain your composure.
- ▶ Follow all police directives.
- ▶ Make no effort to resist arrest; do not fight back.
- ▶ Say as little as possible; never volunteer information.
- ▶ Insist on speaking to a lawyer; say nothing until the lawyer arrives.
- ▶ Do not be intimidated or pressured into making a confession.
- ▶ The police are never the friend of an arrested suspect despite their conduct, so avoid answering any questions.
- ▶ Never make any deals or offer a confession until you speak to a lawyer.
- ▶ Never talk to cellmates because any statements you make can be used against you in court.
- ▶ Tell your lawyer pertinent facts so that he can better represent you; what you tell the lawyer is privileged and confidential.
- ▶ Never represent yourself at any criminal proceeding.

If you are arrested and taken into custody, you will be "booked" at the police station. This involves being fingerprinted and photographed, and disclosing pertinent facts about your identity, residence, and place of work. If the accused crime is serious (i.e., a felony as opposed to a misdemeanor), you will be kept in a cell and your personal belongings taken. You will be issued a receipt that lists all personal items taken. The items will be stored and returned at a later date. Examine the receipt to be sure all items are listed.

Generally, you can make a telephone call to inform someone of your whereabouts. Use the call wisely. Call a lawyer, spouse, relative, or close friend. Do not discuss the facts of the case or guilt or innocence over the phone because such comments may be overheard. Ask your friend or relative to contact an attorney to arrange a meeting as soon as possible.

After being booked, you may be released before the formal arraignment, depending on the seriousness of the crime you are charged with committing. For a misdemeanor, you may be released without bail and told when and where to return to court. For a felony or serious crime, you may be held in jail until the arraignment. An arraignment is a formal proceeding conducted by a judge with you, your lawyer, and the prosecuting lawyer (typically from the district attorney's office) present. You can sit in jail several days before the arraignment, depending on the time and location of the arrest. For example, if the arrest occurred late on a Friday evening in a small town, you may have to sit in jail until Monday morning before the arraignment.

At the arraignment, you will be asked to plead guilty, not guilty, or no contest (nolo contendere). After some discussion by all sides, the judge will determine how much bail is to be set before a release. Bail is the amount of funds to be deposited with the court to ensure a person's appearance at future court proceedings until the case is resolved. The amount of bail is determined by many factors, including the nature and severity of the alleged crime, your background and assets, financial stability, and roots in the community. If there is little risk of your fleeing the jurisdiction and the crime is a minor one, the judge may release you on your own recognizance without the requirement of posting bail.

Virtually all states allow people to post bail with credit cards, so not having sufficient cash on hand for minor infractions may be avoided. Bail bond companies located near prisons and jails are open twenty-four hours to post bail after charging a certain fee (typically, 10 percent of the amount), which is nonrefundable even if you appear at all the court proceedings. If you fail to appear and the bond is forfeited, you will be responsible to repay the bond company for its losses. Many bond companies require people to sign a paper called a lien, which guarantees payment from personal possessions and property and allows the company to seize personal assets in the event of nonpayment.

ASSAULT AND BATTERY

Also see: Crimes and Criminal Law

Also see: Crimes and Criminal Law

In civil law, assault and battery are commonly referred to as intentional torts. These legal causes of action provide for damages against the person who intentionally injures or intends to injure another. Assault and battery are also crimes prosecuted by the state; depending on the severity of the threat or touching, and whether or not a weapon is used, they are felonies with jail time to the accused upon conviction. Victims often wait for a criminal conviction, which requires evidence beyond a reasonable doubt. A civil lawsuit is then filed, and success of the action is presumed since a judge need only conclude a preponderance of the evidence (a lesser standard) to establish fault.

Civil assault is defined as conduct causing another's expectation of immediate harm or offensive contact with his or her body. Words alone do not constitute an assault unless they are accompanied by a menacing act such as threats being made while holding a knife. *Civil battery* is the unjustified harmful, offensive touching of another person's body or anything connected to it. The contact may be made by someone's fists or by a bullet launched by someone shooting a gun. Battery also occurs when actions exceed what is permitted, such as a doctor permitted to biopsy a small section of a person's leg but amputating the entire limb without the patient's formal consent. If someone is threatened (i.e., assault) or physically roughed up (i.e., battery) by a security guard while being detained during a wrongful accusation of shoplifting, the victim may have a claim for damages on both causes of action.

When assault and battery are treated as civil claims, damages are recovered after a victim commences a private lawsuit in court. Compensation can be re-

REQUIREMENTS OF PROOF	HOW TO PROVE IT
Time and place of incident	Your testimony, witnesses
Facts showing the act was intentional	Same as above
Injuries sustained	Photographs (preferably in color and taken as soon after the injury as possible); police report; medical bills; employer's statement of lost wages; medical or hospital report; income tax returns showing lost compensation or profits

Defenses:
1. The incident was provoked
2. Self-defense
3. Reasonable threats or force were used and justified under the circumstances

covered for physical injuries and discomfort (pain and suffering), direct out-of-pocket medical expenses incurred for hospital visits, prescription drugs, lost time from work, and damages for emotional injuries. The table on page 46 illustrates what must generally be proved in order to recover in a lawsuit.

Speak to a lawyer to learn more about your rights if you are threatened or injured by another. Call the police and consider filing criminal charges if the acts are serious. In some cases, criminal charges may be filed against the perpetrator(s) even without your consent.

ASSESSMENTS *See Tax Law*

ATTORNEYS *Also see: Appeals; Consumer Transactions; Crimes and Criminal Law; Litigation; Malpractice*

Laws are unduly complicated, and people often need attorneys to guide them properly. Americans are exposed to hundreds of different kinds of transactions requiring legal services. For example, attorneys are required when buying a house, condominium, or cooperative; reviewing a sophisticated employment contract or equipment lease; preparing a complicated will or trust; getting divorced; or being arrested. People need attorneys to advise them about tax, labor, and other legal regulations.

The time to determine whether an attorney is needed is before legal action is contemplated or necessary. The best way to decide if an attorney is needed is to speak to one. Many attorneys don't charge for brief information given over the telephone.

HOW TO FIND AN ATTORNEY

Select an attorney with care. The right choice can mean the recovery of thousands of dollars or the satisfactory resolution of a conflict or other problem and peace of mind. The wrong choice can cost money and aggravation.

Phone an attorney you know or who is recommended. Describe your problem and ask whether an interview should be scheduled. Recognize that many attorneys who competently represent clients in one area (e.g., criminal law) are not qualified to represent the same clients in unrelated matters (e.g., a personal injury lawsuit) because most attorneys become familiar with certain types of cases, which they handle promptly, efficiently, and profitably. When attorneys accept matters outside the realm of their daily practice, the chances of their making mistakes or not handling matters promptly increase. Ask the attorney what proportion of his working time he spends dealing with the area of law related to your problem. If he says that he does not commonly handle such matters, ask for the names of other attorneys he is willing to recommend. Clients often receive excellent assistance through attorney referrals.

Ask around for recommendations. If you don't know an attorney, ask friends or relatives if they can recommend someone. Be wary of recommendations from people such as bail bondsmen and hospital attendants, who sometimes receive illegal referral fees for recommending clients, because their recommendations may be self-serving.

Call a local bar association. These associations are listed in the phone book, and some maintain lists of attorneys who agree not to charge more than $25 for the first half hour of consultation. If experience is important, tell the person handling the inquiry that you want to contact an experienced practitioner.

Be wary of attorney advertising. Some attorneys have misled the public with their advertising. One common method is to run an advertisement that states that a particular matter costs only $XX. When a potential client meets the attorney, he learns that court costs and filing fees are $XX, but attorney's fees are extra. Also beware of advertisements that proclaim the attorney is a "specialist." Most state bar associations have not adopted specialist certification programs.

THE INITIAL INTERVIEW

After you find a lawyer who will discuss your case with you, set up an initial interview. This interview will help you obtain a sound evaluation of your legal problem and help you decide if you should hire the attorney. This is also the time to discuss important working details, such as the fee arrangement. Bring all pertinent written information to the initial interview (e.g., copies of contracts, checks, letters, bills of sale, and photographs). Tell the attorney everything related to the matter. Communicate all relevant information without inhibition because the discussion is privileged and confidential.

Once the attorney receives all the pertinent facts, he should be in a position of advising if the matter has any legal validity or consequences depending on state law. He should also advise you whether the matter can be resolved through legal assistance. If so, inquire how quickly he thinks the matter can be resolved, what must be done, and how much he intends to charge for the contemplated services.

If a lawsuit is considered, or if you have been sued and need the attorney to assist in defense of the case, the attorney will then:

> ► Decide whether the case has a fair probability of success after considering the law in the state where the suit will be brought
> ► Give an estimate as to how long the lawsuit will last
> ► Make a determination of the approximate legal fees and disbursements
> ► Explain what legal papers will be filed, when and what their purposes are
> ► Discuss the defenses an opponent will probably raise, and how to deal with them

If the attorney sees weaknesses in the case and believes that litigation will be unduly expensive, he may advise a compromise and settlement of the claim without resorting to litigation. In any event, the chosen course of action should be instituted without delay to ensure that the requisite time period in which to start the action—that is, the statute of limitations—will not have expired.

For all matters, the attorney should advise what legal work needs to be done, how long it will take, and how much it will cost. Some attorneys neglect to give honest appraisals. Clients are then misled and spend large sums of money on losing causes. Be wary if the attorney states that "you have nothing to worry about." Prudent attorneys tell clients that "airtight" cases do not exist and that the possibility of unforeseen circumstances and developments is always present.

If applicable, request an opinion letter that spells out the pros and cons of the matter and how much money may be spent to accomplish your objectives. Even if you are charged for the time it takes to draft it, an opinion letter can minimize future misunderstandings between you and your attorney and help you decide whether or not to proceed with a lawsuit or legal intervention. The Sample Attorney Opinion Letter on pages 326–327 in the Appendix illustrates this concept.

It is important to leave the interview feeling that the attorney is open and responsive to your needs, is genuinely interested in helping you, will return your telephone calls promptly, and will prepare and handle your case properly. Although it is difficult to predict how well an attorney will perform, there are certain clues to look for during the interview.

- Does the attorney present an outward appearance of neatness and good grooming?
- Are you received at the appointed interview hour or kept waiting? Some attorneys believe that if clients are kept waiting they will think the attorney is busy and, therefore, good. Keeping you waiting is merely a sign that the attorney is not organized or is inconsiderate.
- Does the attorney leave the room frequently during the interview, or permit telephone calls to intrude? You deserve his complete attention.
- Does he demonstrate boredom or lack of interest by yawning or finger tapping?
- Is he a clock watcher?
- Does the attorney try to impress you by narrating other cases he handled? Good attorneys do not have to boast to obtain clients.
- Does he fail to discuss the fee arrangement up front? Some attorneys have a tendency to wait until all work is done before submitting large bills. The failure to discuss fee arrangements at the initial interview may be a sign the attorney operates this way.

Successful attorneys win cases and make money for their clients. Don't be fooled by appearances. Plush offices, fancy cars, and expensive clothes may signal that you will pay exorbitant fees for routine legal services. Don't be impressed by the school where the attorney graduated. Most law schools do not give their graduates practical experience, and many less prestigious "local" law schools offer superior training, which is what you are paying for.

Be sure the attorney of your choice will be working on the matter. People often go to prestigious firms, expecting their matter to be handled by a partner. They pay large fees and sometimes wind up being represented by a junior associate. Be sure your retainer agreement states that the matter will be handled by attorney X (the attorney of your choice).

The major factor in determining whether a particular attorney should be hired is the amount of experience and expertise he or she has in handling similar legal problems. Use an attorney who devotes at least 50 percent of his practice to such problems. Avoid inexperienced attorneys if possible. Novices charge less, but often require more time to handle a problem. If you are being charged on an hourly basis, you may pay the same amount of money and not obtain the expertise of a pro.

Hire an attorney to whom you can relate. Ask the attorney about his outside activities and professional associations. Inquire if you may speak to any of his previous clients; references can help you learn more about the attorney. If you do not feel comfortable with the first attorney you meet, shop around and schedule appointments with others.

CONFIRMING THE ARRANGEMENT

After you decide to retain an attorney, it is necessary to discuss a variety of points concerning fees to eliminate potential misunderstandings.

Clarify the fee. Most attorneys charge a modest fee for the first visit to the office. Fees should be charged only when actual time is spent working on a matter. Charges are based on the amount of time and work involved, the difficulty of the problem, the dollar amount of the case, the result, the urgency of the problem (e.g., a real estate closing that the attorney must handle the day after he is contacted will command a higher fee than the same closing that takes place in a month), and the attorney's expertise and reputation in handling your type of problem. Operating expenses and office overhead are elements that may also affect the fee arrangement.

Frequently, an attorney cannot state exactly how much will be charged because he is unable to determine the amount of work that is involved. In such a case, ask for an estimate of the minimum and maximum fee you can expect to pay. If it seems high, do not hesitate to question it. If necessary, tell the attorney that you intend to speak to other attorneys about fees.

The fee arrangement is composed of several elements, which you must clearly understand. Costs are expenses that the attorney incurs while preparing a case or working on a matter (e.g., photocopying, telephone, mailing, fees paid to the court for filing documents). Be certain the fee arrangement specifically mentions in writing which of these costs you must pay.

FORM 15. **Sample Hourly Retainer Agreement with Attorney**

Date

Name of Client
Address

Re: Retainer Agreement Regarding Doe v. Doe

Dear (Name of Client),

This letter confirms that you have retained me as your attorney to (state precise nature of engagement, such as to negotiate a settlement agreement with a spouse if that is reasonably possible; or, if not, to represent you in a divorce action). You agree to pay to me promptly an initial retainer of (specify $, such as $1,500). If I devote more than 10 hours to this case based upon accurate time records commencing from the initial conference, which I will prepare and send to you on a monthly basis, you shall pay additional fees counted at the rate of (specify $, such as $150/hour), and I will promptly return any outstanding portion of the retainer previously paid.

If you should decide to discontinue my services in this matter at any time, you shall be liable for my time computed at the rate of $150/hour.

These fees do not include any work in appellate courts, any other actions or proceedings, or out-of-pocket disbursements. Out-of-pocket disbursements include, but are not limited to, costs of filing papers, court fees, process servers, witness fees, court reporters, long-distance telephone calls, travel, parking, and photocopies (billed at 10 cents per copy) normally made by me or requested by you, which disbursements shall be paid for or reimbursed to me upon my request after I furnish you with evidence of same.

I promise to keep you informed of all developments as they occur and to send you copies of all incoming and outgoing correspondence immediately after it is generated/received. I will personally handle all negotiations of your matter, preparing all necessary papers and documents and arguing your case in court if necessary.

I look forward to working with you on this matter. Kindly indicate your understanding and acceptance of the above terms by signing this letter below where indicated.

Very truly yours,
Name of Attorney

I, (name of client), have read and understand the above letter, have received a copy, and accept all of its terms:

_____   Dated: _____
Name of Client

Attorneys use different forms of fee arrangements. In a *flat-fee arrangement,* the attorney is paid a specified sum to get the job done. Most attorneys offer a number of services that are performed on a flat-fee basis (e.g., preparation of a simple will, uncontested divorce, formation of a small corporation, preparation of certain commercial contracts, and other standard services). In a *flat-fee-plus-time arrangement,* a sum for a specified number of hours is charged. Once the attorney works more hours than are specified, the client is charged on an hourly basis. However, most attorneys use an *hourly-rate arrangement,* with the rate ranging from $150 to $300 an hour or more. Under this arrangement, you will be charged on a fixed hourly rate for all work done. If you are billed by the hour, ask if phone calls between you and the attorney are included. If so, ask that you be charged only for calls exceeding a certain number per month. This can be justified by arguing that you should not be charged when the attorney fails to clarify a point, provide additional information, or discuss news regarding the progress of the case. (See page 51 for a sample hourly retainer agreement.)

In a *contingency-fee arrangement,* the attorney receives a specified percentage of any money recovered via a lawsuit or settlement. Contingency-fee arrangements are common in personal injury lawsuits. Many people favor contingency-fee arrangements because they are not required to pay legal fees if their case is unsuccessful. However, some types of contingency fees are not permitted. For example, an attorney cannot agree to structure the size of his fee based on the type of verdict obtained for a client in a criminal proceeding. Contingency fees are also looked upon unfavorably by courts and disciplinary boards in matrimonial actions because they are viewed as encouraging divorces. So, too, are contingency fees in personal injury suits that exceed maximum allowable percentages (typically 40 percent). If an attorney proposes contingency fees in these areas, never accept the arrangement and hire him.

Always spell out contingency arrangements in writing to prevent problems. The agreement should state who is responsible for costs in the event you are unsuccessful. All provisions should be explained so they are clearly understood; be sure to save a copy for your records. (The sample contingency fee arrangement on page 53 illustrates many of these points.)

There are distinct advantages and disadvantages in using different fee arrangements. For example, in a flat-fee arrangement you know how much you will be charged but not how much care and attention will be spent on the matter. The hourly rate may be cheaper than a flat fee for routine work, but some dishonest attorneys "pad" time sheets to increase their fees. In addition, although contingency-fee arrangements are beneficial to clients with weak cases, they sometimes encourage attorneys to settle "winner" cases for less money rather than go to court. This is why, no matter what type of fee is agreed upon, it is essential to hire an attorney who is honest and has your best interests in mind at all times.

Ask for a receipt if you pay for the initial consultation or retainer in cash. If a retainer is required, inquire whether the retainer will become part of the entire fee and whether it is refundable. The retainer guarantees the availability of the attorney to represent you and is an advance paid to demonstrate your desire to resolve a problem via legal recourse. Ask if the retainer and other fees can be paid by credit card. Be sure that interest will not be added if you are late in

FORM 16. **Sample Contingency Fee Arrangement with Attorney**

Date

Name of Client
Address

Re: Retainer Agreement Regarding Doe v. Smith

Dear (Name of Client),

This letter confirms that our law firm will represent you (specify matter, such as in the prosecution of your claim for personal injuries sustained by you on _____ date, as a result of a slip-and-fall accident in _____ store located at (specify location).

We will devote our efforts to this matter for a fee, the amount of which will depend upon the outcome of your claim:

1. If nothing is recovered, you will not be indebted to us for our service and will not be required to reimburse us for any costs or expenses incurred with your case.

2. If we are successful, we will first be reimbursed for any costs and expenses paid by the firm in connection with your matter. We will then receive 25 percent of the net amount obtained for you if no suit is filed, and 33 percent of any amount received after suit is filed.

3. Proceeds, if any, recovered by way of settlement, judgment, or otherwise, shall be disbursed as follows: All our costs which have not been reimbursed by you will be deducted; our fees, as set out in the percentage above, will be deducted and the balance will be immediately paid to you.

4. Should you decide to discharge us and retain another law firm for any reason, we shall receive a reasonable percentage of the other firm's percentage of the proceeds recovered by said firm proportionate to the amount of work done by our firm on your matter.

We promise to keep you informed of all developments as they occur and to send you copies of all pertinent incoming and outgoing correspondence immediately after it is generated/received. (Specify name of lawyer) will primarily handle your matter, including all negotiations, and try the case in court if necessary. This law firm may not be handling an appeal of your case, depending on the outcome of the case, and our mutual discussion and agreement at a later date.

If this letter correctly states our understanding of the terms of our representation, will you please so indicate by signing this agreement in the space below and returning a copy to us immediately.

Sincerely yours,
Name of Attorney for
Law Firm

_____   Dated: _____
Name of Client

paying fees. Request that all fees be billed periodically. Insist that billing statements be supported by detailed and complete time records that include the number of hours (or partial hours) worked, a report of the people contacted, and the services rendered. Some attorneys may be reluctant to do this, but by receiving these documents and statements on a regular basis, you can question inconsistencies and errors before they get out of hand, be aware of the amount of the bill as it accrues, and pay for it over time. (The sample monthly billing statement below is the kind of bill the author prepares for all his clients who are charged on an hourly basis. Insist on nothing less.)

Most important, request the attorney to send copies of all incoming and outgoing correspondence so you will be able to follow the progress of the case.

Understand what legal fees are tax-deductible. Legal fees are tax-deductible provided they are ordinary and necessary business expenses. This means that the cost of legal fees paid or incurred for the "collection, maintenance, or conservation of income" or property used in producing income can be deducted. Deductions are also allowed for legal fees paid to collect, determine, or refund any tax that is owed. Ask the attorney whether fees paid are deductible. Structure the fee arrangement to maximize tax deductions and ask for a written statement that justifies the bill on the basis of time spent or some other allocation

---

FORM 17. **Sample Monthly Billing Statement from Attorney**

Date

Name of Client
Address

Final statement for all services rendered in the matter of the contract negotiation between (name of client) and (name of employer) at the rate of $200 per hour per agreement:

1. 1/05/99	Initial Meeting with Client, 10:30–11:15	NO CHARGE
2. 1/06/99	Review of initial proposed Agreement,	
	7:30–7:55 a.m.	25 min.
	Tel. conv. with Client, 9:05–9:15	10 min.
3. 1/07/99	Tel. conv. with Employer's Attorney, 9:40–9:45	5 min.
	Tel. conv. with Client, 8:45–8:50; 9:50–9:55	10 min.
4. 1/08/99	Draft of Revised Agreement including	
	tel. conv. with client, 6:50–8:25 a.m.	95 min.
	Fax agreement to Employer's Attorney	
	Final Discussion with Employer's Attorney,	
	2:05–2:25	20 min.

Total time spent on Matter from January 5, 1999 through
   January 8, 1999:   165 min. or 2.75 hours
   Amount earned: $550.00

to support the claim. Keep the statement in a safe place until tax time and show it to your tax preparer. Accountants and other professionals often clip copies of the statements directly to the return so the IRS won't question the deduction.

The following is a summary of tax-deductible legal fees:

▶ Attorney fees paid to obtain estate planning, including the preparation of a will

▶ Attorney fees paid to obtain a tax ruling

▶ Attorney fees paid to perfect a patent application, copyright, or other intangible asset

▶ Attorney fees paid to obtain alimony, property, or tax advice incident to a divorce; fees paid to obtain the divorce itself are not

▶ Attorney fees paid to address problems involving bankruptcy, antitrust (except if it relates to the imposition of a fine or penalty), or labor relations

▶ Attorney fees paid to oppose a suspension of a professional license or disbarment

▶ Attorney fees for services tending to increase or protect taxable business income (e.g., defending inherited stock)

OTHER ITEMS TO CLARIFY DURING
THE INITIAL INTERVIEW

Will the attorney be available? Complaints often arise because of poor communication. At the initial interview, ask what the attorney's normal office hours are. Advise the attorney that availability is very important to you since you are paying for this service. Request that he return phone calls within twenty-four hours. Insist that his secretary or associate return phone calls if he will be unavailable for extended periods of time, but make it clear you will not call him unnecessarily.

Will the attorney work on the matter immediately? The legal system is often a slow process. Don't stall it further by hiring a procrastinating attorney. Insist that the attorney begin working on the matter as quickly as possible. Ask for an estimate of when the matter will be resolved. Include this in the retainer agreement for protection.

Are there hidden conflicts of interest? Attorneys must avoid even the appearance of impropriety. For example, when an attorney represents both a husband and wife in a divorce, there is an inherent conflict that limits his ability to zealously promote the best interest of each of them. Ask the attorney up front if he perceives any potential conflict of interest (e.g., is he related to or was he ever employed by the person you are suing?). An attorney must decline representing a client when his professional judgment is likely to be affected by other business, financial, or personal interests. If an attorney is disqualified, his associates and partners are also forbidden to serve you.

How will funds be handled? Attorneys are obligated to keep client funds in separate accounts. This includes unearned retainer fees. The rules of professional conduct state that an attorney cannot commingle client funds with his own and that bank accounts for client funds must be clearly marked as "Client Trust Accounts" or "Escrow Accounts."

An attorney must notify the client immediately when funds are received. You must also receive an accurate accounting of these funds. This consists of a complete explanation of the amount of money held by the attorney, its origin, and the reason for any deductions. Be sure that you receive this. Ask for a copy of all checks received before the attorney deposits the funds into his trust or escrow account. Tell the attorney to place your funds in an interest-bearing escrow account. Later on, when the funds are remitted, be sure the interest is included in the amount returned to you.

PROBLEMS ENCOUNTERED AFTER AN ATTORNEY IS HIRED

You have the right to change attorneys at any time if there is a valid reason. Valid reasons include improper or unethical conduct, conflicts of interest, and malpractice by the attorney. If you are dissatisfied with your attorney's conduct or the way the matter is progressing, consult another attorney for an opinion. Do this before taking action, because you need a professional opinion on whether your attorney acted correctly or incorrectly.

Never fire your attorney until you hire a replacement because you may be unrepresented and your case could be prejudiced or dismissed. If you fire your attorney, you may be required to pay for the value of work rendered. You may also have to go to court to settle the issue of legal fees and the return of your papers, since some attorneys assert a lien on the file. However, these potential problems should never impede you from taking action if warranted.

If you have evidence that your attorney misused funds for personal gain or committed fraud, you may file a complaint with the state grievance committee or local bar association. Don't be afraid to do this. All complaints are confidential. You cannot be sued for filing a complaint if it is later determined that the attorney did nothing wrong.

Another alternative is to commence a malpractice lawsuit against the attorney. Legal malpractice arises when an attorney fails to use "such skill or prudence as attorneys of ordinary skill commonly possess and exercise in the performance of the tasks they undertake." This doesn't mean you can sue if your attorney gets beaten by a better attorney. You can sue only if he renders work or assistance of minimal competence and you are damaged as a result. You can also sue for malpractice when there is a breach of ethics (e.g., the failure to remit funds belonging to a client), in addition to suing for breach of contract and/or civil fraud.

The following are examples of attorney malpractice:
- Settling a case without your consent

- Procrastinating work on a matter (e.g., neglecting to prepare a will after being paid and before the client dies)
- Charging grossly improper fees
- Failing to file a claim within the requisite time period (statute of limitations)
- Failing to competently represent a defendant in a criminal matter

Consult another attorney before embarking on any of these courses of action to learn if you have a valid claim. An honest and unbiased attorney will also tell you what steps should be taken to protect your rights.

Summary of Steps to Take to Use an Attorney Effectively

1. Speak to an attorney before action is contemplated to determine if one is needed.
2. Schedule an interview if necessary; inquire if you will be charged for it.
3. Bring relevant documents to the interview.
4. Do not be overly impressed by plush surroundings.
5. Be sure the attorney of your choice will be handling the matter.
6. Hire an experienced practitioner who devotes at least 50 percent of his working time to your type of problem.
7. Look for honesty and integrity in an attorney.
8. Insist on signing a retainer agreement to reduce misunderstandings.
9. Have the agreement read and explained to you before signing and save a copy for your files.
10. If the attorney cannot state exactly how much you will be charged, get minimum and maximum estimates. Include this in the agreement.
11. Be certain you understand how additional costs are calculated, and who will pay for them.
12. If an hourly rate is agreed upon, negotiate that you will not be charged for a few telephone calls to your attorney.
13. Inquire if you can pay the bill by credit card.
14. Structure the fee arrangement to maximize tax deductions and savings.
15. Insist on receiving copies of incoming and outgoing correspondence and monthly, detailed time records.
16. Be sure the attorney will be available, will immediately commence work on your matter, and has no potential conflicts of interest.
17. Insist that all funds received by the attorney be deposited into an interest-bearing escrow account. Don't forget to ask for the interest later on.
18. Never allow the attorney to pressure you into settling a case or making a rushed, uninformed decision.
19. Consult another attorney before deciding to fire the present one, file a complaint with the grievance committee, or commence a malpractice lawsuit.
20. Do not expect miracles.

AUTOMOBILES

Also see: Arrest; Crimes and Criminal Law; Contracts; Driving While Under the Influence; Litigation; Loans; Traffic Violations

WARRANTIES

Manufacturing defects are often discovered soon after the purchase of a new automobile. While manufacturer's warranties are supposed to correct such problems at no cost, purchasers are sometimes disappointed by the dealer's failure to repair the defect properly and promptly. Full warranties are defined as covering all parts and labor charges for an extended period of time; limited warranties cover reimbursement only for specific parts for a short period of time. Dealers selling a particular make of car are typically obligated to perform repairs covered by warranty even if the car was not purchased from them.

Most used cars are offered "as is" with no warranty or small limited warranties. (See page 328 in the Appendix to review a simple Bill of Sale for an Automobile, which always should be prepared and signed when purchasing or selling a used car.) Try to obtain a full or limited warranty when buying a used car from a car-rental company or used-car dealer and include this in the sales contract. Under federal law, used-car dealers selling more than six cars in a twelve-month period must specify what warranties go with the used car and post this conspicuously on the car. If the used-car dealer fails to honor the warranty, send a letter certified mail, return receipt requested, demanding satisfaction. If no satisfaction ensues, send a demand letter to your state's Department of Consumer Affairs to protect your rights. (See pages 59–60 for examples of these letters.)

If a new-car dealer fails to provide prompt warranty coverage or assistance, consider the following:

Contact the nearest factory zone manager listed in the owner's manual. Ask a representative to meet with you and the dealer's service manager. If the problem affects safety, have the repair made immediately, even if you have to pay, and argue about the refund later.

Send a certified letter to the manufacturer's main office if the problem is not resolved. Describe the problem briefly; explain what the dealer offered and what you think should be done.

Consider suing the dealer or manufacturer. This is done through a small-claims court or a state's lemon law arbitration proceeding. In most states, legislation called "lemon laws" attempts to provide refunds or replacements when the manufacturer is unable, within a reasonable period of time, to remedy a substantial defect. Used with private arbitration as a dispute-resolution mechanism, these laws often help consumers receive quicker and less expensive relief.

FORM 19. **Sample Letter to Used-Car Dealer**

> Your Name
> Address
> Date

(Name), President
ABC Used Car Sales
Address

Dear (Name),

On (date) I bought a used (describe make, model, year, serial number, color) for the sum of (specify $). At the time of the sale, you stated that the car was a "cream puff," in perfect mechanical condition.

It was agreed that your shop would perform any and all repairs if the car malfunctioned for any reason for a period of 60 days after the date of purchase at no cost. This was inserted into the sales contract and initialed by both of us. A copy of the sales contract is attached.

Last week, a mere 10 days after the sale, the car broke down while I was driving to (specify location). An AAA representative towed the car back to my home. Despite several telephone calls to you, the car is sitting in my driveway while you keep telling me "to be patient."

I require the use of an automobile for my business, and I am currently renting a replacement at the sum of $35 a day while your car is inoperative. Unless the car is repaired to my satisfaction immediately per our understanding, and you provide me with a replacement car at no cost while mine is being repaired, I will bring the matter to the attention of the Department of Consumer Affairs, the Consumer Fraud Division of the Attorney General's Office, and the Better Business Bureau. I will also consider instituting legal action against your firm, and you personally to recover all out-of-pocket and other losses.

Hopefully this can be avoided and I await your immediate response and assistance.

> Very truly yours,
> Name of Consumer

cc: to your personal attorney if you have one

▷ Send certified mail, return receipt requested.

Most state lemon laws expand the scope to include leased and used vehicles, increase the length of warranty coverage, and reduce the number of repair attempts that qualify a vehicle as a lemon. Some laws also cover commercial vehicles, trucks, and motorcycles, and the failure to provide a warranty may itself be a violation that may subject a dealer to punitive damages, attorney fees, and costs incurred by an aggrieved consumer, such as renting a replacement vehicle and travel to have the vehicle repaired.

Check applicable state law and contact the nearest Better Business Bureau (BBB) or Department of Consumer Affairs to learn the limits and extent of consumer protection. Notify the dealer, manufacturer, or company where the car was

FORM 20. **Sample Demand Letter to Department of Consumer Affairs**

Your Name
Address
Date

Dept. of Consumer Affairs
Address

Re: Formal complaint against ABC Used Car Sales, license number XXX

To Whom It May Concern:

This letter is a formal complaint against ABC Used Car Sales.

On (date) I purchased a used car (describe make, model, year, serial number, color) from ABC Used Car Sales. A sales contract was signed that stated ABC would perform satisfactory repairs at no cost for a period of 60 days from the date of the purchase.

On (date) the car broke down, and ABC refuses to repair it. This action has caused me significant damages, including (specify).

Please investigate the matter on my behalf. I am enclosing a copy of the sales contract, letter of protest sent to ABC via certified mail, return receipt requested, costs of renting a replacement car, and other documentation for your review.

Please contact me at the above address if you require any additional information or assistance.

Thank you for your prompt cooperation in this matter.

Very truly yours,
Your name

cc: ABC Used Car Sales; Better Business Bureau;
    Attorney General's Office, Consumer Fraud Division

▷ Send certified mail, return receipt requested.

purchased and request that repairs be promptly made. If after several attempts the condition is not alleviated, arbitration can be commenced or a private lawsuit can be initiated to obtain a refund of the purchase price or a suitable replacement car.

The following steps can enhance a claim before filing for arbitration:

▶ Notify the dealer or manufacturer by letter in a timely manner.

▶ State the make, model, vehicle identification number, and other pertinent facts (e.g., date, price, and place of purchase).

▶ Document the problem or defect; include a statement from a mechanic or diagnostic center to support the claim.

▶ Schedule an appointment with the dealer to return the car.

▶ After the car is repaired, ask for a copy of the bill that shows what repairs were performed.

- Save all documents and records.
- Prepare a diary of steps taken to maintain the car in proper working condition (e.g., regular inspections) to prove that the defect was not caused by abuse or neglect.
- Return the car to the dealer if the problem is not corrected.
- Contact a lawyer to determine the appropriate course of action if the problem persists.

File for arbitration. Most state lemon laws require people to use the manufacturer's informal dispute-resolution mechanism before proceeding to court. These include the Ford Consumer Appeals Board, Chrysler Customer Satisfaction Arbitration Board, BBB AUTOLINE, and the National Automobile Dealers Association (AUTOCAP). If successful, you will usually be entitled to a refund of the purchase price or a replacement vehicle. Attorney fees may also be provided in most states.

To begin the process, file a form to describe the problem. The dealer then comments and/or defends against the charges in writing.

Boards are made up of one or more arbitrators, who base their decision on written statements from the parties involved, testimony at hearings, and physical inspection of the automobile. It takes several months from the date an arbitration request is received to the date a decision is rendered. The average cost to the consumer is less than $400. Most states allow consumers to file private lawsuits when they have been unable to resolve the matter through arbitration. If you cannot afford a private lawyer, speak to a local legal referral service or the Legal Aid Society, or contact a local BBB or state attorney general's office for help.

The following strategies are helpful when commencing arbitration:
- Choose the proper avenue for arbitration.
- Read as much as possible about the arbitration program selected.
- Get assistance and advice. The BBB can help you prepare the case and discuss your options. For example, do you want a refund or a comparable replacement vehicle? An in-person hearing or only a written presentation? Where do you want the hearing conducted?
- Prepare for the hearing. Be prepared to submit the contract of purchase and/or financing agreement; proof of the amount of down payment and number of payments made; all attempted repairs within the time period specified by the state's lemon law; the warranty contract (if any); all correspondence to help the case.
- Organize this information chronologically and logically.
- Present all records indicating with whom you spoke regarding the defect, when and where, and make copies of all letters of protest sent.
- Have witnesses testify on your behalf.

- ▸ If an important witness, such as an impartial mechanic who examined repeated repair attempts, refuses to testify, request that the person be compelled to attend by a subpoena.
- ▸ Present the case directly and answer all questions.
- ▸ Attend all required prehearing meetings to familiarize yourself with the opponent.
- ▸ Know the major provisions of the state's lemon law.
- ▸ Review all material presented by the other side, clarify points, and respond to ambiguous statements for the record.
- ▸ Speak to an attorney. A knowledgeable attorney can assist in all informal and formal stages of the arbitration, file an appeal, help you enforce a favorable award, and file a private lawsuit if applicable.

BAILMENTS

A bailment occurs when the owner of personal property (the bailor) transfers the possession, care, and/or control of the property to another person (the bailee) for a limited time and for a special purpose. The laws regarding bailments apply, for example, when you pay to park your car in a parking lot and it is stolen or damaged. Other common instances of bailment occur when a guest in your home borrows your luggage, you check your coat in a restaurant or with an airline, or you pay a fee to have your fur coat stored, and the article is damaged, lost, stolen, or not returned. To prevail in a lawsuit seeking damages, it is generally necessary to prove the following:

WHAT YOU MUST PROVE	HOW TO PROVE IT
1. Time, place, and delivery of the property to a person, business, or company	1. Contract, receipt, canceled check
2. Description of the property and proof of ownership	2. Bill of sale, your testimony, witnesses
3. Value of the property when originally purchased or acquired; current or replacement value	3. Sales receipt, canceled check, appraisal
4. (a) Item is damaged	4. (a) Photographs, estimates of repair, your testimony, witnesses
(b) Item is lost	(b) Your testimony, witnesses, police report, insurance report
(c) Item is stolen	(c) Same as (b) above
(d) Item is not returned	(d) Demand letter, your testimony, witnesses

(continued on page 63)

(continued from page 62)

WHAT YOU MUST PROVE	HOW TO PROVE IT
5. Damages	5. Cost of replacement value, canceled check, appraisal, sales receipt

Typical Defenses Asserted in Bailment Cases:
1. The property was held longer than required.
2. Storage fees were not paid so the goods were disposed of or kept as a lien until payment is made.
3. There is no proof that the goods were delivered to the bailee.
4. There is no proof that the goods belong to you.
5. The goods were returned as promised or under the terms agreed-upon.
6. The bailee assumed no responsibility for the loss since there was no benefit conferred (called a gratuitous bailment).

Whether you can recover damages and prove liability depends on the unique facts of each case. For example, establishing what degree of care is owed by a restaurant or common carrier who agreed to store an expensive coat and whether that duty of care was breached may depend on whether compensation was given by the bailor to the bailee and other factors. When money is specifically paid, the bailee receives a benefit for this service and the law imposes a higher duty of care to safeguard your property. (See pages 329–330 in the Appendix to review samples of property storage and animal boarding contracts.)

BANKRUPTCY

Bankruptcy is a formal proceeding governed by federal law whereby individuals and businesses unable to pay their bills in a regular manner are shielded to a degree from creditors. The procedure is supervised by the bankruptcy court, which is part of the federal bankruptcy system. Depending on circumstances, different types of bankruptcies can be filed, denominated by appropriate sections of the Bankruptcy Code.

TYPES OF BANKRUPTCY

Chapter 7 (or straight bankruptcy) is typically utilized by individuals or businesses that file a petition for bankruptcy with the bankruptcy court located in their city or county of residence. If the petition is approved by the court, virtually all debts (with the exception of liens on property, certain back taxes owed to the government, child support arrears, purchases made with a credit card within twenty days prior to filing the petition), and certain other debts are discharged (i.e., eliminated), permitting a fresh financial start.

After a debtor files for bankruptcy under Chapter 7, the progress of lawsuits and payment of debts is automatically "stayed" (i.e., stopped) and creditors are prevented from starting or continuing any legal action against the debtor. Most of the debtor's assets are collected, sold, and distributed. Once the case is over, most creditors cannot come back and sue for debts that arose prior to the bankruptcy. Creditors are prohibited from contacting the debtor or his employer, and collection agencies cannot make any attempt to collect debts. Once a person has filed for bankruptcy, he or she must wait six years to file again.

In a *Chapter 11* business reorganization, ongoing businesses are permitted to restructure their debts in a timely and responsible fashion without going out of business. A plan to pay off creditors at a reduced rate is developed by the business's management or a court-appointed trustee and must be approved by the creditors and a bankruptcy judge. This type of bankruptcy is most often used by corporations and business partnerships that want to continue to operate, and provides a way to pay all current bills while paying off a portion of previous debt over time.

In a *Chapter 13* reorganization plan, also known as "adjustment of debts," individuals with regular sources of income are given a period of time (up to five years) to pay off all or some of their debts to the extent that they reasonably can out of earnings and other resources. Chapter 13 makes it possible for owners of real property and other assets that could be sold under the terms of a Chapter 7 liquidation to keep their property even though they are behind in their mortgage payments. By filing for Chapter 13 protection up to the moment of a foreclosure sale, debtors can preserve their homes from foreclosure even when a judgment of foreclosure has already been entered.

Only individuals with regular income, unsecured debts (e.g., credit card charges) of less than $250,000, and secured debts (e.g., a home mortgage) of less than $750,000 can utilize this form of financial relief. A negotiated amount of money recommended by the trustee and approved by the bankruptcy judge is forwarded each month to the trustee, who pays each creditor a lesser amount. Typically, this lesser amount is determined by the number of creditors, the total amount of outstanding debt, and what proportionally is fair to the class of creditor. People whose income far exceeds their expenses typically choose to file Chapter 13 as opposed to Chapter 7. But if the debtor cannot maintain payments, the bankruptcy may be converted into a Chapter 7 by a judge's order.

Bankruptcy laws were devised to give individuals and business entities an opportunity to avoid financial oppression. Under many states' laws, people are allowed to keep a small amount of cash, cars up to a certain value (e.g., $2,400), most retirement plans, a portion or all of their homes depending on state law (called a homestead exemption), and contents, professional books, and tools of a trade valued up to $1,500, life insurance policies valued up to $8,000, and modest personal injury settlements of up to $15,000. Thus, filers do not lose everything. These amounts vary by state.

Although filing for bankruptcy may give you immediate relief from creditors and collection agencies, your credit will be impaired, sometimes permanently, and you may find it difficult to obtain reasonable credit. Credit reporting agencies are notified whenever anyone files for bankruptcy protection, wages are garnished, or assets are taken or attached. Once a bankruptcy is filed, credit reporting companies such as TRW or Equifax will state on a credit report that the individual filed for bankruptcy but not state an opinion or give a recommendation as to whether credit should be extended. A bankruptcy filing generally stays on your credit record for ten years, but in certain instances, such as when you apply for a mortgage, some bankruptcy information can be given out for the rest of your life.

Since the credit rating for most people who file for bankruptcy is poor to begin with, they often have nothing to lose. There have been instances where people have received credit-card applications and cards shortly after filing for bankruptcy, and some lending institutions may still lend money although at higher interest rates. Some experts suggest that people who file for Chapter 7 bankruptcy are better credit risks because they are debt-free and can't file for bankruptcy again for another six years.

A person cannot be denied a job because he files for bankruptcy. According to the bankruptcy code, no private employer may terminate the employment of, or discriminate with respect to employment against, an individual who is or has gone bankrupt. Under the federal Fair Debt Credit Reporting Act, employers are generally forbidden to use credit reports for hiring or employment decisions unless the job is security-sensitive or the financial integrity of the applicant is essential to successful job performance. In most states and under the federal Consumer Credit Protection Act, it is illegal for a company to fire a person who has been sued for the nonpayment of a debt or when the company is instructed to cooperate in the collection of a portion of a person's wages through garnishment proceedings. It is even illegal for a person or business engaged in arranging for student loans to allow decisions to be influenced by the fact that the applicant or someone associated with the applicant has filed for bankruptcy.

BEFORE YOU FILE FOR BANKRUPTCY

Bankruptcy is a drastic step and should be considered only after other options have been taken and have failed, since there are more effective means to combat debt problems. Consider taking the following actions before deciding to file for bankruptcy.

Contact creditors directly by letter requesting a reasonable period of time to pay off any debts. Try to reduce the full amount of the debt and have the creditor waive interest and penalties. You can often do this by stating that you will pay the bill now in full if a sufficient reduction is granted. If so, confirm all understandings in a written agreement that accurately reflects the settlement and save a copy for your records.

Attempt to obtain a debt-consolidation loan. This is a short-term solution. Obtain one large loan from a bank or other lending institution and use the proceeds to pay off your creditors, leaving you liable only for the new loan, which is usually at a lower interest rate than credit-card debts.

Seek help from a consumer credit or debt counseling service. There are specialists who, for a modest fee (under $200), will review your income and expenses and advise on how to cut expenses, remedy credit, and obtain a debt-consolidation loan.

Seek legal assistance if you are being sued by creditors. A competent attorney may be able to settle such lawsuits for a reduced amount and avoid your having to file for bankruptcy. Lawyers should be able to structure reasonable payouts with creditors over time or stall litigation proceedings to give you time to explore your options.

Hire a specialist, because a lawyer not familiar with bankruptcy proceedings may not have the time or resources to research a complicated issue that is routine for a bankruptcy attorney. Thoroughly explore the pros and cons of each form of bankruptcy with the attorney before selecting a Chapter 7, 11, or 13 proceeding. Discuss the ramifications of jointly held property (e.g., with a spouse) and special laws if you are in the military. Understand the fee to be charged and insist on receiving a retainer agreement that spells out all fees and costs.

Consider relocating. The amount of property a debtor can keep after a bankruptcy varies from state to state. A few states, such as Florida, allow a person to keep his home and property even if it has a high market value. Some people establish a separate residence in a more favorable state to take advantage of these laws. However, you must live in a new state for a sufficient period of time (e.g., more than a year) to establish residency before taking advantage of that state's particular laws. If applicable, speak to a lawyer for more advice concerning this.

Understand what debts are not discharged. Filing bankruptcy is not a free lunch. While some taxes can be eliminated, they must be more than three years old and meet other criteria. The same is true for student loans guaranteed by the government; they cannot be dismissed unless they became due more than seven years ago. Other debts, such as those arising from driving while intoxicated and causing injury or death, are not dischargeable. A competent lawyer will provide information on the kinds of debts you will still owe, and the lawyer's ultimate conclusion may be to not file for bankruptcy if numerous debts will still remain.

WHAT TO DO IF YOU ARE A CREDITOR

If you are owed money by someone who files bankruptcy or reorganizes under the bankruptcy laws in most states, it will be necessary for you to file a proof of claim form. All creditors are usually listed when a bankruptcy case is filed. For example, if you are owed wages or commissions and your employer goes bankrupt, you will receive a notice from the court listing you as a creditor, specifying the amount of money you are owed, and informing you where to file the form. If you learn that a debtor went bankrupt but do not receive such a notice, contact officials of the company, the company attorney, or other creditors to discover this information.

The bankruptcy trustee assigned to a Chapter 7 or Chapter 13 case is responsible for sorting out and paying off creditor claims. Claims are paid depending on the amount of money (assets) available and in order of priority. Priority claims are typically paid in full before general (unsecured) creditors are paid. Examples of priority claims are for unpaid taxes, creditors (such as banks) with security interests and liens on certain property, and people who are owed salary, commissions, and unpaid benefits (e.g., vacation pay) of up to $4,000 earned within ninety days of the filing of the petition in bankruptcy. (Refer to the sample proof of claim below, which illustrates the discussion that follows.)

FORM 24. **Proof of Claim for Wages, Salary, or Commission**

UNITED STATES BANKRUPTCY COURT
FOR THE CENTRAL DISTRICT OF CALIFORNIA

In re
DEBTOR INC.   Bankruptcy 98-1111
Debtor
(include here all names used by bankrupt/debtor within last 6 years)

PROOF OF CLAIM FOR WAGES, SALARY, OR COMMISSION

    1. The debtor owes the claimant $5,000.00 computed as follows:
       (a) wages, salary, or commission for services performed on April 1, 1998 to
       June 30, 1998, at the following rate or rates of compensation (if appropriate):

                    $5,000.00
       (b) allowances and benefits, such as vacation and severance pay (specify)

                 ———

   Total amount claimed $5,000.00

    2. The claimant demands priority to the extent permitted by Section 507 (a) 5)
    of the Bankruptcy Code. $4,000.00
    3. The claimant has received no payment, no security, and no check or other
    evidence of the debt, except as follows:
    (state whether you were paid any money on this obligation, whether you
    retained any company property, such as a computer to offset the debt, etc.)

Dated:

                 Signed: JOHN DOE_____
                       Claimant
           Social Security Number:_____
                   Address:_____

▷ *Author's note:* The penalty for presenting fraudulent claims can be a fine of up
  to $5,000 or imprisonment for not more than five years or both.)

A Case in Point. Debtor Inc. goes bankrupt on July 1, 1998, and John Doe, a company salesman, has earned $5,000 in commissions within ninety days of the filing of the petition in bankruptcy. If sufficient money is on hand, John Doe may receive up to $4,000 in full. However, if John Doe has earned and is owed over $4,000 within ninety days of the time the company goes bankrupt, he will be entitled only to a general unsecured claim for the money that is owed in excess of $4,000 (typically about ten cents on the dollar for this portion of the claim). Similarly, if Howard Moe has earned $6,000 in commissions one hundred days before the company goes bankrupt, he is entitled only to a general unsecured claim for the entire $6,000 (i.e., perhaps ten cents on the dollar).

Helpful Strategies. If a merchant or employer has not filed for bankruptcy and you are owed money that is due longer than ninety days, have all payments you receive prior to the bankruptcy made specifically on account of your oldest money, salary, or commission claims. For instance, if you have not been paid your weekly salary for five weeks and you then receive a weekly paycheck, have your company note on the check, or in a letter, that the check you received is for your salary that was due five weeks before and is not payment of your current weekly wages. This may allow you to claim a greater portion of the debt as priority. (Note: Creditors who are paid before a bankruptcy are sometimes requested to return the money if certain conditions [called a fraudulent or preferential transfer] exist. Speak to a bankruptcy attorney to discuss your rights and options if applicable.)

Do not delay in filing your claim. If you fail to file a claim, you may not get paid. Do not expect to receive payment quickly; it may take several years before your claim is processed and you are paid. Request the trustee to place your name and address on the mailing list to receive all pertinent correspondence from the bankruptcy court. Such a request is often granted and you will be able to follow the progress of the case.

Attach copies of all documents you file with the bankruptcy court to support your claim. Speak to a lawyer, accountant, or other professional adviser if you have any questions about how to complete the form properly. Finally, it may be possible to take certain tax write-offs as "bad debt deductions" on your federal and state income taxes for any monies that you are not paid, particularly if you operate on an accrual rather than a cash tax reporting basis. Contact your tax consultant to discuss this particular strategy in detail if appropriate.

BANKS   *See Commercial Transactions*

BENEFITS AND RIGHTS   *See Social Security; Unemployment; Workers' Compensation*

BONUSES   *See Employment*

BROKERS *See Independent Contractors*

BUILDING CONTRACTORS *See Independent Contractors*

BUMPING AND OVERBOOKING *See Travel Rights*

BURIAL *See Funeral Arrangements*

BUSINESS SCAMS *See Fraud*

CHECKING ACCOUNTS AND CHECKS
See Commercial Transactions

CHILD ABDUCTION *Also see: Children; Divorce*

Between 25,000 and 100,000 children are victims of child snatching each year. In most cases the abducted child is taken by the noncustodial parent, a relative, or a close friend. Reunion of the child with the custodial parent is the exception, not the rule. Animosity toward the ex-spouse rather than concern for the child is generally the motive for child snatching. Violence sometimes attends these incidents. After the abduction, the life of the child may be unstable; he or she may be moved from place to place because the abducting parent does not want to get caught. This disruption can cause long-term psychological and/or physical trauma.

WHAT TO DO AFTER A CHILD HAS BEEN ABDUCTED

Contact the police immediately. Important leads tend to disappear as time passes. The faster the police are contacted, the more quickly they will be able to gather leads and act on them. Give the police the following information:

Full name
Nickname
Signature and other handwriting sample
Address and home phone number
Citizenship
Any identifying characteristics such as scars or blemishes, blood type, age, sex, race, height, weight, eye color, hair color
Date and place of birth
Medical history and current necessary prescriptions
Social security number
Name of school
Names and addresses of grandparents and other relatives
Recent photographs, fingerprints, and/or videotapes

You may also want to contact the data bank at the National Crime Information Center. The center assists the FBI and police in locating abductors, who may travel from state to state.

Check with friends, neighbors, ex-in-laws, and your spouse's boss. Most child snatchers are not loners. Often they reveal their plans to trusted individuals before they act. You may gain information regarding a child's whereabouts through these people.

Avoid committing illegal acts. Some parents make threats to an ex-spouse's family or friends or take the law into their own hands. Such illegal conduct can expose them to criminal and/or civil penalties and jeopardize the chances of obtaining permanent custody of a child, since some judges view illegal countermeasures as evidence of unfitness as a parent and may revoke a previous award granting custody, or even deny custody.

Consider filing kidnapping charges. Congress passed the Parental Kidnapping Prevention Act in 1980. This legislation extended the Fugitive Felon Act to cases involving child snatching and has been instrumental in reducing the number of child snatchings and in apprehending fugitives from justice, since FBI agents can now assist state law-enforcement agencies in returning abducted children to their custodial parents. Under this law agents also have the authority to bring abducting parents back to the state where the child previously resided to face criminal charges.

In order for the FBI to assist, the following conditions must be met: parental kidnapping must be a felony in the state where it originated; that state must have begun a felony prosecution and issued a warrant; and the local prosecutor must ask the U.S. Attorney General for a federal "unlawful flight to avoid prosecution" warrant.

If you decide to press criminal charges against an ex-spouse for parental kidnapping, the local police and prosecutor will play a major role in the arrest and trial. The police perform the following important roles in child-snatching cases:

- ▸ They receive the complaint from the victimized spouse.
- ▸ They gather the necessary paperwork to support the charges.
- ▸ They obtain witness statements.
- ▸ They confer with and work closely with the prosecutor.
- ▸ They officially communicate with and work closely with other police departments, public agencies, and the FBI.

Prosecutors perform the following key roles in child-snatching cases:
- ▸ They make the decision to arrest the ex-spouse.
- ▸ They interrogate friends and relatives of the ex-spouse who may have information about the whereabouts of the child; concealed information may lead to a conspiracy charge against those who have knowledge but fail to disclose it.

> They request necessary assistance from the police, public agencies, and the FBI.

> They issue legal process for the investigation.

A parent's responsibilities do not end once criminal charges are filed. Often the parent filing charges is asked to help gather information and pursue leads to locate the ex-spouse. That is why it is important to know as much as possible about an ex-spouse. For example, always keep a list of the ex-spouse's banks, credit cards, property holdings, social security number, date of birth, names and addresses of friends and relatives, and other pertinent data such as military service history. A list will simplify the investigative process when or if it must commence.

Hire a private investigative agency. A skilled investigator will be able to contact an ex-spouse's bank and credit-card companies, investigate the ex-spouse's employment history and job skills, and speak to his or her friends, relatives, neighbors, co-workers, and former employers. Usually an investigator will contact school officials to determine if and where a child's records have been transferred; the local post office, to determine if a forwarding address was given; the state Bureau of Motor Vehicles, to determine if a new driver's license or car registration was issued; and utility companies, to find out if the ex-spouse has opened a new account.

Thoroughly investigate the reputation of the agency to be hired. Find out whether the firm is licensed and adequately bonded. Any state Department of Consumer Affairs or local Better Business Bureau will likely require that private investigative agencies be licensed. Some require that agencies post performance bonds and sign affidavits before they can be licensed. Contact these regulatory bodies to determine whether a particular firm is licensed. A license does not guarantee the reliability or competence of an investigative agency, but it is a step in the right direction. Inquire whether any complaints or lawsuits have been lodged against the investigative agency in the recent past.

When hiring a private detective who practices alone, check out the investigator's credentials and make sure he or she is licensed. Some forty-five states require private detectives to be licensed. At a minimum, this means they are required to have some training or equivalent law-enforcement experience, pass a qualifying exam, and have no past criminal record. In addition, the state agency that monitors private investigators can advise if any complaints have been filed against the detective. Don't forget to ask about this.

Before hiring an investigative agency or a private detective, it is also a good idea to ask for references. Ask for the names of other clients who have used the investigator's services and confirm these references. How much will be charged for the work involved? What about costs? If you decide to hire an agency or private detective, write up an agreement stating your understanding of what

FORM 25. **Sample Retainer Agreement with Private Investigator Service**

Your Name
Address
Date

(Name), President
Name of Firm
Address

Dear (Name),

This will confirm that I have retained the services of your private investigative agency to assist me in locating my 6-year-old son (name) who was taken from me by my former spouse. You agree to use your best efforts in locating the whereabouts of my ex-spouse and son; however, you agree not to "snatch back" my child. Rather, the full extent of our agreement is for you to locate the whereabouts of these individuals and report this information to me for use by my attorney.

For your services, I shall pay you at the rate of $75 per hour. I have paid you an initial retainer of One Thousand Dollars ($1,000) to be applied against your hourly rate. In the event my child is returned to me or you discover his whereabouts before the retainer has been depleted, or I decide to discontinue your services for any reason, you agree to promptly return the unused balance within one (1) week from my written request. I understand that your hourly rate does not include costs and expenses. These include, but are not limited to, long-distance phone calls, travel, parking, and photocopies made by you to be billed at 10 cents per copy. They also do not include the fee for your assistant's time, for which you advise I will be billed at the rate of $40 per hour.

Per our agreement, you shall confer with me on all expenses exceeding $100, which I shall approve before they are incurred. In addition, you shall bill me monthly with respect to all services performed and costs incurred and shall send me complete, accurate, itemized monthly statements with receipts to prove same. In the event you spend a sufficient number of hours to deplete the retainer, I shall be advised before additional work is incurred to determine if I want you to proceed, and how much additional time I authorize you to devote to this matter. In no event are you to incur more than (specify $) to this matter.

As notice of your acceptance of this agreement, please sign below where indicated and return a signed copy to me immediately. I look forward to working with you.

Very truly yours,
Your Name

Accepted and Agreed to:
Name of Private Investigative Agency
By: _____
        Name of President or Owner

the agency or private detective will do and your obligations, and ask the person in charge to sign it. (See the sample retainer agreement letter on page 72.) If the agency or individual detective does not send signed confirmation of the agreement back to you, either do not retain the person or agency or discuss in detail the reasons why.

Be specific about what you want the investigator to do. Give instructions not to "snatch back" the child; this may cause legal problems and harm the child emotionally as well. After you receive a report on the location of the child, discuss your legal options with a lawyer.

Pursue your rights under the Federal Educational Rights and Privacy Act. Under this law, for example, it may be possible to obtain the name, address, and telephone number of the school to which a child's records have been transferred. Speak to a lawyer about this.

Seek international help if the child was abducted to a foreign country. The Convention on the Civil Aspects of International Child Abduction was ratified by Congress and an automated fax system was instituted by the Department of State in 1996. Many foreign countries participate in this treaty and can help locate and retrieve a child abducted internationally. Speak to a lawyer familiar with this treaty for more details if applicable.

CHILD CUSTODY   *Also see: Children; Visitation*

More than one million children experience the divorce of their parents annually, and too often, the children become the victims of divorce. Some experts are calling for the creation of special courts so that judges, with the assistance of trained psychiatrists and social workers, can preside solely over child-custody-related disputes, unhampered by general court calendars and other responsibilities.

GENERAL PRINCIPLES OF CHILD CUSTODY

Years ago the law stated that the father was the exclusive custodian of a couple's children. However, when women became emancipated in the nineteenth century, the law recognized that both spouses had equal rights to the custody of their children; upon divorce custody was awarded to the spouse deemed most emotionally and financially stable.

The law now generally states that a judge must make determinations of custody according to the child's best interest and overall welfare. What constitutes a child's "best interest" depends on the facts and circumstances of each case. Custody issues, more than most litigated matters, are determined primarily by their unique patterns; judges are supposed to weigh carefully all significant factors relevant to a child's welfare and best interest.

In determining what constitutes a child's best interest, judges are theoretically not supposed to consider the following:

- Whether the parents agreed by contract with whom the child would live
- The "tender-years" doctrine, whereby custody of a young child is automatically granted to the mother, particularly if the young child is a girl
- Which parent fights harder to gain custody of the child

The judge will typically focus on the following:
- The atmosphere and stability of each parent's home
- The amount of care, affection, and concern demonstrated by each parent to the child
- The child's stated preference, particularly when he or she is relatively mature (e.g., thirteen or older)
- The ability and availability of each parent to care for the child
- The financial standing of each parent and the financial capability of each to support the child
- The morality of each contesting parent and past conduct toward the other
- Whether or not the child will be forced to relocate or suffer other disruptive changes
- A parent's compliance with court rules and orders
- A parent's religious beliefs that may seriously threaten the child's welfare

Custody awards are not aimed at rewarding or punishing parents, since the court's paramount concern is for the child's welfare and judges are supposed to consider all of the above factors in making a determination of custody.

Judges will not usually reverse an earlier decision of custody unless the custodial parent is unfit. Examples of unfitness include incidents of open homosexuality in front of the child, immoral conduct, alcoholism or habitual drug use, history of child abuse or neglect, serious physical or mental impairments, or the inability to provide a suitable home environment for the child. Other factors might be a past history of child or wife beatings, failure to pay child support, and an extensive criminal record.

Frequently, neighbors, baby-sitters, household employees, schoolteachers, clergy, and relatives are requested to testify on behalf of one of the contesting parents. In addition, since the testimony of a psychiatrist, psychologist, or therapist is often crucial in determining whether the parent is fit or what is in the child's best interest, the opinions of such experts are usually given great weight by a judge.

HOW TO AVOID A CUSTODY BATTLE
Custody litigation is time-consuming, messy, and expensive. To avoid a complex custody battle:

Try to settle custody disputes privately before the divorce. Courts are not bound by the parents' agreements concerning custody and visitation, and are free to modify them, particularly if the agreement is determined not to be in the child's best interest. Discuss and settle the question of the child's best interest before resorting to expensive litigation and court intervention.

The following is a comprehensive checklist of points concerning visitation and custody matters that should be explored by parents commencing divorce proceedings. Once a settlement is reached on a majority of these points, they can be incorporated into a written custody agreement with the help of a lawyer.

- ▸ What type of custody (i.e., joint legal custody or sole custody) is desired?
- ▸ With whom will the child principally reside?
- ▸ What form of visitation rights will the noncustodial parent receive? (How many visits per week? When? Is notice to the custodial parent required before each visit?)
- ▸ Can visitation take place in the custodial parent's home, or must the child be taken from the house?
- ▸ How much extended visitation (e.g., vacations) with the noncustodial parent will be permitted?
- ▸ Is the custodial parent permitted to move the child to relocate or must he or she live within a certain geographic territory (e.g., within a fifty-mile radius) of the noncustodial parent? What happens if the child is moved? Can the other parent cut off support or regain custody?
- ▸ If the custodial parent is permitted to move to another state with the child, who will pay for the traveling expenses incurred when the child visits his or her noncustodial parent?
- ▸ How much decision-making power and authority does the custodial parent have regarding the child's education, health, religious training, vacations, trips, and other matters? Does the noncustodial parent have the right to be notified of said matters before decisions are made? If so, does he or she have the right of consultation or veto power?
- ▸ Are there circumstances under which custody will change? If so, what are they?
- ▸ Do both parents agree not to alienate the affections of the child by speaking poorly about the other or promising gifts or favors in return for the child not loving the other parent? What actions may the injured parent take if alienation of affection is attempted?
- ▸ If the children are to be in the ex-wife's custody, are they permitted to assume the name of the wife's second husband if she remarries? May they call the second husband "father"? May he legally adopt them?
- ▸ If the children are to be in the ex-husband's custody, and he remarries, may the children call the second wife "mother"? May she legally adopt them?
- ▸ If the noncustodial parent contributes child support, may he or she suspend support payments when the children visit him or her on extended vacations?

FORM 26. Pertinent Custody and Visitation Clauses to Consider Including in a Separation Agreement

(a) Optional: The parties shall have joint custody of the unemancipated children of the parties, irrespective of whether the children shall reside with the Mother or the Father and each shall be equally responsible for the supervision, control, and care of the children. The arrangement will afford both parties ample opportunity to enjoy the children's society and to participate in a harmonious policy best calculated to promote the interests of the children.

Or: Legal custody of the unemancipated children of the parties shall be given to the (specify).

(b) The parties acknowledge that the children's wishes are to be considered in connection with the exercise of visitation rights, and each party agrees that he or she shall encourage the children in anticipating periods of visitation with the other.

(c) Each of the parties hereto agrees to keep the other informed at all times of the whereabouts of the children when with the Father, or the Mother, respectively, and they mutually agree that if either of them has any knowledge of any illness or accident, school problems, or other circumstances affecting the children's health or general welfare, the Father or the Mother, as the case may be, will promptly notify the other of such circumstances.

(d) The parties shall consult with each other with respect to the children's education, illnesses and operations (except in emergencies), health, welfare, and other matters of similar importance affecting the children whose well-being, education, and development shall, at all times, be the paramount consideration of the Father and Mother.

(e) Each party agrees that, in the event of acute illness of the children at any time, the other party shall have the right of reasonable visitation with the children at the place of confinement.

(f) Each parent shall be entitled to complete, detailed information from any pediatrician, general physician, dentist, consultant, or specialist attending the children for any reason whatsoever and to receive, upon request, copies of any reports given by them, or any of them, to the other parent;

(g) Each parent shall have the right of reasonable, unhampered telephone communications with the children and shall provide to the other parent a telephone number for that purpose;

(h) From the date hereof, the children shall reside with (specify, for example, the Mother). The Father shall have liberal visitation rights. While the children are residing with the Mother, the Father shall have the right to visit the children outside the Mother's residence during two (2) weekday (Monday through Thursday) evenings per week between 7:00 and 9:00 p.m. and two (2) weekends (Friday between 7:00 and 9:00 p.m. through Sunday between 7:00 and 9:00 p.m.) per month in accordance with arrangements mutually made with the Father and the children on reasonable (72-hour) prior notice by the Father to the Mother;

(i) Notwithstanding the foregoing, the children shall reside with the Father for (specify) full weeks during each and every Summer, such visitation being on a consecutive basis; and on Father's Day if at that time they are residing with the Mother. For at least four (4) hours on the child's birthday, the parent with whom the child is not then living shall have the right of visitation in accordance with arrangements mutually made with the visiting parent and the child on reasonable prior notice by the visiting parent to the other parent;

(j) The parties shall alternate visitation on major school holidays from year to year; for example, the children shall reside with the Father for four (4) days from 9:00 a.m. Thursday to 7:00 p.m. Sunday every other Thanksgiving; for a full week every other Christmas and Easter holiday, etc.

(k) Optional: If either party shall fail to comply with any of the provisions of this Article, or in the event a dispute or controversy should arise among the parties hereto, the subject matter of this Agreement or the Agreement, the parties agree to submit their dispute to binding arbitration in (specify location) under the then prevailing rules of the American Arbitration Association. The decision of the arbitrator shall be final and binding and the party obtaining a favorable decision may initiate a proceeding in any court having competent jurisdiction for the purposes of enforcing an award hereunder.

Or: If either party shall fail to comply with any of the provisions of this Article, the other party shall have the right to initiate a proceeding in the (specify) Court, for such relief as may be appropriate under the circumstances. The prevailing party shall be entitled to recover all reasonable attorney fees and costs incurred as a result of such an action;

(l) Although the parties hereby acknowledge that nothing herein contained shall be construed as an obligation or duty on the part of a party to exercise rights of visitation, nevertheless they acknowledge the need for planning activities for the children and further acknowledge that disappointing a child may have serious, adverse effects upon the child. Accordingly, each party agrees that on all occasions when he or she does not plan to exercise rights of visitation or expects to be early or late in so doing or intends to return the children at an earlier or later hour, as much advance notice as reasonably possible will be given to the other party in order that appropriate plans will be made for the children;

(m) The parties shall exert every reasonable effort to maintain free access and unhampered contact between the children and each of the parties and to foster a feeling of affection between the children and the other party. Neither party shall do anything which may estrange the child from the other party or injure the children's opinion as to the Mother or Father or which may hamper the free and natural development of the children's love and respect for the other party;

(n) Each party covenants, represents, and warrants not, at any time or for any reason, to cause the children to be known or identified or designated by any name other than (specify) and both parties covenant, represent and warrant that they will not initiate or permit the designations of "Father" and/or "Mother" or their equivalent, to be used by the children with reference to any person other than the parties hereto;

(o) In no event shall the children be adopted without express, prior written consent of each of the parties;

(p) Nothing herein shall bar or limit the parties from discussing and agreeing upon modifications of the provisions set forth in this Article;

(q) Reference herein to "child" shall refer to the unemancipated (Note: under 18 to 21 depending on the law in your state) children of the parties;

(r) Should either party die or become seriously incapacitated mentally or physically while the children are still of minor age, the guardianship and custody of the minor children shall remain wholly and exclusively with the other party;

(s) It is the parties' intention to exercise fully all rights of visitation as herein provided but the exercises thereof shall be entirely optional, and failure to exercise such right on any particular occasion shall not be deemed or construed or constitute a waiver of a right thereafter to full compliance with the provisions hereof;

(t) Neither party shall remove the residence of the children beyond a radius of fifty (50) miles from their present residence without prior, written consent of the other party. If (specify, for example, the Mother) shall remove the residence of the children beyond said radius without the consent of the Father or the Court, such failure to obtain consent shall be presumptive of the right of the Father to obtain legal custody of the children and to terminate further payments under this agreement to the Wife for her support and maintenance. In addition, it shall entitle the Father to pursue all other remedies available to him under the circumstances, including (specify).

Confirm the agreement in writing. Agreements regarding custody are typically incorporated into a master separation agreement with separate sections for custody and child support. (The list of clauses on pages 76–77 illustrates the kinds of provisions that are frequently drafted.) The separation agreement is then approved by a judge during divorce proceedings. Since the courts have authority to decide all matters pertaining to the general welfare of children, custodial agreements between parents are subject to close judicial scrutiny. To be workable and lasting, a custody arrangement must be consistent with the children's welfare. Courts are free to modify a prior agreement between the parties when circumstances have markedly changed. However, without a showing of changed circumstances, an agreement between the parties concerning custody, maintenance, and education of the child that is clearly in the child's best interest probably will not be overturned.

Consult a lawyer experienced in custody matters to be certain that a custody agreement is clearly drafted and is fair to the child.

Understand the difference between joint and exclusive custody and decide which is best for you and the child. Both parents can have an equal role in raising a child. "Joint custody" or "coparenting" provides that each parent share in the parental authority and day-to-day responsibilities regarding the child. This differs from the traditional concept of exclusive or sole custody, where the child resides with one parent who has sole legal authority to make decisions about the child's education, health, religious training, and vacations, while the noncustodial parent merely has rights of visitation.

While the concept of joint custody sounds reasonable, it doesn't always work in practice. Generally, the determination of whether a joint custody arrangement is in the child's best interest depends on whether the parents are able to cooperate and agree on important decisions affecting the child. It rarely works when parents are spiteful or harbor resentment toward each other.

Obtain a complete legal appraisal of rights to custody if a settlement cannot be effectuated. To determine if a valid case exists, a competent lawyer will inquire into the following:

▶ What are the client's objectives? Are his or her motives sincere?

▶ Has an earnest effort been made to reach an amicable resolution? If so, why have negotiations broken down?

▶ Why is the client better qualified as the custodial parent?

▶ What witnesses will be able to verify this? What will their testimony be?

▶ Has the client remarried? If so, what kind of relationship does the child have with the new spouse? Has the newly married couple considered the change that custody will have on their marriage?

▶ What is the child's stated preference? Is the child old enough so that his or her desires will carry weight with the court?

▸ What are the relative strengths and weaknesses (in terms of financial disparity, age, and general health) of the contesting parents?

Recognize that it is not easy to obtain a modification of an earlier custody agreement or court decree.

Understand custody and visitation rights of grandparents, stepparents, and extended family members. Some state laws allow grandparents to petition state courts for visitation privileges following the dissolution of a marriage. Other courts are specifying that stepparents can stand in place of parents when questions of child abuse, neglect, financial support, medical consent, and inheritance arise. Some courts have granted visitation rights, and even exclusive custody, to grandparents after it was shown that the grandparents had established a close relationship with the children, the parents had died, and/or it was in the best interest of the children.

Understand the law concerning visitation. The right of the noncustodial parent to visit the child is practically absolute, unless exceptional circumstances have been presented to the court. This means that a judge cannot revoke visitation privileges unless the child's welfare is in danger. Even unwed fathers are entitled to visitation privileges, unless it is not in the child's best interest.

Contact an attorney immediately if the custodial parent is denying access to a child or is flouting court-ordered visitation benefits (e.g., not allowing you to visit your child on the days previously agreed to, or shortening or canceling the visitation period without notice, etc.). This should be done particularly if your former spouse intends to move the child to a distant place.

TIPS ON WINNING A CONTESTED CUSTODY CASE

In order to win a contested custody case, proper planning is essential. Cases are often lost because of the inability of counsel to prepare a case properly or because of failure to produce expert witnesses (e.g., psychiatrists) to help prove the case.

Avoid making yourself look like the "bad guy." Do not commit acts that place you at a disadvantage, for example, by deliberately moving a child to a distant location, thereby depriving the noncustodial parent of visitation rights.

Try to make a good impression at the trial.

Never force a child to live with you against his or her will.

Be sure to introduce witnesses at the trial to support a claim. Ask the witnesses to recall, in advance of the trial, specific incidents that illustrate why you are better suited for custody and more dedicated to the child. Let each witness know where in the sequence of the trial his or her testimony will come in. Since the testimony of a child psychiatrist or psychologist is important, obtain the services of a well-respected, well-qualified professional who has rendered opinions for child-custody cases in the past.

Work up a strategic plan. Be prepared to show where the child will live, how he or she will be transported to and from school, and who will care for the child when he or she is not in school and you are not physically present. The judge will seek answers to such questions as:

> ▸ Whether the child will have adequate room and sleeping accommodations
> ▸ Whether the child has a good relationship with your friends, relatives, and neighbors
> ▸ Whether you and the child have common interests

Little things like how much time you spend with a child can be more important than material possessions. Become active in the business, religious, and social activities of a church or synagogue. Devote some free time to civic endeavors such as Little League or Girl Scouts. This type of involvement may impress a judge.

Prepare a detailed list of provable reasons why the other parent should not be awarded custody or that there should be no change in custody.

Be prepared to show and prove that the child's life would be disrupted by a change of custody. It is a good idea to prepare a list of close playmates, school friends, and social activities that the child enjoys and participates in.

Prepare color photographs to prove your claim. Take pictures showing where the child lives, goes to school, and plays.

CHILD SUPPORT

Also see: Child Custody; Children; Divorce; Mediation

A natural parent has a continuing duty to provide support for an unemancipated child. This means that if a parent has sufficient means (or is able to earn the means), he or she will be required to pay a fair and reasonable sum for the child's support until the child reaches eighteen years of age (twenty-one in some states), marries, permanently abandons the home, moves out, or gains full-time employment and becomes fully self-supporting. In most states, the amount of support given to a child depends on the particular circumstances of each case and the financial abilities of each parent.

LEGAL INTERVENTION

If divorced parents cannot agree on the amount of child support, or if special circumstances have occurred that warrant a modification of the amount previously awarded, it may be necessary to petition the court for an order of child support. Although you can do this without a lawyer, it is not advisable; speak to a lawyer immediately to protect your rights and consider the following:

Speak to a clerk at the family court. A clerk may be able to provide names of local attorneys who specialize in handling similar matters. Ask for information on how to obtain a court order for support; how to identify and discover what real and personal property is available for attachment; how to collect from a spouse who is self-employed; and what to expect in court.

Attempt to resolve the problem through mediation. Family mediation is a process in which a trained professional guides structured discussions between family members and encourages them to reach an agreement that is acceptable to all parties. It is not for everyone. If the custodian of the children is significantly unequal in financial and/or emotional strength, he or she may do better being represented by an attorney rather than participating in the mediation process. In addition, a mediator who is not a lawyer may not be sufficiently knowledgeable about the tax consequences involved in a support agreement.

Contact an attorney who specializes in domestic relations. Choose a lawyer with whom you can discuss your needs and who can represent your interests in working out all aspects of the agreement (custody, visitation, child support, division of property, and other financial arrangements). See a lawyer even if you think you are unable to afford the fees, and explain your financial situation. Ask for a reduced fee and ask about having the court order the noncustodial parent to pay all or some of your legal expenses and court costs.

Contact a legal clinic, such as Legal Aid, for assistance. One problem with legal clinics, though, is that several different lawyers may work on a case.

Contact a local office of the Child Support Enforcement Administration. Services available from the Child Support Enforcement Administration include the receipt, disbursement, and record keeping of child-support payments; assistance in locating absent parents; referrals to the state attorney general's office and other enforcement agencies; implementation of state tax refund intercept programs, the federal tax refund offset program, and unemployment benefits intercept programs; assistance in establishing support orders by consent when possible; assistance in enforcement; and referrals to the IRS for collection services.

Contact a local branch of your state attorney general's office. Many state's attorneys are empowered to prosecute nonsupport and paternity cases, and some employ staff attorneys for this purpose.

Contact a self-help organization such as the Association for Children for Enforcement of Support (ACES), located in Toledo, Ohio, for advice and assistance. ACES and other not-for-profit groups employ skilled staff members to help locate deadbeat parents.

Know your rights. There are basically two court systems to turn to for redress: criminal and civil. It is possible to proceed with civil litigation and criminal prosecution at the same time in some states. When a civil order exists and it is not being honored, a criminal action may be entered. The following remedies may be used for civil enforcement:

WAGE LIENS. In a civil case, you may request a wage lien when the person ordered to pay support is more than thirty days behind in payments. Some states do not have wage-lien statutes, however, so check to see if this is applicable by state law.

GARNISHMENT. Garnishment is a remedy used to attach a portion of a debtor's income to satisfy a debt, including settlement of arrears in child-support cases. There are limitations, however, on the amount of a debtor's income that can be taken through garnishment, typically not more than 50 percent of a person's weekly salary, up to a maximum of $300. Garnishment can be applied to all earnings except federal employee worker's disability benefits; earnings that can be attached include annuities, pensions, social security, nonfederal disability income, unemployment compensation, railroad retirement, individual retirement accounts (IRAs), wages, retirement of armed services personnel, and federal employees' wages and retirement.

GARNISHMENT OF MILITARY PAY. Federal law authorizes legal process against members of the U.S. military forces for garnishment of pay to collect child support and alimony arrears. The law provides a limit of 50 percent on the amount subject to garnishment.

ATTACHMENT OF A SPOUSE'S REAL AND PERSONAL PROPERTY. This is done by obtaining a court order that gives the right to attach the respondent's assets to collect the obligation. Typically, a request is made that the court file the support judgment in the amount of money which the court determines is owed as a lien in any county where the debtor has real estate, a bank account, a car, or other assets. A judgment remains in effect for a limited period of time, typically six to twelve years. After a judgment is obtained, you must then take additional court action to enforce it. For example, a support judgment usually becomes final after thirty days. You must then record the final judgment and pay a small sum of money to the clerk of the court to obtain a writ. Once a writ is obtained, you can then contact the sheriff, marshal, or other licensed individual to attach the property of the debtor, secure a voluntary wage lien, or obtain a lump-sum payment. In many states, the person obtaining the writ must pay for storage and auction costs. A debtor is more likely to be amenable to payment of arrears when faced with imminent loss of a valued possession.

ASSISTANCE FROM THE IRS. The Child Support Enforcement Administration in your state may apply to the IRS for full collection process after other means of collection have failed. The IRS may enforce a levy for child-support obligations against income or assets of the noncustodial parent. Property may be seized and sold for payment of the delinquency. The IRS typically charges about $125 for this service. For further information, contact a local county child-support agency. In addition, the IRS is allowed to intercept federal income tax refunds due to the noncustodial parent who is at least $150 or three months in arrears in child-support payments. The money is sent directly to the state, which then disburses the funds according to a predetermined formula.

ASSISTANCE FROM STATE GOVERNMENT. Most states provide for automatic attachment of wages, permit automatic withholding of all state and federal income tax refunds, require that all child-support payments be made through a court so delinquencies can be monitored and pursued, and authorize the use of liens on property and other capital holdings of a noncustodial parent who is twenty-five days or more in arrears.

By law, most states must conduct delinquent support searches within seventy-five days of a court judgment. Wage withholding is the most effective method of collecting money by state agencies. And although it is more difficult to collect arrears from self-employed people, some states will help you obtain support orders that allow withholdings from commissions, dividends, retirement benefits, and lottery winnings.

Speak to a state agency caseworker for more details. An agency caseworker may help you obtain information from an ex-spouse's bank, stockbroker, or mortgage company; conduct a vehicle or property search; and help locate real property through deeds and property assessments to determine assets. Inquire whether your state has implemented a license revocation program. More than twenty states have passed laws authorizing the suspension of a delinquent parent's driving privileges or professional license (e.g., an attorney's license to practice law) in the event the nonsupport exceeds a certain period of time (i.e., four months). You may need a judge to approve this after a hearing, so seek competent advice where applicable.

Seek assistance from an appropriate agency if you have difficulty locating your ex-spouse. There are a number of ways to locate nonpaying absent ex-spouses. Some effective techniques are:

▸ Ascertain the ex-spouse's address if he or she is still living in the state by contacting the motor vehicle bureau.
▸ If the telephone number is unpublished, obtain the absent parent's address from the local police department's crisscross telephone directory.
▸ Contact nationwide credit bureaus, labor unions, and financial institutions to uncover this information.

In addition, your state may have a parent locator service. Contact a local department of social services for further details.

Sue the ex-spouse for breach of contract or specific performance of a properly executed separation agreement. An agreement, if properly written and executed, is a contract. Failure to pay child support, including medical support where specified, is a breach of contract, and a court may enter a money judgment for the unpaid arrears and may order that payments be made in the future. It is best to proceed with the assistance of a lawyer.

Seek to hold the nonpaying ex-spouse in contempt. A petition to cite for contempt is the most commonly used method of civil enforcement of child or spousal support. It may be filed by anyone having direct knowledge that the support order is not being obeyed. In most states, judges hearing such complaints have the power to punish the offender by fine or by imprisonment for an indefinite time, or to order payment of the arrears either within a set time or by an addition to the regular payment. Usually, judges are reluctant to impose a jail sentence on a first offender.

To be found in contempt, the noncustodial parent must have had the ability to pay when he or she defaulted. Quitting a job without a new one or voluntarily changing jobs to one that pays less is generally no excuse. However, closing a business in order to retire is not contempt if the noncustodial parent is of normal retirement age. If there is no previous court order or decree, contempt of court is not typically available as a remedy.

Bring criminal charges against the nonpaying ex-spouse. Many states have laws that make willful failure to support a spouse or child a crime. To file criminal nonsupport charges, you will have to appear in court and swear out a formal complaint. Some states require screening by a local district attorney's office before charges can be brought. Criminal prosecution for nonpayment has many advantages, including:

> ▶ When the action is handled by the district attorney's office, there is no cost to you.
> ▶ Criminal cases normally proceed faster than civil cases.
> ▶ A finding of contempt may result in jailing for an indefinite period; this may force the offending person to pay all or part of his or her arrears to avoid incarceration.
> ▶ No prior order is needed to file a criminal action.
> ▶ Pertinent facts can be placed on the FBI interstate computer through a local police department.
> ▶ If a warrant is issued, authorities in other jurisdictions may be alerted so that locating and arresting an offender can be done significantly faster.
> ▶ The stigma of a criminal conviction may prompt the offending parent to start support payments.

The disadvantages of criminal (and civil) prosecution include:
> ▶ Court costs and lawyer fees can make proceedings costly unless the court orders the noncustodial parent to pay a portion of the costs.
> ▶ It may take a long time before a hearing is scheduled and the matter is disposed of.
> ▶ Service of process upon defaulting individuals may be difficult, especially when you don't know where the defaulting party lives.
> ▶ If the noncustodial parent pays a fine or serves time in jail for nonpayment of a support order, the conviction may result in wiping out arrears that have accumulated under the order.

- The judge may reduce, change, or modify a defaulting party's prior support offer after the party has served time in jail.
- Imprisonment usually eliminates or reduces a person's income and therefore may not serve your cause.
- Criminal conviction may affect employment in some occupations and the standard of evidence required for conviction is proof beyond a reasonable doubt (a higher standard than used in civil proceedings).

Speak to an experienced attorney before deciding what course of action to take. In most situations, resort to criminal prosecution for nonpayment of child and/or spousal support should be done only after all other methods fail.

STRATEGIES TO INCREASE THE CHANCES OF RECOVERING SUPPORT ARREARS

Plan ahead. Arrange for child support while the divorce action is proceeding and include a written separation agreement or other document. This will allow you to proceed quickly in court if the ex-spouse fails to pay the specified amount; it will also prove that there was an agreement and what the agreement was.

Negotiate the support provisions in the separation agreement carefully. Be sure child support is listed separately from alimony and other obligations and that a separate amount for each child is listed in the agreement rather than a lump sum for all the children. The agreement should also include provisions for (1) the medical, dental and the special needs of the children, including insurance coverage of these items; (2) child-support payments from the noncustodial parent's estate in the event of his or her death; (3) the child's education needs (including college); (4) a provision for a salary lien in case the noncustodial parent ceases payment in the future; (5) an escalation clause providing for an automatic or cost-of-living increase in the amount of payments when either the noncustodial parent's income or the child's need increases; and (6) the amount of payment and the intervals of payment. Specifying these items in the agreement will anticipate problems before they occur and make it easier to enforce arrears in the event the support clauses are not observed. (Review the list of clauses on pages 86–87 to get a better idea of the kinds of points to include in a separation agreement.)

Assert yourself. Educate yourself about what services are available and what new laws are being passed. Check the phone book to find referral services and information groups in your area. Contact a local child support enforcement agency, state attorney general, district attorney, or county attorney office for information and assistance. Learn the local procedures for filing court papers if you cannot afford a lawyer. Contact the clerk of a local family

FORM 27. **Pertinent Child Support Clauses to Consider Including in a Separation Agreement**

1. As and for the support, maintenance, and education of each child, (specify, for example, the Father) shall pay to the Mother the sum of (specify $) per week, per child, payable on each and every Friday of each week commencing on (specify date).

2. The aforementioned $X per week, per child, payment for each child shall continue with respect to each such child until an Emancipation Event as is hereinafter defined shall have occurred to any such child. Upon the occurrence of any such Emancipation Event, the Father shall no longer be responsible for the payment of such $X weekly amount for the particular child so emancipated.

3. During the period that support payments are paid for the children or either of them, the Father shall be exclusively entitled to list them or either of them, as the case may be, as his dependents on his income tax return and the Mother shall not be entitled to list either of them as her dependents on her tax returns.

4. All obligations under this Article shall terminate in the event of the death of the Wife or the Husband. The parties contemplate that in the event of the death of the Wife, then with respect to such of the children concerning whom an Emancipation Event has not previously occurred, the Husband shall have such obligation as is imposed by law with respect to the support of any such child or children. In the event of the death of the Husband, all obligations set forth in this Article shall immediately terminate.

5.(a) In addition to the support provided herein, the Father agrees to furnish at his own expense medical insurance (specify type) for the benefit of the children of the parties until the remarriage of the Wife and/or emancipation of the children and to pay for one-half (or specify all) of all reasonable medical, dental, orthodontia, and drug expenses (hereinafter collectively called "medical expenses") of the children of the parties. The Mother shall advise the Father of any medical insurance which may be furnished to her by an employer in order that the Father need not duplicate coverage for the children. If the Mother is required to pay for such coverage of the children, the Father may elect to utilize said coverage for the children and shall promptly pay for or reimburse the Mother for such expense or to provide his own coverage. For uninsured medical and dental expenses, the parties shall share such costs equally, provided he or she, as the case may be, shall have given consent for such expenses, which consent shall not be unreasonably withheld (unless medical or dental treatment is required in such short time that it is impossible or impractical to obtain such consent).

(b) The Mother agrees that she will promptly fill out, execute and deliver to the Father all forms and provide all information in connection with any application he may

court for further information, including forms and instructions for representing yourself in court.

Don't be intimidated if the ex-spouse has moved to another state. The law allows each state to honor another state's orders and decrees regarding child support. Even federal laws allow a child support case to move into the federal make for reimbursement of medical, dental and drug expenses under any insurance policies which he may have. He shall promptly refund to the Mother any medical expenses paid for by her either directly or if insured, out of the proceeds of an insurance claim which the Husband shall promptly file.

(c) The Father will furnish to the Mother at her request documentation and other proof of his compliance with the provisions of this Article, and the Wife, in addition, is hereby authorized to obtain direct confirmation of compliance or noncompliance with any insurance carrier.

(d) In addition to the foregoing, the Father shall pay promptly one-half (½) of all reasonable expenses for the tuition, fees, transportation, and outfitting of the children at a summer camp, or for summer or vacation travel or similar summer or vacation activity, if the children desire to pursue such activity and if the Father consents thereto, which consent will not be unreasonably withheld. The Mother agrees to consult with the Father regarding each such activity and to consider such suggestions and comments which he deems shall be in the best interests of the children. In no event will the Father be required to pay for any of the said expenses incurred for the participation of the Mother in such activity or activities.

(e) It is agreed that the Father's obligation for support of the children herein shall be suspended during any period when the children are residing with the Father for an extended period of time, such as during the summer, or for summer camp or other activities which necessitate the children staying away from home at the Father's expense.

(f) In addition to the foregoing, if the children of the parties have been recommended by a teacher, guidance counselor, or other educational adviser or administrator to obtain tutoring help with respect to any academic lessons or courses, the Father agrees to pay promptly for one-half (½) of the reasonable cost of such tutoring.

(g) In addition to the foregoing, if the children of the parties desire to attend religious school or receive private religious training, or attend college, the Father agrees to pay promptly for one-half (½) of the reasonable cost of such education or training. Both parties shall encourage the use of financial aids, grants, loans, and scholarships to help defray expenses, and they agree to cooperate with each other and the child toward that end. The expenses referred to in this subparagraph shall include, but shall not be limited to, application and testing fees, tuition, required books, uniforms, materials and supplies, reasonable transportation, and incidental expenses.

Optional: With respect to college expenses, the Father shall only be liable to pay one-half (½) of the costs of a four-year education, including room and board, at a public state university.

courts when state court efforts have been exhausted. Many people do not realize that a state order filed in one state can be carried out in another.

Obtain a court order as soon as possible. A petition for a court order for child support can and should be filed the day the noncustodial parent leaves. This will enable you to proceed with other enforcement mechanisms in the event of nonpayment. A separation agreement is not a court order; it is simply a contract between two parties that must be reduced to a court order as soon as possible.

Review all legal papers. Always be sure that the court order or decree specifies the amount of support to be paid and the payment intervals. Do not depend on a lawyer to take care of this for you. Check all papers carefully upon receipt. Verbal agreements are unenforceable, even if stipulated in court, unless they are specified in the written order or decree.

Locate the ex-spouse as soon as possible. If it can be shown that the absent parent is preparing to leave the state and is in arrears with child-support payments, you may be able to petition the court to order him or her to remain in the state. Usually the absent parent will be required to post a bond in the amount of the arrears. If he or she then leaves the state without payment, the bond may be forfeited and the money turned over to you or an appropriate child-support agency. Speak to a lawyer or other trained professional for further details about this if it seems appropriate.

Take steps to establish paternity or parenthood rights. A natural father or mother may have the legal responsibility to support a child born out of wedlock. A properly drafted and signed acknowledgment of paternity or parenthood (see page 331 in the Appendix for examples) may protect your child's rights. Seek legal advice concerning this where applicable.

COLLEGE EDUCATION

Generally, parents are not legally responsible for paying the costs of a college education or of special training for their children. However, in cases where this is an issue, a court will look at the educational background of the parents, the environment in which the child grows up, the child's academic ability, and the economic status and occupations of the parents. Often, a combination of these factors will demonstrate a finding of special circumstances in which the child is expected to attend college. In addition, the facts of the case may indicate that a parent's actions reflected the desire that the child attend college and the assumption that the parent would pay for it (e.g., a parent makes specific promises in front of witnesses, or the parties acknowledge their intentions to pay for college education in their separation agreement). Certainly, where the parent is capable of paying such support and has encouraged the child to obtain higher or special education, the court will be more willing to order that payments be made.

The obligation to pay college costs does not necessarily mean that the child must attend a private college. A parent seeking to obtain support from an ex-spouse for college education or other related expenses should be reasonable. It is often difficult to predict how much money courts will award in this area;

being reasonable may save unnecessary legal expense and aggravation and may help achieve support for a child's college education.

CHILDREN   *Also see: Child Abduction; Child Custody; Child Support; Contracts; Crimes and Criminal Law; Divorce*

A child, or minor, in most states is a person under the age of eighteen. Numerous federal, state, and local laws are designed to protect children. For example, minors are typically forbidden from entering into legal contracts because the law presumes they lack requisite mental capacity. Most often, a minor's parents' or legal guardian's consent is necessary and such a contract will be valid only if no fraud, duress, or other illegal factors are involved in the making of the contract.

AGE

The age of a minor has direct legal consequences in many areas of the law. For example, youngsters under fifteen who commit serious crimes are typically tried as minors in juvenile court. Statutory rape is generally defined as unlawful sexual intercourse with an underage child (under sixteen in some states) even though consent is freely given and there is no threat of force. Age also determines a young person's right to obtain a driver's license, legally purchase an alcoholic beverage (twenty-one in virtually all states), get married without parental consent (often eighteen or older, but younger with parental consent or the consent of a judge), and receive child support. The responsibility of paying child support ends when the child becomes emancipated, and one of the elements of emancipation is defined as sufficient age. Thus, when a child reaches the age of twenty-one or even eighteen in some states, a parent is not legally obligated to continue supporting that individual.

BEST INTEREST OF THE CHILD STANDARD

In the area of family law, children have many protections, including a bill of rights that many states have incorporated into their court proceedings. These provisions generally state that children must not be treated as pawns and have the right to grow up in a home environment that will best guarantee an opportunity to achieve mature and responsible citizenship. As a result of this bill of rights, judges are required to take an active role in the affairs of children and periodically review custodial arrangements and child-support orders as the parents' circumstances and the child's benefit require. Most states automatically provide separate legal representation for children and appoint guardians ad litem to represent them in protracted divorce, custody, and support cases. A guardian ad litem is an impartial lawyer who presents evidence to the court during a hearing or proceeding so neither parent can distort the truth or manipulate the child. Speak to a lawyer for more details concerning this if applicable.

The law requires a judge to make determinations according to the child's best interest and overall welfare. "Best interest of the child" is the legal standard most often used by judges when making decisions regarding adoption, custody, and child support. For example, when awarding custody to either parent, the award is not aimed at rewarding or punishing parents, since the court's paramount concern is for the child's welfare. Judges are legally obligated to consider a number of factors when determining what is in the best interest of the child. An attorney can appeal the decision if an error is made in applying this legal standard.

CIVIL RIGHTS   *Also see: Employment; Travel Rights*

Americans possess many civil rights that are guaranteed by the United States Constitution, the Bill of Rights, and numerous federal and state laws. Such protections cover freedom of religion, freedom of speech, freedom from unreasonable search and seizure, the right to bear arms, and rights of privacy. Personal liberties have been expanded in such diverse areas as employment, education, and voting. This section discusses major civil freedoms and offers strategies by which individuals can protect their rights.

FREEDOM OF RELIGION

Religions in this country are allowed to flourish with no harmful governmental interference. Religious organizations are entitled to property and other tax exemptions. People are free to practice their religious beliefs, and the government cannot promote or favor one religion over another.

The Civil Rights Act of 1964 prohibits religious discrimination and requires employers with more than fifteen workers to reasonably accommodate the religious practices of employees. For example, employers must regularly give time off for the Sabbath or weekly holy day (except in an emergency) for employees who religiously observe even if such observances conflict with their work schedules. In such cases, the employer may give leave without pay, may require equivalent time to be made up, or may allow the employee to charge the time against any other leave with pay except sick pay. Employers may not be required to give time off to employees who work in key health and safety occupations or whose presence is critical to the employer on any given day. Also, they are not required to take steps inconsistent with a valid seniority system or incur overtime costs to accommodate an employee's religious practices.

If you are a religious observer experiencing difficulties with an employer, speak to a lawyer immediately or contact a regional office of the Equal Employment Opportunity Commission (EEOC) for advice and investigation. If you believe a violation is occurring in the public schools concerning school practices or clothing regulations, or there is government intrusion upon religious practices, consult the American Civil Liberties Union (ACLU) or the Anti-Defamation League of the B'nai B'rith for direction and guidance.

FREEDOM OF EXPRESSION

The First Amendment guarantees Americans the right to freedom of speech, the press, and assembly. This right is not absolute, and courts balance the free exchange of ideas with the protection of the general population. Limits for obscenity, libel, symbolic speech (e.g., burning a draft card or the American flag), protests, and other issues are being interpreted by the courts all the time or have been decided by the United States Supreme Court. For example, notwithstanding the general right of free speech, it is illegal to:

▸ Defame someone
▸ Stand outside a jail and talk to prisoners
▸ Incite riots
▸ Sell obscene materials to minors

Speak to a lawyer immediately if you believe your rights of free speech are being infringed or violated.

RIGHTS OF PRIVACY

Examples of privacy rights (which may differ depending on the state where an incident occurs) include:

▸ The right not to have confidential details regarding your medical or credit history disseminated to virtually all third parties.
▸ The right not to have your home or other private area entered without your consent.
▸ The right not to have your name or photograph used commercially without your consent.
▸ The right not to have your telephone conversations overheard.

Wiretapping and eavesdropping of telephone and private conversations are regulated and to some extent limited by federal and state law. Title III of the Omnibus Crime Control and Safe Streets Act prohibits the deliberate interception of private oral communications, including telephone conversations. For example, employers are forbidden from eavesdropping on the private conversations of employees (e.g., in a restroom or locker room). In some states, it is illegal to tape the telephone or direct conversation of another without his or her consent except when a warrant is issued by a judge in a criminal investigation.

In other states, it is legal for one party to the conversation to tape it. It is essential to know the laws of your state to act properly in this area. When in doubt about any perceived privacy right or violation thereof, consult a representative from a regional ACLU or a private attorney for guidance.

Several federal laws, including the Freedom of Information Act, govern the collection of, access to, and control of government information. Individuals can request copies of all documents collected by a federal agency concerning themselves or others to ensure that they are not haunted by wrong or misleading agency records. The two sample letters on pages 332–333 in the Appendix illustrate the kinds of letters that may be sent by certified mail, return receipt requested, to protect your rights in this area.

Finally, the term "right of publicity" refers to the right of an individual to protect himself or herself from the unauthorized commercial exploitation or appropriation of his or her persona, or the right to control the commercial use of his or her identity. At least fourteen states have adopted statutes that recognize a related right of privacy in this area. For example, if you discover that your picture appeared in a commercial ad and you did not authorize or receive compensation for its use, you may have a claim in this area. Speak to a lawyer for more details where applicable.

RIGHT TO PEACEFUL ASSEMBLY

People can be charged a fee to purchase a permit to hold a rally and pay for the costs of clean-up and police protection. Towns, cities, and county governments can issue the permit and require people to conduct the meeting only during reasonable hours and at certain places. However, people are allowed to express their views without prohibition during such rallies or demonstrations, even for causes or beliefs repugnant to the general population.

RIGHT TO BEAR ARMS

In about forty states, bans have been imposed prohibiting individuals from joining private military organizations and engaging in paramilitary training. But these laws do not prohibit citizens from owning their own firearms. However, under the federal Brady Law, there is a period of time (several days) a person must wait before being able to purchase a handgun while his background is investigated and it is determined he is not a prior felon. Most states prohibit the carrying of a concealed weapon on one's person in public without a permit and may have other gun regulations.

RIGHT TO DUE PROCESS

Due process of law is defined as the benefit of written laws, including full understanding of obligations and the right to be heard procedurally when deprived of life, liberty, or property, guaranteed by the Fifth and Fourteenth Amendments to the U.S. Constitution. In the United States, people have the following due process rights:

> ▶ Land cannot be taken by the government in an eminent domain proceeding without providing fair compensation.
> ▶ The opportunity to be given notice of, prepare for, and adequately respond to any form of charges in a criminal trial or civil lawsuit.
> ▶ The right to a fair hearing before an impartial panel and the right not to be forced to take the stand and testify against oneself.
> ▶ The right not to be tried a second time for a crime (known as double jeopardy) when found innocent the first time.

The right to due process has far-reaching consequences to individuals in all phases of life such as marriage, family, abortion and reproduction, freedom to travel, and rights of privacy. For example, states cannot prohibit the sale of contraceptives to married couples. With certain exceptions (e.g., minors having to discuss their decision with a parent or having to wait twenty-four hours before going through with the decision in some states), women generally have the unencumbered right to abort a fetus during the first trimester of pregnancy without governmental interference. People may sue the government for personal injuries when they are injured by the negligence of a government employee. If you believe your due process rights have or are being violated, consult an attorney immediately for advice and assistance.

RIGHT TO EQUAL PROTECTION

Each citizen has the same rights and obligations as any other, and federal, state, and local governments may not favor one group of people or an individual over another on the basis of age, color, race, national origin, or sex. The right to equal protection applies to all areas, including employment, education, and public accommodations and housing. For example, private employers typically with more than several workers, labor unions, state and local government agencies, and employment agencies are prohibited from:

> ▶ Denying an applicant a job on the basis of race, color, national origin, sex, or age
> ▶ Denying promotions, transfers, or assignments on the basis of race, color, national origin, sex, or age
> ▶ Penalizing workers with reduced privileges, reduced employment opportunities, and reduced compensation on the basis of race, color, national origin, sex, or age
> ▶ Firing a worker on the basis of race, color, national origin, sex, or age

If you have been treated unfairly on the job, react quickly and correctly to protect your rights. Speak to a competent attorney or a representative from an agency empowered to investigate a claim, such as the EEOC or your state's Commission on Human Rights, as soon as possible. Time is of the essence, since in most situations complaints must be filed within 300 days of the alleged illegal act or within ninety days in federal court after you receive a decision from the state's Commission on Human Rights, to avoid expiration of the statute of limitations. If you are protesting illegal activity but have not been fired, no one can stop you from filing a complaint. The law forbids employers from threatening reprisals or retaliation. To increase the chances of winning a case:

> ▸ Speak to other minority employees to determine if they have received similar discriminatory treatment.
> ▸ Discuss the problem with friendly witnesses who are willing to testify on your behalf and help prove a claim.
> ▸ If you receive an unfavorable performance evaluation or warning that is subjectively tainted, submit a written response that documents why the appraisal or warning is incorrect. This may document the protest and prove that you did not acquiesce through silence or inaction to the employer's version of the facts.
> ▸ Consult an experienced labor lawyer before taking any action.

In the area of accommodations and facilities, people cannot be refused service by a public restaurant or other retail establishment because of their sex, race, color, or national origin. However, a private facility, such as a men's club supported by private membership dues, can generally exclude women or members of other groups.

To reverse years of discrimination by educational facilities and in employment, the federal government instituted affirmative action programs to increase the opportunities for minorities. One example of an affirmative action plan is the government's requirement that certain types of construction jobs be awarded to companies owned and operated by minorities. In education, a university may consider an applicant's race in the context of promoting ethnic diversity among its student body. However, the U.S. Supreme Court recently ruled that all affirmative action plans must pass a strict test as to fairness if they are to be upheld as constitutional.

Under the federal Fair Housing Act and Title VII of the Civil Rights Act of 1968, among other laws, many forms of housing discrimination are illegal. Homeowners are prohibited from making adverse decisions to lease or sell real estate because of a person's age, religion, sex, color, or national origin. In some states, people cannot be denied a lease on the basis of sexual orientation. It is also against the law for real estate agents to steer prospective buyers away from certain areas. If you are discriminated against because your offer to buy a house at the full asking price was denied, yet the house is still listed on the market, or you are not shown houses in the neighborhood you requested, contact a lawyer or representative from the federal Department of Housing and Urban Development. However, if the seller can prove that the transaction did not occur because of purely economic reasons, such as the prospective buyer's inability to obtain a mortgage, a discrimination case may not stick and monetary losses, legal fees, court costs, and other damages will not be awarded.

Older persons, women, disabled Americans, and many other minorities have rights in the areas of employment, education, and housing.

RIGHT TO COUNSEL

The Supreme Court ruled more than thirty years ago that every defendant in a criminal case is entitled to an attorney of his or her choice and that if the defendant cannot afford the costs, a lawyer must be appointed. In most states, the organization responsible for providing indigents with competent, free lawyers is the Legal Aid Society.

RIGHT TO TRAVEL FREELY

You cannot be required to disclose your travel plans or be precluded from traveling freely within or without the United States except in certain limited circumstances such as the following:

- ▸ During a custody dispute in which a judge is supervising the parental arrangement and the court directs a parent to surrender a child's passport
- ▸ After an arrest while a person is out on bail
- ▸ After a conviction while a person is on parole
- ▸ If someone desires to travel to a foreign country that has no diplomatic relations with the United States

See the section "Travel Rights" for a discussion of what to do when you are "bumped" or suffer lost luggage.

RIGHT NOT TO RECEIVE CRUEL AND UNUSUAL PUNISHMENT

According to the Eighth Amendment of the Constitution, it is illegal to impose excessive bail on a person after an arrest; to inflict torture after an arrest; or to impose an extremely long jail sentence on a person for a minor criminal violation. Speak to a competent attorney who specializes in criminal law to protect and defend your rights in this area when applicable.

WHERE TO GO FOR HELP

In summary, a number of federal and state agencies should be contacted whenever you believe that your civil rights have been violated. The following is a brief listing of important agencies and private groups:

For civil rights violations, contact:

Commission on Civil Rights, Washington, DC

American Civil Liberties Union, New York, NY

National Association for the Advancement of Colored People,
 Washington, DC

National Organization for Women, New York, NY

For discrimination in education, contact:

U.S. Department of Education, Washington, DC

Equal Employment Opportunity Commission, New York, NY

Immigration and Naturalization Service, Washington, DC

For housing discrimination, contact:

Office of Fair Housing and Equal Opportunity, Washington, DC

Equal Employment Opportunity Commission, New York, NY

For discrimination concerning the elderly, contact:

American Association of Retired Persons, Washington, DC

National Council on the Aging, Washington, DC

American Association of Homes for the Aging, Washington, DC

Social Security Administration, Washington, DC

Equal Employment Opportunity Commission, New York, NY

For discrimination against the handicapped, contact:

Equal Employment Opportunity Commission, New York, NY

U.S. Department of Transportation, Washington, DC

State Attorney General's Office

Pension and Welfare Benefits Administration, Washington, DC

Social Security Administration, Washington, DC

COHABITATION *See Living Together*

COLLECTION AGENCIES *See Credit*

COMMERCIAL TRANSACTIONS

Commercial law defines the rights and duties of persons engaged in commerce
and the transaction of business. Several common topics are discussed below.

BANKS

A bank's primary obligation to its customer is to honor his or her checks when
the customer has sufficient funds on deposit. A bank must also maintain the
customer's signature on file so that forgeries can be detected before any payment

is made. A bank may be liable when it mistakenly pays out a check to a person who forged an endorsement. A customer who promptly reviews his or her bank statements and is not otherwise negligent has the right to have an account re-credited for checks bearing the customer's forged signature or another person's forged endorsement.

Other common problems with banks include:

Electronic fund and account mix-ups

Imposition of unwarranted fees

Holding a customer's checks beyond the maximum amount of time required to pay for such deposits

Bank credit card errors

Misrepresentation of credit charges (e.g., not disclosing the annual percentage rate on loans)

Failure to specify adequate reasons for denying credit

Engaging in discriminatory lending decisions on the basis of race, gender, age, marital status, national origin, religion, or because the applicant is on welfare or in the past has filed a complaint about the bank

If a problem occurs, first attempt to resolve it directly with the bank. Discuss the problem in person, and follow up all meetings with a letter confirming the substance of the meeting and what was promised (e.g., immediate action). Send the letter by certified mail, return receipt requested, to prove delivery. If the matter is not resolved quickly, appeal to a supervisor or an officer of the bank. Send a final letter warning that legal action will be taken if the problem is not resolved.

You can hire a lawyer to take further action, or contact an agency that oversees, regulates, and handles complaints against banks in your jurisdiction. These include a state's banking department, Federal Home Loan Bank, U.S. Comptroller of the Currency, Federal Reserve Bank, and the Federal Deposit Insurance Corporation. If you are having trouble reaching the appropriate agency, contact a regional or local department of consumer affairs as a last resort. Most consumer affairs agencies will intervene on a consumer's behalf or can guide you in this area.

CHECKS AND BANK CARDS

Rules governing the handling of checks are contained in a set of laws called the Uniform Commercial Code, which is followed by financial institutions throughout the United States. The following list summarizes basic information about checks:

- ▸ A bank may charge a fee for every check you write.
- ▸ If someone forges your signature on a check made payable to you which the bank pays by mistake, you are entitled to receive damages. If a bank's

FORM 32. **Negotiable Promissory Note**

Amount of Loan (specify $)   Place

                                                          Date

THIS PROMISSORY NOTE (the "Note") is effective as of the date it is executed by (specify name of Maker), "Maker," located at (specify address), for the purpose of evidencing an obligation from Maker to (specify name of Payee) "Payee," located at (specify address).

1. PROMISE TO PAY. For value received, Maker promises to pay Payee at (specify address), or at such other place as may be designated in writing by the holder of this Note, the total sum of (specify $) (specify with or without interest, costs, and fees) to be paid (specify the dates and amounts of payments). The checks for all installment payments are to be made payable to (specify name) and mailed directly to (specify address).

2. NOTICE OF NONPAYMENT. If Maker fails to make a payment set forth above on its due date, Payee shall give Maker written notice of such nonpayment. The date of such notice shall be deemed to be the date that Payee transmits such notice by certified mail or facsimile at the following address (specify). Maker shall have ten (10) days from the date of such notice to make said payment.

3. NO OFFSETS. Maker agrees to pay this Note free from any offset, deduction, or counterclaim.

4. PREPAYMENT. This Note may be prepaid in whole or in part at any time.

5. DEFAULT AND ACCELERATION. Maker shall be immediately in default upon the occurrence of any of the following events: (a) Maker fails to pay any amount due hereunder in full when due and Maker fails to make such payment pursuant to the ten-day notice provisions of Paragraph 2 hereinabove; (b) Maker violates or otherwise fails to perform or observe any term, covenant, or agreement contained in this Note; (c) the winding up, liquidation, or dissolution of Maker; (d) sale or transfer of substantially all of Maker's assets; (e) a receiver is appointed for all or any part of Maker's property; (f) Maker makes an assignment for the benefit of its creditors; or (g) Maker files or has filed for protection under any bankruptcy law. In the event that Maker defaults under this Note, then, at the option of the holder of this Note, the entire unpaid balance of principal shall become immediately due and payable.

mistake was intentional, additional damages for loss of credit or damage to reputation may also be awarded.

▸ A bank is liable once a timely stop-payment order is made but not followed (i.e., the check is paid). Oral stop-payment orders are valid for fourteen days, but they can be extended in writing. Written orders last for six months and can be extended. See pages 334–335 in the Appendix for examples of Stop Payment Request and Notice of Bad Check letters that you can send to protect your interests.

▸ Banks may refuse to honor a check with an entry that has been crossed

6. WAIVERS. Maker waives presentment, protest and demand, notice of protest, dishonor and nonpayment of this Note and expressly agrees that this Note, or any payment hereunder, may be extended from time to time at the written consent of the holder, all without in any way affecting the liability of Maker.

7. ATTORNEY'S FEES AND INTEREST. If an event of default has occurred and the holder of this Note refers it to any attorney for collection, Maker agrees to pay all costs and reasonable attorney's fees incurred by the holder of this Note in connection therewith. Interest shall accrue from the date of default at the rate of (specify %) per annum or the maximum legal interest rate, whichever is greater.

8. CONSTRUCTION. This Note shall be governed by and construed and enforced under the laws of the state of (specify).

9. SUCCESSORS. The terms and conditions of this Note shall inure to the benefit of and be binding jointly and severally upon the successors, assigns, heirs, survivors, and personal representatives of Maker and shall inure to the benefit of any holder, its legal representatives, successors, and assigns.

10. NO BREACH. No breach of any provision of this Note shall be deemed waived unless it is waived in writing. Waiver of any one breach shall not be deemed a waiver of any other breach of the same or any other provision of this Note.

11. AMENDMENTS. This Note may be amended or modified only by written agreement duly executed by Maker and Payee or the holder of this Note.

12. NO DEFAULT. If the due date of any payment under this Note falls on a Saturday, Sunday, or public holiday, such payment may be made on the next business day without constituting a default in payment under this Note.

13. DISHONORED CHECK. In the event that any payment on this Note is made by check that is dishonored by the drawee bank, for any reason whatsoever, there shall be added to the amount owing under this Note the sum of Fifty Dollars ($50.00) to cover the banking charges and expenses related to such dishonored check.

"Maker"

_____
Signature of Maker

Witness: _____

Dated: _____

out or written over, even if the change has been initialed by the payer.

- ▸ A check is technically valid for six years, unless a time limitation is printed on the front, but most banks are reluctant to honor a check more than 180 days old.
- ▸ Banks are not liable for paying checks after a customer's death unless they are timely notified.
- ▸ Banks are not liable for mistakes or forgeries that go unreported or undetected because a customer does not accurately and timely examine account statements and notify the bank of mistakes.

▸ Under the federal Electronic Funds Transfer Act, customers have limited liability for charges on lost or stolen bank cards and are required to be given receipts of computer terminal transactions and all wire transfers.

Unless you have acted with gross irresponsibility (e.g., given a checkbook and identification to a stranger), you will probably not be responsible to a merchant for reimbursement if someone steals your checkbook and signs and presents the check to a merchant. Never admit liability if you are contacted. Contact the police when your checks are stolen or misused and file a police report at the time the loss is discovered. Ask for a copy of the police report and notify the bank immediately. Speak to a lawyer for further details if applicable.

Read bank statements immediately after receiving them. If you notify the bank that issued your automated teller machine card of a loss or theft within two business days after an occurrence, damages are limited to $50. If you wait longer than two days, liability increases to $500. If you fail to report an unauthorized transfer that appears on a bank statement within sixty days, you could be liable for the full amount of all unauthorized withdrawals.

Report any lost or stolen bank cards by phone and then by letter immediately. If the bank fails to credit an account properly for any missing funds, you can file a complaint with the Board of Governors of the Federal Reserve System in Washington, D.C. Under the Electronic Funds Transfer Act, you can also sue the bank and recover up to three times the amount improperly withheld from an account, plus $1,000 in punitive damages. The same is true for reporting lost or stolen credit cards. Contact your credit card company immediately. Then send a letter confirming the conversation and your request. The sample Notice of Lost Credit Card on page 336 in the Appendix illustrates this procedure.

LOANS

Mortgage, home equity, business, and personal loans are common bank loans. Generally, a spouse will not be liable for a separate business loan entered into by the other spouse unless he or she cosigned (guaranteed) the loan. However, for most home equity or mortgage loans, both parties are typically personally liable for the unpaid debt, especially if they live in a community property state where all marital assets and debts are presumed shared equally.

All sophisticated loan agreements are presented in written form. Read such agreements carefully before signing. Question all fine print and ambiguous language. Get advice from a lawyer before signing any complicated loan agreement. Understand all aspects of the loan including:

How and when it will be repaid

Total cost of the loan

Interest, finance, legal, and additional charges

Whether the lender has a security interest in the property covered by the loan or other items to ensure the collectibility of the loan

Notice and acceleration provisions when the borrower is in default

Procedural guidelines in the event of default

Effect and extent of personal guarantees

Conditions that may extend the loan

Documents to be returned after the loan is paid off

Tax implications: deductibility of the interest, finance, and other payments

Get written confirmation when lending money. Never lend large sums of cash without a receipt because there may not otherwise be sufficient proof that a loan was made. It is always preferable to make a loan by check with the word "loan" marked in the bottom left corner. Some people prepare promissory notes similar to the one on pages 98–99 as proof of the loan. Specify whether it is a demand note ("payable immediately on demand") or whether the loan is to be repaid in installments over time. Specify in the note the rate of interest to be charged and be sure the rate is not excessive (i.e., greater than 18 to 24 percent per annum in many states) to avoid charges of usury and avoid penalty.

When litigation ensues either in small-claims court for small loans (i.e., under $3,000) or in regular court, the issue basically boils down to credibility. If you lend money and it is not repaid in a timely fashion, the following must be proved to win the case:

WHAT MUST BE PROVED	HOW TO PROVE IT
1. Date and place you lent the money	1. Your testimony, witnesses
2. Whom you lent the money to	2. Your testimony, witnesses, note of indebtedness, loan agreement, canceled check
3. Amount of money lent	3. Same as #2 above
4. Amount and time intervals of repayment	4. Same as #2 above
5. Timely demand was made for repayment	5. Your testimony, witnesses, copy of demand letters sent certified or registered mail
6. The amount has not been repaid	6. Your testimony, witnesses

Typical defenses raised by the defendant (the person being sued) include the following:
The amount of interest charged is excessive and not permitted by law (i.e., usurious).
The loan was really a gift.
The loan was forgiven.
The loan was repaid.
There is no proof that the loan was ever made.

The Appendix contains a Sample Loan Agreement (page 337) that illustrates the kind of document you may be required to sign when making a purchase or when borrowing or lending money. If you are the lender in such an agreement and are not repaid in a timely fashion, your first step should be to send a Notice of Default letter by certified mail, return receipt requested, to the defaulting party (see page 338 in the Appendix for an example). Such a notice of default will help you if you seek to enforce the debt or contract.

Speak to a lawyer before making a loan involving a significant sum of money or if you are unable to recover a loan that you have made. If the case is successful, there are several courses of action a lawyer can take if the defendant fails to pay the judgment amount. These are called *supplemental proceedings* and include filing a lien, commencing a foreclosure action on real property involved with the loan, repossessing an item subject to the loan (e.g., a car), or garnisheeing a portion of the debtor's salary if his or her employer can be located.

COMMISSIONS *See Contracts; Employment*

CONDOMINIUMS *See Real Estate*

CONSUMER TRANSACTIONS

Numerous federal, state, and local laws have been enacted to strengthen the rights of consumers in the past twenty years. However, it takes common sense and knowledge to avoid the numerous pitfalls consumers face every day when making purchases and entering into agreements with merchants. An informed consumer:

asks questions

reads the fine print

investigates credentials and checks references

gets the terms of any deal in writing

sends a letter of agreement confirming the deal if none is received

keeps careful records

protests unfair or illegal treatment

follows up with stronger action if satisfaction is not received

researches applicable law and consults an attorney immediately when necessary

knows his or her rights

This section briefly discusses common types of consumer transactions and how to enhance your legal position in each area. Your state's consumer protection office can advise you on how to resolve many of the kinds of disputes that consumers become involved in. See pages 339–342 in the Appendix for a list of state consumer protection offices with addresses and telephone numbers.

MAIL FRAUD

The Federal Trade Commission (FTC) is the federal agency empowered to protect consumers from unfair and deceptive merchant practices. According to a policy promulgated by the FTC called the Mail-Order Merchandise Rule, companies that sell by mail or telephone must ship an order within thirty days of the time they receive it unless the purchaser authorized a longer period of time. Consumers must be informed of any delays, and be allowed to cancel the order and receive a refund check within seven days. The Mail-Order Merchandise Rule does not apply to COD purchases. *For maximum protection, pay by credit card for all consumer purchases to be delivered later, because if the order doesn't arrive on time, it is easier to cancel without waiting for a refund.*

UNORDERED MERCHANDISE

Merchants who send unordered merchandise violate the Federal Trade Commission Act. Unordered merchandise does not have to be paid for and, in most states, does not have to be returned. Contact the local postmaster or the Federal Trade Commission in Washington, D.C., when you receive offensive, unordered merchandise. The FTC has nationwide jurisdiction over deceptive, unfair marketing practices. Contact a local Better Business Bureau for advice and assistance if you receive unordered or substituted merchandise.

MAIL-ORDER PURCHASES

When purchasing by mail, compare different offers and apply the following rules:
- ▸ Check the advertising claims.
- ▸ Keep a copy of the ad or catalog from which you ordered.
- ▸ Check to see if there is a money-back warranty if you're not satisfied.
- ▸ Check the time limit on delivery and cancel the order by letter if it does not arrive when promised.
- ▸ Do not send cash. Pay the correct amount (i.e., extra charges, shipping, handling, and sales tax) by check.
- ▸ Check the order immediately when it is received. Return it to the sender if it is not what was ordered. Notify the company in writing and keep a copy of the letter.
- ▸ If you believe you are the victim of mail-order fraud, contact your local postmaster for assistance. Request a formal investigation of the matter by sending a letter like the one on page 104.

RETURN POLICIES

Consumers are generally entitled to a refund for defective or damaged goods not marked "as is" and misrepresented items. Most states have no typical refund law that applies to all retail establishments. Depending on the merchant, refunds range from "100% money-back guarantees" to no refunds or exchanges. Some

FORM 38. **Sample Letter Regarding Mail-Order Fraud**

Your Name
Your Address
Date

Local Postmaster
Address

Dear Postmaster,

I believe I have been the victim of an illegal mail fraud.

On (date) I responded to an advertisement in (specify). The ad stated that I would obtain (specify name of product), provided I sent $29.95 to (specify address of company).

Over two months have passed since I sent my check (which was cashed), and I have not received my purchase. In addition, I sent the company a letter certified mail, return receipt requested on (specify date) to document my protest, and I have not received a reply.

Please investigate this matter on my behalf. I can be reached at the above address if you require additional information.

Thank you for your cooperation in this matter.

Sincerely,
(your name)

Enclosures: copy of ad, canceled check, letter of protest

▷ Send certified mail, return receipt requested.

---

states require that all refund policies be listed in every contract of purchase and refunds be given when policies are not properly posted at each cash register or store entrance. For more details, call a local Better Business Bureau.

Under the laws of many states, businesses that sell home furnishings and major appliances are required to list the delivery date or range of dates in a contract at the time the order is taken. If the company fails to deliver the goods by the promised date, and the customer does not consent to the delay, the customer can:

▸ Cancel the contract and obtain a full refund of the deposit or full payment within two weeks of the company's receipt of a request
▸ Negotiate a new delivery date
▸ Cancel the contract and obtain a credit for the deposit
▸ Select new merchandise

The above relief may not be available if the merchant is unable to deliver the merchandise as a result of factors not in his control, such as labor strikes or floods.

Most contracts for the purchase of expensive items, such as cars and houses, allow consumers to cancel the transaction for any reason within a specified period of time (e.g., three days). This is referred to as a cooling-off period. If your state has such a law, check the details before signing a contract to know whether you may change your mind legally without incurring penalties or damages, and how much time you have to do so.

The Appendix contains a Receipt Form and a group of five useful letters (pages 343–347) to send whenever you seek redress in this area. For example, if you have a disputed account, have purchased defective merchandise, wish to return goods, cancel delayed or back-ordered goods, or desire to cancel a home solicitation agreement within three business days after signing it, always prepare and send an appropriate letter by certified mail, return receipt requested, to the seller or retail establishment and save a copy for your records. The letter can serve as proof of the arrangement that was agreed on, or to document and strengthen a claim.

WARRANTIES

Before signing any contract for the purchase of goods, be sure that any warranties offered verbally are contained in the contract. Under the law, express warranties are created when a manufacturer (through its salespeople or literature) makes a statement of fact about the capabilities and qualities of a product or service. When consumers rely on these factual representations in purchasing the product or service and the statements then prove to be false, consumers are entitled to recover damages.

Although sellers are not obligated to put warranties in writing, if they do, the warranties must contain important points such as how long the product purchased will last, what parts the warranty covers, what steps the consumer can take if something goes wrong, who offers the warranty, and the consumer's legal rights. The purchaser of a product also receives various implied (automatic) warranties from the manufacturer and the merchant. One is that the item is fit for a particular purpose (called an implied warranty of fitness); the other is that the item is adequate for the purpose for which it was purchased (called an implied warranty of merchantability). In many states consumers can enforce their rights with respect to implied warranties up to four years after a purchase.

Try to negotiate additional warranties before making a purchase. These differ from sales contracts because you may have to pay extra. If a warranty is offered, try to get it extended to cover extra parts and time even if you have to pay additional money. Watch out for disclaimers in sales contracts that reduce or minimize standard warranties. Understand the warranty offer and compare warranties from competing brands before making a purchase. Negotiate the longest, strongest, most comprehensive warranty you can. Questions to ask include:

What is the term of the warranty?

When does it start?

Will it pay for all repairs?

What is covered?

What must you do to enforce your warranty rights?

How long do you have?

Can you lose the warranty, for example, by not following a regular maintenance program?

Where must you return the product for it to be repaired?

Who pays for shipping?

How long must you wait before it is returned?

SWEEPSTAKES AND PRIZES

Legitimate sweepstakes and prize awards rarely require people to purchase anything in order to win. If you have doubts about any offer, contact a local Better Business Bureau or state, county, or city department of consumer affairs. Find out if the FTC has any pending cases against the company.

MAIL-ORDER BUSINESSES

Most mail-order promoters are not interested in helping people make money from their homes but in selling expensive advice and cheap products. They deal through the mail to make it as difficult as possible for dissatisfied consumers to find them. Always:

- Study the business being offered and learn about potential pitfalls as well as opportunities.
- Evaluate the risks of starting a business with no experience.
- Contact a local Better Business Bureau for advice before investing in any home business by mail.
- Check the performance claims made for the products and be sure they are supported by facts.
- Demand proof of earnings from others who have launched similar ventures. Get references and talk to these people. Verify the information with the people whose earnings are reported.
- Carefully review any contract or agreement before signing.
- Before making any investment, set a limit on the total amount you want to make available for investing and never exceed this limit.
- Speak to an attorney for advice before investing any significant (e.g., more than $2,500) money in a mail-order business.

TELEPHONE SALES

With regard to telephone solicitations, remember the following points:

- If the deal or proposal seems too good to be true, it probably is.

- Do not reveal a credit-card number and do not converse with strangers on the telephone.
- Ask for and review a written prospectus before investing.
- Speak to a lawyer before investing significant sums of money in a telephone solicitation.
- If you have been the victim of telemarketing fraud, contact the local Better Business Bureau, Federal Trade Commission, state attorney general's office, U.S. postal inspector, or other appropriate agency.

TIME-SHARES

Time-shares are offers to purchase a residence or vacation property for a period of time each year. Speak to a lawyer or competent adviser before making any time-share investment. Read the fine print carefully. Inspect the premises thoroughly before deciding to invest. Can you sell the time-share if you're not satisfied or your needs change? If so, to whom and for how much? These are just a few of the questions that should be answered before you decide to invest.

VOCATIONAL SCHOOLS

Choosing a trade school should be treated like any other consumer transaction. Rule out schools that do not have a state license and accreditation from an independent agency approved by your state's Department of Education. Call the Better Business Bureau; find out if the school has had problems in the past.

PETS

Many states require merchants to give customers detailed information regarding a pet's pedigree, health, and medical care. As with any other purchase, if you are dissatisfied with the pet, contact the merchant or place you purchased the animal immediately and demand either a replacement or a complete refund. Send a letter documenting the telephone conversation by certified mail, return receipt requested, and follow up this letter with other letters if the matter is not resolved quickly. If satisfaction is not received, consider suing the merchant in small-claims court. Contact the Better Business Bureau for additional information and advice.

DOOR-TO-DOOR SALES

Whether products or home-improvement services are offered, the seller must give notice-of-cancellation rights under federal and most state laws. This cooling-off notice must be stated in a contract or on a receipt. It begins once the seller gives you a notice-of-cancellation form, advising how long you have to change your mind and how to effect cancellation. If you have not received this form, you can cancel by notifying the seller in any manner. Contact a local Better Business Bureau for details about your state's cooling-off law.

MOVING COMPANIES

Regulation of household movers is typically split between individual states, for intrastate moves, and the U.S. Department of Transportation, for moves between states. Federal law requires interstate movers to offer arbitration for damage or loss claims of $1,000 or less, although consumers can be required to pay a fee for the arbitration. To reduce potential problems with movers, take the following steps:

1. Before the move, call the U.S. Department of Transportation and/or your state's Department of Transportation to determine if the moving company is licensed, insured, and bonded. Contact the nearest Better Business Bureau to learn if an unusually large number of complaints have been made. Obtain written estimates from several companies before making your decision. Demand a cap on the amount of the final bill. Be sure the company will adhere to the estimate given so that you will not run the risk of paying unanticipated charges before your belongings are unloaded. Review a copy of the company's contract and insurance coverage; purchase extra insurance that exceeds the mover's liability coverage where warranted.

2. Before the move, examine all of your property and inventory it. Take all valuables such as jewelry with you. Review all forms presented to you and question ambiguous or confusing language. Save copies for your records.

3. After the move, immediately send a letter documenting any claim to the company if you discover that any property was damaged or lost in transit. Send the letter certified mail, return receipt requested, and save a copy for your records. If the matter is not resolved, notify your insurance carrier (or the company's carrier), a state Department of Transportation, or the Federal Department of Transportation, and file a formal complaint. An agency may intercede on your behalf or you may be able to settle the matter with the carrier. Consider suing the moving company in small-claims court for matters under $3,000. Contact a lawyer if your damages exceed this amount.

A FINAL NOTE ON CONTRACTS

The language in a consumer contract can greatly affect credit terms and personal finances beyond what the actual deal would lead you to believe. For example, the contract may preclude you from suing the merchant in the state where you reside, having a jury trial, or contain other unfair provisions such as limiting damages only to the purchase price. You may not be sufficiently compensated for losses, so read the fine print in any consumer transaction very carefully. The list on page 109 summarizes the associations, licensing boards, and other entities to which you should complain when you receive shoddy goods and services. Consult the yellow pages for the local address of each.

FORM 39. **Where to Complain**

Accountants — State Education Department
Airlines — U.S. Department of Transportation, Federal Aviation Administration
Animals — Animal Affairs Bureau, Society for the Prevention of Cruelty to Animals
Architects — State Education Department
Automobiles — National Highway Traffic Safety Administration
Auto Rentals — Department of Motor Vehicles, Better Business Bureau, Department of
    Consumer Affairs
Banks — U.S. Comptroller of the Currency, Federal Reserve Bank, state banking depart-
    ment
Charities — State Attorney General
Chiropractors — State Education Department, State Health Commission
Computers — Department of Consumer Affairs
Contractors — Better Business Bureau, Department of Consumer Affairs
Dentists — State Education Department, State Health Commission
Discrimination — Division of Human Rights, Equal Employment Opportunity Commission
Doctors — State Health Department, American Medical Association, State Health Commis-
    sion
Dry Cleaners — Better Business Bureau, Department of Consumer Affairs
Food — Food and Drug Administration, U.S. Department of Agriculture, State
    Department of Agriculture and Markets, Department of Consumer Affairs
Funerals — State Health Department, Federal Trade Commission, Better Business Bureau,
    Department of Consumer Affairs
Furniture — Department of Consumer Affairs, Better Business Bureau
Garbage — Department of Sanitation
Home Improvements — Department of Consumer Affairs, Better Business Bureau
Insurance — State Insurance Department, Attorney General's Office
Lawyers — Legal Referral Department of Lawyers Disciplinary Committee,
    American Bar Association, Attorney General's Office
Mail-order Sales — Department of Consumer Affairs, Federal Trade Commission,
    Postal Service
Moving and Storage — Interstate Commerce Commission, Department of
    Transportation, Department of Consumer Affairs, Better Business Bureau
Noise — Department of Environmental Protection
Notaries — State Education Department
Nursing Homes — Department of Health, Attorney General's Office
Pharmacists — State Education Department
Police Misconduct — Civilian Complaint Review Board
Potholes — Department of Transportation
Real Estate Brokers — State Education Department, Department of State
Repairs — Department of Consumer Affairs
Restaurants — Department of Health
Social Workers — State Education Department
Stockbrokers — Securities and Exchange Commission, National Association of
    Securities Dealers
Taxis — Taxi and Limousine Commission
Veterinarians — State Education Department
Utilities — Public Service Commission
Water — Department of Health

CONTRACTS

A contract is an enforceable agreement that can be written, oral, or implied by the actions or intentions of the parties. The words *agreement* and *contract* legally mean the same thing.

WHAT MAKES A CONTRACT VALID?

To determine if a valid contract exists, it is necessary to prove the following:

The parties entering into the contract were of sound mind (i.e., were not insane) and had the required legal capacity and mental ability. In many states, minors under eighteen are legally incapable of making a binding contract. As for required mental ability, if, for example, a person has agreed to purchase an expensive car while intoxicated or disoriented because of medication, he should contact a lawyer because he may be able to exculpate himself and not honor the agreement.

There was mutual acceptance of the agreed-upon terms. All contracts require an offer and an acceptance. An offer is the presentment of terms, which, when accepted, may lead to the formation of a contract. The terms offered have to be definite and clearly understood by the person receiving the offer. For example, when an offer is extended to buy something, the price, quantity, and other important terms, such as an accurate description of the item to be conveyed must be clearly understood. The offer must be certain and not an invitation to bargain or negotiate. The acceptance must be clearly made for the same thing offered in the manner specified by the offer. For example, if the offer says that response must be in writing by mail, a verbal acceptance may not be legally sufficient.

Consideration was given. Consideration is an essential element of an enforceable contract; it is something of value given or promised by one party in exchange for an act or promise of another. The amount of consideration paid in money is typically not important in determining whether the contract is valid (e.g., one dollar could be sufficient as consideration).

Consideration does not have to be money. It can be a promise to refrain from doing something, or a promise to do something. It cannot be a gift because one of the parties is not required to do anything in return for receiving the gift.

The subject matter was legal. For example, if you wish to sue someone for failure to pay for illegal drugs, you could not resolve the matter in court, because the subject matter of the underlying transaction was illegal.

Contracts can be *express, implied by conduct,* or *implied in law.* An express contract is either an oral or a written agreement whose terms are manifested by clear and definite language. An implied contract is an agreement inferred from the conduct of the parties. This occurs where the parties may not have precisely agreed on all key terms but the contract was performed anyway. An implied-in-law contract (also called a quasi contract) is created by operation of law to avoid unjust enrichment of one party at the expense of another. In a quasi contract there has been no agreement or meeting of the minds; one party has conferred a benefit on another under such circumstances that fairness and equity require compensation. This occurs for example when a doctor renders assistance to an unconscious patient. The patient later on receives a bill for the doctor's services. Since competent medical care was provided by the doctor with the expectation of being paid, the patient will be required to pay for the reasonable value of the doctor's services.

Although many contracts can be oral and still enforceable, certain types of agreements must be in writing to be valid. For example, contracts:

> ▸ involving the sale of land in most states or a property interest (except for leases of less than one year)
> ▸ involving the sale of goods exceeding $500 in value
> ▸ not able to be fulfilled within a year
> ▸ concerning one's offer to pay for the debt of another
> ▸ involving promises made in consideration of or affecting a marriage (e.g., prenuptial agreements or property distributions on divorce) must be evidenced in writing and signed by the party to be charged (i.e., to which the contract applies) to be valid.

The Simple Suggested Contract on page 348 in the Appendix contains the essential terms that must be included to make almost any contract legally valid.

When a legal dispute arises concerning the terms of an oral contract, a court will resolve the problem by examining all the evidence that both parties offer and weighing their testimony to determine whose claims should be upheld. A problem with oral contracts is that the same words discussed and agreed upon by both parties (assuming what was said can be proved) often have different interpretations. To avoid problems, insist on a written document that clarifies and confirms the terms of any contract that has been agreed upon. Whether you are about to hire a contractor to do house repairs, purchase an insurance policy, or be employed, obtain a written contract that spells out the understanding and clarifies your rights. In important jobs, for example, executives should request a written contract that confirms important terms defining compensation, benefits, job security, notice of termination, and other considerations. The employer should provide such information to you.

You can protect yourself by sending a letter spelling out any oral agreement you have reached with another party. In many instances, the letter can act in lieu of a written contract, provided the letter states that if any of the terms are incorrect or incomplete, an immediate reply is necessary. (The letter on page 112 illustrates this concept.) Write the letter with precision, since ambiguous or unclear language will work against you. Keep a copy of the letter for your records. Send it certified mail, return receipt requested, to prove delivery. If the other party does not respond to the letter or does not raise objections to the stated understanding, a written contract may be deemed by a judge to exist. That is how you can turn an oral handshake into a legally enforceable written contract!

When a contract is formed, all parties must live up to the promises set forth in the agreement. Breach of contract is the unjustified failure of a party to

FORM 47. **Sample Contract by Letter with Employer**

Your Name
Address
Telephone Number
Date

Name of Corporate Officer
Title
Name of Employer
Address

Dear (Name),

Per our discussion, it is agreed that I shall be employed by (specify employer) as a (specify job title) for an initial term of (specify, such as one year), beginning on (specify date). As compensation for services, I will receive a salary of (specify $) per year payable in equal biweekly installments on the first and fifteenth day of each month during the employment term.

In addition to my base salary, I will receive an annual bonus of (specify $) payable in equal quarterly installments and the company will promptly reimburse me for all reasonable business expenses on presentation of appropriate vouchers and records. This bonus will be given as compensation for additional services to be rendered. Upon termination of this agreement for any reason, I shall be entitled to receive my bonus and salary for the remaining period of the quarter in which my separation occurs.

If any of the terms in this letter are not correct, please advise me immediately in writing. Otherwise, this letter shall set forth and accurately reflect our understanding of this matter.

I look forward to working for (specify employer).

Sincerely,
(Your name)

▷ Send certified mail, return receipt requested.
▷ *Author's note:* Send a similar letter whenever you reach an agreement with anyone concerning any matter. If the letter is clearly drafted, sent certified mail, return receipt requested, and you do not receive a response, this will help turn an oral handshake into a written contract! Be sure to save a copy of the letter and the proof of receipt as evidence.

perform a duty or obligation specified in a contract. If the contract is impossible to perform because of force majeure, such as a flood or strike, this may be a defense. Other defenses typically raised to defeat the validity or enforceability of a contract are:

- No consideration was given.
- Subject matter of the contract required it to be in writing.
- Contract was entered into through fraud.
- Important terms were intentionally misrepresented.
- Contract was entered into under duress or coercion.
- The parties were unclear about key points of the deal.
- Contract required someone to do or sell something illegal.
- Contract was entered into with someone who lacked requisite mental capacity or was underage.
- Contract was entered into with a person who lacked the legal authority to bind another (e.g., a low-level bank employee who did not have the legal power to verbally approve a million-dollar loan).

If any of the above is applicable, contact a lawyer immediately if you wish to disavow (i.e., get out of) a contract. The longer you wait to take action, the worse your chances may be, so seek legal help as soon as possible.

Always review any contract or business document thoroughly before signing. Question all ambiguous and confusing language, including common ("boilerplate") clauses. Consult a lawyer if you do not understand the meaning of any terms. Submitted contracts often contain clauses that work to your disadvantage, and you cannot typically use the defense "I didn't read it carefully" or "I didn't consult a lawyer" to get out of it. Never be pressured into signing a contract without first reading it carefully.

Be sure that all changes, strikeouts, and erasures are initialed by both parties and that all blanks are filled in. If additions are necessary, include them in a space provided or attach them to the contract. Then, note on the contract that addenda have been added and accepted by both parties. This prevents questions from arising if addenda are lost or separated, because it is often difficult to prove that there were any without mention in the body of the contract.

When dealing with a business entity, such as a corporation, or with an agent, be sure the contract is signed by a person with legal authority (i.e., one authorized to bind the company to important terms) such as the president or other officer. Ask to see a written document authorizing that individual to act on behalf of another. Obtain a signed copy of the executed agreement and keep it in a safe place.

Once a contract is made, it cannot generally be changed without the consent of all parties involved. A contract modification is the alteration of contract terms. The best way to avoid a unilateral modification (i.e., a change without approval of one of the parties) is to have a clause in the contract that states that all changes must be in writing and signed by both parties. When presented with a contract modification you don't agree with, always protest the change, preferably in writing, because if you do nothing, a judge may find that you waived your rights or accepted the change by conduct.

The best way to protect yourself in this area is to prepare a new contract whenever you desire to extend, modify, terminate, or assign a preexisting contract. See pages 349–350 in the Appendix for a sample contract that illustrates this legal concept and a checklist of important points regarding contract execution.

BREACH OF CONTRACT

Breach of contract is a legal cause of action for the unjustified failure of one party to perform a duty or obligation specified in an agreement. When a contract is deemed to be breached, damages are awarded to the innocent party as compensation for financial loss or injury. In order to recover damages, it is necessary to prove that a contract existed, that there was a breach, and that a party was injured or damaged as a result. If damages are nominal, a small amount of money (e.g., one dollar) or the actual nominal amount may be recovered. If damages are significant, the injured party will be compensated by a sum of money to make him or her whole—for example, payment for lost profits or income that would have been earned through the duration of an employment contract. If the breach is minor, a party can treat the contract as continuing and seek reimbursement for damages. Typically, in the event of a material (i.e., major) breach, the contract is treated as being unjustifiably terminated, relieving the nonbreaching party of obligations and allowing that party to seek compensation.

The law does not allow people to recover money in excess of their damages as the result of a breach of contract. Parties to a contract are required to make reasonable efforts to reduce losses ("mitigate damages") as much as possible. This could mean purchasing a similar car from another merchant if the first dealer cannot sell you the car you agreed to purchase. Or, if you found a new job after being unjustifiably fired prior to the expiration of a contract, your damages would be reduced by the amount of earnings received from the new position.

Some contracts contain written clauses that stipulate what damages are to be paid in the event that the contract is breached. These are referred to as *liquidated damages.* If a judge or jury is unable to calculate the actual damages sustained, a liquidated damages clause may be enforceable. In many situations, however, liquidated damages clauses are not honored by the courts because they are deemed to be a penalty and not representative of actual losses incurred by the breach.

In some situations, parties considered by a judge to be in breach may be ordered to continue performing terms of the contract. This is referred to as *specific performance.* For example, if one party in a contract is required to sell property to another and unjustifiably backs out of the deal, a judge may require that person to go through with the deal as previously contracted.

Sometimes parties will settle a contractual dispute by compromise. For example, suppose you were to receive $50,000 over time for the purchase of a business. After making $30,000 in payments, the buyer cannot afford further payments and states that you misrepresented the amount of sales the business was supposed to generate. Rather than go to court, you agree to accept $10,000 more in full and final settlement.

Be careful whenever you receive checks marked "payment in full" or words to that effect. If the check is written in an amount less than you believe is due and you cash the check, you may not be able to obtain the additional amount owed. In some states, you can write a restrictive endorsement on the back of the check (i.e., "Under Protest. Endorsement of this check does not constitute a waiver of any and all claims for additional monies owed") and you may still be able to sue for the balance. In other states, your cashing the check will constitute an "accord and satisfaction" and will preclude you from recovering anything further, despite any protest language. Before cashing any dubious check, speak to a lawyer to get an opinion as to how state law applies. It's also a good idea to photocopy any such check before cashing it and save the copy.

The following sections briefly analyze various kinds of contracts and discuss points that should be understood or included in each.

EMPLOYMENT CONTRACTS

Always discuss the terms and conditions of employment before you agree to work. Be sure to understand your employment duties and responsibilities, title, job security (e.g., the initial contract period and provisions for renewal and termination notice); compensation package including salary, salary increases, bonus program, and requirements; and other details, including an explanation of your fringe benefits, vacation and sick time, and reimbursement for relocation. Even if an employer has promised lifetime employment (e.g., "You have a job here with us as long as you want to work"), if the promise isn't in writing, you can probably be fired on a moment's notice.

Avoid signing contracts that contain *restrictive covenants* (also referred to as covenants not to compete). A restrictive covenant is a provision in a written contract that forbids an employee from doing a certain act, such as working for a competitor, soliciting customers that he previously called on, or starting a competing business. Although every case is different, some judges are reluctant to restrict an employee's livelihood. When judges decide that a restrictive covenant is too harsh, they will either modify the terms, making it less restrictive (e.g., reduce a one-year covenant to six months), or declare it to be totally unenforceable and of no legal effect. The relevant factors typically considered by a judge are:

- ▸ Any unfairness in length or geographic limitations (e.g., greater than one year; the entire United States)
- ▸ The degree of hardship on the employee if the covenant is enforced
- ▸ Any additional compensation given to the individual as inducement to sign a contract containing such a clause
- ▸ Special skills or training of the employee and the amount of time, money, and effort expended by the employer to train the employee
- ▸ The bargaining power of the parties
- ▸ The status of the individual: whether he or she is an independent contractor (rather than an employee), which may make it more difficult in some states to restrain the contractor
- ▸ The hardship to the employer's business if the covenant is not enforced
- ▸ Special knowledge (trade secrets) or confidential information acquired by the employee
- ▸ Possible breaches by the employer of any of its own obligations (e.g., failure to pay salary), releasing the employee from any obligations under the contract

Even if a restrictive covenant battle can be won in court, the legal bills incurred may be prohibitive. Thus, avoid signing employment contracts containing such clauses whenever possible. *Seek legal advice before signing any employment agreement.*

SERVICE CONTRACTS

When hiring a building contractor, architect, or other professional, several rules typically apply. *Never hire the individual without first interviewing him or her.* Examine the person's academic and professional experience and credentials. What associations does the person belong to? Is he or she registered, licensed, or bonded with an applicable agency? Depending on the service, most states require formal registration and testing to ensure competence. If applicable, review samples of the person's work. Obtain references; speak to people who previously hired the individual. For example, when hiring an architect, talk to customers, contractors, builders, landscapers, and planners who worked on job sites with the architect. Look at the actual homes or offices designed by the architect whenever possible.

Ask for a written estimate of fees and compare this with estimates of other individuals before making a decision. Request a written contract that clearly describes the duties to be performed, responsibilities of both parties, how modifications in the contract will be handled and billed, and other points such as deadlines (also referred to as *time of the essence clauses,* which require performance to be completed by a specified date) and term of the agreement. If the contract is complicated or if a considerable fee is involved, retain the services of a lawyer familiar with the particular subject to review the agreement and negotiate additional terms on your behalf.

CONTRACTS FOR THE PURCHASE OF GOODS

Laws prohibiting unfair and deceptive trade practices in all consumer transactions have been enacted in every state. For more information, please consult the section "Consumer Transactions."

Under the laws of many states, businesses that sell home furnishings and major appliances are required to list the delivery date or range of dates in a written contract at the time the order is taken. The business must deliver the merchandise by the latest stated delivery date unless you are notified of the delay and agree to the revised delivery date. If the company fails to deliver the goods by the original promised date and you do not consent to the delay, you can:

- ▸ Cancel the contract and obtain a full refund of the deposit or partial or full payment within two weeks of the company's receipt of your request
- ▸ Negotiate a new delivery date
- ▸ Cancel the contract and obtain a credit for the deposit
- ▸ Select new merchandise

If the delay was caused by a factor not in the retailer's control, such as a labor or shipping strike, or it was your fault, you may not be able to seek the above relief. If you do not receive goods on time, document the cancellation in writing, sent by certified mail, return receipt requested. The letter should state the amount of money to be refunded and when you expect to receive it. It should also state the name(s) of the persons spoken with and other pertinent facts.

Most contracts for the purchase of expensive items (e.g., a house) contain provisions allowing you to call the deal off within a specified period of time. This is referred to as a *cooling-off period*. If your state has a cooling-off law, check the details before you sign the contract so you know how much time you have to change your mind and back out of the deal.

Some states have passed "plain English" laws requiring that consumer contracts use nontechnical, simple words. Federal and state truth-in-lending laws require that companies offering credit provide detailed information about credit contracts and terms in simple language. Insist on this whenever possible. Never sign complicated contracts for the purchase of goods if such contracts contain "fine print" clauses you do not understand or agree with. Speak to a lawyer if you signed a complicated contract to see if the defense of *adhesion* can be used to get out of the contract. Adhesion means you had little or no bargaining power when you signed the agreement, which by law was required to be drafted in simpler language. Don't assume you are precluded from recovering damages if you sign a standard contract with a disclaimer limiting your remedies. Although the law varies considerably from state to state, many judges find such clauses unconscionable, and therefore unenforceable.

LEASE CONTRACTS

Most lease contracts involve real estate or purchases of property (e.g., automobiles). When it comes to renting real estate, such as an apartment or office, be sure you understand who pays the broker for helping you find the apartment or negotiate the lease. If you are a landlord, avoid giving a broker an exclusive right to rent the property; retain the right to rent it yourself or to allow other brokers to assist you. Carefully review any broker's agreement before signing.

Never rent an apartment or office based on the basis of a floor plan. Inspect the premises carefully before you sign the lease. Do not be pressured to make a snap decision. Read the lease carefully before signing. If leasing property on behalf of a business or company, never personally guarantee payment of a lease if you can help it. If applicable, sign the lease in your official capacity (e.g., "Steven Jones, President," not "Steven Jones").

Other terms to consider include: (1) negotiating for the security deposit to be placed in a separate interest-bearing account, with interest going to you on a yearly basis; (2) negotiating for the right to lease with an option to buy the property over time to substantially reduce the final purchase price; and (3) negotiating for the painting, upgrade, or replacement of old appliances.

Avoid signing leases with clauses that:

- Eliminate the right to trial by jury.
- Force you to pay large attorney fees if the landlord unfairly commences legal proceedings.
- Provide for large increases on top of the base rent. Hidden costs in leases often include tax escalation provisions, construction and alteration of the premises fees, insurance obligations, utility charges, labor escalation costs, and many other expenses; understand the total bill to be incurred before signing on the dotted line.
- Give the landlord the automatic right to evict you if the rent is not paid within a certain number of days after the beginning of the month. Although some states restrict the right to automatic evictions without proper notice, others don't, so retain the right to be notified in writing before any legal action is taken so you will have additional time and the right to cure any alleged violations of the lease.

Leases are complicated documents that should be reviewed carefully by an attorney or accountant before you sign. Even if you use the standard form of lease found in a stationery store, review it carefully; such forms often contain clauses that cause difficulty later.

When leasing equipment, an automobile, or other product, read the contract carefully. The lessor (the entity leasing the goods) is required to provide a dated, written statement describing the leased property and the total amount of payments, including the amount of any refundable security deposits and advance payments or trade-in allowances to be paid or credited to the lessee (the person renting the goods). The contract should also make clear any extra government and registration fees and disclose certificates of title, license fees, and taxes. Understand how much is to be paid for the item at the end of the lease if you want to purchase it. This is called a buy-back clause. Discuss the advantages of leasing as opposed to buying with a professional adviser. Question excessive charges to be imposed if the goods are not returned in perfect condition. Include express warranties for extra protection. Understand how long the lease will last, the amount, how late charges will be computed, and the conditions under which either party may terminate the lease prior to the expiration of the lease term. These are just some of the many points to be aware of and negotiate in a lease.

If you are a landlord, vendor, or contractor, request money up front as security to cover a portion of an agreement. For large leases or purchases, assurances from other parties who can guarantee payment are advantageous. Consider including an arbitration provision in any agreement. In the event of a dispute, arbitration is usually quicker and cheaper than formal litigation. Using arbitration may allow you to enforce your rights quicker and with less legal cost when the other party fails to make timely payments.

SURETY CONTRACTS

A surety contract is an agreement by one person or entity to pay the debt of another. This is also referred to as a personal guaranty and must be in writing to be enforceable. (See page 351 in the Appendix for an example of a personal guaranty.) The surety may be a cosigner on a loan or the guarantor of the loan under the terms of a separate document. If you are making a loan, insist on cosigners or guarantors to increase the chances that the individual receiving the loan will pay it off. Speak to a lawyer for advice if you are borrowing money and are asked to sign a complicated loan document or if you are making a loan and want to include a surety provision.

CONVICTIONS   *See Crimes and Criminal Law*

COOPERATIVES   *See Real Estate*

COPYRIGHT

A copyright is an owner's exclusive right to print, reproduce, sell, and exhibit written material, musical compositions, works of art, photographs, theater and movie scripts, data systems, software, and other intellectual property placed in a tangible form, which, when registered, indicates that the copyright exists. The holder (owner) of the tangible form of expression is protected by the copyright. Once copyrighted, your work cannot be copied, adapted, or reproduced without your permission or compensation.

Copyrights are governed by federal law. A copyright lasts for the life of the creator, plus fifty years. Copyrights predating 1978 (the effective date of the revised federal law called the Copyright Act of 1976) may last for as long as seventy-five years. Additional changes to copyright law came into effect in 1989 with the signing of the Berne Convention, which established generally equal treatment of copyrights throughout most of the world. It is now possible to bring an infringement suit based on a U.S. copyright in another country that has signed the Berne Convention.

The Copyright Act of 1976 classifies copyrightable material into about a dozen groups depending on subject matter. Certain items do not fall into these categories and cannot be copyrighted. These include words and short phrases (e.g., names, titles, and slogans) and works such as telephone books, time cards, and diaries that are designed for recording information.

The exclusivity of a copyright as to use, unlike that of a patent, is subject to a number of exceptions. The "fair use" exception permits, among other applications, limited use and noncommercial reproduction for libraries, archives, and classroom purposes in an educational context when the use does not adversely or commercially impact the market. For example, it also allows authors and others to incorporate several lines of text from another work (but not necessarily poetry) without obtaining permission from the copyright holder.

Owning a copyright grants certain benefits, including the exclusive right to prevent others from using the work and to establish the terms and cost of its use. These rights come into effect when an original work of authorship is reduced to a tangible form (written down on paper). Two or more authors can be joint (not necessarily equal) copyright holders depending on the extent of their contributions or the existence of a formal agreement indicating the manner of joint ownership. The copyright, like any other form of intangible property, can be sold, assigned, and bequeathed in a will. The copyright owner can sell different rights to the same work to different people. Transfer of some of the rights is done via a license arrangement. A license can either be limited to one entity (called an exclusive license) or several entities (called a nonexclusive license).

To secure a valid copyright, it is important to place a proper designation on the front page of all copies of the work that are distributed to the public. For example, stating the following, "Copyright © 1998 by Steven Mitchell Sack. All rights reserved." will serve as a valid copyright notice so that it cannot be claimed that the work is in the public domain, free for anyone's use. It is not necessary to file the work with the Copyright Office in Washington, D.C., unless you want to institute a lawsuit for alleged infringement. However, registering the work with the Copyright Office is strongly recommended, because if you have registered the work before you learn of an alleged infringement or within three months after the work's first publication, the law allows a successful litigant to receive attorney fees and minimum damages (called statutory damages). If you register the work after learning about a potential infringement, you may receive only the damages sustained or the infringer's profit. Contact the Library of Congress in Washington, D.C., or a copyright attorney for information about the correct form to file. Follow the instructions on the form to be sure it is filled out correctly. The cost of registering a copyright is small (about $10); always save copies of the application with proof of payment for your records. It is a good idea to register all your works even if they have not been published (in the case of a book).

To win a copyright infringement case, the following three elements must generally be proved:

1. That you are the copyright owner
2. That the person accused of taking your work had access to it
3. That the infringing work is substantially similar to yours

To reduce the likelihood of problems and prove a claim, place a copyright notice on all copies of your work that you send to others. File a copyright application with the Copyright Office as soon as practical. Contact the Copyright Office to inquire about the status of the application if you do not receive a registration within several months. Save copies of the cover letter whenever you send a screenplay or musical composition to others. Send everything certified mail, return receipt requested, to prove when and to whom the property was delivered. These strategies can help establish elements 1 and 2 above in the event of a lawsuit.

However, you will need a competent attorney specializing in intellectual property (copyright law) to assist you in proving "substantial similarity," and each case is decided on its unique set of facts. If someone developed a similar idea independently or if the work in question has only minor similarities, you may not be able to sustain your claim.

Money damages, attorney fees, and costs are awarded to people who win a copyright infringement case, provided the work was registered with the Copyright Office before an alleged infringement. In certain instances, a judge may order the guilty party to cease using your copyright immediately through an injunction. Money damages range from lost profits to the reduction of the property's market value now that it has unlawfully been used by another. When your damages cannot be proven or when the amount of revenue or profits derived by the infringer is small, a judge may award statutory damages (a specific money award imposed by law) of up to $10,000 for each violation. For deliberate and intentional (i.e., willful) violations, additional money for each violation can be granted.

Always consult a competent attorney specializing in copyright matters for further information and advice.

CORPORATIONS

A corporation is a legal entity typically created to conduct business. The rules governing the corporation and its formation are controlled by the law of the state where the corporation is established. Once a corporation is formed, a distinct entity exists that is separate from the shareholders who own it, and this entity does not automatically dissolve upon the death of its owners. The corporation can conduct business, make purchases, pay its own taxes, sue or be sued, and enter into contracts. Perhaps its most significant feature is that, unlike a sole proprietorship, joint venture, or partnership, the owners (shareholders) are not generally personally liable for corporate debts or activities.

A closely held corporation is typically owned by a small number of shareholders who actively assist in the management and running of the business. A publicly held corporation is generally owned by thousands of investors who are not involved in the running of the business.

Corporations can take several forms for tax and other purposes. Common varieties include C Corporations (C Corp.), S Corporations (S Corp.), Professional Corporations (PC), and Limited Liability Corporations (LLC).

A *C Corporation* first pays a tax on its net taxable income. If it distributes profits in the form of dividends to its shareholders, they must also pay a tax on this distribution. This is a major disadvantage of a C Corporation, since stockholders are often taxed twice on profits unless they receive money some other way (frequently in the form of salary in lieu of dividends, which is a deductible expense of the corporation, so a tax is paid only once by the shareholder after receiving salary). An advantage of a C Corporation is that many fringe benefits, including medical premiums and profit-sharing plans funded on behalf of its owner-employees, are fully deductible by the corporation.

An *S Corporation* does not pay any tax on its net profits. All income and deductions are passed directly through to the shareholders, who pay tax on their proportional share of the profits. Unlike in a C Corporation, however, S Corporation shareholders are personally liable for any losses.

Professional Corporations are typically established by professionals such as doctors, dentists, and attorneys. Many professionals prefer to incorporate for tax reasons and to shield themselves from personal liability in many activities, such as signing leases or taking loans. However, professionals still may be personally liable to their patients or clients for wrongful acts they commit, or when they operate or act (e.g., make personal promises and commitments, don't hold regular board of directors meetings, or issue stock) as though the corporation does not exist. This is referred to as "piercing the corporate veil."

Limited Liability Corporations have recently become popular. These entities allow companies to be structured in a way that permits them to be taxed as a partnership while retaining the limited liability protection of a corporation.

The advantage of being taxed like a partnership (which is a voluntary association between two or more persons engaged in a business as co-owners for profit) or an S Corporation is that members can deduct partnership or corporate losses from their personal tax returns if the entity loses money.

These are the major advantages of a corporation:

▶ A corporation has a totally independent existence apart from those who own and operate it.

▶ Shareholders are not usually personally liable to the creditors of a corporation. If the venture loses large sums of money, shareholders will lose only what they have invested in the corporation.

▶ The corporation can continue in existence no matter what happens to its shareholders.

▶ Shares of stock can be freely bought, sold, given away, and inherited.

▶ Even minority shareholders (those with a small percentage of ownership in the corporation) have the right to review the books and records of the company and receive an accurate accounting. In many situations, they have a say ("dissenters' rights") in how the company is run and can even force a dissolution (winding down and liquidation of the company's assets) in the event of an impasse, or sue the directors or officers if they disagree with corporate decisions made by those individuals.

The key disadvantages of a corporation include:

▶ The tax rate on profits may be higher than personal rates.

▶ Additional costs, such as those of forming the corporation (i.e., incorporation fees); filing annual state franchise and business returns, and paying fees and taxes; paying accounting and bookkeeping fees to prepare yearly federal, state, and local corporate tax returns; and other administrative costs, will be incurred.

▶ Higher rates for expenditures such as telephones and insurance.

▶ Inability to make decisions freely and quickly without answering to other shareholders.

▶ Shareholders are taxed on distribution of profits after the corporation pays a tax on its earnings (i.e., known as "double taxation")

Shareholders of a corporation own common or preferred stock, and the class of stock often determines whether shareholders have voting rights and other powers. For example, common stock usually allows shareholders the power to vote while preferred stock may provide a separate, higher dividend. Shareholders have the right to elect directors and approve all major decisions such as the sale of the company's stock in a merger. They do not have the authority to run the company, which is a function of the directors or the officers (i.e., president, vice president, secretary, and treasurer) appointed by the directors. Generally, the bylaws of a company determine the number and qualifications of the directors. However, directors cannot use corporate assets for personal gain and cannot acquire stock at bargain rates. All decisions must be taken to benefit the corporation and not for personal gain.

When considering forming or investing in a closely held corporation, it is essential to seek proper legal, accounting, and tax advice. Always negotiate, draft, and sign a comprehensive shareholders agreement that spells out the rights, duties, and obligations of all the owners of the business. Provisions to include in such an agreement are:

> The structure of the corporation (as an S, C, PC, or LLC corporation).

> How to value the shares of the corporation, especially in the event of a dispute

> How daily decisions to run the company will be made (i.e., is unanimous consent or majority consent required?)

> Whether shares must first be offered for sale to the other stockholders with right of first refusal before being offered to the outside world

> Disposition of stock and other benefits in the event of death or disability of a stockholder

> Number of signatures required for checks to be issued by the corporation

> Location of bank accounts and all deposits

> The right to inspect the company's books and records at all times at reasonable hours

> Employment contracts with restrictive covenants for all officer/shareholders of the company

> Method for resolving disputes, such as arbitration, to avoid expensive and protracted litigation

> Designation of officers and number of directors

> Special powers and compensation for all directors and officers

This list is an initial summary of the kinds of concerns that must be addressed. A lawyer, accountant, and other professional adviser can help resolve these and many other points and structure a deal to maximum advantage.

COURTS

A court is a place where trials are held and/or the law is applied. Depending on a litigant's choice and other factors, a trial may be conducted and decided by a judge alone, or by a judge and a jury. In some appellate courts and the United States Supreme Court, only judges are present to hear arguments and make decisions.

A court can preside only over matters of which it has jurisdiction. Courts of original jurisdiction are the first courts to preside over a matter. A court of appellate jurisdiction is a higher court that reviews cases removed by appeal from a lower court.

Each state has its own court system, which operates separately from the federal court system. There are basically two levels of state courts: trial courts and appellate courts. General trial courts are typically divided into two separate, distinct courts, one to hear criminal matters and one to adjudicate civil matters. Civil trial courts may be further divided depending upon the amount of money or the subject matter at issue. In New York, for example, original jurisdiction small-claims courts adjudicate civil matters up to $3,000, the Civil Court adjudicates matters up to $25,000, and the Supreme Court presides over civil matters involving more than $25,000 or other issues. The Family Court hears issues pertaining to support, domestic violence, and problems affecting juveniles, while the Surrogate Court is involved in matters affecting probate, estates, and wills.

The federal court system is divided into twelve districts or circuits and generally has jurisdiction (1) when a person or an entity (i.e., a corporation) is suing a person or an entity residing in another state and the amount in controversy exceeds $50,000; (2) when a federal law governing such issues as bankruptcy, copyright, patents, maritime matters, and postal matters is involved; and (3) when one state is suing another state.

Within the federal system are separate limited jurisdiction courts that hear matters exclusively pertaining to bankruptcy (U.S. Bankruptcy Court), tax issues (U.S. Tax Court), suits against the federal government (U.S. Court of Claims), and disputes concerning tariffs and customs (U.S. Court of International Trade).

The United States Supreme Court is the country's highest court. It considers cases from the highest courts of each state, appeals decided by the U.S. Court of Appeals (the highest federal appeals court), and cases involving the constitutionality of federal laws.

The vast majority of lawsuits originate in state courts. If you are thinking of filing a lawsuit, speak to a lawyer or visit the clerk of any local court to determine where the correct place is to start. Each state has its own unique filing, procedural, and jurisdictional requirements, which must be correctly followed so the case will not be dismissed. It is essential to get proper advice before starting any legal process.

COVENANTS NOT TO COMPETE
See Contracts; Employment

CREDIT *See also: Employment*

Obtaining credit and maintaining a good credit rating are essential to financial success. When financial institutions, credit card companies, retailers, and credit bureaus fail to update credit reports or make mistakes regarding your credit history, you can take steps to protect your rights. You can also take effective action if a lender discriminates by denying you credit or you suffer collection agency harassment.

CREDIT REPORTING RULES

After you apply for a loan, a credit bureau examines your credit history and issues a report. Under the federal Fair Credit Reporting Act, credit reports cannot be furnished for illegitimate purposes or to people unauthorized to receive such reports. Reports cannot contain information on judgments, tax liens, or arrest records more than seven years old except when the company or person requesting the information is considering extending credit or providing insurance of more than $50,000, or offering employment in a job paying more than $20,000. Past bankruptcies may be reported for up to ten years. Once notified that a report is inaccurate, a credit bureau must investigate and correct false information. At the loan applicant's request, a reporting agency must clearly and accurately disclose, to the applicant, the source, nature, and substance of all information it has about the applicant in its files.

Any company or person who asks for a credit report about an applicant must promptly notify him or her in writing, and the applicant can receive a copy of the final report by asking for it in writing. Any company that turns down a request for credit, insurance, or employment partly because of information contained in a consumer credit report must supply the name and address of the agency that furnished the report. More important, the Equal Credit Opportunity Act prohibits lenders from discriminating against anyone on the basis of sex, marital status, religion, national origin, color, or age. The fact that an applicant is receiving workers' compensation, social security, or disability benefits cannot be used to deny credit, discourage applying for a loan, charge a higher interest rate, or limit the applicant to a smaller loan if the applicant otherwise meets the lender's criteria for loan approval. A lender cannot ask about childbearing plans, a spouse or ex-spouse, or whether any reported income comes from alimony or child support. Financial institutions must provide written notice of a loan rejection within thirty days, along with the reason given by the credit bureau.

Women and elderly persons often encounter credit problems and have difficulty obtaining loans. The Equal Credit Opportunity Act prohibits a lender from discrimination on the basis of sex or age. However, it may be difficult for women who married before 1977 (when the law was enacted) to obtain credit in their own name because their credit activities may still be reflected on a husband's report. For alleged discrimination violations, consumers must sue creditors and lenders within two years of the illegal acts and may recover, if successful, actual damages, up to $10,000 in punitive damages, court costs, and attorney fees, and receive the credit they were denied.

HOW TO CORRECT AN ADVERSE CREDIT RATING

There are simple steps to take to remedy an unjustifiably poor credit rating without the assistance of a credit agency or attorney. The basic aim is to find out what credit information is being reported to others, correct or delete inaccurate or incomplete information, and, if necessary, have the credit agency renotify recipients of reports. First, request a credit report from a major credit bureau to check for accuracy and that no adverse credit information has been reported by mistake. Local offices of major credit bureaus can be located in a telephone directory. Consumers will not be charged for a credit report if they contact TRW Information Service and request the report by letter no more than once a year. Include pertinent information, such as social security number, full name, current address, and other pertinent facts.

If you receive an inaccurate report, ask in writing for an explanation of the discrepancy and a complete report of your credit history. (Refer to the sample letters on pages 128–129 as guides.) The law requires that credit bureaus honor these requests. Speak directly with any establishment that denied you credit to discover why your credit rating is impaired. Make an appointment to visit a local credit bureau. A representative must agree to see you if you have been denied credit within the last thirty days and have proof (e.g., a photocopy of the denial letter). Dealing with the agency in person often speeds up the process.

A consumer victimized by a reporting agency's intentional carelessness or disregard of its legal duties can sue for actual and punitive damages, as well as court costs and attorney fees. Contact a regional office of the Federal Trade Commission, the regulatory agency empowered to oversee credit bureaus, within two years of the reporting agency's misconduct to obtain information and assistance. The bureau can also be sued under guidelines contained in the Fair Credit Reporting Act.

There is no guarantee of a favorable credit rating in instances where no credit file has been established or a person previously filed for bankruptcy protection or had his wages garnisheed, assets repossessed or attached, or was found guilty of delinquent child support. The same is true if someone recently moved and is unable to prove employment and income, furnish credit references, or complete credit applications.

Note: A federal law now makes it easier for consumers to discover when their credit report has been used against them, and to contest incorrect information in a report. Key provisions of the law require credit bureaus to:
- ▸ Establish toll-free numbers answered by people (not automated responses)
- ▸ Investigate consumer complaints and notify consumers of the result within thirty days
- ▸ Shift the burden of proof from consumers to the credit bureau
- ▸ Provide a free copy of a consumer's credit report if it resulted in any

FORM 52. **Sample Letter to a Credit-Reporting Agency**

Your Name
Address
Social Security #
Date

Reporting Agency
Address

To Whom It May Concern:

On (specify date) I was notified by (specify) that my application for credit had been rejected. Enclosed is a copy of the notice.

Pursuant to the Fair Credit Reporting Act, please immediately send me a copy of my present credit file and summary history. I understand that there will be no charge for this service.

Since my credit is being wrongly impaired and time is of the essence in correcting any inaccurate or incomplete information that may be contained in my file, I request that you promptly provide me with the report so that corrective action may be taken. This can be done via a telephone appointment if you prefer, and I thank you for your prompt attention and assistance in this matter.

Very truly yours,
(your name)

▷ Send certified mail, return receipt requested.

FORM 53. **Sample Letter Requesting Information Concerning an Investigative Report**

Your Name
Address
Telephone Number
Date

Company Requesting Report
Address

To Whom It May Concern:

Thank you for your letter of (date) notifying me that you were requesting my consumer credit history from (specify).

Please advise me in writing why you have requested such information. In addition, I expect to receive a copy of the report so that I can correct any incorrect information.

Your cooperation is greatly appreciated.

Very truly yours,
(your name)

▷ Send certified mail, return receipt requested.

FORM 54. **Sample Letter Disputing Information in Your Credit File**

> Your Name
> Address
> Telephone Number
> Date

Credit Bureau
Address

To Whom It May Concern:

On (date) I received a copy of my credit history, enclosed, which contained inaccuracies that are severely affecting my credit. The following items are incorrect: (specify reported items and why they are incorrect).

Please promptly investigate these items and make the necessary corrections. Furthermore, please notify (name of subscriber or company seeking information or turning you down for credit) immediately of the corrections.

Feel free to get in touch with me at the above address if you need further information. Thank you.

> Very truly yours,
> (your name)

▷ Send certified mail, return receipt requested.

---

adverse action to the consumer in the areas of credit, employment, licenses, insurance, or housing

▶ Make credit reports easier to understand
▶ Take reasonable steps to ensure that incorrect information does not reappear in a consumer's file after it has been removed

These changes should enhance the rights of individuals dealing with credit report problems.

CREDIT CARDS

Under federal law, credit-card companies may not send cards unless a consumer requested one or submitted an application for one. If the consumer already owns a card, however, a renewal card can be sent automatically or in substitution of a current card.

One legal advantage to using credit cards is that consumers can withhold payment if they are unsatisfied with purchased items. The credit-card issuer cannot report the amount withheld as delinquent on a credit report until the disputed amount is either settled or a court determines that the reported dissatisfaction has no validity.

If a card is lost or stolen, report this within twenty-four hours by phone and letter so you will not be responsible for unauthorized charges in excess of $50 per card. Although loss of a card may not cause financial harm, it can interfere with a person's credit if the loss is not reported immediately. Never lend a card or disclose an account number over the telephone to strangers, and check all statements promptly for unauthorized transactions.

BILLING ERRORS

The Fair Credit Billing Act offers significant protection against billing errors made by a card issuer or merchant. Billing errors for which the issuing bank is responsible include failure to record payments and mathematical errors in totaling charges or calculating the finance charge. Billing errors for which merchants are responsible include charges for:

- items not ordered or not received
- items delivered to the wrong address
- items delivered in the wrong quantity
- items delivered so much later than promised that the bill arrived before the item
- items that turned out to be different from what you ordered

Notify the issuing bank in writing within sixty days after receiving a statement that contains an error. While the dispute is pending, you may withhold payment of the disputed amount but must pay the rest of the balance. During this time, the card issuer may not close your account or threaten your credit rating by reporting you as delinquent. The card issuer must respond to any letter within thirty days and must, within ninety days, investigate a complaint. If the claim turns out to be justified, the charge is canceled; if not, you must pay the amount plus any interest charges that have accrued.

COLLECTION AGENCY HARASSMENT

Although many collection agencies follow acceptable practices, the debt collection area continues to be a major source of consumer complaints. People receive persistent telephone calls at inconvenient hours and threatening letters and telegrams, including phony legal subpoenas. Illegal collection charges are tacked onto the debt, and people are misled into thinking that their unpaid bills will ruin their credit. However, due to the passage of the federal Fair Debt Collection Practices Act more than a decade ago, collection agencies are forbidden from repeatedly calling people at home or sending threatening letters. They cannot legally contact neighbors, relatives, or employers. Debt collectors who engage in false representations, unfair practices, and abuse while trying to enforce a debt are liable for actual damages, statutory damages of up to $1,000, court costs, damages for mental anguish, money spent for medical treatment and lost wages (if the debtor got sick from such wrongful acts), and attorney's costs.

The law protects people against abusive practices of private collection agencies, lawyers who regularly engage in consumer collection activities (even when those activities consist of litigation), professional collectors, and companies that service mortgage loans. Debt collectors cannot use obscene language or publicize your debt (i.e., publish "shame" lists of people who allegedly refuse to pay their debts) except to a credit bureau. They cannot represent themselves as attorneys when they are not, or threaten you, your property, or your reputation. They cannot reverse telephone charges before revealing the purpose of the communication. Late charges, interest, collection fees, and expenses cannot be added to the amount of money owed unless this is permitted under state law and you originally agreed in writing to such an arrangement before a purchase was made. If allowed, such fees must be outlined in the first written notice, but not in subsequent correspondence.

No communication is allowed before 8:00 A.M. or after 9:00 P.M. Although collectors can reach you by mail, telephone, telegram, or fax, you cannot be called at work if the collector is told that the employer forbids personal telephone calls. Collectors cannot make threats (such as state that they will seize your wages or file a lawsuit) unless they intend to follow through. They cannot write you by postcard; letters cannot be sent to your employer asking him to discuss the debt with you. If you hire a lawyer, contact can be made only through the lawyer, unless he allows the collection agency to communicate with you. The Sample Consumer Demand Letter on page 352 illustrates the kind of demand letter that is acceptable under federal law.

Once you are contacted by a collection agency, request verification of the debt. (You can model your letter on the one on page 132.) The agency is required to tell you the amount of the debt and the name and address of the original creditor. You then have the right to dispute the debt. During a dispute, all collection agency activity must stop until the agency contacts the creditor to determine if the debt is correct or the agency sends you written notification about the debt.

If you need more time to organize your finances and the collection agency threatens to sue unless payment is made immediately, send a letter to the agency requesting written verification of the debt. This will effectively stall agency action for some time. Even if a debt is legitimately owed, you can notify the agency in writing to stop all further contact and this request must be honored. This can be done before or after you request written verification of the debt. The agency then cannot contact you, except by letter, stating that all collection efforts are being stopped or that specific legal action to recover the debt has been started. The agency's only alternative may be litigation. However, persons with small debts or those who forbid collection agencies to contact them often have their debts "wiped out" since the amount of money owed may not justify the time and expense of a lawsuit. (Note: A person's credit rating, however, can be impaired by the failure to pay a legitimate debt.)

FORM 55. **Sample Letter Requesting Verification of Debt**

Your Name
Address
Date

Name
Title
Name of Collection Agency
Address

Re: Request for written verification of my disputed debt with (name of creditor)

Dear (specify name),

On (specify date), you contacted me by (specify letter, telegram, fax, in person) concerning a purported debt I owe to (name of creditor) in the amount of (specify $).

I do not owe such a debt because (specify billing error, merchandise returned, merchandise damaged, merchandise unsatisfactory).

I will be contacting (specify name of creditor) in an effort to resolve this matter. In the meantime please:

1. Verify the amount of the alleged debt with (name of creditor).
2. Send me a copy of the written verification.
3. Stop all collection efforts until I receive a copy of this written verification.

Thank you for your immediate attention and cooperation in this matter.

Very truly yours,
(your name)

cc: creditor

▷ Send certified mail, return receipt requested.

Speak to a lawyer if collection agency harassment occurs. The lawyer can decide whether to sue the collection agency under state law or the Fair Debt Collection Practices Act, or to contact the FTC. (An example of the kind of letter you can send to the FTC is on page 133.) If suit is brought under the Fair Debt Collection Practices Act, it must be filed within one year from the offensive incident(s). Consult the law in your state to determine whether the state imposes stronger penalties than federal law. If so, file a lawsuit in state court. Consider allowing the FTC to commence an investigation on your behalf. The FTC can impose a variety of sanctions on a collection agency, including the return of money or property, fines, and a public announcement of wrongdoing.

CREDIT CHECKS

Employers, creditors, and others generally cannot conduct random credit checks into a person's background without his or her consent. If they do so, they

FORM 56. **Sample Letter Protesting Credit Harassment**

Your Name
Address
Telephone Number
Date

Director
Regional Office
Federal Trade Commission
Address

Re: Violation by (name of agency) of the Fair Debt Collection Practices Act

Dear (name),

    I am writing to you regarding the unfair practices of (name of agency) located at (address).

    On (dates) I was illegally harassed by said agency (explain how). This arose out of a disputed debt with (name of creditor).

    I (state what you told the agency, whom you spoke with, and why your requests have not been honored).

    I enclose copies of correspondence with (name of agency). I would appreciate it if you would investigate this matter to eliminate such outrageous conduct for myself and others that might have suffered similar abuse.

    You can reach me at the above address if you need further information. Please notify me of all developments in this matter.

    Thank you for your cooperation.

Very truly yours,
(your name)

cc: collection agency; creditor

▷ Send certified mail, return receipt requested.

▷ *Author's note:* Although an agency such as the Federal Trade Commission may investigate and stop alleged misconduct, it may not be able to get you damages for any wrongdoing. If you receive a favorable disposition, consider speaking with a private attorney for the purpose of suing the collection agency under the Fair Debt Collection Practices Act and applicable state laws.

can be held liable under such legal theories as defamation and intentional infliction of emotional distress. They may commit other violations of the law when references are not investigated properly or are leaked to nonessential third parties. In one case a man terminated from a company discovered that his former boss, in reference checks, called him "untrustworthy, disruptive, hostile, paranoid, and irrational." He sued, and a jury decided that those characterizations were out of line, a mistake that cost the company $1.9 million.

To avoid potential liability, employers, creditors, and others involved in conducting background and credit checks typically require that a person to be investigated give them written permission to do so. This consent is obtained via the employment or credit application or a separate signed release. However, most typically in the area of employment, even if damaging information is discovered, federal bankruptcy laws prohibit private employers from terminating the employees or discriminating against job applicants who currently are bankrupt or who previously filed for bankruptcy. Under the Fair Debt Credit Reporting Act, employers are forbidden from using credit reports for hiring or firing decisions unless the job is security sensitive or the financial integrity of the applicant is essential to successful job performance. Additionally, Title VII of the Civil Rights Act of 1964 as amended and the Equal Employment Opportunity Commission prohibit employers from refusing to hire minority applicants who have poor credit.

If your employer or creditor has requested permission to conduct a credit investigation, request a copy of any report received, together with the name and address of the credit agency supplying it. Explain any errors that need to be corrected on credit reports. If you are treated unfairly, such as denied a job, or learn that inaccurate information about your background was disseminated to nonessential third parties, speak to a lawyer immediately to protect your rights.

CREDIT CHECKS   *See Credit; Employment*

CRIMES AND CRIMINAL LAW   *Also see: Arrest*

When a person commits a crime, he or she is engaging in an act that is prohibited by law and for which there is a punishment or a penalty. Civil and criminal cases differ in the nature and subject matter of the wrong that is committed. A civil action is a legal proceeding instituted to enforce a private right or remedy. A crime is typically a public wrong, committed with intent or some other criminal state of mind, for which the law provides punishment or recompense to society. For example, while a civil contract may concern property, the subject matter of a dispute may not be the stealing of an item but the refusal to pay for it. In many cases, a failure to act (e.g., not filing an income tax return) is also a crime.

Crimes are classified as either felonies or misdemeanors. Felonies are serious crimes (e.g., murder, rape, arson, armed robbery, tax evasion, possession of illegal drugs with the intent to sell or distribute, and forgery and larceny involving property valued in excess of a certain amount) that are punishable by incarceration in jail. Misdemeanors are less serious crimes (e.g., simple assault, disorderly conduct, disturbing the peace, malicious mischief, and possession of a small amount of illegal drugs with the intent merely to use them) that are punishable by little jail time (e.g., less than one year), fines, or probation.

To prove a crime, typically the accused must have committed an act and had the requisite intent to do so. In many situations, if a person hurts someone else in self-defense or can prove that it was an accident, no conviction of a crime will ensue. But there are occasions when a person can be charged for an unintentional act, such as criminal homicide while driving in a reckless manner. Although the trend is to prosecute minors for serious crimes such as murder or flagrant assault, children below a certain age (sixteen or seventeen in most states) are presumed not to have sufficient mental capacity (i.e., the ability to understand the consequences of their acts) and may not be prosecuted as adults. The same is true for mentally infirm individuals and those who are insane. That is why people often plead they were insane at the time a crime was committed. However, being intoxicated or on drugs when a crime was committed may not be a viable defense.

Although no one can be prosecuted for merely thinking about committing a crime, a person can be charged when his or her actions go beyond the thinking stage. For example, the crimes of solicitation (asking for someone's help to commit a crime), conspiracy (an agreement between two or more people to commit a crime), and attempt (starting to commit a crime but getting caught before the actual act) are punishable. And, if a person incites or helps someone to commit a crime, or is there when the crime is committed, he or she may be considered an accomplice or an accessory, which may be just as serious.

Some crimes have different degrees that provide for different forms of punishment. For example, larceny usually involves the "unlawful taking and carrying away of another person's personal property with the intent to deprive the owner thereof." The difference between grand larceny, which is a felony, and petit larceny, which is a misdemeanor, is determined by the value of the property taken. Each state has its own rules for classifying crimes and the degrees of crimes as well as the punishments for each. That is why it is best to consult an attorney who practices primarily in criminal law for advice and information regarding laws in your state.

MISDEMEANORS

See page 136 for a list of common misdemeanor crimes and their typical penalties.

FELONIES

Felonies are grouped according to crimes of theft, crimes involving property, crimes against a person, drug-related crimes, and victimless offenses such as prostitution and gambling. Virtually all carry minimum jail sentences in excess of one year.

Crimes Involving Property

1. Larceny: the theft or attempted taking of someone's personal property without force or deceit with intent to permanently deprive the owner of such property.

CRIME (MISDEMEANOR)	DEFINITION	PENALTY
1. Loitering and vagrancy	Standing around a public place with nowhere to go	Small fine of under $100
2. Disturbing the peace	Making too much noise in a public place	Small fine of under $100
3. Malicious mischief	Destruction or mutilation of public property	Fines ranging from $100 to $500
4. Simple assault and disorderly conduct	Fighting	Fines ranging from $250 to $2,500; no jail time for first offenders; probation
5. Public drunkenness	Drinking in public	Fines of up to $250
6. Petit larceny	Stealing an item worth less than a certain amount	Fines of up to $1,000; no jail time for first offenders; probation; jail time of up to a year for repeat offenders
7. Possession of small amounts of drugs with intent to consume		Same as #6 above
8. Driving while intoxicated (no harm caused)		Fines of up to $2,500; no jail time for first offenders; suspension or revocation of license for repeat offenders; jail time

Note: Minor offenses, such as violations of city ordinances or traffic violations, may not be classified as misdemeanors but as infractions in some states. For such violations there is no jail time or record of the proceeding or conviction; fines are smaller than those for misdemeanors (e.g., $25).

2. Motor vehicle theft: unlawful taking or attempted taking of an automobile with intent to permanently or temporarily deprive the owner of it.

3. Burglary: entering a structure at any time to commit a crime or steal something.

4. Embezzlement: the wrongful taking of property entrusted to one's care.

5. Forgery: altering or making a writing of legal significance with intent to benefit from the wrongful act (e.g., signing someone's name to a check without his or her consent).

6. Receiving stolen property: taking possession of property that is known to be stolen.

7. Robbery: the use of force, or threat of immediate force, for the purpose of taking property belonging to another.

Crimes Involving People

1. Robbery: see definition above.
2. Rape: unlawful sexual intercourse with a person by force, without consent, or when the person is underage.
3. Assault: unlawful intentional inflicting, or attempted inflicting, of injury upon the person of another. If the assault is caused by a dangerous weapon, or an attempt is made to cause death or serious injury, the crime is called aggravated assault. If the injury is minor or is done without a weapon, it may be classified as simple assault.
4. Arson: an attempt or act to destroy someone's property by means of fire or an explosion.
5. Kidnapping: the forcible taking of another against his or her will.
6. False imprisonment: the deliberate confinement of a person without his or her consent and legal justification.
7. Homicide: causing the death of another person without legal justification or excuse. Homicide is divided into crimes of murder, voluntary manslaughter, and involuntary manslaughter.
   a. Murder: unlawful killing of one human being by another with malice aforethought (i.e., in an evil state of mind evidenced by an intentional killing, killing someone during the course of a dangerous felony, or killing someone while doing something with a high risk of death or serious injury in disregard of the consequences).
   b. Voluntary manslaughter: an intentional killing without malice aforethought such as killing in the heat of passion.
   c. Involuntary manslaughter: an unintentional killing such as killing someone while driving recklessly.

Other Crimes

1. Prostitution: engaging in sexual activity in exchange for money or property
2. Pimping: soliciting on behalf of a prostitute for personal gain
3. Bribery: influencing a public official through gift or favor
4. Mail fraud: using the mails to commit a crime

WHAT HAPPENS AFTER AN ARREST

After an arrest, an arraignment or initial appearance is conducted. An arraignment is a proceeding whereby an accused person is brought before a judge to hear the charges filed against him or her, and to enter a plea of guilty, not guilty, or no contest. In some states, an arraignment is the same as a preliminary hearing, where a judge determines whether enough evidence exists to proceed to trial. Other states conduct grand juries for the same purpose. A grand jury is a closed proceeding whereby a number of citizens (usually twelve or more) examine evidence and hear about the case from the prosecutor (typically, the district attorney). During these pretrial stages, the accused may file motions through an attorney. These motions often seek to exclude (i.e., suppress) illegally obtained or irrelevant evidence.

After an arrest, an accused person has many due process rights, including:

▶ The right to be released if the complainant decides to drop the charges for a minor crime
▶ Prompt and complete notification of all criminal charges
▶ Full opportunity to prepare and defend against all charges
▶ The right not to be subjected to excessive bail and remain incarcerated prior to the trial for a lengthy period of time without good cause
▶ Fair and impartial adjudication of all the facts and issues
▶ The opportunity to testify and present his or her side of the facts
▶ The right to be defended by a competent lawyer
▶ Access and opportunity to consult with a lawyer to prepare a defense and examine evidence to be introduced at the trial by the prosecutor
▶ The opportunity to confront and cross-examine all adverse witnesses
▶ The right not to be compelled to testify against himself or herself or be forced to offer any confessions
▶ The right to a speedy trial
▶ The right to close the pretrial proceedings to the public or sequester the jury during the trial to avoid undue influence from the press
▶ The right to exclude illegally obtained evidence, such as perjured testimony or evidence obtained without a search warrant, from the trial
▶ The right to a speedy appeal upon conviction

Once the case proceeds to trial, the defendant can request a jury or judge to issue the decision. One advantage of a jury trial is that all members of the jury must find that the accused committed a crime beyond a reasonable doubt. If one or several vote no, a "hung jury" results, which means no conviction. If you are a defendant, discuss this issue carefully with a lawyer. The same is true be-fore you decide to plead guilty to a lesser offense (called plea bargaining). Before you are allowed to plea-bargain, a judge must be certain you understand the consequences and are doing so freely and with consent. You must understand what punishment you will receive; some judges often surprise defendants and their attorneys by accepting a guilty plea, but enforcing a harsher sentence than you bargained for. *Get assurances from the prosecutor before pleading guilty to any offense.*

Typical arguments and defenses raised in criminal cases include:

▶ Guilt cannot be proved with certainty beyond a reasonable doubt. This is contrasted to the easier standard of proof in civil matters, which is proof by a preponderance of the evidence.
▶ The victim consented to the acts.

- The accused was not at the scene when the crime occurred (i.e., "an alibi defense").
- The accused was induced to commit the crime by entrapment.
- The statute of limitations expired for a misdemeanor crime (typically, there is no statute of limitations for felonies).
- Double jeopardy requires a dismissal of the charges because the accused was already tried once for the same or related offense.
- The act was committed in self-defense (defending yourself, someone else, or your property). However, in most states, you cannot use deadly force to protect property.

If you are convicted of a misdemeanor or a lesser crime, ask your lawyer to have the conviction or records of the proceeding sealed or expunged if possible. Some judges will grant this request, particularly for first-time offenders and minors who subsequently stay out of trouble and need an unblemished record to apply for certain jobs or graduate school. Never overlook this important request if applicable.

The defendant has the right to appeal a conviction or ask for a new trial. To prevail, a lawyer must demonstrate that substantial prejudicial errors were committed at the trial, which, if they had not occurred, would have caused the verdict to be different. Generally, to win an appeal, it must be proved that evidence:

- was introduced at the trial that should have been excluded
- was obtained in violation of the defendant's constitutional rights
- was not available for examination before the trial to help the lawyer properly prepare an adequate defense
- was discovered after the trial (e.g., new evidence) and would have made a major difference

Other grounds for a new trial include situations where a jury is given wrong instructions by a judge concerning the definition of the crime or what must be found to determine guilt. Formulating and writing criminal appeals is an art. It is important to hire a lawyer experienced in writing criminal appeals for maximum success.

If you are convicted of a felony, you may have to serve time in jail. If you are fortunate, if the conviction is a first offense, or if there are mitigating factors (e.g., stealing for necessities), and you are not deemed to be a threat to the community, you may be sentenced to probation rather than go to jail. This means you will be allowed to function in society but must report to a probation officer on a periodic basis. The probation officer's job is to determine that you are meeting all the conditions of probation, such as being drug-free or attending counseling, working in a steady job, and so on. If the terms of the probation are violated, you may be sent to jail or resentenced.

Minors accused of crimes are usually tried in juvenile courts instead of regular courts. The difference between juvenile courts and regular courts is that juvenile courts are less formal and are supposed to offer rehabilitation and counseling rather than punishment; and a judge rather than a jury decides guilt or innocence and makes all sentencing decisions.

When youths are found guilty, they are declared juvenile delinquents. Depending on their condition and circumstances, minors can be sent back to their parents, placed in foster homes, or sent to work camps. However, before and during a trial, minors are entitled to be represented by counsel, afforded all similar protections and due process rights as adults, and must be proven guilty beyond a reasonable doubt.

After serving a prison term, a convicted criminal is released from prison. Some convicted criminals are paroled earlier because of good behavior. A few may be pardoned by a governor or the president. If criminals are pardoned, all their rights are restored as if the conviction never occurred, such as the right to vote and serve on a jury. Anyone convicted of a crime and paroled may lose many rights, including the rights of citizenship. However, in some states, parolees cannot be denied employment. Speak to a lawyer for more details if applicable.

Finally, if you are a victim of a crime, be aware that thirty-seven states have enacted laws that allow crime victims and their families to play a role in plea bargains and address the court during sentencing. In a few states, you have the right to be notified before a convict is released from jail and to provide the parole board with written statements on why that person should be denied early parole.

DAMAGES

Damages are compensation or relief awarded to the prevailing party in a lawsuit. Damages can be in the form of money or a directive by the court for the losing party to perform or refrain from performing a certain action.

The following are brief descriptions of the kinds of damages that can be awarded:

Compensatory damages. This is a sum of money awarded to a party that represents the actual harm suffered or loss incurred. To collect compensatory damages, one must prove what the actual out-of-pocket losses are since damages cannot be presumed. For example, projections of future lost profits will not be awarded unless they are definite and certain.

Incidental damages. Traditionally, these are direct out-of-pocket expenses for filing a lawsuit and related court costs (e.g., process server fees). These direct costs of litigation are typically awarded to the prevailing party in a litigation as part of the party's loss.

Liquidated damages. This is an amount of money agreed upon in advance by parties to a written contract to be paid in the event of a breach or dispute. If it is not possible to compute the amount of the loss, a judge may uphold the amount specified. However, in many circumstances, when the amount specified has no actual basis in fact, a judge may disregard it, viewing the amount merely as a penalty.

Nominal damages. This is a small amount of money (e.g., one dollar) awarded by the court. Sometimes, a party may win the lawsuit but not have proved suffering or any actual damages.

Punitive damages. Also called exemplary damages, punitive damages represent money awarded as punishment for a party's wrongful acts beyond any actual losses. When punitive damages are awarded, a judge is often sending a signal to the community that similar outrageous, malicious, or oppressive conduct will not be tolerated. Under the laws of many states, punitive damages can be awarded only in certain types of lawsuits, such as personal injury and product liability actions, and not lawsuits to enforce contracts or business agreements. Recently the Supreme Court agreed with the IRS and ruled that most punitive damage awards, intended to deter wrongdoing, are not awarded on account of personal injuries and therefore are taxable to the recipient.

Specific performance. This is a directive by the court for the party being sued (i.e., the defendant) to perform a certain action such as sell a business or not work for a competitor pursuant to a clause in an employment contract. Specific performance is typically not awarded if monetary damages can make the party seeking the relief whole.

Injunction. This is a court order restraining one party from performing or refusing to perform an action.

Mitigation of damages. This is a legal principle that requires in some cases that a party seeking damages make reasonable efforts to reduce damages as much as possible; for example, to locate a new buyer to purchase a house at the same or similar price if the old buyer unjustifiably backs out of the deal.

DEFAMATION

Defamation occurs when a communication (either oral or written) is made about a person that tends to so harm that person's reputation as to lower him or her in the estimation of the community or to deter others from associating or dealing with him or her. Defamatory statements in written form constitute libel; defamatory statements in oral form constitute slander; and the penalties are similar for each. Defamatory acts are quite common, such as when a newspaper reporter misstates a private person's comments during an interview, when a former employer maliciously provides an improper job reference, and when false gossip is repeated.

For defamation to occur there must be:

▸ a false statement made about someone;

- to a third party;
- that injures the person's reputation; and
- no absolute or qualified privilege exists as a legal bar to the lawsuit.

No defamation exists when a poor opinion about someone is given. To be actionable, the comment offered must be a statement of fact and not an opinion. If the statement is true, this is a valid defense. If the person alleging defamation is not mentioned by name, a valid case will exist if it is clear that he or she was the one being talked about and the statement was made to a third party.

Damages do not have to be proved in all instances. The law treats certain statements as defamatory per se, which means that the person or business does not have to prove actual damages to win a verdict; money can be recovered simply because the statement is untrue.

Examples of per se statements are:

- Accusing a person of serious misconduct in his or her business, trade, or profession (e.g. that a doctor or group medical practice he is affiliated with has trouble paying its bills, is discontinuing its operations and filing for bankruptcy, is financially unstable, incompetent, of poor moral character, unreliable, or dishonest).
- Imputing to a person the commission of a criminal offense.
- Charging a person with dishonesty (e.g., "He is a crook and steals money from the company.")
- Accusing a person of serious sexual misconduct (e.g., "She is a whore.")
- Stating that a person has a loathsome or deadly disease (e.g., AIDS).

In certain situations, such as in court proceedings and the employment context, people have an absolute or qualified privilege to make defamatory statements without legal consequences. For example, statements made about people by judges, witnesses, and lawyers during trials are absolutely privileged. Employers have a qualified privilege to talk about former employees when giving job references. However, this doesn't mean that an employer can talk maliciously about a former employee and tell untruths in an attempt to embarrass and scuttle future job opportunities.

To avoid problems, think first before disclosing private information concerning others. For employers, potentially damaging information in performance reviews and comments to prospective employers should be reviewed by a supervisor. Avoid having damaging memos about a person read by nonessential third parties. In many states, such as Connecticut, any dissemination of private employment data to prospective employers other than the dates of employment, position held, and latest salary figures is illegal. Many states prohibit the dissemination of confidential private medical information as well.

Avoid disseminating any information about anyone that can even remotely be considered private. Do not repeat unconfirmed gossip or trade gossip, especially about the financial condition of a competitor, business, or product. If you might be a victim of defamation, speak to a lawyer immediately to protect your rights.

DISABILITY   *See Employment*

DISCRIMINATION   *See Civil Rights; Credit; Employment*

DISPUTE RESOLUTION   *See Mediation*

DIVORCE   *Also see: Alimony; Annulment; Separation*

Marriage is a civil contract between two people of the opposite sex. Once two people marry, a unique legal status is created, the obligations of which cannot be transferred or assigned, and which can be dissolved only by divorce or through annulment. In most states, it may also be altered by a decree of separation. Once a couple has decided they no longer wish to continue their marriage and are not interested in obtaining a legal separation, either or both spouses must file certain documents in court to obtain a divorce. A divorce is a formal court proceeding in which a marriage is dissolved. The laws governing divorce vary from state to state, and each state can grant divorces only to its own residents (by definition, people who have lived within the state for a minimum period of time, usually at least six months).

The law in each state governs marriage, divorce, annulment, separation, and related matters. For example, many states provide for divorce merely on the showing of "incompatibility," "irreconcilable conflict," or "breakdown of the marriage." In other states, there must be a showing of grounds such as cruel and inhuman treatment, abandonment of one spouse by another for a requisite period of time, living apart for a specified period of time, refusal to have sexual relations, imprisonment for more than a specified term, or adultery. Some states also allow other "no-fault" events like living apart under a separation agreement or decree for more than a year; this automatically ripens into a divorce after papers are filed in court.

A large number of married couples will wind up divorced during their lifetime. The law has tried to keep pace with this phenomenon by making it easier for couples to obtain a divorce. No-fault divorce laws passed in many states have eliminated the need to prove improper conduct by one or both spouses (which used to be essential in obtaining a divorce). However, although the actual divorce may be easier to obtain, equitable-distribution and community-property laws have made the focus of court inquiry primarily economic in nature. No longer does a wife have to think in terms of receiving only alimony (also called maintenance). How to value and divide assets and property acquired during the marriage, including the value of pensions, a wife's homemaking services, and professional degrees, has made the process sometimes quite complicated, with huge financial consequences for the divorcing couple.

Consult the law of the state where you reside to determine what standards are necessary to obtain a divorce. Speak to a competent matrimonial attorney for advice and direction. For example, a small but growing number of states make the process quite simple for couples who mutually agree to end the marriage. These states allow divorces simply on submission of sworn affidavits and consents forwarded to the court. You must know the procedures in order to process the case properly.

The fifty states also have different concepts with respect to who gets what when a divorce is obtained. Typically, the manner in which property is divided and distributed upon divorce is characterized by several different methods, and states are categorized accordingly as community-property states, equitable-distribution states, and common-law states.

Community-property states recognize marriage as a community of which each spouse is a member and to which each contributes equally through his or her labors. All property acquired during the marriage is regarded as community property in which both parties share equally, no matter who owns legal title to the property. Since each community-property state has its own peculiar rules under which marital property can be divided, contact an experienced lawyer for further information.

Under the laws in *equitable-distribution states,* each spouse is a partner to the marriage and the assets and property the partnership produces. Judges are empowered to distribute marital property equitably, not necessarily equally, after considering the following factors:

- ▶ The duration of the marriage
- ▶ The respective age and health of the parties
- ▶ The parties' pre-separation standard of living
- ▶ Contribution of each party toward the acquisition, preservation, or appreciation of the marital property
- ▶ Contributions of the homemaker spouse
- ▶ Present and prospective earnings of each party
- ▶ Vocational skills of each party
- ▶ Desirability of the custodial parent working or remaining at home to care for the children

Virtually all non-community-property states are equitable-distribution states. Typically, both kinds of states do not consider fault in rendering a distributive award. Thus, for example, it may not matter if the husband has committed adultery when deciding what share of marital property he should keep.

However, some states do consider economic dissipation of marital assets a factor in awarding less property to one spouse. An example of this would occur where, for example, one spouse is accused of mismanaging the couple's investments, running a couple's business into the ground, or creating huge gambling debts.

A few states are called *common-law states* because they do not include the value of homemaking services, companionship, professional degrees, or pensions in making decisions of property. In these common-law states, the courts have no general or equitable power to distribute property upon divorce; title alone controls. Thus, for example, if a husband buys a house and puts it under his wife's name, it's hers. If he owns all the stock in a business, it's his, and the wife is not entitled to share in the ongoing profits of the business, the appreciated value of the business during the marriage, or anything else.

Obviously, common-law states have created tremendous inequities for spouses, particularly women, and the trend is for those states to change their laws, becoming either equitable-distribution or community-property states. It is very important to know how the law in your state deals with distribution of property upon divorce. This should be the first question to ask a lawyer. Speaking to an experienced lawyer will enable you to learn more about your rights and options.

DISTRIBUTION OF ASSETS

While some people are able to obtain a divorce on their own, this is not recommended where the couple has acquired marital assets such as a house and other property, liquid assets (stocks, bonds, and savings), or other assets. Most people are unaware of the kinds and amount of property distribution they are entitled to. For example, some states allow wives a share of their husband's professional practices, businesses, and pensions as well as benefits derived from homemaking services. Only a competent lawyer can advise what constitutes marital property subject to distribution in a state, how it is located, and how much it is worth.

When a client seeking a divorce goes to a lawyer, the client should be required to provide specific data and the events that form the basis of his or her case. The lawyer needs certain forms to be filled out, disclosing such things as:

- ▶ The economic history of the marriage (who bought what with whose money?)
- ▶ A financial affidavit listing the assets of the marriage
- ▶ A pre-separation standard-of-living questionnaire
- ▶ A current breakdown of monthly living expenses
- ▶ Information revealing where key assets are kept and the identity of such assets

The Appendix contains two comprehensive document and property checklists (pages 353–354) that you should prepare and review before meeting with your lawyer. All this information will assist the lawyer in determining both spouses' income and the value of their assets prior to entering settlement discussions. Acquiring this information is necessary in attempting to resolve the divorce by settlement.

Marital property is defined as all property acquired by either or both spouses during the marriage and before the execution of a separation agreement or the commencement of a matrimonial action, regardless of the form in which title is held. This means that, depending on the state, a spouse would be en-titled to receive either an equitable (fair) or an equal share of the present value of the following:

Life insurance policies, including their cash values
Annuities
Pensions
Profit-sharing plans
Keogh and IRA plans
Closely held businesses
Professional licenses and degrees
Tax-shelter investments
Real estate acquired during the marriage
Living trusts
Patents, copyrights, and royalties
Bank accounts
Leasehold interests and mortgages
Stocks and bonds
Stock options
Household furniture and furnishings
Art objects, coins, jewelry, antiques, collectibles
Oil and mineral rights
Promissory notes, tax refunds, security deposits
Value for homemaking services
Other assorted items

In order to recover a fair share, it is necessary to discover the existence of these assets and then determine their value. A lawyer should assist a client in this process, provided that copies of tax returns, insurance policies, bank records, stock-brokerage records, registry of deeds and mortgage records, employment records, and pension, profit-sharing, and retirement plans can be produced. If a lawyer is satisfied that the existence and location of all assets have been ascertained, it is then essential to evaluate how much these marital assets are presently worth. Often the assistance of experts such as brokers, accountants, and appraisers is required in this process.

The economic history of the marriage must also be analyzed to determine the amount and types of assets that are *separate property,* not subject to division upon divorce. Separate property is defined as property acquired before marriage or property acquired by bequest, devise or descent, or gift from a party other than the spouse. In some states, separate property also includes:

▶ Compensation for personal injuries

▶ Property acquired in exchange for or the increase in value of separate property, except to the extent that such appreciation is due in part to the contributions or efforts of the other spouse (e.g., when a wife remodels a house that was owned by the husband before their marriage and substantially increases its value)

▶ Property described as separate property by written agreement between the parties

What constitutes separate and marital property, and the value of each asset, is often a difficult legal question, and some divorce trials take more than several weeks to resolve these issues.

MAINTENANCE PAYMENTS

A husband, and in rare cases a wife, is liable for the support of his spouse and/or children. If the parties cannot agree, the court will determine the amount. This payment, called maintenance or alimony, can be made payable on a temporary or permanent basis. For more information, see the section "Alimony."

SOCIAL SECURITY, ACCIDENT, AND HEALTH-INSURANCE BENEFITS

A divorced party is entitled to receive social security benefits based on an ex-spouse's earnings. The party may also be able to participate in the divorced spouse's accident and health insurance plans according to the law in certain states. Discuss this with an experienced attorney if applicable.

ATTORNEY FEES

A party may also be entitled to attorney fees incurred in connection with a divorce when he or she has few assets (e.g., a nonworking spouse). Many states require a spouse to pay for the expert and lawyer fees of the other. Ask for this when applicable.

HOW TO PROTECT YOURSELF IN DIVORCE PROCEEDINGS

1. Know the laws in your state with respect to obtaining a divorce and distributing property and other assets.
2. Hire an experienced, competent attorney to represent you. The more money the marital estate is worth, the more there is riding on the competence and skill of an attorney. The best divorce lawyers are well trained

in financial analysis, tax aspects of divorce, and business litigation, and can speak intelligently with accountants and other experts. Choose an attorney whom you trust and one who possesses proven litigation and business experience.

3. Try to obtain copies of important business records before commencing divorce proceedings. Key financial documents sometimes disappear after legal proceedings begin. By collecting as much information as possible about a spouse's finances and businesses, you will help your lawyer properly evaluate the case.

4. Be sure your lawyer spends sufficient time investigating all aspects of your marital history. A competent divorce lawyer thoroughly learns all pertinent aspects of a case. If the lawyer is careless or irresponsible, make him work harder. If you are still not satisfied, shop around for another lawyer before it is too late.

5. Recognize the value of your services if you are a nonworking wife. Conversely, be prepared to offer evidence demonstrating a wife's self-centered, nonproductive drain on the family partnership if you are a husband.

6. Assist your lawyer in developing a realistic approach to the case. Present a good image. Avoid doing things such as clearing out safe-deposit boxes, closing checking and savings accounts, tapping phones, and withholding visitation of the children, without proper discussion and the consent of the lawyer.

7. Spend time to trace all marital assets and purchases, including what was purchased, when, and the source of funds.

8. Establish evidence to support your side of the case in matters of employability. For example, be prepared to show that your spouse is a healthy, college-educated, capable individual, and to demonstrate any health or employment problems of your own. Judges have wide discretion in determining the amount and duration of maintenance payments, so great care should be taken to establish a spouse's ability to enter the job market and be self-sustaining and/or your inability to do the same.

9. Never underestimate the value of financial experts. Although they are expensive, experts are playing a large role in complex divorce cases. If your lawyer is not using an expert, question him or her about this.

10. Get advice regarding what is considered separate property not subject to division upon divorce. Never leave everything up to the lawyer. Question what you are not entitled to receive and be sure to get adequate explanations. If you have doubts, get a second legal opinion.

11. Never agree to pay more than you can afford. Some husbands, out of guilt or fear, agree to pay more money in settlement than they can afford. Later they learn they are paying out so much money in child support, alimony, and other expenses that they have no money for themselves.

FORM 58. **Comprehensive Living Expenses to Calculate Support and Financial Need For: (Designate Husband, Wife, Children, or any combination)**

	Per Week	Per Month	Per Year

A. Housing Expenses
   1. Rent
   2. Mortgage payment
   3. Property taxes (if not included in
      mortgage payment)
   4. Appliance and house service contracts
   5. Home repairs
   6. Gardening expense
   7. Exterminator
   8. Fuel oil
   9. Gas and electric
  10. Water
  11. Sewer
  12. Garbage collection
  13. Telephone (including portable and
      car phones)
  14. Cable television
  15. Homeowner's association
  16. Tips to doormen, mailmen, etc.
  17. Snow removal
  18. House insurance
  19. Household help
B. Food
C. Cleaning and household supplies
D. Laundry and dry cleaning
E. Clothing
   1. Clothing for self
   2. Clothing for children
   3. Clothing for spouse
F. Medical insurance premiums
  Medical expenses not covered
    by insurance
   1. Doctors for self
     Doctors for spouse
     Doctors for children
   2. Dentists for self
     Dentists for spouse
     Dentists for children
   3. Hospital
   4. Psychotherapy

(continued on page 150)

FORM 58. *(continued from page 149)*

	Per Week	Per Month	Per Year

F. Medical insurance premiums *(continued)*
Medical expenses not covered
by insurance *(continued)*
  5. Medicine (drugs)
  6. Vitamins
  7. Medical specialists
  8. Orthodontia
  9. Allergy expense
  10. Other:
G. Auto expenses
  1. Gasoline and oil
  2. Maintenance and repairs
  3. Loan payments, lease payments,
    or rental payments
  4. Registration fees
  5. Insurance
  6. Depreciation
  7. Parking and tolls
  8. Car washes
H. Other transportation expenses
  1. Commutation
  2. Taxis and buses
  3. Other
I. Child-care expenses
  1. Lunch money
  2. Allowances
  3. Baby-sitter
  4. Day care
  5. Grooming
  6. Summer camp
  7. Religious education
  8. Tutoring
  9. After-school clubs
  10. Lessons (music, dancing, etc.)
  11. Pet expense
  12. Other education expenses
J. Personal expenses
  1. Tobacco
  2. Grooming
  3. Cosmetics
  4. Lunches
  5. Entertainment (includes dinners out)
  6. Vacations

	Per Week	Per Month	Per Year
7. Club dues and expenses			
8. Religious dues and expenses			
9. Gifts and presents			
10. Hobby expenses			
11. Sports expenses			
12. Education expenses			
13. Books, magazines, records, etc.			
14. Charitable contributions (other than religious)			

K. Business expenses
    1. Dues (union, etc.)
    2. Subscriptions, books
    3. Other nonreimbursed expenses (specify)
    4. Retirement contributions

L. Insurance Premiums
    1. Life insurance
    2. Medical insurance
    3. Accident insurance
    4. Disability insurance
    5. Other (specify)

M. Recreational expenses (not otherwise mentioned above)
    1. Other real estate (second home, etc.)
    2. Boat expenses
    3. Airplane expenses
    4. Expenses to visit ailing parents, children from a previous marriage, etc.

To assist your attorney, please assemble and bring to the office the following items:
1. All income tax returns for the past five years
2. All bank books, certificates of deposit, and bank statements for the past three years
3. Listing by expense category of all checks written for the past two years with separate totals for each year
4. Copies of deeds to all real estate
5. Insurance policies
6. Copies of existing wills
7. Retirement plans and statements for yourself and spouse
8. Recent paycheck vouchers for yourself and spouse

▷ *Author's note:* The above list is also helpful in calculating whether you can afford a mortgage for a house purchase and many other financial decisions.

Be realistic. Recognize you will need ample funds for your own life after the divorce. Have the lawyer prepare a comprehensive monthly expense sheet to determine current and estimated future financial needs. (The list of Living Expenses outlined on pages 149–151 constitutes a comprehensive guideline.)

12. Be aware of the tax consequences of divorce. Failure to know how taxes affect overall finances in a divorce or separation can lead to devastating consequences. Be sure the lawyer has considered all tax angles when structuring the property settlement. For more information on this subject, see the section "Taxes."

13. Understand the legal distinction between an annulment, a separation, and a divorce. Question the lawyer about the advantages and disadvantages of each before the divorce is finalized. Choose the form best suited for your needs and requirements.

14. Confirm your deal in writing. The comprehensive Separation Agreement (on pages 355–366 in the Appendix) for a couple divorcing with no children will give you a better idea of the kinds of clauses that should be drafted in writing for your protection. (Note: Refer also to the Property Settlement Worksheet on page 367 in the Appendix for assistance in keeping track of all the marital assets to be divided and documented in the separation agreement.)

DOMESTIC HELP *Also see: Employment*

Most people fail to realize that when they hire nannies and other domestics to work in their homes, they become employers and must conduct themselves appropriately. The tax issues in hiring a domestic employee are frequently overlooked, along with workers' compensation entitlement for injuries suffered in the home, immigration and naturalization requirements, reporting of wages and tips, and exposure to sexual harassment suits.

For example, if you pay a baby-sitter, house cleaner, or domestic over 18 years of age more than $1,000 per calendar year, you must make quarterly Social Security payments on those wages and withhold the employee's share of Social Security. You must also pay annual taxes in accordance with the Federal Unemployment Tax (FUTA), using IRS Form 940 or 940-EX. You may be liable to pay unemployment insurance under your state's law in addition to workers' compensation coverage. You may also be liable for overtime pay at the rate of one and one-half times the regular rate for all hours worked exceeding 40 in a given week, and you may be required to pay the minimum wage imposed under federal or state law.

These requirements do not address problems relating to promises of job security, severance, and other traditional employer-employee issues that arise on termination. When hiring domestic help, you should consider implementing a contract such as the one for child care on page 153 or the one for housekeeping services on page 368 in the Appendix. And you should always speak to a lawyer for more details when you are in doubt about your legal position as an employer.

FORM 63. **Contract for Child Care**

This Contract for Child Care, is made by and between (Name of Individual or business "Employer", located at: _____) and (Name of Individual or business "Employee", located at: _____) on (specify date).

WHEREAS, the parties desire that Employee provide child care for the following children: (specify names and ages); and

WHEREAS, Employee accepts such responsibilities and to perform such duties as specified herein;

NOW, THEREFORE, FOR VALUABLE CONSIDERATION SET FORTH HEREIN, THE PARTIES AGREE AS FOLLOWS:

1. This Agreement will commence on (specify date).

2. The Employee agrees to perform the following duties: (specify in detail, such as housecleaning, ironing and laundry, shopping, cooking, bathing the children, errands for the family, assisting in transportation, etc.).

3. Set forth other pertinent conditions, such as term of the contract, whether it can be extended after the initial term, living arrangements for the Employee and reporting hours.

4. Specify payment. This should include the hourly or weekly rate, and what taxes will be deducted from the Employee's regular paycheck. (For example: The Employee will be paid a weekly salary of $X. The following deductions will be taken to comply with appropriate law including Social Security; federal, state, and local employment taxes; workers' compensation and unemployment insurance; charges for personal telephone calls; and other deductions discussed and mutually approved by the Employee in advance. Said payment will be made each Monday by 5:00 p.m. (Author's Note: Consult your local or state law regarding overtime and maximum weekly working hour requirements.)

5. The Employee will receive the following benefits: (specify, such as room and board, meals, sick leave, vacation days, personal days, holidays, health insurance, life insurance, transportation, or use of an auto).

6. Termination. The Employee is hired AT WILL. Either party can terminate this Agreement at any time with or without warning, notice, or cause.

7. Severance Pay. At the termination of this Agreement, Employee shall receive X week's severance pay plus all accrued wages and benefits earned up to the termination date.

8. This Agreement supersedes all prior agreements and understandings and may only be modified in writing and signed by both parties. This Agreement is in force when signed below.

9. This Agreement cannot be assigned without the prior consent of Employer.

10. This Agreement shall be governed by the law of the state of (specify).

_____
Name of Employer

Dated: _____

_____
Name of Employee

DRIVING UNDER THE INFLUENCE

Also see: Arrest; Crimes and Criminal Law; Traffic Violations

Driving under the influence of alcohol or drugs is illegal. In some states, you can be charged with breaking a law even if a car is not in motion. Such laws are called operating under the influence (OUI) statutes, and you can be arrested if you are in actual physical control of a car; that is, you are sitting in the driver's seat, in possession of the ignition key, and capable of starting the motor. In other states, you can be arrested only while actually driving under the influence (DUI) of illegal and even legal prescription drugs or while intoxicated (DWI).

To stem the tide of drunk driving, numerous state laws have been enacted making it easier to test whether a driver is intoxicated, automatically suspending or revoking a driver's license for a first offense, and restricting a person's ability to plea-bargain away a DWI charge to a lesser offense (e.g., pleading guilty to a charge of reckless driving).

When a police officer suspects someone of driving under the influence, he will stop the driver and put him through a variety of tests to measure alertness and physical condition. Do not refuse to take these tests in most cases, because in most states your license may be suspended automatically even if you have done nothing wrong. Say as little as possible to the police officer. Try to alter the test conditions to your advantage. For example, at night, ask that the tests be performed in a well-lighted area, preferably on level, clean concrete. Inform the officer of any physical disabilities that could affect your performance. Ask the officer to repeat any instructions you do not understand. Ask the officer to demonstrate what you are supposed to do. It is best to have a witness view all procedures to ensure that the officer acts reasonably and correctly.

Most states permit a police officer to insist that you submit to a Breathalyzer test on the spot rather than travel to the police station. If you refuse, you may risk suspension or revocation of your license. To be sure, ask the police officer about the consequences of refusing to submit to such a test.

If the Breathalyzer reveals that the alcohol content in your blood exceeds the legally permissible limit, you will be taken to a local police station and arrested. If you fail field tests or a Breathalyzer test, the police may have the right to search you and the contents of your car. If illegal drugs, weapons, or contraband is discovered during the search, you may be charged with committing other criminal violations.

Once arrested for driving under the influence, you face many serious consequences, including having your insurance company cancel coverage or raise your rates after a conviction, receiving a suspension or revocation of your driver's license, facing jail time and/or large fines for first or repeated offenses, and being exposed to lawsuits and required to pay for the injuries or property losses suffered by others as a result of your acts. If you are arrested for driving under the influence, it is a good idea to hire a criminal lawyer who handles such cases on a regular basis. A competent lawyer may know how to obtain and challenge test results, properly question police officers at the trial, and get the charges dismissed or reduced via a plea bargain to a lesser offense.

For a first DUI offense, consider pleading no contest ("nolo contendere") where state law permits. The advantage of this plea is that your license may not be suspended or revoked and you may not be required to serve jail time. Also, if you became intoxicated because a business, party host, bar, restaurant, or liquor store provided or sold you alcohol knowing that you were drinking too much, you may be able to sue that person or entity under your state's "dram shop" law. Speak to an attorney for advice if applicable.

DUE PROCESS *See Civil Rights*

EAVESDROPPING *See Civil Rights; Employment*

EMPLOYMENT *Also see: Domestic Help; Independent Contractors*

Years ago, the law favored employers when it came to resolving employment disputes; employers could fire workers with or without cause or notice and have little fear of legal reprisal. This has changed. Federal and state laws now give employees rights against discrimination, sexual harassment, unfair parental leave policies, mandatory lie detector tests, failure to keep stated company promises and commitments, and numerous other protections. This section discusses key areas of importance before hiring, while working, and at termination.

ADS AND INTERVIEWS

Advertisements and brochures cannot discriminate on the basis of age, color, race, national origin, religion, or sex. For example, an advertisement that states "age 25 to 35 preferred" discriminates against the employment of older persons and is illegal. The laws apply equally to advertisements that favor men over women, whites over blacks, and any other class of people to the detriment of protected minorities. If an ad denies you access to any job or interview, contact the nearest Department of Consumer Affairs office, Equal Employment Opportunity Commission (EEOC) office, or state attorney general's office. You may be able to file charges, obtain damages (e.g., be hired), and force the employer to rewrite the ad.

It is illegal for employers to ask discriminatory questions at a hiring interview. Generally, employers may ask questions to learn about a candidate's motivation and personality. The questions can relate to former job responsibilities and outside interests. However, inquiries into an applicant's race, color, age, sex, religion, and national origin that further discriminatory purposes are illegal under Title VII of the Civil Rights Act of 1964, as amended. This law applies to all private employers, employment agencies, and labor organizations. For example, it is illegal to ask women "Do you have children?" or "Are you married?" and to ask applicants if they have ever filed a workers' compensation claim or have any illnesses the company should know about. It is even illegal to ask applicants how old they are and whether they rent or own a home.

Employers are not permitted to ask questions about past arrests, since these often end in acquittal, dismissal, or withdrawal of charges. If discriminatory questions are contained on a medical history form, applicants have the right to refuse to answer them. See pages 369–370 in the Appendix for a Checklist of Legal and Illegal Hiring Questions (based on federal law). Each state has its own discrimination laws, which often go further than federal law in protecting the rights of applicants during job interviews. If you believe that an illegal question was asked at a hiring interview (or even at lunch after the formal interview but before the decision to hire was made), speak to a labor lawyer or contact a regional EEOC office for guidance. The letter on page 157 illustrates how to initially request an investigation for illegal conduct in this area.

It is also important not to be exploited by an unscrupulous employment agency, search firm, or career counselor. The main purpose of an employment agency is to find people jobs. Career counselors and search firms offer additional services, such as resume and letter preparation and training in interview techniques. Career counselors do not obtain jobs for applicants.

To avoid problems:

▸ Understand the terms of any arrangement. What services are you receiving? Who pays the costs involved? What if you do not take a job that is offered?
▸ Confirm everything in writing.
▸ Never pay money in advance of results.
▸ Speak to a lawyer or contact a local Better Business Bureau or the Department of Consumer Affairs if you have been exploited. These agencies are empowered to investigate alleged mistreatment. The letters on pages 158 and 159 are examples of how to protect your rights.

ILLEGAL PREHIRING PRACTICES

Before they hire, some employers take actions that are illegal. These involve the following areas:

Applicant references. Most states limit an employer's ability to make pre-employment inquiries about criminal arrests and convictions and restrict the use of such information. Employers cannot obtain credit and other confidential (e.g., medical) information about applicants without their consent. When such information is communicated to a nonessential third party, causing harm, an

FORM 65. **Sample Complaint Letter to Human Rights Commission (or other appropriate state agency)**

Your Name
Address
Telephone Number
Date

Director of Appropriate Agency
Address

Re: Formal Protest against ABC Employer for Illegal Hiring Practices

To Whom It May Concern,

This letter is a formal complaint against (specify employer), located at (address).

On (date), I was interviewed by (name of employee) for the position of (title). The interview took place at (location). During this interview, I believe I was asked a variety of illegal questions. The following are the specific questions asked: (list them)

Although I answered some of the questions, I politely chose not to answer others on the basis of irrelevance and illegality. After the interview, I was told by (name) that the company never hired anyone who refused to answer these questions. Although extremely qualified, I was denied the job.

I believe I was the victim of illegal and discriminatory hiring practices. I understand that your agency has the authority to investigate these charges and institute legal proceedings, if appropriate on my behalf, seeking restitution and possibly enabling me to be hired by the company. Therefore, please investigate this matter on my behalf. You can reach me at the above address and telephone number if you require any additional information or assistance.

I am available to meet with a representative of your agency to discuss the matter in greater detail if necessary. Thank you for your cooperation in this matter.

Very truly yours,
(your name)

▷ Send certified mail, return receipt requested.

applicant may have the right to sue for defamation or intentional infliction of emotional distress.

Lie detector tests. As a result of the federal Polygraph Protection Act, employers are generally forbidden from asking applicants to submit to lie detector tests in all preemployment screenings. Many states have also enacted strong laws protecting job applicants from stress tests, psychological evaluation tests, and other honesty tests. If you are asked to submit to such a test as a condition of being offered a job, and believe the test is unfair, harmful, or distasteful, investigate pertinent state law.

FORM 66. Sample Complaint Letter to Job-Search Firm

Your Name
Address
Telephone Number
Date

Name of Officer
Name of Firm
Address

Dear (Name),

On (specify date) I responded to an advertisement your firm ran in (specify newspaper or magazine). The ad specifically promised that your firm could find a job for me as a salesperson in the cosmetics industry. The ad stated that a ($XXX) advance was fully refundable in the event I could not obtain a job paying more than $20,000 per year.

Per your request, and after several telephone conversations, I sent you a check for ($XXX) which was cashed. That was four months ago. Since that time I have received one letter from you dated (specify), which states you are reviewing my employment history.

In view of the fact that you have not obtained full-time employment on my behalf, I hereby demand the return of ($XXX), per our agreement.

If I do not receive the money within 14 days from the date of this letter, be assured that I shall contact the Department of Consumer Affairs, Better Business Bureau, the frauds division of the attorney general's office, and my lawyer to commence a formal investigation.

Hopefully this can be avoided and I thank you for your immediate cooperation in this matter.

Very truly yours,
(your name)

▷ Send certified mail, return receipt requested.

Job misrepresentation. This occurs when employers make promises regarding guaranteed earnings or commissions not supported by fact. For example, the Federal Trade Commission considers the statement "If you come to work for us, you'll make at least $100,000 in commissions this year" an unfair and deceptive trade practice if the promise exceeds the average net earnings of comparable sales employees or executives. However, a company does not commit fraud merely by painting a job with glowing colors and suggesting that a great future awaits a prospective employee. When a company representative predicts probable earnings, the predictions are mere opinions and not statements of fact actionable by law. However, company representatives should be careful about making special promises based on conditions that do not presently exist.

Preemployment drug and alcohol testing. Drug and alcohol tests have

---

FORM 67. **Follow-Up Letter to Department of Consumer Affairs**

Your Name
Address
Telephone Number
Date

Commissioner
Department of Consumer Affairs
Address

Re: Formal Complaint Against ABC Employment Agency, License #

Dear Commissioner,

I hereby make a formal complaint against (specify name of firm). I believe the firm has committed the following illegal acts (specify).

The facts on which I base my allegations are as follows: (state the facts in detail).

On (specify date), I sent the agency a formal demand letter requesting the return of my deposit. This letter was sent by certified mail, was received by the firm, yet I have received no response. I enclose a copy of the letter for your review together with all pertinent documentation from my files.

I request that you convene a formal investigation regarding this matter. Feel free to contact me at the above address if you need further assistance or information.

Thank you for your cooperation and attention.

Very truly yours,
(your name)

cc: the employment agency, your attorney, Better Business Bureau, and the frauds
    division of state attorney general's office

▷ Send certified mail, return receipt requested.

---

generally been upheld as legal with respect to job applicants (as opposed to employees who are asked to submit to random tests as a requisite for continued employment). Applicants have fewer rights to protest such tests than employees, and these tests are not viewed as violating privacy rights, since applicants are told in advance that they must take and pass the test to get the job and that all applicants must submit to the test even to be considered for employment.

However, taking the test does not give potential employers the right to handle the test results carelessly. Unwarranted disclosure of test results can result in huge damages. Speak to a lawyer immediately if you are denied employment or fired shortly after accepting employment for allegedly failing a drug or alcohol test when you know that the results are impossible or if the results of a failed test are conveyed to nonessential third parties, causing humiliation and embarrassment.

TERMS OF ACCEPTANCE

Never accept employment until key terms, conditions, and responsibilities have been discussed and clarified, no matter what type of job is offered. When important terms, including the compensation arrangement and benefits package, are not agreed on before the hiring, the law will not generally impute such rights and employees cannot force employers to give them valuable benefits not promised before the starting date. Salary, title, and duties are fair game for negotiation. On the other hand, fringe benefits and profit-sharing and pension programs are typically fixed and not open to negotiation. Reviewing a prospective employer's personnel manual may reveal what benefits cannot be negotiated.

The following is a list of recommended points to clarify before accepting any job.

- ▸ Am I considered an employee or an independent contractor for tax and insurance purposes?
- ▸ Will I be given job security (as opposed to merely being "hired at will," which gives the employer the right to terminate my job at any time with or without notice and with or without cause)? If so, what kind of job security is being offered?
- ▸ Is a bonus part of my compensation package? How can I be sure I will receive a fair amount of bonus every year?
- ▸ Are periodic raises given? What is the procedure for merit raises and job advancement?
- ▸ Does the employer have a definite stated policy regarding severance?
- ▸ Who administers the company's pension plan? Is it a reliable company? How often are employees notified of their benefits?
- ▸ How are commissions earned? What happens to commissions for orders accepted prior to a termination that are shipped and paid for after I leave the job for any reason?
- ▸ What fringe benefits will I receive?
- ▸ What happens to my benefits if I resign? How much advance notice do I have to give in the event I want to resign?
- ▸ What happens to my benefits if I am terminated? How much advance notice will I receive in the event I am terminated due to a budget cutback or reorganization?
- ▸ Are expenses reimbursable? If so, when will I receive reimbursement and what must I submit to get reimbursement?
- ▸ Are relocation expenses paid? What happens if I am asked to relocate and the job doesn't pan out after a short period of time. Will the company still reimburse me for moving expenses?
- ▸ What is the company's policy toward maternity/paternity and other leaves of absence?

- If vacation pay is not used in the year offered, will it be accrued the following year or is it forfeited?
- What are the company's short-term and long-term disability policies?
- Are personal leave days given? If so, how many?
- What are my job duties? Can these change?
- What are my responsibilities?
- Is overtime offered? If so, at what rate?
- How long must I work before qualifying for health and other benefits?
- Will I receive a contract confirming the points that have been discussed and agreed on?

After agreement on key employment terms, ask your employer to put these terms in writing. This will reduce potential misunderstandings and decrease your chances of being fired unfairly. With a written agreement, it is easier to prove the terms of your employment, since oral agreements are often interpreted differently by employers and employees. A handshake confirms only that you accepted employment; it does not prove what was contracted for. Some employment contracts say that terms cannot be changed without the written consent of both parties. If such a clause was included in your contract and your employer attempted to unfairly reduce your salary or other benefits, this could not be done without your written approval. You are also protected if you are fired in a manner prohibited by the contract.

Whenever you obtain an employment contract or any business document, read it carefully. Question all ambiguous and confusing language. Consult a lawyer if you do not understand the meaning of any terms. Be sure that all changes, strikeouts, and erasures are initialed by both parties and that all blanks are filled in. Most important, always obtain a signed copy of the executed agreement and keep it with your other valuable documents in a safe place.

The Appendix contains two useful documents: a Sample Employment Agreement for Executives (pages 371–375) and a Sample Confidentiality and Noncompetition Agreement (pages 376–378). Always discuss such a document with your attorney or adviser before signing it.

If the company fails to send a written agreement, it is often advisable to write a letter yourself confirming any oral agreements related to your job. The letter can serve as a written contract provided you can prove delivery and it is not ambiguously drafted. The key is to state at the close of the letter that if any terms included in the letter are ambiguous or incorrect, the company must respond within a specified period of time; otherwise the letter shall be considered to set forth the entire understanding of the matter. If the company fails to respond within the stated time, the letter can serve as a valid contract. Send all letters by certified mail, return receipt requested, or have them hand-delivered. This is how you can turn an oral handshake into a written agreement. The sample sales

FORM 68. **Sample Sales Representative Agreement**

Your Name
Address
Telephone Number
Date

Name of Corporate Officer
Title
Company Name
Address

Dear (Name),

This letter will confirm the terms of my engagement as a sales representative for your company. I agree to represent the company in the following territory (specify states), for a minimum period of one year, beginning on (specify date).

The above-named territory will be covered exclusively by me, with no other salespeople covering the territory. There will be no house accounts in the territory.

I will be paid a commission of (specify %) of the gross invoice for all accepted orders in my territory, regardless whether the orders are sent by me, received by the company through the mail, or taken at the company's place of business without my assistance.

There will be no deductions from my commission for credit or returns. Commission checks together with accurate commission statements will be sent to me on or before the (specify) day of the month following the month my orders are accepted.

I will be considered an independent contractor and will be responsible for all applicable social security, withholding, and other employment taxes.

This contract will be automatically renewed for successive one-year terms so long as my yearly gross volume of accepted orders exceeds that of the previous year (or specify other circumstances).

If any of the terms of this letter are incorrect, please advise me immediately in writing. Otherwise, this letter shall set forth our understanding of this matter, which cannot be changed except in a writing signed by both of us. I look forward to working for you.

Very truly yours,
(your name)

▷ Send certified mail, return receipt requested.

representative agreement above should be sent by all sales reps who do not receive a written agreement from a principal.

ON-THE-JOB RIGHTS

Employees possess many on-the-job rights. For example, the federal Polygraph Protection Act bans virtually all employers from requiring regular workers to submit to lie detector tests. If you are pressured to take such a test, speak to a lawyer immediately. Avoid signing any waiver that releases the employer from liability. See page 379 in the Appendix for a typical Lie Detector Test Disclaimer and Release.

Employers are permitted to search an employee's office if there is a reasonable basis for suspecting the employee of wrongdoing, but the search must be confined to nonpersonal areas of the office. Clearly visible personal items cannot be searched. If you are grabbed, jostled, held, or physically threatened during a search, the employer may be liable.

Summaries of many other important rights follow.

Access to records. Some states have passed laws allowing employees access to their personnel records to correct incomplete or inaccurate information. In many other states, however, they generally do not have the right to review their records. However, most states prohibit employers from distributing confidential information, such as medical records, to nonessential third parties and prospective employers.

Wiretapping and eavesdropping. In most states you have the right to be told before a phone conversation, interrogation, or interview is taped. Wiretapping and eavesdropping policies are generally regulated and to some degree prohibited by federal and state law. Title III of the Omnibus Crime Control and Safe Streets Act of 1968 prohibits the deliberate interception of oral communications, including telephone conversations. Thus, conversations between employees that occur with the expectation that they are private (e.g., take place in the women's restroom) are confidential, and employers are forbidden from eavesdropping. Employers who fail to comply with this federal law are liable for actual and punitive damages and criminal liability for willful violations.

Right to unionize. The National Labor Relations Act allows employees to unionize and bargain collectively. Employers are prohibited from interfering with the exercise of these rights; they cannot fire, lay off, or demote workers who participate in such activities. Contact your union, regional labor relations board, state department of labor, or a private labor attorney if you believe your rights have been violated.

Right to work in a safe environment. The Occupational Safety and Health Act requires employers to provide a safe and healthful workplace. The Occupational Safety and Health Administration (OSHA) is the federal agency created to enforce the law in this area. The law protects employees who band together to protest wages, hours, or working conditions. Under this law, workers are allowed to refuse to perform in a dangerous environment (e.g., in the presence of toxic substances, fumes, or radioactive materials) and to strike to protest unsafe conditions. Employees can also initiate an OSHA inspection of alleged dangerous working conditions by filing a safety complaint and cannot be retaliated against for taking this action when justified. It may not be a good idea to walk off the job suddenly when you believe you are working in a dangerous or unhealthy environment unless the work is placing you in imminent danger of injury, but you should always discuss objectionable conditions with a supervisor, union delegate, management, or OSHA representative. This will make your demands seem more reasonable and minimize potential conflict. Contact your union, the regional office of the National Labor Relations Board (NLRB), an OSHA representative, an attorney, or the state department of labor if you believe your rights have been violated.

Right to work in a smoke-free environment. Most states have passed laws recognizing the rights of nonsmokers to work in a smoke-free environment. Various federal agencies, including the Merit Board and the EEOC, have ruled that employers must take reasonable steps to keep smoke away from workers, and OSHA has issued similar requirements to enhance safety in the workplace. If you have any problem in this area, gather the facts and speak to management. State all grievances in writing to document your claim. If you receive no response, send a follow-up letter. (See the letters on page 165 as models.) If you receive a negative response, speak to a lawyer to protect your rights. Contact an appropriate agency for further information. Your regional Department of Labor, Department of Health, or OSHA office will provide you with more information. Finally, speak to a doctor about workers' compensation. If you incur medical expenses due to a smoke-related on-the-job illness, discuss filing a workers' compensation claim with your doctor.

Right to be warned before a massive layoff. Employees are entitled to be warned of large layoffs under the federal Worker Adjustment and Retraining Notification Act. Employers with more than one hundred workers are required to give employees and their communities at least sixty days' notice or comparable financial benefits (sixty days' notice pay) of plant closings and large layoffs that affect fifty or more workers at a job site. Speak to an experienced labor attorney or contact the nearest regional office of the Department of Labor for more information. Companies must be careful when contemplating a substantial reduction of their workforce, and a representative from the Department of Labor can advise employees if their rights are being violated.

Testing for AIDS, drugs, and alcohol. All forms of employee testing raise significant issues of potential violations of an employee's privacy rights. Additionally, due to the enactment of the Americans with Disabilities Act (ADA), all such tests are closely scrutinized. AIDS testing is permitted in certain states only in limited circumstances where the job involves public health and safety, such as for food handlers, hospital workers, and members of the military. Most genetic testing is prohibited. Some states entirely prohibit drug and alcohol testing, but state law varies dramatically. For example, Utah generally permits employee testing with required procedural safeguards to ensure the testing is done in a reasonable and reliable manner with concern for employees' rights of privacy. Connecticut permits individual tests only when an employee is suspected of being under the influence of drugs or alcohol and his or her impaired state

FORM 69.

Sample Letter Demanding a Smoke-Free Work Environment

Date

Name and Title
Department
Company Name
Address

Dear (Name of Supervisor or Officer),

This will confirm the conversations we have had regarding the need to provide me (us) with a work environment free of tobacco smoke. Enclosed is information to support the request to eliminate smoking in work areas.

Also enclosed is a petition signed by employees in our work location. (If this is an individual request and there is no petition, disregard this paragraph.)

As my (our) ability to work is constantly undermined by the unhealthy, toxic pollutants to which I (we) am (are) chronically exposed, I (we) will appreciate your giving this request priority. May I (we) expect a reply by (date)?

Very truly yours,
(your name)

P.S. If a prompt response is not received, please be advised that I (we) may be forced to contact an OSHA representative for assistance. Hopefully, this will not be necessary.

▷ Send certified mail, return receipt requested.

▷ *Author's note:* Send a similar version to management whenever you are exposed to any potentially unhealthy working hazard.

FORM 70.

Sample Follow-Up Letter Requesting Smoke-Free Environment

Date

Name and Title
Department
Company Name
Address

Dear (Name),

As of this date, I (we) have received no reply to my (our) request of (date). (If temporary or interim measures were tried but were unsuccessful, identify them here.)

To protect my (our) health while in your employ, it is vital that the company provide me (us) with a smoke-free work area so as to comply with the laws of this state (specify applicable statute). I (we) have asked organizations that are expert in the area of occupational health to provide you with additional information on my (our) behalf.

I (we) will appreciate your immediate response to this urgent matter.

Sincerely,
(your name)

▷ Send copies to middle management, president of company, medical director of company, union representative, and personal physician.

adversely affects job performance. However, under Connecticut law, employees who test positive cannot be fired if they consent to participate in and successfully complete a rehabilitation program.

Since the law varies from state to state, is constantly changing, and may be even more stringent as a result of ADA, speak to a lawyer or a representative from the Department of Labor or the EEOC for advice in this area if applicable.

Constitutional protections. Employers risk potential lawsuits based on the invasion of privacy, intentional infliction of emotional distress, and wrongful discharge, among other causes of action, for violations stemming from unlawful interference in an employee's private nonprofessional life and relationships. Beginning in the late 1960s, the U.S. Supreme Court ruled that government employees could not be fired in retaliation for their exercise of free speech. The area of free speech, privacy, freedom from discharge as a result of whistle-blowing, and related constitutional protections has now been expanded to private-sector employees, particularly in states that have enacted broad civil rights laws. In many states, an employer cannot discipline, fail to promote, or fire an employee because the company does not agree with the employee's comments on matters of public concern. A majority of states have laws that prohibit employers from influencing how their employees vote. Attempts to regulate off-duty conduct are also prohibited. For example, attempts to curb legal off-the-job behavior, such as restrictions against smoking or consuming alcoholic beverages after office hours, are illegal.

However, employers have the right to regulate behavior in some areas. Management rules aimed at curbing intra-office romances, prohibiting employees from distributing literature, and setting standards in dress and personal appearance may be legal if the company's rule is reasonable and serves a legitimate interest.

Employment discrimination. Although employment discrimination is illegal, hundreds of thousands of cases are reported to the EEOC and filed in federal and state courts each year. Federal and state laws prohibit employers from discriminating against employees or potential employees on the basis of age, race, color, creed, religion, national origin, sex, marital status, disability, or physical handicap. Discrimination can occur during any employment stage: recruiting, interviewing, hiring, promotion, training, assignment, discipline, layoff, or discharge. (See page 380 in the Appendix for a Sample Demand Letter Alleging Discrimination.)

AGE DISCRIMINATION. Federal and state age discrimination laws protect workers forty years old and older. Private employers, labor unions, and state and local government agencies cannot deny an applicant a job on the basis of age, impose compulsory retirement before age seventy, coerce older employees into retirement by threatening termination, fire employees because of age, or deny promotions, transfers, or assignments because of age. It is also illegal to penalize older workers with reduced privileges, employment opportunities, and compensation. However, employers can fire older workers for inadequate job performance, reasonable business decisions having nothing to do with age (e.g., a company reorganization), or for cause (e.g., tardiness or insubordination). It is also legal in most cases for employers to entice older workers into early retirement by offering bigger pensions, extended health benefits, and substantial raises.

If you suspect you were denied a job or fired on the basis of age, demand an explanation from the employer for the action taken. Contact the EEOC if you are not satisfied with the answers given. After you discuss your case with a compliance officer, the EEOC can conduct an investigation on your behalf. You should also consider speaking to a labor attorney for more information and advice. Your case will be strengthened if fellow older employees were also victimized.

SEX DISCRIMINATION. The law requires similar employment policies, standards, and practices for males and females. For example, it is illegal for an employer to refuse to hire women with preschool-age children or fire pregnant workers. Another prohibited form of sex discrimination is sexual harassment. Unwelcome sexual advances, requests for sexual favors, and verbal or physical conduct of a sexual nature constitute sexual harassment when:

> the person must submit to such activity in order to be hired
> the person's consent or refusal is used in making an employment decision such as a raise or promotion
> such conduct unreasonably interferes with a person's work performance or creates an intimidating, hostile, or offensive working environment

In order to prove sexual harassment, you must document your claim. Send the company a letter by certified mail, return receipt requested, that describes the offensive acts. (The letter on page 168 illustrates this.) Judges are more willing to award damages when a formal complaint was made in writing but the harassment continued. Discuss the incident(s) with co-workers to discover if any of them have been victims of similar harassment. If you can prove that after being notified the employer failed to take corrective action or retaliated against you by demoting, transferring, or firing you instead of the accused, your case may be strengthened.

RACE DISCRIMINATION. Federal and state laws protect minority workers from discrimination. You cannot be denied a job, fired, or treated unfairly (e.g., denied a transfer or promotion) on the basis of race. Prerequisites for employment that have a discriminatory impact (asking a minority applicant at the hiring interview if he or she has an arrest record or poor credit background) are illegal. If you believe you were fired or denied an employment opportunity on the basis of race, color, or national origin, contact your local EEOC office or a private labor attorney for assistance.

FORM 71. **Sample Letter Protesting Sexual Harassment**

Your Name
Address
Telephone Number
Date

Name of Supervisor or Officer
Title
Name of Employer
Address

Dear (name),

While working for the company, I have been the victim of a series of offensive acts that I believe constitute sexual harassment.

On (date), I (describe what occurred and with whom). I immediately (describe your reaction) and ordered that such conduct stop. However, on (date), another incident occurred when (describe what occurred and with whom).

I find such behavior intimidating and repugnant. In fact, (describe the physical and emotional impact on you), causing me to be less efficient on the job. Please treat this letter as a formal protest of such conduct. Unless such conduct ceases immediately, or in the event the company illegally retaliates against me for writing this letter, I will contact the Equal Employment Opportunity Commission to enforce my rights.

I do not wish to take such a such drastic measure. All I want to do is perform my job in a professional environment.

Thank you for your cooperation in this matter.

Very truly yours,
(your name)

CONFIDENTIAL

▷ Send certified mail, return receipt requested.

HANDICAP DISCRIMINATION. In 1990, Congress passed the Americans with Disabilities Act to strengthen the rights of handicapped workers. As a result of ADA, it is now illegal to deny employment to a handicapped person who is capable of performing the job in question, and decisions not to hire an applicant because of a physical or mental condition are closely scrutinized. For employers with fifteen or more workers, it is now illegal to establish negative classifications of job applicants or employees because of disability. Employers are required to make existing facilities used by employees readily accessible to and usable by individuals with disabilities and provide disabled workers with more liberal part-time or modified work schedules. Generally, however, employers are permitted to terminate workers who are physically unable to perform their duties due to a physical or mental impairment.

RELIGIOUS DISCRIMINATION. The EEOC has created guidelines with respect to religious discrimination. Employers have an obligation to make reasonable accommodations to the religious needs of employees and prospective employees. An employer may be required to allow you the right to wear special clothes (e.g., a hat or shawl) that do not interfere with a company's reasonable public image business objective and give you time off for the Sabbath or holy day observance, except in an emergency. In such an event, the employer may give leave without pay, may require you to make up equivalent time, or may allow you to charge the time against other leave with pay except sick pay. This general rule, however, may not apply to private employers who can prove that an employee's absence would create a severe business hardship.

ENFORCING YOUR RIGHTS. Recognizing discrimination is merely part of the battle; you must take proper steps to enforce your rights. Federal law entitles victims of discrimination to recover a variety of damages. They include job hiring; reinstatement; wage adjustments; back pay and double back pay; promotions; recovery of legal fees, expert witness fees, and filing costs; damages for emotional pain and suffering up to $300,000; punitive damages; instituting an affirmative action program on behalf of fellow employees; obtaining a jury trial, and in some cases, future wages where reinstatement is not possible.

Although you can hire a private attorney to commence a discrimination lawsuit in federal court, most litigants file a formal complaint with the EEOC or the appropriate state agency. There is no cost involved. Once a formal complaint is received, an EEOC investigator attempts to resolve the matter informally at a no-fault conference. If a settlement is not reached, the EEOC will conduct a formal investigation by interviewing witnesses and reviewing the company's business records. Once a decision of probable/no probable cause is found, you have several options: the EEOC may refer the matter to an appropriate state or local human rights agency for action; the EEOC or Department of Justice may commence a lawsuit for you and/or others similarly situated (a class action lawsuit); or you can hire a lawyer and sue the employer privately. The advantage of suing an employer privately is that you may reach a settlement faster. However, private lawsuits can be expensive. Always speak to a labor lawyer for more details and to learn your options when applicable.

Pregnancy and maternity/paternity leave. The federal Family and Medical Leave Act protects employees who work for companies with more than fifty workers. An eligible employee (defined as having worked at least 12 months for the employer or 1,250 hours during the 12-month period prior to taking the leave) is allowed to take up to 12 weeks of unpaid leave in any 12-month period for the birth of a child; the adoption of a child; to care for a child, spouse, or parent with a serious illness; or to convalesce from a serious health condition. A person taking leave must be restored to his or her position or to an equivalent position, with equivalent benefits, pay, and other terms and conditions of employment, upon returning to work. As a result of this law, you or your spouse cannot be fired for becoming pregnant or taking time off for child-bearing or other valid health-related reasons. Speak to a labor lawyer if your rights are being violated.

Right to receive overtime pay. The federal Fair Labor Standards Act provides that, for any time worked in excess of forty hours per week, an hourly worker must be paid at a rate not less than one and one-half times the regular rate that employee earns. Exempted from this overtime requirement are employees classified as "employed in a bona fide executive, administrative, or professional capacity." Typically, a salaried professional is not entitled to receive overtime pay. However, if a company utilizes compensatory plans that offer unpaid leave to these professionals, such as allowing workers time off without pay or allowing them to work more than forty hours one week to make up for working less than forty hours in a previous week, such policies may be illegal. The Department of Labor ruled recently that if a company allows or requests salaried professional employees to take time off without pay, the workers automatically become hourly employees entitled to overtime.

Contact a representative at your state's Department of Labor or the Wage and Hour Division of the U.S. Department of Labor if you are having a problem collecting overtime pay. Significant damages can be awarded in the event an employer fails to pay overtime or fails to include you in the group of employees eligible to receive overtime. The act makes employers who fail to pay required overtime liable for the unpaid overtime compensation and an equal amount as liquidated damages, plus attorney fees and costs. Damages may also include all earned overtime up to two years (ordinarily) or three years back in the event of a willful violation finding, plus potential punitive damages. Since a claim for overtime can go several years back, always keep accurate records of overtime worked to substantiate a claim.

Right to receive workers' compensation. Each state has enacted its own peculiar rules with respect to workers' compensation, which provides aid for employees who suffer job-related injuries. Under state compensation laws, the amount of money paid in benefits is linked to the worker's rate of pay prior to the injury and the kind and extent of injuries suffered. Workers' compensation is a substitute for other remedies the worker may have against the employer, such as bringing a private lawsuit for negligence. In many cases, the issue becomes one of determining whether the injuries suffered were job-related. The reason is that workers typically prefer to sue the employer privately and obtain greater damages than are typically awarded under workers' compensation statutes.

Since the outcome of each workers' compensation case varies depending on the particular facts and unique state law, always seek the advice of a lawyer specializing in workers' compensation law. Issues such as how long you may delay before filing a claim, whether coverage is available for stress-related injuries, and what kinds of injuries are covered, together with strategies to help maximize the benefits received, can become complicated and typically require a lawyer's assistance and advice.

Summary of Steps to Take While Working for an Employer

1. Save all correspondence, copies of records, and other documents.
2. Notify your employer immediately if you discover errors in your salary, bonus, commissions, compensation, or benefits.
3. Do not accept reductions in your salary or other benefits, particularly if you have a written contract that prohibits oral modifications of important terms.
4. Write letters to protest illegal actions, such as to complain about sexual harassment or health and safety violations in the workplace. This is important so you will not be deemed to have consented to such treatment by your lack of action.
5. Write a rebuttal to any subjective or incorrect performance review or evaluation you receive. Explain why you perceive the review to be inaccurate.
6. Recognize your rights to privacy, to unionize, and to health and safety in the workplace and seek competent legal counsel at once if your rights are violated.

WHAT TO DO IF YOU ARE FIRED

The postemployment phase is just as important as knowing how to be hired properly and enforcing your on-the-job rights. Many workers are fired unfairly, and millions of dollars are forfeited each year by people who fail to recognize what they are legally entitled to. Many state and federal laws protect workers from unfair discharge. Dismissals based on the following may be illegal, even if you were hired at will without a written contract.

1. Fired to deny accrued benefits. The law obligates employers to deal in good faith with longtime employees. If you are fired just before you are supposed to receive anticipated benefits such as an earned bonus, accrued pension, profit sharing, or commissions due, consult a lawyer immediately. However, if an employer fires you for a lawful reason—that is, for cause—the fact you are about to become eligible for a substantial benefit may not make the firing illegal.

2. Fired due to a legitimate illness or absence from work. You cannot be fired (a) if you are absent due to an injury that occurred on the job and you have filed a workers' compensation claim; (b) if you are absent for a medical reason relating to pregnancy; or (c) if you take maternity/paternity leave of less than twelve weeks in any given one-year period. However, an employer may have the right to fire a worker who is excessively absent due to illness. Your option may be to file for and collect benefits under the company's short- or long-term disability plan.

3. Fired for serving on jury duty or in the military, or for voting.

4. Fired for whistle-blowing. Various state Whistle-blower's Protection Acts protect workers who reveal abuses of authority. These statutes penalize employers who retaliate against workers who report suspected violations of health, safety, or financial regulations or laws and provide specific remedies, including reinstatement with back pay, restoration of seniority and lost fringe benefits, litigation costs, attorney fees, and fines. To find out if your state has such a law, speak to an experienced labor lawyer, legal referral service, or the American Civil Liberties Union (ACLU) in your area. People who work for federal agencies are also protected from reprisals for whistle-blowing.

5. Fired for attempting to unionize, complaining about health or safety violations, or for legal off-the-premises conduct.

6. Fired in a manner inconsistent with company handbooks, manuals, and disciplinary rules. Some employers have written progressive disciplinary programs for employees that have to followed before a firing. Failure to follow these rules, such as giving a formal warning or placing an employee on probation before a firing, can give rise to a lawsuit based on violation of an implied contract in some states.

7. Fired because you are over forty, belong to a protected minority group, are female or handicapped, or engage in a religious observance, primarily because of such personal characteristics. Also, if you belong to a minority group and are fired for an infraction such as reporting to work late, but other male, young, or white workers with worse attendance records are only given a warning, you may allege discrimination based on preferential treatment.

8. Fired as part of a massive layoff and not given at least sixty days' notice or sixty days' severance pay.

9. Fired after you received a verbal promise of job security or other rights that the company failed to fulfill.

10. Fired in violation of rights granted according to a written contract or collective bargaining agreement if you belong to a union.

STEPS TO TAKE WHEN YOU ARE FIRED

Most employers fire workers without warning. However, the fact that you are axed suddenly does not mean you should accept fewer benefits than you are entitled to. The following strategies can help increase severance benefits and/or damages in the event of a firing.

1. Stall for time. Do not panic or scream at your boss when informed of the bad news. Request extra time to think things over. This may allow you to learn important facts and negotiate a better settlement. If possible, avoid accepting the company's first offer.

2. Review your employment contract or letter of agreement. If you signed a written contract, reread it. Review what is says about termination,

FORM 72. **Sample Letter Demanding True Reason for Discharge**

Your Name
Address
Date

Name of Officer of Employer
Title
Name of Employer
Address

Re: My termination

Dear (Name of Officer),

On (date) I was fired suddenly by your company without notice, warning, or cause. All that I was told by (name of person) was that my services were no longer required and that my termination was effective immediately.

To date, I have not received any explanation documenting the reason(s) for my discharge. In accordance with the laws of this state I hereby demand such information in writing immediately.

Thank you for your prompt attention and cooperation in this matter.

Very truly yours,
(your name)

▷ Send certified mail, return receipt requested.

▷ *Author's note:* Many states have no laws requiring an employer to furnish a true reason for the discharge upon demand. Thus, use this letter only where state law permits.

because if the company fails to act according to the contract, your rights may be violated.

3. Ascertain why you are being fired. This can help in the event you decide to sue your former employer. For example, once you receive a reason for the firing, the employer may be precluded from offering additional reasons at a trial, arbitration, or unemployment compensation hearing. Some states have service letter statutes requiring companies to specify in writing the reasons for an employee's termination. If the employer refuses to tell you why you were fired, or tells prospective employers other reasons later, you may have grounds for a lawsuit under the laws of these states. The letter above illustrates how to demand a true explanation of the reasons for your discharge.

4. Learn who made the decision to fire you. You may discover you were fired for a petty reason such as jealousy and can be reinstated. Or, perhaps the punishment for a long-term worker "did not fit the crime," since other workers were not similarly treated. Sometimes, however, short of commencing a lawsuit, there is little you can do other than negotiate a better severance package.

5. Ask to see your personnel file. Some states permit terminated workers to review and copy the contents of their personnel files. Sometimes these files do not support firing decisions because they contain favorable recommendations and comments. If you can be fired only for cause and the company gives you specific reasons why you were fired, your file may demonstrate that such reasons are factually incorrect and/or legally insufficient. In this event, you may have a strong case against your former employer for breach of contract. If you have received excellent performance reviews and appraisals and the file indicates you received merit salary increases, you may use this information to successfully fight the firing, negotiate more severance than the company is offering, and better prepare you for future interviews with prospective employers.

6. Reconstruct promises. If promises regarding job security were previously given, recall the time, place, and whether the statements were made in the presence of witnesses. Some courts are ruling that oral promises from high-ranking company officers (e.g., the president) concerning job security are binding.

7. Request an additional negotiating session to discuss your severance package. Generally, a company has no legal obligation to pay severance unless you have a written contract stating that severance will be paid, oral promises were given regarding severance pay, there is a documented policy of paying severance in a company handbook or manual, the employer voluntarily offers to pay severance, or other employees in similar positions have received severance pay in the past. Although lower-level employees may have difficulty arranging a negotiating session, most managers, employees in supervisory positions, and executives will be granted another interview.

8. Negotiate the severance package properly. At the interview, avoid threatening litigation. Appeal to corporate decency and fair play instead. For example, it is better to say "I am fifty-eight years old and have to pay for two children in college right now and your offer of four weeks' severance is inadequate since it is unlikely I can find a comparable job in the next four weeks" rather than say "If you don't pay more money I will sue."

Ask for an amount of severance pay equal to one month for each year on the job. Discuss an additional bonus, pension and profit-sharing benefits, medical coverage, and other benefits paid by the company for an extended period of time. Discuss a favorable letter of reference, entitlement to unemployment insurance benefits, and how the company will announce the separation (called your "cover story"). Send the employer a letter (similar to the one on pages 176–177) confirming your severance package if you don't receive one from the company.

9. Confirm all agreements in writing to document the final deal. Insist on receiving more money and other benefits before signing any release or waiver of a discrimination claim. Exit agreements, releases, and covenants not to sue can deprive you of valuable rights. Never sign one without the advice of a lawyer.

10. Apply for unemployment benefits. Unemployment benefits are available under state law. However, you may be denied benefits if you voluntarily left your job, were fired for misconduct, or refused a valid job offer. You can request a hearing if you feel benefits were unfairly denied. Speak to a lawyer or a representative from your local Department of Labor if you are actually fired but the company asks you to resign (you may unknowingly forfeit unemployment benefits), if your benefits are contested by the company, or if you require representation at an unemployment hearing.

11. Do not be intimidated or forced into early retirement. Recognize that you may have rights, particularly if your early retirement causes you to lose large, expected financial benefits.

12. Enforce your ERISA rights. The Employee Retirement Income Security Act prohibits the discharge of any employee who is prevented from attaining immediate vested pension benefits or who was exercising rights under ERISA and was fired as a result. ERISA also entitles employees to certain rights as participants in an employer's pension and/or profit-sharing plans. Plan participants are entitled to examine without charge all plan documents, including insurance contracts, annual reports, plan descriptions, and copies of documents filed by the plan with the U.S. Department of Labor. If you have not received a proper accounting or payment of your retirement benefits, send a letter to your employer certified mail, return receipt requested, asking for summaries of each plan's annual financial report. If you do not receive the information within thirty days, you can file a lawsuit in federal court. In such a case, the court may require the plan administrator to provide the materials and pay you up to $100 a day until you receive them (unless the materials were not sent for reasons beyond the administrator's control). Find out the name and address of the administrator of any of your retirement plans. If the company is stonewalling you by not returning your calls, providing information, or paying your retirement benefits, consult a labor lawyer for advice.

13. Enforce your COBRA rights. The federal Consolidated Omnibus Budget Reconciliation Act requires private employers who employ more than twenty workers on a typical business day to continue to make group health insurance available to workers who are discharged from employment. All employees who are discharged as a result of voluntary or involuntary termination (with the exception of those who are fired for gross misconduct) may elect to continue plan benefits currently in effect at their own expense provided the employee or beneficiary makes an initial payment within thirty days of notification and is not covered under Medicare or any other group plan. The law also applies to qualified beneficiaries who were covered by the employer's group health plan the day before the discharge. Thus, for example, if you choose not to continue coverage, your spouse or dependent children may elect to continue coverage at their own expense. The extended coverage period is eighteen months after

FORM 73. **Letter Documenting Severance Arrangement**

Date

Name of Corporate Officer
Title
Name of Employer
Address

Re: Our Severance Agreement

Dear (Name of Corporate Officer),

This will confirm our discussion and agreement regarding my termination:

1. I will be kept on the payroll through (specify date) and will receive (specify) weeks' vacation pay, which shall be included with my last check on that date.

2. (Name of Company) shall pay me a bonus of (specify) within (specify) days from the date of this letter.

3. (Name of Company) will purchase both my nonvested and vested company stock, totaling (specify) shares at a price of (specify $) per share, or at the market rate if it is higher at the time of repurchase, on or before (specify date).

4. (Name of Company) will continue to maintain in effect all profit-sharing and retirement plans, medical, dental, hospitalization, disability, and life insurance policies presently in effect through (specify date). After that date, I have been advised that I may convert said policies at my sole cost and expense and that coverage for these policies will not lapse. I will receive information concerning the conversion of my retirement plan savings within the next few weeks.

5. I will be permitted to use the company's premises at (specify location) from the hours of 9:00 a.m. until 5:00 p.m. This shall include the use of a secretary, telephone, stationery, and other amenities at the company's sole cost and expense to assist me in obtaining another position.

termination of the covered employee; upon the death, divorce, or separation of the covered employee, the benefit coverage period is thirty-six months for spouses and dependents.

Be sure you know your rights under COBRA in the event you are fired. If an employer refuses to negotiate continued health benefits as a part of a severance package, fails to explain your rights and options, or fails to notify you of the existence of such benefits within thirty days of the discharge, contact the personnel office immediately. Follow up the telephone call with a letter sent certified mail, return receipt requested. If the employer refuses to offer continued COBRA benefits after a discharge for any reason, consult a labor lawyer immediately.

14. Take action if the employer is providing negative references to prospective employers. This includes sending letters by certified mail, return receipt requested, to protect your rights (see page 178 for an example of such a letter). The letter can document what you have learned and put the employer on

6. I will be permitted to continue using the automobile previously supplied to me through (specify date) under the same terms and conditions presently in effect. On that date, I will return all sets of keys in my possession together with all other papers and documents belonging to the company.

7. (Name of Company) will reimburse me for all reasonable and necessary expenses related to the completion of company business after I submit appropriate vouchers and records within (specify) days of presentment.

8. (Name of company) agrees to provide me with a favorable letter of recommendation and reference(s) and will announce to the trade that I am resigning for "personal reasons." I am enclosing a letter for that purpose, to be reviewed and signed by (specify person) and returned to me immediately.

9. Although unanticipated, (name of company) will not contest my filing for unemployment insurance benefits after (specify date) and will assist me in promptly executing all documents necessary for that purpose.

10. If a position is procured by me prior to (specify date), a lump-sum payment for my remaining severance will be paid within (specify) days after my notification of same. Additionally, the stock referred to in Paragraph 3 will be purchased as of the date of my employment with another company if prior to (specify date) and the proceeds will be paid to me within (specify) days of my notification.

If any of the terms of this letter are ambiguous or incorrect, please advise me immediately in writing specifying the item(s) that are incorrect. Otherwise, this letter shall set forth our entire understanding in this matter, which cannot be changed orally.

(Name of Corporate Officer), I want to personally thank you for your assistance and cooperation in this matter and wish you all the best in the future.

Very truly yours,
(your name)

▷ Send certified mail, return receipt requested.

notice of your desire to take prompt legal action if the problem persists. Many states have enacted antiblacklisting statutes that punish employers for maliciously or willfully attempting to prevent former employees from finding work. In some states, untruthful job references are treated as crimes. You can also assert a lawsuit based on defamation and emotional distress if you discover that private employment data and confidential personnel records (e.g., medical information) were leaked to outsiders without your consent.

15. Resign from a job properly. It is best to request and sign a written contract with your new employer when you are hired. This protects you if the new employer decides not to hire you after all or tries to fire you after a short period of employment. If you signed a contract with your old employer when you were hired, review what it says regarding termination and comply with those terms if you decide to resign. For example, if the contract states that you can resign provided written notice is sent by certified mail sixty days prior to the effective

> FORM 74. **Sample Letter Protesting Unfavorable Job Reference**

Your Name
Address
Telephone Number
Date

Name of Employer
Address

Dear (Name),

On (specify date), I applied for a job with (name of potential employer). At the interview, I was told that your firm had submitted an inaccurate, unfavorable reference about me.

(Specify name) supposedly said the reason I was fired was that I was an uncooperative and complaining worker (or specify facts).

This is untrue. In fact, my personnel file, which I copied, contains not one derogatory comment about me.

You are hereby requested to cease making inaccurate statements about my job performance to anyone. If you do not comply, I will contact my lawyer and take appropriate legal action. Hopefully this will be avoided and I thank you for your cooperation in this matter.

Very truly yours,
(Your name)

cc: potential employer

▷ Send certified mail, return receipt requested.

termination date, you must send that timely notice. Failure to do so can result in your former employer suing you for breach of contract. (See the sample Letter of Resignation Requesting Benefits on page 381 in the Appendix.)

Be aware: Many people mistakenly believe that it is better to resign than to be fired. This is not always true. By resigning, you may waive valuable benefits, including severance pay, bonuses, unemployment benefits, and other monies. Thus, always think twice about resigning if the employer gives you the option. In fact, the author prefers that his clients be fired rather then resign whenever possible, since potential damage claims and severance benefits may remain intact.

16. Return company property. Items such as automobile keys and samples must be returned to avoid claims of misappropriation, fraud, and breach of contract. When returning items by mail, be sure to get a receipt to prove delivery. If the company owes you money, you may consider holding the company's property to force a settlement. However, speak to a lawyer before taking such action, since many states do not permit employees to retain company property as a lien.

17. Speak to a labor lawyer to enforce your rights, especially if you are owed wages or other compensation, or you believe the employer violated the law.

Consult the Appendix to review the series of letters (pages 381–390) you or your lawyer can send certified mail, return receipt requested, to enforce your rights and collect monetary benefits. The Appendix also contains a summary of things to consider if your job is in jeopardy (page 392) and a list of negotiating strategies to help you maximize severance pay and retirement benefits (page 393).

ENGAGEMENT   *See also: Divorce; Marriage; Separation*

Millions of people get engaged each year. Except for the handling of gifts given and promises made during the betrothal period, little legal significance pertains to the engagement process because the parties are not yet legally married.

A serious problem that sometimes arises concerns the exchange of gifts and the disposition of the engagement ring when the engagement is broken and the marriage does not occur. Ownership rights to engagement gifts are governed in most states by case decisions (i.e., common law); few states have passed laws governing this area. What this means is that each case is decided by a judge based on its particular facts and circumstances. Different kinds of gifts are exchanged, including personal gifts, holiday gifts, birthday gifts, and gifts in contemplation of marriage. Third parties also give gifts to the couple. The reason for the gift, the actual item given, and the date on which it is received sometimes play a significant role in determining legal ownership.

Generally, a gift is a voluntary transfer of property to another that is made gratuitously and without consideration. The person receiving the gift (referred to as the "donee") is considered to have title to that property. However, some gifts are not absolute (i.e., they do not convey complete title) but are given with the intent that the marriage take effect before legal title is transferred. Thus if you decide, for example, that you cannot go through with a planned marriage, you may be legally obligated in most states to return any gifts you received that were conditioned on performance of the marriage. For a woman, this includes the engagement ring, any other gifts given on the assumption she was going to marry, wedding presents, and shower gifts.

In most instances, it is difficult to prove that a gift was given only in contemplation of marriage. Because of this, the law generally makes an exception with respect to engagement rings. Courts view engagement rings in the nature of a pledge for the contract of marriage, and the ring is usually considered a conditional gift because of its symbolic significance, which sets it apart from other gifts. If both parties mutually consent to the breaking of the engagement, the donor (the person giving the gift) will normally acquire the right to retain the ring. If the donee breaks the engagement without legal justification—for example, because of a liaison with another man—she is probably required, upon demand, to return the ring. But if the donor breaks the engagement without legal justification, the donee will normally be entitled to keep the ring.

Other gifts given before and during the engagement period (frequently referred to as "gifts of pursuit") are more difficult to recover in a lawsuit, especially when they were received on the donee's birthday, an anniversary, a holiday, or a special occasion. This is because when the gift is given on a special occasion, the defense that the gift was conditioned on the upcoming marriage is considerably weakened.

Each engagement has its own unique and varying events that may or may not change the outcome of legal ownership of gifts. However, if you are giving a gift in contemplation of marriage, for additional legal protection you may wish to:

▸ Stress that the gift is conditional upon consummating the marriage.
▸ Announce these intentions in front of witnesses if possible.
▸ Demand the prompt return of the item once the engagement is broken by the other party, preferably in writing.
▸ Avoid giving gifts on special days if possible.
▸ Recognize that you may have difficulty recovering the gift, even the engagement ring, if you are the one who breaks the engagement or provokes the breakup.

If the recipient of your gifts never intended to marry you even when receiving conditional gifts, you may be able to recover these items on the grounds of fraud. However, if you are engaged to a minor (e.g., a person under eighteen), you may not be able to recover any gift under any circumstances. Finally, you are probably legally obligated to return all shower and wedding gifts to third parties after the engagement is called off, particularly if you are responsible for that decision.

In the past, some women sued men who failed to go through with a promise to marry for breach of contract. However, such "heartbalm" actions have now been abolished by statute in most states, along with lawsuits for fraud and misrepresentation. A few states still allow jilted parties to sue third persons for emotional pain and suffering if the third party caused a breakup of the engagement or marriage. However, the vast majority of states do not recognize such "alienation of affection" actions. Speak to a domestic relations lawyer for advice if applicable.

EQUITABLE DISTRIBUTION *See Divorce*

ERISA *See Employment*

EVIDENCE   *Also see: Crimes and Criminal Law; Litigation*

Evidence is information in the form of oral testimony, exhibits, physical items, or affidavits used to prove a party's claim. Evidence can be presented in many forms. For example, exhibits are tangible evidence presented in a court proceeding for the purpose of supporting factual allegations or arguments. Testimony from expert witnesses may be introduced as evidence. In certain kinds of criminal cases, physical evidence such as fingerprints or hair samples can be helpful in proving who harmed a victim if no witnesses were present.

In a civil case, the plaintiff has the burden of proving its case by a legal standard called preponderance of the evidence ("more likely than not") through witnesses, charts, documents, photographs, and other forms of physical evidence. In a criminal case, the prosecution must prove a person's guilt beyond a reasonable doubt. This is a more difficult standard to achieve.

During the trial one side will try to get certain evidence admitted into the court record for consideration by a judge or jury when deciding the case. The other party, through his or her lawyer, will seek to exclude such evidence through objections—for example, by stating that the evidence is irrelevant or inadmissible. A judge will either deny the objection and allow the evidence to be admitted or sustain the objection and exclude the evidence. The introduction of evidence in any case depends on an attorney's arguments and the judge's interpretation of that state or federal court's rules. Certain types of evidence, such as evidence taken without a search warrant or hearsay evidence (a witness's testimony about what someone else said outside the courtroom), must be excluded (and may be excluded in advance of a trial).

Each party has the opportunity to discover what evidence the other intends to introduce at the trial to prove its version of the facts. This is done through depositions where a witness's testimony is taken under oath and during discovery procedures whereby records and other physical information are turned over to the other side for evaluation. In a criminal matter it is against the law to destroy evidence.

Because the success or failure of a case often depends on the type of evidence introduced and admitted (or excluded) from the record at a trial, it is important to hire a lawyer who is very knowledgeable about the rules of evidence. For maximum success, always hire a lawyer who possesses competent trial skills.

FELONY   *See Crimes and Criminal Law*

FORECLOSURE   *See Real Estate*

Fraud is a false statement or representation of fact that is relied on by and causes damages to the defrauded party. Typically, the false statement or representation must be material (important), not an opinion (but a statement of fact), and stated knowingly to deceive and induce the defrauded party to do something (e.g., pay money, sign a contract, or make an investment). Sometimes it is difficult to prove fraud in a lawsuit because of the necessity of demonstrating that the person making the untrue statement knew it was false at the time.

Lawsuits based on fraud, misrepresentation, and deceit (terms typically used interchangeably) can be either criminal or civil, depending on the circumstances and the parties involved. For example, when a fraud is perpetrated on an insurance company, the IRS, or a consumer who purchases a used car based on a false mileage (i.e., odometer fraud), it is considered a crime against society, imposing potential jail sentences for proven acts. On the other hand, when a fraud affects limited parties, such as a business person who relies on false promises in a transaction or an individual who is swindled by a deceitful stockbroker, the fraud is typically considered civil in nature. There are times when both criminal and civil fraud lawsuits can arise out of one fraudulent act, so speak to an attorney to learn more about when this is applicable.

Business agreements, consumer contracts, and marriages induced by fraud can be set aside (voided) in certain cases. Wills can be contested and voided when proof of fraud in the preparation of the will is demonstrated. (For example, a false page of a will is inserted in place of the original by a person who wants to inherit more money.)

To avoid business and investment fraud, never be pressured into making a quick decision. If you are told a once-in-a-lifetime deal will pass you by unless you act quickly, chances are good that you are being swindled. Never invest in a deal until you receive written information. Analyze how your money will be used. Consult a lawyer, accountant, financial adviser, or other professional before investing more than $1,000 in any venture. Insist on an agreement that accurately reflects how the money is being used. Hire a lawyer to analyze any business or complicated investment agreement or to prepare one for your protection.

If you are successful in bringing a lawsuit based on fraud, you may recover recompense for the harm suffered. Additionally, in egregious situations, the law sometimes allows victims to recover additional sums to punish the wrongdoer and serve as a deterrent to others. These are called punitive damages.

FUNERAL ARRANGEMENTS

The Federal Trade Commission has enacted legislation to protect consumers from unfair and deceptive trade practices by funeral providers. Regulations require funeral homes to give complete information over the telephone concerning prices and services. During a visit, you must be given a written, itemized list of all funeral goods and services and prices. Funeral providers must obtain express permission from a representative before charging a fee for embalming, not require you to purchase a casket for use in a cremation service, not misrepresent state and local legal requirements for burial or cremation to enhance fees, and not misrepresent the existence of markups on cash-advance items (i.e., state that items such as flowers are sold at cost when this is not true). A few states have enacted laws even tougher than the FTC funeral rule. In those states, funeral establishments are required to follow the tougher law.

In some states, funeral homes are licensed by the health department. In other states, the Department of Consumer Affairs is responsible for investigating matters under dispute and conducting formal hearings. Both agencies often attempt to resolve complaints informally. If these attempts are unsuccessful, fines can be imposed and licenses suspended or revoked for blatant violations, such as for charging highly excessive fees, cremating a person's body by mistake against a family's wishes, or not having the proper burial plot available (although it was previously paid for).

Ask for a detailed summary of all possible costs before making any purchase. Insist on a written agreement that itemizes all charges. Read the contract carefully before signing. Speak to a lawyer or contact a regional office of the FTC if you have been misled, are a victim of fraud or misrepresentation, or believe the funeral establishment failed to render agreed-upon services (and is therefore liable for breach of contract). Some parties have sued and won damages for emotional pain and suffering when the funeral home commits a highly offensive act (e.g., burying the wrong body) or when the wishes of the family or deceased are not properly followed.

In most cases, you will want to sue the funeral home in small-claims court when the amount in dispute is relatively small (i.e., under $3,000).

GARNISHMENT *See Child Support*

GENERAL PARTNERSHIP *See Partnership*

GIFT *See Engagement; Probate; Taxes; Trusts; Wills*

GUARANTY *See Contracts*

GUARDIANS *See Child Custody; Children; Wills*

GUILTY PLEA *See Arrest; Crimes and Criminal Law*

HOMOSEXUALITY AND THE LAW

Also see: Adoption; Civil Rights; Employment; Living Together; Marriage

The legal rights of homosexuals have been strengthened in many areas. (In a few states, homosexual sodomy is still considered a crime, although such laws are rarely enforced.) Some states and cities have passed laws prohibiting discrimination against anyone in housing, employment, and civil rights because of his or her sexual orientation. Under the laws of these states, for example, it is illegal to fire, refuse to hire, or offer an apartment lease to a person because of a stated or apparent sexual preference. Gay couples who live together have many of the same rights and obligations as heterosexual couples who live together, and lawsuits can be brought for palimony and support claims after the breakup of the relationship.

Hawaii was the first state to recognize the legality of same-sex marriages. Its highest court ruled that prohibiting one individual from marrying another on account of his or her gender violated that state's constitutional guarantee of equal protection since no compelling reason was shown to ban same-sex marriages. Thus, in the absence of a U.S. Supreme Court ruling to the contrary, gay couples may soon be free to marry in Hawaii.

Some states allow heterosexual and homosexual cohabitants to register as domestic partners to receive benefits typically afforded only to married persons. These benefits include continued occupancy of an apartment, health insurance benefits, and visitation rights in correctional and hospital facilities.

Adoption is not limited to children. A majority of states have laws providing for the adoption of adults as well as minors. If one gay partner dies without a will, the other partner usually cannot make a claim against the estate as a spouse, heir, or next of kin. However, if an adoption between homosexuals is approved, inheritance and succession rights of tenancy or occupancy rights with respect to a lease or real estate are permissible.

Gay couples typically still have difficulty in adopting a child and being awarded custody. In custody disputes, many judges are disposed to believe that a parent's nonmarital homosexual relationship may cause significant stress on a child and is not in his or her best interest. Such a relationship is often viewed as a negative factor against the parent who seeks custody, sometimes resulting in a finding that the parent is unfit. However, this premise is not universally accepted and each case is decided on its own unique facts and circumstances.

Speak to an experienced lawyer to understand, enforce, or protect your rights in any of these areas if applicable.

HOUSES   *See Real Estate*

Quotas and immigration policies affecting the legal admission of immigrants into the United States, the exclusion and deportation of illegal immigrants, the granting of political asylum, work visas, and resident status, and the regulation of immigrant-related employment practices are all areas governed by federal law. The major immigration law is the McCarran-Walter Act, also known as the Immigration and Naturalization Act. That law authorized the U.S. Immigration and Naturalization Service (INS) to supervise and enforce immigration policies. Revisions to that law have followed over the years. For example, in 1965 restrictions on the entry of Asians were abolished as well as the national origins quota system.

The U.S. Immigration and Control Act of 1986 (IRCA) required employers to hire only U.S. citizens and aliens authorized to work in the United States. To discourage aliens from illegally entering the country by eliminating job opportunities, the 1986 regulation required companies to verify the eligibility of every worker hired in order to avoid civil fines and criminal penalties. Verification guidelines must now be followed regardless of an employer's size or the number of hires. New employees are required to fill out their portion of the I-9 Employment Eligibility Verification Form when they begin work, and employers must, within three business days, check documents, including a driver's license or Social Security card, to establish the employee's identity and eligibility to work. See page 394 in the Appendix to review a detailed list of documents employers must request to comply with this federal law.

The Immigration Act of 1990 (IMMAC) further revised immigration rules by allowing 750,000 more people to be admitted into the U.S., providing 10,000 visas for permanent residence to foreigners who will invest more than $1 million in the U.S., and expanding the number and origin of persons who can apply for asylum. Those who qualify can now receive "temporary protected status" and be allowed to work in the U.S. for up to eighteen months without being deported.

All immigration and naturalization laws relate to the treatment of aliens. An alien is a person who is not a citizen or national of the U.S. Immigrants are defined as persons who wish to become citizens and/or remain in the U.S. permanently; residents are defined as persons who wish to travel, work, or study in the U.S. on a temporary basis. All aliens must obtain a visa or an entry permit when entering the U.S. Aliens typically first apply for visas at an American embassy or consulate in their own country.

Many different kinds of nonimmigrant or temporary visas are issued. For example, "green cards" are given to permanent residents. A prospective U.S. employer can make an application on behalf of an alien who is waiting abroad. However, in addition to the pitfalls of hiring undocumented aliens, employers of foreign workers are also exposed to discrimination charges by disgruntled U.S. applicants because the IMMAC requires that such employers seek labor certification from the Department of Labor and that any qualified U.S. worker must be hired first (i.e., given a preference).

Because any qualified U.S. workers applying for a job must be given preference, employers can take proper steps to avoid potential problems. For example, employers should list and describe every job requirement, document all recruitment efforts made for any applicant, and keep a record of all interviews to prove they were not a sham and to support the reasons for any rejection of an applicant. When someone is denied a job, the reasons must relate directly to listed job requirements. Employers should save all records to fight any Department of Labor challenge that may arise.

If you are:

- An alien already in the U.S. who wishes to apply for an advantageous change in nonimmigrant status
- A professional with an advanced degree, a professor or researcher with extraordinary ability, or a foreign executive or manager working temporarily in the U.S. who wishes to continue employment
- An employer unfamiliar with immigration and labor rules as they pertain to hiring workers
- A person who wishes to reunite (i.e., sponsor) a close family member or relative living abroad
- A person who knows someone seeking refuge or asylum status

speak to a representative from a local Department of Labor or INS office for advice where applicable. (Note: Some lawyers charge fees for providing information you may learn free of charge from an INS office. Thus, speak to a qualified immigration attorney only when necessary.) It is often not necessary to reveal your name or address when asking a question over the telephone or in person.

Under provisions of IMMAC, many foreign tourists may visit the U.S. for up to ninety days without obtaining a visa. Most important, due to the passage of the Social Security Domestic Employment Reform Act of 1994 (commonly referred to as the "Nanny Tax law"), people who hire baby-sitters, chauffeurs, housekeepers, maids, and others who work in or around the home have added responsibilities concerning the payment of employment taxes and filing paperwork for these people. Beginning with wage payments made in 1994, you are not required to pay Federal Unemployment Tax (FUTA) and file a Form 940 unless you pay a worker more than $1,000 during the year. However, like any employer, you must comply with the requirements of the IRCA by checking each worker's documents proving identity and eligibility to work, having each worker complete his or her part of Form I-9, completing the employer's portion of Form I-9 (which contains an attestation that you have seen the worker's green card, passport, or other documents), and keeping the form on hand for at least three years. You cannot knowingly hire aliens ineligible to work, and there is no exclusion in the law just because you hire household employees. Once you hire a nanny or other household employee, you must apply for an employer identification number with the IRS, pay state unemployment taxes, pay state workers' compensation taxes and/or disability insurance, and withhold state income taxes.

Depending on the facts of each case, if the worker is an independent contractor, you may not be required to comply with the tax-related filing requirements mentioned above. Speak to an accountant or professional adviser to learn the facts and avoid violating the law with respect to hiring aliens and others who provide household help.

INCOME TAX   *See Tax Audits*

INDEPENDENT CONTRACTORS
Also see: Employment; Taxes

There is no precise legal definition of an independent contractor. Each state has its own laws to determine whether an individual is an employee or an independent contractor. According to the IRS, employees follow instructions about when, where, and how work is to be performed; contractors establish their own hours and have no instructions regarding how the job should be completed. Most employees may quit or be discharged at any time while independent contractors are typically discharged or may leave only after a job is completed to avoid breach of contract liability. Rather than receiving pay in regular amounts at stated intervals, contractors are typically paid in a lump sum on the completion of a job or project, or by some other arrangement, such as on a commission basis. Also, employees typically work for one "boss" while independent contractors may work for several persons or firms simultaneously.

When you hire an architect, home contractor, or electrician to do extensive work (in your home, for example), there are significant legal and tax benefits to treating these individuals as independent contractors rather than employees. Independent contractors are generally not treated as agents, which means that you cannot be deemed responsible to third parties for an independent contractor's promises or actions even while he is working for you. If the independent contractor injures someone while working for you, you may not be legally responsible for his negligence, as you may be for an employee. (Note: You can still be directly responsible if the contractor is injured on your property in the course of his work. Also, if the contractor was hired to transport something dangerous, like toxic chemicals, the law can make you strictly liable for the independent contractor's acts.)

By hiring an independent contractor, you are not required to withhold or collect income or employment taxes, such as Federal Unemployment Tax (FUTA), Federal Insurance Contributions Tax (FICA), and various state and local taxes. Likewise, if you are an independent contractor, no taxes can be withheld from your pay, but you must file state and federal tax returns on which you report your gross income and business-related expenses. And if an independent contractor is injured while working, he is entitled to sue the person or entity causing the injury in court instead of being forced to collect smaller damages under state workers' compensation laws.

The most significant factor that enters into a legal decision of whether an individual is an employee or an independent contractor is the degree of control and supervision asserted by the person doing the hiring. When few instructions and little training are given and when the worker is hired to achieve a certain result (like being paid a flat fee to paint a house rather than being paid by the hour), it is more likely that the worker will be deemed to be an independent contractor. The same is true when an individual or a company does not work full-time or only for you, supplies the tools and materials, and carries indemnity and liability insurance. (The summary of rules on page 189 provides guidance in determining employee versus independent contractor status.)

When hiring any independent contractor, request a written agreement that states that, in the event of a tax audit, the individual or company being hired will indemnify and hold you harmless (i.e., reimburse you for any losses, expenses, and attorney fees incurred) from an adverse ruling that the contractor was actually an employee for tax purposes. The agreement should also state that you will not be liable for any acts or statements made by the independent contractor (or his workers) and that the contractor carries sufficient liability insurance to protect you and others from any damage or injuries arising while the work is being performed.

As with any arrangement, the nature of the work being performed, the cost of the job, the time period in which the job will be completed, and a schedule of progress payments should always be negotiated and included in any agreement. (See the sample consulting or independent contractor agreement on pages 190–191.) If time to complete the job is important, be sure the agreement includes a "time is of the essence" clause. Include a penalty if the job is not completed on time—for example, a 20 percent reduction of the contract price. Be sure the contract includes all the terms, duties, responsibilities, and conditions you discussed with the contractor. Under the doctrine referred to as the statute of frauds, the law presumes that all discussions and oral agreements are incorporated into a written document; in most cases, judges will not hear testimony about what was agreed to orally when there is a written contract.

When dealing with a home-improvement contractor, specify that the contractor must procure all permits required by law, such as certificates of

FORM 93. **Summary of Rules to Determine Employee vs. Independent Contractor Status**

1. Instructions. Employees generally follow instructions about when, where, and how work is to be performed; contractors establish their own hours and have no instructions regarding how the job should be completed.
2. Training. Employees typically receive training via classes and meetings regarding how services are to be performed; contractors generally establish their own procedures and receive no training.
3. Services rendered personally. Services are typically performed personally by the employee; contractors may utilize others to perform job tasks and duties.
4. Supervision. Most employees are supervised by a foreman or representative of the employer; contractors generally are not.
5. Set hours of work. An employee's hours and days are set by the employer; contractors dictate their own time and are often retained to complete one particular job.
6. Full time required. An employee typically works for only one employer; contractors may have several jobs or work for others at the same time.
7. Work on premises. Employees work on the premises of an employer or on a route or site designated by the employer; contractors typically work from their own premises and pay rent for their own premises.
8. Manner of payment. Employees are generally paid in regular amounts at stated intervals; contractors are paid upon the completion of the job or project, in a lump sum or other arrangement, such as on a commission basis.
9. Furnishing of tools and materials. Employees are usually furnished tools and materials by employers; contractors typically furnish and pay for their own tools, materials, and expenses.
10. Profit. Employees generally receive no direct profit or loss from work performed, while contractors do.
11. Job security. Employees may be discharged or quit at any time without incurring liability; contractors are typically discharged after a job is completed and are legally obligated to complete a particular job to avoid liability.

▷ *Author's note:* Many of these rules are followed by the IRS when determining employee or independent contractor status. Speak to an accountant or other professional for more advice where applicable.

insurance for workers' compensation, public liability, and property damage. Insist on having copies of these permits forty-eight hours before work begins. The contract should also state that your deposit will be returned in full immediately if copies of these documents are not received. The contract should also have a cancellation ("right of rescission") notice. Such a notice will let you back out of a deal with any independent contractor within a specified number of days. The Contract for Home Maintenance or Extensive Repairs on pages 395–396 in the Appendix illustrates these points.

FORM 94. Sample Consulting or Independent Contractor Agreement

This Consulting Agreement (the "Agreement") is entered into this (specify date) by and between (specify parties; "Consultant" and "Company").

WHEREAS, the Company is in need of assistance in (specify area); and

WHEREAS, Consultant has agreed to perform consulting work for the Company;

NOW, THEREFORE, the parties hereby agree as follows:

1. Consultant's Services. Consultant shall be available and shall provide the following efforts (specify) as requested.

2. Consideration. The Company will pay Consultant (specify payment such as at an hourly rate, flat fee, or a commission). If for an hourly rate, then state: Consultant will submit written, signed reports of the time spent performing consulting services, itemizing in reasonable detail the dates on which services were performed, the number of hours spent on such dates, and a brief description of the services rendered. The Company will receive such reports no less than once a month and the total amount of work will not exceed (specify $). The Company shall pay Consultant the amounts due within (specify) days after such reports are received.

3. Expenses. Additionally, the Company will pay Consultant for the following expenses incurred while this Agreement exists: (specify, such as all travel expenses to and from work sites, meals, lodging, and related expenses). The Consultant shall submit written documentation and receipts itemizing the dates on which such expenses were incurred and the Company will pay for such expenses by separate check no later than (specify) days after receipt of same.

4. Independent Contractor. Nothing herein shall be construed to create an employer-employee relationship between the parties. The consideration set forth above shall be the sole payment due for services rendered. It is understood that the Company will not withhold any amounts for payment of taxes from the compensation of Consultant and that Consultant will be solely responsible to pay all applicable taxes from said payments, including payments owed to its employees and subagents.

5. Consultant's Warranties. The taxpayer I.D. number of the Consultant is (specify). The Consultant is licensed to perform the agreed-upon services enumerated herein and covenants that it maintains all valid licenses, permits, and registrations to perform same and on behalf of its employees and subagents.

6. Insurance. The Consultant will carry general liability, automobile liability, workers' compensation, and employer's liability insurance in the amount of (specify). In the event the Consultant fails to carry such insurance, or such insurance coverage lapses while this Agreement is in effect, it shall indemnify and hold harmless Company, its agents and employees, from and against any such damages, claims, and expenses arising out of or resulting from work conducted by Consultant and its agents or employees.

7. Competent work. All work will be done in a competent fashion in accordance with applicable standards of the profession and all services are subject to final approval by (specify) prior to the Company's payment.

8. Representations and Warranties. The Consultant will make no representations, warranties, or commitments binding the Company without the Company's prior written consent.

9. Confidentiality. In the course of performing services, the parties recognize that Consultant may come in contact with or become familiar with information which the Company or its affiliates or subsidiaries may consider confidential. This information may include, but is not limited to, information pertaining to (specify), which may be of value to a competitor. Consultant agrees to keep all such information confidential and not to discuss or divulge any of it to anyone other than appropriate Company personnel or their designees.

10. Term. This Agreement shall commence on (specify date) and shall terminate on (specify date), unless earlier terminated for any reason by either party hereto upon Thirty (30) days prior written notice.

11. Notice. Any notice or communication permitted or required by this Agreement shall be deemed effective when personally delivered or deposited, postage prepaid, by first-class regular mail, addressed to the other party's last known business address.

12. Entire Agreement. This Agreement constitutes the entire agreement of the parties with regard to the subject matter hereof, and replaces and supersedes all other agreements or understandings, whether written or oral. No amendment, extension, or change of the Agreement shall be binding unless in writing and signed by both parties.

13. Binding Effect. This Agreement shall be binding upon and shall inure to the benefit of Consultant and Company and to the Company's successors and assigns. Nothing in this Agreement shall be construed to permit the assignment by Consultant of any of its rights or obligations hereunder to any third party without the Company's prior written consent.

14. Ownership. All ideas, plans, improvements, or inventions developed by Consultant during the term of this Agreement shall belong to (specify).

15. Governing law. This Agreement shall be governed by the laws of the state of (specify). The invalidity or unenforceability of any provision of the Agreement shall not affect the validity or enforceability of any other provision.

WHEREFORE, the parties have executed this Agreement as of the date first written above.

By _____
   "Consultant"

Company
By _____
   Name and Title

▷ *Author's note:* If you are hiring a consultant or independent contractor, modify this Agreement where applicable with the assistance and guidance of a professional adviser and amend any reference of the "Company" to yourself.)

FORM 95. **Sample Letter of Protest to Contractor**

Your Name
Address
Telephone Number
Date

Name of Contractor
Address

Dear (Name),

I hereby make a formal demand for you to cure the breach of our written agreement dated (specify).

Our contract specifically states that "time is of the essence" and that you will finish the job (state what was agreed to) by (date).

You are now ten (10) days late under the contract. Therefore, I demand (indicate what you want the contractor to do to remedy the situation, such as complete work immediately, or reduce the final purchase price).

Unless I hear from you immediately and the matter is resolved satisfactorily, I shall refrain from making any further payments, contact my attorney, and file a formal complaint with the Department of Consumer Affairs.

Thank you for your anticipated cooperation in this matter.

Very truly yours,
(your name)

(Optional) P.S. I am sending a copy of this letter to the Complaint Division of the Department of Consumer Affairs to remain on file.

▷ Send certified mail, return receipt requested.
▷ *Author's note:* Many contractors are anxious to receive the final payment and will attempt to accommodate you if your demands are not unreasonable. Sending a letter may help. Additional strategies: Always agree to make the final substantial payment when the job is completed. Never agree to changes in the original contract unless the changes are agreed to in writing and initialed by both parties. This is for your protection.

Deal only with a licensed building contractor and make sure you understand everything in the contract before you sign. Speak to an accountant, attorney, or other professional for advice if applicable. Always send a letter of protest (like the one above) if the contractor is not honoring the terms of your written agreement. File a written complaint (like the one on page 193) with the Department of Consumer Affairs or other appropriate agency if you do not receive satisfaction.

Sample Complaint Letter

Your Name
Address
Telephone Number
Date

Director
Regional Office, Complaint Division
Department of Consumer Affairs
Address

Re: Request for Commencement of Investigation Against (Name of Contractor)

Dear (Name),

I hereby request you to commence a formal investigation of (name of contractor), located at (address), license # (specify).

On date, I signed a written contract with (name of contractor) to receive (specify work to be performed, where, at what price, etc.). After the job was supposedly completed (state what happened, what you observed). I immediately contacted the contractor several times by telephone and letter and requested he complete the job in the manner specified in our contract. On (date), I spoke with (name) and (state what was said). On (date) I wrote a final demand letter to the contractor. To date, all of my requests have been ignored.

I enclose a copy of the contract, color photographs showing the condition of the premises as they presently exist, and additional correspondence, including a formal demand letter which I sent by certified mail, return receipt requested, which although received, went unanswered.

It is my understanding that your agency has the authority to investigate and schedule a hearing. I would appreciate that this be done as quickly as possible because (state the reason). I am available at (give your telephone number) during business hours to assist you at your convenience. Kindly notify me of all developments and thank you for your cooperation and courtesies.

Very truly yours,
(your name)

P.S. I am demanding (state how you have been damaged and what you wish to recover).

cc: copy sent certified mail to contractor

▷ Send certified mail, return receipt requested.
▷ *Author's note:* Wait a few days after sending the letter, then follow it up by calling the agency. If you do not receive appropriate action, consult a lawyer to determine your legal rights and options.

INHERITANCE RIGHTS *See Probate; Trusts; Wills*

INJUNCTION *See Litigation*

INJURIES *See Accidents; Negligence*

INSURANCE *Also see: Accidents; Contracts*

Some of the more common forms of insurance are accident, automobile, disability and health, homeowner's, liability, life, property, and unemployment. For a sum of money paid up front and/or on a regular basis (a premium), an insurance company (the insurer) issues a contract, called a policy, that provides benefits and/or reimbursement to the insured (the person or entity purchasing the policy) in the event of a loss or happening generally causing economic loss. Legal problems commonly occur when people do not understand the coverage they are receiving, fail to correctly understand clauses in their insurance contracts, and have trouble collecting insurance proceeds from their carrier after filing a claim.

BEFORE BUYING INSURANCE

As with most contracts, ambiguities in insurance agreements are supposed to be interpreted against the insurance company because it is the contract drafter. However, since virtually all insurance contracts and applications are complicated documents, it is important to read them carefully before signing. Be aware of exclusion clauses that limit the insurance company's obligation to pay. These sometimes appear in bold type but may be difficult to understand. It is essential to know what coverage you will not be receiving before you buy an insurance policy. Exclusions are often stated in the fine print. Ask the insurance agent (the person who, acting on behalf of the company, sells you the policy) for a thorough explanation of all confusing or ambiguous clauses. If you are not satisfied with the answers, consult an attorney or an independent broker for clarification and advice.

Complete the application truthfully. Insurance companies often attempt to deny reimbursement for a loss on the basis that prior conditions or problems existed but were not revealed. This is called a material misrepresentation or an omission. Not all misrepresentations will deprive the insured of benefits, because erroneous answers are sometimes provided by applicants who are confused by the questions or who forget to include important facts. For a company to be able to void the policy, it generally must be able to prove that the misrepresentation was willful (i.e., fraudulent) and/or significant. This is decided first by an insurance adjuster and, if the matter is not resolved, by a judge according to the unique facts of each case. If a company was aware of the misrepresentation but continued to accept and cash the premiums anyway, it may not be able legally to refuse to pay benefits.

Insurance policies can be canceled by either party, so it is important to pay premiums on time. Most policies prescribe the time and method for paying premiums as well as what constitutes a late payment. They also contain grace periods to allow for late payments and prevent a lapse of coverage. If a payment is made beyond the outside allowable date, the insurance company may be able to deny a claim or cancel your policy upon giving required notice, usually in writing.

The policy may also not be enforceable if there is no insurable relationship between the purchaser and the insured or if certain acts are illegal (e.g., filing a false claim). Most policies do not allow the owner to change the beneficiary without prior written notification (and sometimes consent) of the insurance company.

WHILE THE POLICY IS IN EFFECT

For homeowner's and property insurance policies, maintain a complete inventory of all belongings insured and keep a separate copy outside your home. Have a video or pictures taken of special items (e.g., jewelry) and save all sales receipts when purchasing expensive items to prove the existence and value of covered property. Save all repair bills, receipts, proof of payment, and pertinent documents. Maintain complete records of repair and replacement costs, medical bills, and so forth. Pay by check; the canceled check will serve as proof of payment. Review all insurance policies regularly if gaps exist because of changed circumstances, such as increasing coverage limits if your house has increased in value. Contact your insurance agent (or the company directly if you didn't buy the policy through an agent) or an independent broker to get answers to your questions about the application of any policy.

Perform all duties specified in the policy to eliminate an insurance company's defense. For example, if you are required to maintain your boat, house, or other property in proper working condition or obtain annual medical checkups, do so to avoid breaching the contract.

FILING A CLAIM

Never file false claims or exaggerate your loss. Such acts may provide a basis for the insurance company to refuse to pay the claim. Even worse, it may expose you to criminal liability. Most insurance policies have a time limitation by when you must report a claim to the carrier or lose the coverage for that claim, so talk to an insurance agent or adjuster as soon as possible. Follow up the phone call with a letter to prove that a claim was filed. Contact all companies having any possible connection to your case.

File a police report immediately in the event of an accident, theft, or break-in; the report will be proof of your loss when filing an insurance claim. Take photographs of damaged property before and after it is repaired or of recent injuries when filing accident and disability claims.

Contact your insurance company immediately in writing if you have difficulty collecting on your claim. Draft the letter carefully since it may be used as evidence of the insurance company's lack of diligence in handling your claim. Consider having a lawyer analyze your claim and represent you if you are claiming a large amount of money and not receiving satisfaction. Insurance companies frequently err in their analysis of written policies and their duty to pay the customer for a loss covered under a policy. The law requires them to act in good faith, and a willful denial of a legitimate claim or other misconduct may leave the insurer liable for punitive damages.

Your lawyer may consider filing a lawsuit based on breach of contract or negligence. You may also file a grievance with your state's insurance department. Most state insurance departments investigate complaints against insurance companies, brokers (generally, independent contractors who procure insurance on behalf of an insured but who have no power to bind the insurance company as an agent does), agents, adjusters (people who investigate and settle claims on behalf of an insurance company), and public adjusters (people who typically represent an insured against the insurance company), and many attempt to mediate disputes regarding premiums, coverage, and renewals. When amicable attempts to resolve matters fail, these agencies can commence formal investigations and hearings on a consumer's behalf, particularly when a certain aspect of an insurance company's conduct has affected many consumers (a class action).

Never automatically accept an unfavorable insurance company decision if you believe that the denial or settlement offer is unfair. For example, do not cash a check for reimbursement if the amount of the check seems inadequate because acceptance may constitute a settlement of the claim in full. Speak to a competent attorney to get an explanation of your options and to protect your rights.

INTESTACY LAWS *See Wills*

INVASION OF PRIVACY *See Privacy*

INVENTIONS AND PATENTS
Also see: Copyright; Trademarks

An invention is a new and useful process or machine. The rights of the creator of the invention are protected by a patent. A patent is an agreement between the federal government and an inventor that gives the inventor (and his heirs or assigns) or holder of the patent the exclusive right to use, manufacture, and sell the device to the public for a fixed period of time (usually seventeen years) after disclosing the invention to the public. The U.S. Patent and Trademark Office maintains a list of prior patents to determine whether a proposed patent is similar to or conflicts with a previously issued or pending patent.

To be patentable, an invention must primarily be original. An idea behind a new product, machine, manufacturing process, or design must be new or a significant and innovative improvement to an existing product, machine, process, or design. The Patent Office will reject an application for an invention that is similar to one with a patent already on file. Also, an idea that does not have value or cannot be implemented cannot be patented.

Patents (as well as copyrights, trademarks, and trade names) are considered a form of intellectual property. Patents are classified into several categories depending on the type of idea or thing invented. Separate patents exist for a process, a machine, a design, or an improvement on an existing patent, among other categories. Only qualified individuals, including patent attorneys or patent agents (nonlawyers), are permitted to submit and argue patent applications before the Patent Office, and such individuals must pass a specialized technical examination before being allowed to do so.

Patents typically cannot be renewed. Once the period of the patent expires, it enters the public domain, where anyone can use or sell it without paying compensation to the patent holder (usually the inventor). However, it is possible to alter or add to unpatented or lapsed works and create a new, patented invention.

The usual procedure for obtaining a patent begins with submission of the invention to a patent attorney, who may conduct a preliminary search to determine if the invention is unique and original. If it is, the attorney will draft and submit a patent application, including a description and sketch of the invention. Once the application and fee (at present about $600) are received at the Patent Office in Washington, D.C., an examiner will review the application for originality. If the invention has been described in any printed publication or was in public use or offered for sale anywhere in the U.S. for more than one year prior to the time an application is filed, a patent will not be issued. If a patent application is rejected, the attorney can appeal the decision first to a Patent Office appeals board and then in court if necessary.

It can take several years to obtain a patent once the application is filed. During this period, many inventors attempt to protect their creation and inform others that a patent has been filed by placing the phrase "patent pending" on the product or in advertising. Once a patent is issued, it must then be assigned and recorded so others cannot use the invention without paying compensation (typically royalties) in the form of a license. If a person or company wrongfully manufactures or sells a patented article or makes unauthorized use of a patented invention, that party is guilty of infringement. Often the patent owner will ask a court to issue an injunction prohibiting the unauthorized use of the patent and/or sue for damages equal to lost profits or the gross revenue obtained by the infringer. Such lawsuits are typically lengthy and very expensive. For example, it took the inventor of a windshield wiper mechanism more than a decade and millions of dollars in legal fees and costs to settle out of court with a few major automobile companies and win tens of millions of dollars in royalties against other car companies after a trial and appeals process.

If you create an idea or invention on company time, your employer may own the rights to your invention. Most inventions and processes developed on the job are called work for hire. A work for hire is defined as a work prepared by an employee within the scope of his employment or work specifically ordered by the employer. When an employee is requested to develop a new product, process, or machine, is provided with the means and opportunity to resolve the problem or achieve the result, and is paid for that work, then the employer is generally entitled to the fruits of the employee's labors. Often the employee has already signed an agreement stating that all inventions created on the job belong to the employer and that the employee agrees not to disclose or use such inventions without the employer's consent. Also, an idea is presumed to be a work for hire if it is offered voluntarily without entering into a formal compensation agreement.

If you were not hired to invent or solve a particular problem, you may have a claim to the rights of your invention depending on the facts of the case. Under a legal theory called the shop right concept, when an employee makes an invention or discovery that is outside his employment but utilizes the employer's resources (e.g., equipment, materials, and facilities), that invention may be owned and patented by the employee subject to a shop right on the part of the employer. This shop right can, in certain instances, give the employer a nonexclusive irrevocable license to use the invention for a lengthy period without having to pay a royalty.

HOW TO REDUCE THE POSSIBILITY OF EXPLOITATION

Many inventors give away valuable ideas without understanding their rights. The following strategies can reduce the possibility of exploitation.

1. **Articulate your idea, method, or process in writing.** It is difficult to prove that you are the creator of a valuable idea unless it is set down on paper.

2. **Be sure the writing is detailed and specific to increase the chances of proving that the idea is a protectable property interest.**

3. **Avoid volunteering ideas if the entity receiving the idea is under no obligation to pay anything if it is used.** Prepare an "acknowledgment of receipt of idea" (similar to the one on page 199), which will prove that you conveyed the idea with the expectation of receiving compensation.

4. **Talk to a patent lawyer if you have an idea you plan to pursue.** By conducting a preliminary search early on, you can avoid expending a significant amount of effort and expense before learning that a proposed invention is already patented by someone else.

FORM 98. **Sample Acknowledgment of Receipt of Idea**

On this day, I have received from (person or employee's name) an idea concerning (specify), which was presented in the form of (specify).

I (or the company) acknowledge that the idea is creative and original and has not been used in the past by me (us). If used, (person's or employee's name), will be compensated according to the following (specify).

I (or the company) agree to maintain the confidentiality of the material submitted to us by (name of person or employee) and agree not to disclose it, or the ideas on which it is based, to any person, firm, or entity without (name of person or employee's) consent.

Dated:

Name of Person or Employer By:_____

Name of Person or Employee Who Submitted Idea

▷ *Author's note:* If compensation is difficult to determine at the time the acknowledgment is prepared, it can state that the person or employee will be compensated in a manner mutually agreed upon by the parties and that the idea will remain the property of that person or employee until such formula is determined.

5. **Take the correct steps to protect the patent.** Some people try to save money by placing a "patent pending" symbol on an invention when discussing it with investors before filing a formal patent application with the Patent Office. Such a move will not help if no patent is pending and may expose you to criminal penalties. It is unlawful to state that any invention has a pending patent unless an application has been filed with the U. S. Patent and Trademark Office.

6. **Be cautious when choosing a company that offers assistance in developing your inventions.** Check out all companies with the Better Business Bureau and ask for references. Most important, never sign an agreement that allows any company to market your ideas without first having the contract reviewed by a patent attorney.

7. **Avoid signing any agreement or contract with work for hire provisions.** Some companies request job applicants and employees to sign agreements and releases that state that all inventions authored or conceived by the employee belong to the employer. The Work for Hire/Invention Agreement on page 397 in the Appendix illustrates this practice. Avoid signing such an agreement whenever possible.

8. **Negotiate a predetermined method of compensation and have the understanding acknowledged by your employer.** If you must sign the kind of agreement discussed in #7 above, or if you are submitting an idea to someone for consideration, ask for a letter (called an "acknowledgment of receipt of

idea"), or prepare one yourself, stating the kind and amount of compensation you will receive if the invention is used. The acknowledgment letter should also include an agreement not to disclose, assign, or transfer the idea or its value to anyone else without your consent.

9. **Get a receipt. If you are unable to obtain a signed acknowledgment, you must be able to prove delivery of a valuable idea to another to protect your rights.** For example, it is often wise to send a certified letter stating that your idea was submitted in confidence with the expectation of payment for its use.

10. **Make copies.** Keep copies of all material and letters that you send to others. Some people even prepare duplicates of all documents and mail them in one package to themselves. The postmark date on the front of the unopened package or envelope may establish the time sequence (when the package was sent) and that you were the sender of the package in the event of a dispute.

JOB APPLICANTS *See Employment*

JOINT CUSTODY *See Child Custody*

JUDGMENT BY DEFAULT *See Litigation*

JURY *See Crimes and Criminal Law; Litigation*

JUVENILE CRIMINAL CASES
See Crimes and Criminal Law

KIDNAPPING *See Child Abduction; Crimes and Criminal Law*

LAWSUITS *See Litigation*

LAWYERS *See Attorneys*

LEASES *See Contracts*

LEGAL SYSTEM *See Courts; Crimes and Criminal Law; Litigation*

LEMON LAWS *See Automobiles*

LIMITED LIABILITY COMPANIES *See Corporations*

LIMITED PARTNERSHIPS *See Partnerships*

LITIGATION

Also see: Attorneys; Courts; Crimes and Criminal Law; Evidence

Millions of civil lawsuits are filed in state and federal courts annually. The most common lawsuits are matrimonial (divorce) cases and related actions, including custody, paternity, and support matters filed in each state's family court, located in the plaintiff's county of residence. Lawsuits arising out of employment matters, including discrimination and breach of contract actions (to collect wages, commissions, and vacation pay) are brought in a state or federal court, depending on the facts. Lawsuits seeking damages due to an accident or other form of negligence are typically brought in state court, as are workers' compensation claims, business litigation, and consumer-related actions.

To avoid having a lawsuit initially dismissed, the party commencing the lawsuit (called the plaintiff) must have proper subject-matter and personal jurisdiction. Having subject-matter jurisdiction means filing the action in the appropriate court. For example, a bankruptcy action must be filed in a federal bankruptcy (district) court; a child custody case cannot be filed in a small-claims court. Speak to a lawyer or other adviser to be sure you are filing your case in the proper court before starting a lawsuit.

It is also necessary to demonstrate personal jurisdiction. Typically, if the person or business being sued (called the defendant) lives or works in the state where the action is filed, or has close ties with that state (e.g., ships goods into or travels to that state to conduct business), a judge may determine that personal jurisdiction exists. It is also necessary to select the correct venue (the proper county) where the lawsuit should be filed. For example, in a personal injury lawsuit, the proper venue may be the county where the accident occurred or where the plaintiff or defendant resides. Since venue laws vary from state to state, it is advisable to speak to an attorney to avoid having the case thrown out of court. Also, ask your attorney about the advantages and disadvantages of commencing the lawsuit in either state or federal court, where applicable. Some experts believe that federal court judges are generally more highly regarded for their legal skills than state judges. Litigants are often able to obtain a trial quicker in federal court than in state court. Conversely, if you are the person being sued (the defendant), it may be advantageous to try to keep the case in a state court to "slow down" its progress.

Ask your lawyer whether your case has merit. For example, does the defendant have a strong defense? Will you be able to prove your case? Will the defendant be interested in settling the matter before protracted and expensive litigation begins? Carefully examine the strengths and weaknesses of your case before proceeding. Analyze whether the defendant has sufficient assets (e.g., money in the bank or property). After going through the lengthy and expensive legal process (if the matter is not settled out of court), you don't want to win your case but then be unable to collect the award. An investigative company can, for a fee, advise you about the defendant's assets. Your lawyer can tell you how to contact such a company. You may also find them listed in the yellow pages.

A civil lawsuit must be commenced (i.e., filed) within a certain period of time after the dispute or accident occurred to avoid dismissal on the basis of being untimely (called the statute of limitations). Each state and federal court has its own rules concerning the maximum amount of time you can wait before a lawsuit must be filed, and it is crucial to know how much time you have before contemplating litigation. If you want to join others in one suit (called a class action), it is necessary to contact the law firm representing the class within the required period of time to be able to be included in the lawsuit.

A lawsuit is started when a plaintiff prepares a summons and complaint. A summons is a single piece of paper, typically accompanied by a complaint, which, when served on the defendant, notifies him or her of a lawsuit. The complaint is the legal document that starts the lawsuit. It alleges pertinent facts and legal causes of action that the plaintiff will rely on in his or her attempt to collect damages. For a lawsuit to proceed, the summons and complaint must be served on the defendant either in person (usually with the help of a process server or sheriff) or by certified mail, return receipt requested, in states that permit mail service. If the defendant is not notified of the existence of the lawsuit (i.e., is not served or served improperly such as by slipping the documents under the wrong apartment door) or if the complaint is not drafted accurately and fails to state a legally recognized cause of action, the case may eventually be dismissed.

Once the summons and complaint have been served on the defendant, they must be filed with the proper court together with the payment of the initial filing fee (which can be as much as $250 in some states). Filing these documents is rather easy. At the courthouse, a clerk accepts the fee and documents, stamps the papers to indicate the date and time received, and issues a receipt. The documents then become part of a file that is stored at the court. The file is given to the presiding judge of the case when appropriate (e.g., during oral arguments before trial and at the trial). Usually, a judge is randomly assigned to preside over every filed case. The judge will rule on various pretrial motions, move the case along to the trial, conduct the trial, and render a judgment based on the evidence when a jury is not involved.

After being served with the summons and complaint, the defendant has a period of time (usually no more than thirty days) to submit an answer. The answer is the defendant's reply to the plaintiff's charges in a civil lawsuit. Properly drafted answers typically deny most of the plaintiff's charges, list a number of legal reasons called affirmative defenses why the case should not proceed, and may or may not contain a counterclaim. A counterclaim is a claim asserted by the defendant in a lawsuit. Sometimes the plaintiff loses his or her case and the defendant wins the case through his or her counterclaim. Each case is decided by its unique facts. The fact that someone is the plaintiff only means that he or she filed the lawsuit first; it does not guarantee success of the matter in any way. However, if the defendant fails to respond to the lawsuit by filing an answer, he or she may lose the case by default. Always consult an attorney after receiving a complaint to ensure that you file a timely answer.

Sometimes the plaintiff is interested not only in obtaining damages, but also in seeking to stop the defendant from doing something (e.g., establishing a competing business or working for a competitor). An action called a preliminary injunction will be commenced, and the moving party will request a hearing immediately after the lawsuit is filed. A request for an immediate hearing is often called an order to show cause. Sometimes, a party is stopped from doing anything by a judge's order (called a temporary restraining order) pending the hearing. If a judge rules in favor of the plaintiff, the injunction will be granted. If a judge rules in favor of the defendant, the injunction will be denied, but depending on the circumstances and the question of damages, the case may be allowed to proceed like any other lawsuit.

After the answer is received from the defendant, the discovery phase of the case begins. Several pretrial devices, including interrogatories, depositions, and motions, are used by lawyers to elicit information from the opposing side, gather evidence, and prepare for the trial. The discovery phase can last several years in a complicated case and be very expensive in terms of attorney fees and the costs of taking depositions, procuring documents, and paying for postage and related expenses.

Interrogatories are written questions sent to an opponent to be answered under oath. One problem with interrogatories is that the opposing party's attorney may draft the responses to prevent, insofar as possible, any damaging statements from being conveyed. Depositions often lasting several days are taken by both sides. A deposition is a pretrial proceeding in which a witness is questioned under oath by a lawyer. A stenographer is present to record all statements and preserve the testimony. Depositions are used to collect information and facts about the case, narrow the issues to be proven at trial, and discredit (impeach) the testimony of witnesses. It is essential that lawyers properly prepare and advise their witnesses before their depositions are taken. Many cases have been lost due to unprepared responses elicited from a witness at a deposition. If a witness's testimony at the trial is materially different (inconsistent) from statements the witness gave at the deposition, his or her credibility may be seriously undermined; if the witness gives a totally different statement about something at the trial, that side's chances of winning the case can be dramatically reduced. Also, incorrect answers at the deposition may give the opposing attorney grounds to file a motion for summary judgment to dismiss the case in its entirety or throw out certain causes of action. A motion to dismiss, sometimes called a demurrer, states that even if the plaintiff's allegations are true and there is no genuine issue as to important facts, no legal basis exists for finding the defendant liable.

Sometimes attorneys file motions to get a ruling on admissibility of evidence (called a request for admission) or ask the court to assist in obtaining documents and records that have not been turned over by the other side although promised. These motions may delay the progress of the case until a judge renders a decision (i.e., denies or grants the motion).

Once the discovery phase of the case is completed, the judge will order a pretrial conference. Both attorneys are asked to appear to discuss the case and the possibility of settlement. Some judges make quite active attempts to settle cases at these conferences. If the conference is successful and the case is settled, the parties will prepare a written stipulation of settlement that describes the terms of the settlement. Typically, the judge will review and approve all settlements before they are implemented.

If you are a litigant, think carefully before accepting or rejecting any settlement. Most civil actions take up to five years to be tried. By accepting a fair settlement early on, you'll be able to invest the settlement money to earn more money. You may also eliminate large legal fees, court costs, and the possibility of eventually losing the case after a trial. However, if you have a good case, it may pay to wait before discussing and accepting a settlement, especially in personal injury lawsuits. Most trial attorneys believe that large settlements are obtained for their clients by waiting until the case reaches the courthouse steps. In personal injury cases, it sometimes appears that insurance companies do not negotiate in earnest until the moment before a case is to be tried. Time is on the side of defendants and their insurance carriers. It often benefits them to wait and see if the case is valid (i.e., that it is properly prepared, that strong testimony from witnesses is available, and that the evidence will prove the claim). In large cases, insurance companies continue to make money on settlement funds by keeping them invested until the very last minute.

The decision on whether to accept a settlement should always be made jointly with your attorney. The attorney knows the merits, pitfalls, and true value of the case better than you do. However, do not allow your attorney to pressure you into accepting a smaller settlement than you think you deserve. Some attorneys seek smaller immediate settlements out of laziness, and the settlement represents money in the bank to them.

Instruct your attorney to provide you with a detailed explanation of the pros and cons of settling your case and say that you prefer to make the final decision to settle or not to settle. Do not let your attorney push you around. Your attorney cannot settle the case without your approval. If he does, he can be sued for malpractice. If you are not satisfied with your lawyer's advice or conduct, consult another attorney for a second opinion before settling the matter. Do this before taking action, because once you sign the settlement papers you may not be able to change your mind and continue with the case, since releases contained in such documents prohibit you from doing so.

If the case cannot be settled, the judge will discuss with both attorneys how the case will proceed. For example, the identity and order of witnesses and exhibits to be submitted at the trial will be agreed to before the trial begins. In some types of lawsuits (but not divorce actions, for example), either party can request that a jury decide the case rather than a judge. A jury trial usually involves twelve people, although some states allow as few as six. In criminal cases, the jury's decision must be unanimous. Some states permit a civil jury's decision to be less than unanimous.

If a jury has been requested by either party, the first step of the trial is jury selection. Prospective jurors are questioned (the voir dire) to see if they are qualified to sit on the panel. Lawyers seek answers to certain questions in an attempt to learn if a person has an open mind and is not biased. After attorneys for both sides dismiss certain people and retain others, the jury is picked and the trial begins.

The plaintiff's lawyer begins the trial with an opening statement. This is a speech designed to tell the judge or jury about the nature of the case, what the plaintiff intends to prove from the facts, and what kind of damages are sought.

Then the defendant's attorney gives an opening statement, after which the trial begins. Witnesses are called by the plaintiff and give direct testimony under oath. The opposing attorney has the right to requestion (cross-examine) each witness in turn. All other evidence, such as documents, exhibits, and the testimony of expert witnesses, is submitted.

After the plaintiff's case is completed, the defense presents its case. When both sides are finished, each attorney gives a summation. This is a review of the facts and testimony and other evidence. If no jury is involved, the judge will render a decision. Typically, both parties have to wait a period of time (up to thirty days) before receiving the judge's written decision.

If a jury is involved, the judge instructs its members as to what law is applicable to the facts and statements they have heard. The jury then leaves the courtroom and returns later with its determination. In rare cases, a judge may disregard the jury's findings and grant a motion for judgment notwithstanding the verdict when he believes there was insufficient evidence to support a jury's conclusion.

After the judgment is made, either party can appeal the decision by filing a written document called a brief. Often, the losing party must post a bond for the judgment amount if he or she wants the appeal to be processed. Interest on the award continues to accrue during the appeal. It is also important to take proper steps to collect the judgment if the losing party doesn't pay. This may involve placing a lien on real estate property owned by the losing party; attaching such property to prevent its transfer, assignment, or sale without your consent; or garnisheeing the person's wages and salary, among other remedies. Speak to your attorney for more information about how this can be accomplished.

Litigation is complicated, time-consuming, and subject to many hazards. Unless absolutely necessary, or if you have a small case that you can handle by yourself in small-claims court, *do not attempt to file papers and represent yourself in a lawsuit without an attorney.*

The following is a summary of key strategies to follow in any lawsuit, whether you are the plaintiff or the defendant.

1. Hire a lawyer skilled in conducting trials. Many attorneys do not litigate cases, which is a specialty.

2. Play an active role in all phases of the case. Request that your attorney routinely send you copies of all incoming and outgoing correspondence on a regular basis. This will help you monitor and question the progress of your case.

3. Never ignore a summons and complaint if you are served. Ignoring a summons and complaint can result in the imposition of a default judgment with huge damages, penalties, and interest assessed against you without your filing a defense. Speak to a lawyer immediately to protect your rights.

4. Never ignore a subpoena if you are summoned to court to appear as a witness. A subpoena is an order requiring your presence to testify. It differs from a summons, which is a document served on a defendant in a lawsuit notifying him or her of a pending lawsuit. If for some reason you cannot be present on the date specified, speak to the clerk of the court for advice and guidance. Ignoring a subpoena can result in a fine, imprisonment, or both. Speak to a lawyer about possible grounds to "quash" or void a subpoena.

5. Be prepared at all times. Competent attorneys work with their clients in anticipation of the upcoming deposition and trial. There should be no surprises in what you will testify to and what the opposing lawyer will ask you. Your lawyer should advise you how to react if you do not understand a question or do not want to answer.

6. Consider alternative methods to settle your dispute. These include arbitration and mediation (which are discussed in other sections of this book). Ask your lawyer to actively seek and encourage a settlement where warranted.

7. Determine if the opposing party has sufficient assets to pay a successful verdict before starting any action.

8. Assess the chances of winning or losing and how much a lawsuit will cost to commence or defend before getting in too deep.

(Note: For illustrative purposes, pages 398–416 in the Appendix contain a group of forms pertaining to litigation, including a lawyer's business litigation retainer agreement, which you should always request and review prior to hiring a lawyer when commencing an action or being defended in litigation. A sample verified complaint and verified answer in a sales commission case, and a stipulation extending the time to answer the complaint, are also provided. The request for interrogatories will give you a better understanding of the kinds of documents often requested by lawyers during litigation. Last come examples of documents often prepared when an action is settled and payment is due. These include a stipulation discontinuing an action, supported by an affidavit for judgment by confession, and examples of two different settlement agreements with releases.)

One final caution: Always defer to your lawyer's guidance in preparing any legal documents during litigation, and never use them without a lawyer's assistance, except as noted above.

LIVING TOGETHER   *Also see: Contracts; Marriage*

The vast majority of the millions of unmarried heterosexual and gay couples who live together are unaware of the legal and financial consequences of their status. Serious problems frequently arise on the death of one partner or when a couple decide to separate. Disputes typically concern disposition of the couple's residence (apartment, co-op, or house) and property purchased with joint funds. Statements such as "I'll support you for life" are sometimes viewed as legally binding promises enforceable in lawsuits. A variety of legal entanglements may ensue over the birth of a child to parties living out of wedlock.

GENERAL POINTS TO REMEMBER

Unlike marriage (which the law favors), the law does not automatically allow for the distribution of property acquired during cohabitation. The law treats marriage as a partnership or joint venture between parties; it does not accord such treatment to a nonmarried relationship that exists in the absence of a contract. A nonmarital partner has a legal right to his or her property acquired during the cohabitation. Personal assets purchased by one of the cohabitants belong to the individual with title or to the one who can prove ownership. For example, the person whose name is on the automobile registration and certificate of title typically is deemed to own the auto and is liable for paying the insurance.

Unlike a married partner, an unwed cohabitant is not automatically entitled by law to a share of a deceased partner's estate. If an individual wants to leave property to an unmarried cohabitant, it must be done by will. If there is no will (i.e., if the person dies intestate), the surviving unwed cohabitant will probably get nothing. In addition, in the absence of a contract or an agreement, nonmarital cohabitants are not entitled to future support or to a property settlement when the relationship ends. Compensation, such as alimony, is awarded only when a judge has evidence of a legal marriage. Thus partners who live together do so at their own risk. If you are not married, you get nothing when you split up except for property that is in your own name or was specifically designated by contract.

Most states do not have specific laws regarding cohabitation. This means that the ramifications of such a relationship remain subject solely to judicial decision. When the couple decide to separate or are not in agreement, a judge will interpret the rights and responsibilities of the parties and attempt to render an award that is fair and reasonable. Factors used in rendering a decision will include the presence or absence of a valid agreement (preferably written) between the parties, the duration and nature of the relationship, and the presence or absence of children.

Most judges will enforce the terms of an express contract between nonmarital partners, provided the contract is not explicitly founded on the furnishing of sexual services. Sexual services are not valid consideration for a contract, since most states, as a matter of public policy, have criminal statutes making prostitution illegal. Thus, for example, if a woman was promised that she would share in the proceeds of her lover's book if she slept with him on a continuous basis, such a promise might not be enforceable. However, if the woman was promised a half share in the proceeds of the book in return for her care of the author's sick mother, such an agreement might be upheld, provided it could be proved.

While a marriage certificate may be "just a piece of paper," it gives married couples superior rights over unmarried cohabitants. The advantages include inheritance rights, lower insurance rates, and injury and death benefits for the surviving spouse, including workers' compensation, social security, pension, and military benefits. Recently some states and localities have adopted laws allowing "significant others" to obtain succession rights to an apartment and certain health benefits and coverage even though the couple are not married. Check the law of your state to determine whether such benefits exist if applicable.

STRATEGIES TO PROTECT AND ENFORCE YOUR RIGHTS

1. **Get an express agreement.** The fact that unmarried cohabitants live together and engage in a sexual relationship does not invalidate agreements between them relating to their earnings, property, or expenses. Typically, such agreements fail because they cannot be proved, are ambiguous or uncertain, or are founded solely on the furnishing of sexual services by one of the parties. Express agreements, preferably written, that discuss the treatment of shared earnings, written trusts, partnership and joint ventures, and other matters of concern can be drafted. The Appendix contains three examples of such agreements (pages 417–422) that can be used when couples want to share assets jointly or keep property separate. Never draft such documents without a lawyer's assistance and review.

2. **Execute a written cohabitation contract whenever you enter a prolonged relationship.** A contract gives both parties legal control over the distribution of their finances and property and protects the parties if the relationship breaks up. In the event the couple must go to court to litigate a dispute, the focus of judicial inquiry will be on the contract rather than the couple's personal relationship. The contract can also contain an arbitration clause to protect the

couple's privacy, since arbitration is conducted behind closed doors. With a written contract, you lower the risk of the agreement not being proved or being thrown out due to a legal principle called the statute of frauds, which requires agreements concerning the disposition of real estate worth more than $500 to be in writing to be enforceable.

Cohabitation contracts can cover many issues, including:
- ▸ Disposition of estates and jointly accumulated property on termination of the living-together arrangement
- ▸ Agreements to furnish reasonable support and maintenance for a specified period of time after the parties separate or on the death of one of the cohabitants
- ▸ Title and interest to specified real estate, citing who is responsible for the mortgage, taxes, and insurance
- ▸ Agreements to keep property separate
- ▸ Agreements that all money transferred by one party to the other or on behalf of the other shall be treated as a loan to be repaid over a certain time and at a certain rate
- ▸ Agreements with respect to business ventures or enterprises commenced or operated by the parties
- ▸ Agreements to establish joint bank accounts or maintain separate accounts
- ▸ Agreements to specifically waive any claims for palimony or support from the other in the event of a termination of the living-together arrangement
- ▸ Agreements with respect to apartment leases and who gets the apartment in the event it goes co-op
- ▸ Statements that the parties agree not to hold themselves out as man and wife
- ▸ Agreements concerning regular finances, such as the treatment of credit cards and who will pay for the rent or mortgage. Are these expenses reimbursable? If so, to what extent and when?
- ▸ Agreements with respect to an acknowledgment of paternity and obligations of custody, support, and care for a child

The sample living together agreements on pages 210–211 incorporate many of these points.
Child support, custody, and visitation rights for children born during the cohabitation or for children from previous marriages currently living with an unmarried couple should be incorporated into the contract when appropriate, and the couple may want to define the extent of any obligations if a breakup occurs. However, each state has its own laws pertaining to what is in the best interest of the child. This means that provisions for child support in a cohabitation contract may be overruled if they conflict with state law.

FORM 110. **Sample Property and Support Agreement**

Date

Dear (name of cohabitant),

You and I have been living together since (specify date), and we intend to continue to do so.

In consideration of your (specify domestic, personal, or extraordinary business services and giving up your career as a _____, assisting me in my career and otherwise taking care of the household), I agree that you will be entitled to (specify, such as share equally in any and all property, real or personal, that I may acquire during the period of our living together), commencing (specify date), through earnings and accumulations acquired other than by inheritance. Such property will include all of our household goods but not (specify).

All real and personal property and accumulations from such property listed on Schedule A, attached hereto and incorporated in this Agreement by reference, shall remain my separate property forever. Likewise, all real and personal property and accumulations from such property listed on Schedule B, attached hereto and incorporated in this Agreement by reference, shall remain your separate property forever.

You will receive your share of the property, in money or its equivalent, when and if we cease living together, or upon my death if we are living together at that time. You will have, by reason of this agreement and our living together, no claim against me or my estate other than for that specified above, but you will, of course, be entitled to receive anything additional that I may choose to leave you in my will.

(Note: Discuss important issues such as treatment of a joint bank account, normal monthly living expenses, support, expenditures for improvements in the parties' residence, and other major items here.)

In the event we, in the future, do get married, the terms and conditions specified herein will apply only with respect to the period of time of this cohabitation and will thereafter terminate, although the property rights acquired during this period shall not.

The purpose of this letter is to protect you as much as myself, and to avoid any possible dispute later on. You should consult an attorney about the terms and conditions of this letter before signing and agreeing to them. This letter was drafted by my attorney (name, address, and telephone number).

In order to indicate your agreement to the foregoing, please sign and date this letter where indicated below.

Sincerely,
Name of Working Party

Dated: _____
Witness: _____

Agreed to and accepted:
Name of Cohabitant

Dated: _____
Witness: _____

▷ *Author's note:* This sample letter agreement lacks many formal clauses and phrases that are preferred in a more formal agreement. Do not draft a letter like this without a lawyer's help.

FORM 111. Sample Termination of Living Together Arrangement

It is hereby agreed that (specify name) and (specify name), who have been living together at (specify address and nature of premises, such as an apartment with a lease in the name of _____ or a house owned by _____), shall separate and go their own way, and as of this time have no intention of resuming their former living together arrangement.

It is also agreed that the property and furnishings owned by either party shall be taken with each party, respectively, as follows: (specify list of items belonging to each person). It is further agreed that the following items have been purchased with both parties contributing money toward the purchase, and these items have been divided in order to make a fair and equal division of the value of the jointly purchased items: (specify list of items belonging to each person).

It is further agreed that the joint bills and obligations shall be disposed of in the following manner: (specify each creditor, amount of obligation, and the person who will pay off the obligation).

It is further agreed that both parties are leaving the shared premises, or, in the alternative, that (name of person) is leaving and (name of person) is staying, and the one staying shall assume all responsibility for said premises henceforward, except for those common debts incurred heretofore. The party who is leaving agrees not to reenter the premises without the remaining party's permission, nor to remove anything therefrom. (Specify how the proceeds will be divided if a house jointly owned is to be sold.)

It is further agreed that neither party shall have a claim against the other's business, pension or retirement funds, insurance proceeds or refundable policies, rights of inheritance or estates, or any other property not described in this Agreement.

It is further agreed that neither party shall have a claim to compensation from the other for services rendered during the time that they lived together, for "spousal support," or "palimony," or for any other property, assets, or money not described in this Agreement.

It is further agreed that should litigation or the services of an attorney be necessary in order to enforce this Agreement, the defaulting or losing party shall pay to the prevailing party such reasonable attorneys' fees and costs as may be fixed by the Court.

The parties acknowledge that they have consulted independent legal counsel during the negotiation and drafting of this Agreement, in its entirety, and that they rely solely on the meaning, construction, and legal effect of this Agreement as given to each individually by their own independent legal counsel (state names and addresses of such counsel). Each party shall be solely liable for his or her respective attorney fees and costs incurred in all consultations and reviews.

Each party states that he or she has entered into this Agreement freely and voluntarily without fraud, duress, threats, or coercion.

In no event may the parties modify this Agreement except in a writing signed by each of them.

Dated: _____   Signature of Parties _____

Witness: _____

▷ *Author's note:* Some agreements that are prepared at the commencement of a living together relationship state the terms of separation when the relationship ends. Speak to an attorney for further advice before drafting a similar agreement.

Although it is not necessary to have a lawyer draft or review a cohabitation contract, this is recommended when the agreement is complicated and involves significant assets. Each party should have his or her own lawyer review and offer advice on a complicated agreement to avoid claims of fraud, undue influence, or coercion (which, if proven, will cause a nullity of the agreement).

3. **Prepare a will that accurately reflects your desires.** All possessions, including property, go to the next of kin in the absence of a will. A will is vital for cohabitants who want to enable partners to receive their possessions in the event of death. Speak to a lawyer for further information.

4. **Act in your own best interest whenever you move into an apartment or co-op with a lover or friend.** This includes trying to get your name on the lease. The person who signs the lease is the lawful tenant. The signer has the right of occupancy and is the person who is first offered the right to renew the lease. Conversely, he or she is the person the landlord sues for nonpayment of rent. An unmarried occupant does not have the same rights or obligations. Even if you have lived with someone for many years and have contributed all the rent, your partner has first claim on the apartment, especially if he or she signed the lease alone, occupied the apartment before you, and although taking your money to pay the rent each month, used his or her personal check. (Note: If you are planning to stay only a short period of time, this strategy may not be worthwhile.) Try to have the lease amended to list you as a joint tenant. Many residential leases expressly limit occupancy to the named tenant and his or her immediate family. Review the lease and take all necessary steps to avoid this problem. This includes signing a separate residence agreement with your cohabitant that spells out all the rights, duties, and obligations while living together (e.g., who pays the rent, what happens when the lease expires, and so forth).

5. **Document your intentions with other evidence.** For example, by paying a utility bill directly instead of giving your lover the money, you may be able to prove that a formal agreement exists to share assets and bills.

6. **Get a receipt when you contribute money for the purchase of property or assets used by both cohabitants.** Property acquired during a cohabitation may be apportioned between the couple even in the absence of an express agreement where an implied-in-fact agreement is found to exist. This results when the conduct of the parties evidences an appropriate intent to pool and share earnings and property during a relationship. In the absence of a written agreement, the goal is to obtain evidence establishing your contribution and ownership in property purchased with your funds.

One way of demonstrating an implied-in-fact arrangement is by obtaining a receipt indicating that your funds were used to purchase cohabitation property. For example, if you give a live-in partner $2,000 to buy $4,000 worth of living room furniture, and your partner pays for the furniture, it is best to get a receipt from him or her that acknowledges payment of $2,000 to strengthen a claim you owned half of the furniture. Better still, try to get a brief letter acknowledging that you contributed half of the money and own half of the furniture. If this is not practical, advance the funds by check (never cash) and write your check for $2,000 with a notation on the face of it such as "50% contribution toward the purchase of equal, jointly owned living room furniture."

7. **Learn how the law in your state treats common-law marriage.** A few states recognize common-law marriage. This means that a couple may be considered to be lawfully married if they hold themselves out to be husband and wife for a lengthy period of time, regardless of whether they obtain a marriage license, have blood tests, or participate in a civil ceremony. For example, if you accept mail under the names of "Mr. and Mrs.," file joint tax returns, and tell people you are married, you may be considered married in a common-law marriage state. Be sure you know the law of your state and act accordingly. If you want to preserve your singles identities but live in a common-law marriage state, it is important to execute a valid cohabitation contract evidencing your intentions.

8. **Avoid making promises you don't intend to keep.** As jilted lovers become more aware of their rights, a larger number of palimony cases are being filed each year. Thus, never make a promise regarding the amount of support or property you will give a cohabitant unless you intend to keep it. Avoid documenting any promise in a letter or written instrument if possible.

9. **Speak to an experienced lawyer if you believe you have been victimized.** Judges are applying a variety of legal theories in awarding damages to cohabitants. These include declaring the existence of an implied business partnership or joint venture when a couple work together or awarding money under an equitable theory called quantum meruit (also known as unjust enrichment) when homemaking services and child care are provided with the expectation of reimbursement. If you have been denied promised benefits or support from a lover and business partner, consult an attorney experienced in family law. You may learn that you are entitled to a greater share of assets and property accumulated during the cohabitation than you imagined.

10. **Check the law in your state.** Laws concerning the rights of cohabitants vary dramatically. For example, some states enforce both express and implied agreements while others recognize only written agreements signed by both parties. Still other states will not enforce any type of agreement between live-in couples.

11. **Be aware that concurrent marital status can decrease your claims.** Many states refuse to enforce promises made by one lover to the other while one or both are still legally married.

12. **Avoid signing a release or any other document indicating your relinquishment of any claims without receiving anything in return or before consulting a competent lawyer to analyze, discuss, and protect your rights.**

LIVING TRUSTS *See Trusts*

LIVING WILLS *See Wills*

LOANS *See Commercial Transactions; Contracts*

MAINTENANCE *See Alimony*

MALPRACTICE

Also see: Attorneys; Litigation; Negligence; Patients' Rights

Malpractice is the failure of professionals to perform work, labor, services, or skills with minimal competence. Professional misconduct sometimes is also considered malpractice. The two most common forms of malpractice arise in connection with services performed by physicians and attorneys.

MEDICAL MALPRACTICE

Medical malpractice is defined as a legal cause of action where one party seeks to recover damages against a doctor, medical assistant, or health-care provider for failure to render services or skills of suitable (minimal) competence in the community where medicine is practiced. Physicians may be guilty of malpractice if they carelessly deviate from accepted standards of medical care and injury results. They may be sued for malpractice in the case of a patient's injury due to their failure to recommend a safer alternative. An error may not result in malpractice unless the doctor failed to follow standard procedures. The fact that a person becomes ill or dies under a physician's care may not constitute malpractice. Only if the doctor failed to render reasonably appropriate or common standards of care or failed to diagnose an illness that should have easily been detected, thereby causing death or injury, will a possible cause of action arise.

Your legal rights as a patient begin when you enter a hospital emergency room, doctor's office, or health maintenance organization (HMO) office. Examples of medical malpractice include:

- ▸ Removing a healthy organ instead of a sick one
- ▸ Operating on a patient while intoxicated, causing injury
- ▸ Engaging in sexual abuse while a patient is medicated
- ▸ Using an unsterilized needle, resulting in infection
- ▸ Prescribing incorrect medication or wrong doses of medication
- ▸ Recommending inappropriate surgery
- ▸ Rendering a misdiagnosis

Massachusetts was the first state to release information about malpractice payouts, disciplinary actions against doctors, and physicians' criminal records. Under Massachusetts law, those who want information on a doctor's background, including education, honors and awards, hospital affiliations, insurance plans, specialties, and history of malpractice claims can call the Board of Registration in Medicine's toll-free hot line and get as many as ten profiles faxed or mailed to them free of charge. The profiles list malpractice claims that have resulted in a payment. Other states are also considering laws requiring the disclosure of doctor records.

LEGAL MALPRACTICE

Legal malpractice arises when a lawyer fails to use such skill or prudence as lawyers of ordinary skill commonly possess and apply in the performance of the tasks they undertake. This doesn't mean that you can sue if your lawyer gets beaten by another lawyer. You can sue only if he or she fails to render work or assistance of minimal competence and you are damaged as a result. You can also sue for malpractice when there is a breach of ethics (e.g., failure to remit funds belonging to a client), and you may also sue for breach of contract and/or civil fraud.

The following are examples of lawyer malpractice:

- Settling a case without the client's consent
- Procrastinating work on a matter (e.g., neglecting to prepare a will after being paid and before the client dies)
- Charging grossly improper fees and failing to provide detailed, accurate time sheets to compute fees
- Failing to file a claim within the requisite time period (the statute of limitations)
- Failing to include a wife's claim for a husband's military pension in a divorce matter in a state that awards the wife a share in such a pension
- Failing to represent competently a defendant in a criminal action (e.g., dozing off during a crucial stage of the trial)
- Failing to keep a client advised of major developments in an important matter to the client's detriment
- Failing to disclose that a conflict of interest exists (e.g., neglecting to inform the client that the attorney or someone from his law firm previously represented an opponent)

ACCOUNTANT MALPRACTICE

Accountants, like other professionals, can also commit malpractice. They are required to perform services according to generally accepted accounting principals. The following are examples of accountant misconduct:

- Failing to file your tax return
- Failing to provide basic, correct tax advice regarding current tax laws
- Using information learned while conducting a tax audit for personal gain (e.g., purchasing the stock of a client after learning that the company is about to go public)

Before deciding to file a malpractice action against any professional (including architects, real estate brokers, accountants, psychologists, and others), speak to a competent attorney who specializes in suing professionals in that field. His advice is essential in deciding if you have a valid claim. He should also tell you what steps to take, such as filing a complaint against the professional with your state's disciplinary board, to protect your rights. Fortunately, a great number of professionals are now willing to testify against each other. If your complaint to a state's disciplinary board is viable, it will be investigated (the process may take months). An investigative committee will decide whether the case should be given a hearing or referred to the appropriate peer group of a local medical, legal, or other society. After a thorough investigation, the board may make recommendations for disciplinary action against the professional, including a formal reprimand, suspension from practice, or revocation of the professional's license (which is rare).

You may file a lawsuit against the professional in addition to requesting that such an investigation ensue. In such a lawsuit, the professional, who generally carries malpractice insurance, may be defended by lawyers from his insurance carrier. Whether malpractice has actually occurred is a question of fact to be decided by a judge or jury. Due to the complexity of most malpractice cases, and the fact that the lawsuit will be vigorously defended, it is critical to seek advice from a skilled attorney.

MARRIAGE
Also see: Divorce; Prenuptial Agreements; Living Together; Separation

Marriage is an agreement between a man and woman of sufficient age (usually eighteen or older) to live together as husband and wife. Although it is a private bond between two individuals that requires freedom from state intervention, many aspects of marriage are regulated by governmental processes and all fifty states have created procedural prerequisites to a valid marriage and established certain rights and duties incident to marriage. For example, in a few states, people as young as fourteen are permitted to marry with parental consent, and many states permit marriages of people between the ages of sixteen and eighteen with parental consent. Most states consider a couple to be married when the ceremony ends, but a few states allow a spouse to have the marriage annulled if it is not consummated by sexual relations.

DIFFERENT TYPES OF MARRIAGE ARRANGEMENTS
In a traditional marriage, two people of opposite sex who are not currently married are eligible to marry (although each state imposes its own requirements as to age, health, and other factors). It is generally necessary for one or both of the proposed partners to apply for a marriage license from an appropriate state or

county agency, pay a fee, and submit to blood tests. The most common method of getting married is the ceremonial marriage. A ceremonial marriage consists of the presentation by the couple of the marriage license to an authorized state official. This can be a judge, a court clerk, or a member of the clergy. The authorized official will then conduct a civil or religious ceremony according to state laws and issue a marriage certificate, to be filed shortly after the ceremony. Other than the promise to marry, the content of the ceremony is within the discretion of the couple.

A few states still recognize common-law marriages. These are arrangements in which a couple live together as husband and wife and present themselves to others as such (e.g., they are listed on their post-office box as "Mr. and Mrs." or they introduce themselves as married people). Most states have revoked recognition of the common-law marriage because of misunderstandings and fraud that have resulted from this status in the past. Be aware that even if you think you are, you may not be properly "married" under common law in your state. Even if you live together in a state that recognizes common-law marriage, you will not be deemed married unless you declare yourselves in front of others and act as if you are husband and wife. To be safe, if you do not want to be considered legally married in these states, execute a written agreement that disclaims any such intention.

Although unusual, other kinds of marriages may be legally valid. For example, in a proxy marriage, where one partner is in prison or serving in the military and is unable to be physically present at the ceremony, a few states allow another person to stand in his or her place at the wedding. One or two states allow for parties to be married confidentially with no witnesses present. Marriages of convenience, where people marry not for love but for other reasons (e.g., to be socially acceptable), are legal. And mixed marriages between persons of different races, which were once prohibited in many states, are now legal in all fifty states. However, virtually all states do not recognize homosexual (same-sex) marriages or marriages whereby one man has several wives (polygamous marriages).

However, if a marriage is entered into under false pretenses, as a result of fraud, or between close relatives (e.g., first cousins) or underage parties, the marriage may be deemed void and capable of being annulled. Furthermore, a marriage entered into solely to defraud the U.S. Immigration and Naturalization Service (called a sham marriage) to enable one of the parties to become a permanent resident of the United States may be disallowed and criminal penalties imposed as well as deportation.

THE CONSEQUENCES OF MARRIAGE

Certain obligations and legal responsibilities are assumed upon marriage, governed by state law where you live. One of the most common consequences is that the wife assumes the surname of her new husband, although this is becoming less common. In most states, a woman who wants to use her husband's surname and her own in combination need only start and continue to use the chosen name. In a few instances, where applicable, it will be necessary for the wife to formally remove her birth name and change her name on legal documents (e.g., an employer's retirement benefits plan, airline miles program, and others).

Each spouse owes the other the legal duty of financial support. This means that if a spouse is in need of financial support and the other spouse is able to provide it, he or she is obliged to do so. This applies equally to wives and husbands. The extent of support depends on the facts of each case; however, one spouse may not allow the other to become a public charge provided he or she has the financial means to prevent this. In a majority of states, each spouse retains control over the property he or she brings into the marriage. Each spouse has the right to buy, sell, and borrow money or claim profits from his or her "separate property." However, a spouse may voluntarily relinquish control over separate property by holding it jointly with the other spouse, such as by transferring stock in a business to the husband or transferring money and establishing a joint bank account.

Generally, neither spouse is responsible for the premarital debts of the other. For example, the property a wife brings into marriage cannot be encumbered for the debts the husband incurred prior to their marriage. Similarly, a husband is liable for his wife's premarital debts only up to the amount of property she conveyed to him at the time of their marriage. (Any debt incurred in your unmarried name may be your sole responsibility, to be collected from your assets. But if you incur a debt while married, your spouse may be obliged to pay it.) If you have been paying your spouse's bills and no longer want to do so, you must notify all appropriate credit-card companies and merchants (preferably in writing) before you abrogate responsibility.

In the past, a woman relinquished her personal credit when she married, but this has changed. The federal Equal Credit Opportunity Act prohibits discrimination based on sex when a person applies for credit. Creditors are not allowed to ask about a person's marital status in an individual credit application. However, a creditor can ask for information about your spouse if you are relying on your spouse's income to support your credit application.

Once married, you have the right to file joint income tax returns with the IRS and state taxing authorities. Speak to an accountant about whether separate or joint filing is to your advantage. You may also be able to claim an estate tax marital deduction, form a marital life estate trust and other family trusts, create a family partnership, and participate in other financial vehicles designed to reduce estate and tax obligations. Upon the death of a spouse, you may be automatically entitled to a share of his or her estate even if the spouse died without a will. Each state has its own formula for awarding the surviving spouse a percentage of the estate. Generally, this ranges from one-third to one-half of the estate (which may depend on whether there are minor surviving children and the nature of the property transferred).

Insurance companies sometimes offer lower insurance plans for married couples. Some people can escape deportation as a result of marital status. Also, being married allows partners to seek damages for wrongful death, loss of companionship (e.g., when a spouse is injured in an accident by another's negligence and the noninjured spouse is deprived of affection and sexual activity), and other legal claims.

In most states, the working spouse's pension and any money set aside for retirement are treated as property of the marriage. A surviving spouse may be provided with the deceased spouse's pension in certain circumstances. A few company-sponsored pension plans allow a surviving spouse to receive a majority of the benefits a spouse received while alive. A surviving spouse may also receive social security benefits based on his or her spouse's earnings if the survivor is sixty-two years of age or older and was married to the decedent for more than one year. These monies may be one-half of the spouse's benefits and may be reduced by other benefits accruing. Other monies that may be received due to a marriage are disability, military pension, and public assistance benefits. Speak to an accountant, attorney, or other professional adviser and someone from a regional office of the Social Security Administration for more details.

Although it is usual for a married couple to live together, it is not legally required. However, it is expected that spouses will remain sexually loyal to each other; in many states, adultery is still illegal, although this criminal offense is rarely prosecuted. Generally, one spouse may not deny the other sex without good cause, and denial may allow the denied spouse to obtain a divorce on the grounds of constructive abandonment. However, a husband may not rape his wife to obtain sex. Some states have written into their criminal laws that marriage is not a defense to rape. Also, one spouse may be liable to the other for transmitting a sexual disease such as herpes or AIDS, particularly if he or she had the disease prior to marriage or contracted it with another partner during the marriage and did not inform the innocent spouse in time to prevent him or her from contracting the disease.

Generally, a woman's right to have children or not is solely her own choice. Women do not need their spouse's consent to use birth control, and a woman has the sole right to decide whether to abort a pregnancy during the first three months. The U.S. Supreme Court has ruled that states are allowed to regulate abortion procedures in the second trimester of pregnancy and the notification of the other spouse before the abortion takes place. After the sixth month and during the third trimester, a woman may no longer have a legal right to abort, no matter what her own or her husband's wishes are.

Although both husbands and wives are free to testify against each other in court, as in divorce or custody proceedings, many states still recognize the right of either spouse to invoke the privilege of a marital communication. This means that husbands or wives cannot be forced to testify in court by a third party about a conversation they held privately when they were married.

Finally, parties are free before or during a marriage to enter into a contract that defines how they will treat their assets and property and support each other at the time of a divorce. Such agreements differ from cohabitation (living together) contracts and are discussed in the section "Prenuptial Agreements."

MATERNITY LEAVE *See Employment*

MEDIATION *Also see: Arbitration; Litigation*

Mediation (also referred to as a form of alternative dispute resolution) is an alternative to formal litigation or arbitration for resolving disputes. In mediation, a neutral intermediary (the mediator) defines the conflicting interests of the parties, explains the legal implications, and attempts to help the parties reach and prepare a fair settlement. When settlements are achieved, they are typically arrived at more quickly and cheaply because opposing parties have not hired opposing counsel to fight it out in court. Landlord/tenant, personal injury, commercial, and divorce disputes are now being resolved this way in greater numbers every year. For example, when a couple realize that their marriage has ended, they may prefer to work out their problems by themselves in the privacy of a business suite instead of a crowded public courtroom, negotiating the terms of a separation agreement based on their best mutual interests and those of their children. When a mediator (usually a trained lawyer, business person, or retired judge) is retained to assist in the process, he or she will not make decisions for the parties but will assist them in reaching a realistic agreement.

Disagreements involving family businesses, inheritances, divorce negotiations, cohabitants, and others who want to settle their disputes in private are often resolved through mediation. Some states now require mediation when automobile lemon laws, complaints about product warranties, or consumer complaints involving local Better Business Bureaus are the subject of a dispute.

To resolve a dispute successfully by mediation requires that both parties agree to participate in the process in good faith. However, critics contend that mediation is not an effective mechanism when one party enjoys a stronger negotiating position and can bully the other party into submission or when one party strongly believes that he or she is entitled to punitive or extra damages that can be awarded only by a judge via litigation.

HOW IT WORKS

Various community associations, private enterprises, and the American Arbitration Association (AAA) offer mediation services. The AAA is most often selected to

FORM 115. **List of Mediation and Dispute Resolution Organizations**

DISPUTE RESOLUTION
American Arbitration Association (AAA)
140 W. 51st Street
New York, NY 10020
(212) 484-4000

American Bar Association
Section of Dispute Resolution
740 15th Street NW
Washington, DC 20009
(202) 662-1680

National Institute for Dispute Resolution
1901 L Street NW, Suite 600
Washington, DC 20036
(202) 862-7200

CONSUMER INFORMATION
Council of Better Business Bureaus
4200 Wilson Boulevard, Suite 800
Arlington, VA 22203
(703) 276-0100

CONTRACTOR ASSOCIATIONS
Remodeling Contractors Association
  (RMA)
1 Regency Drive
Bloomfield, CT 06002
(203) 242-6823

National Association of Home Builders
  (NAHB)
15th and M Streets NW
Washington, DC 20005
(202) 822-0200

National Kitchen and Bath Association
  (NKBA)
687 Willow Grove Street
Hackettstown, NJ 07840
(908) 852-0033

ARCHITECTS AND DESIGNERS
American Institute of Architects (AIA)
1735 New York Avenue NW
Washington, DC 20006
(202) 626-7300

American Society of Interior Designers
  (ASID)
200 Lexington Avenue
New York, NY 10016
(212) 685-3480

▷ *Author's note:* The above organizations may be able to provide additional information about specific areas of dispute resolution. Many offer catalogs of publications, as well as brochures of general information.

assist parties in the mediation process. It is a public-service, nonprofit organization that offers dispute-settlement services to business executives, employers, trade associations, unions, consumers, farmers, communities, families, and all levels of government. Services are available through AAA's national office in New York City and twenty-five regional offices in major cities throughout the United States. See the list above of other organizations that offer dispute resolution services. Some offer catalogs of publications, as well as brochures of general information.

Once both parties agree to try to solve their differences through mediation, a joint request for mediation is usually made through a regional office of the chosen mediation service. The request identifies the individuals involved in the dispute, gives their current addresses and phone numbers, and briefly describes the controversy and the issues involved. If the AAA is used, the parties should include whatever information will be helpful in appointing a mediator.

The AAA assigns a mediator from its master list. The parties are then given information about the mediator. In most cases, the mediator has no past or present relationship with the parties. A mediator recommended by the AAA is free to refuse the appointment or resign at any time. Likewise, the parties are free to stop the mediation or ask for the services of a different mediator if they wish. If any mediator is unwilling or unable to serve, or if one of the parties requests that the mediator resign from the case, the parties may ask the AAA to recommend another mediator. The mediator is compensated on either an hourly or a daily basis. Both parties are informed of potential mediator fees and are sometimes requested to sign a document evidencing approval of the compensation arrangement and an agreement to split the fees equally.

Before settling on a mediator, you should first find out whether the mediator's approach is suited to your needs. At the initial interview, feel free to ask the following questions to be certain you are choosing the right individual:

▸ How does the mediator operate?
▸ How much experience and training does the mediator have?
▸ What is the mediator's background?
▸ How many sessions will be required?
▸ How much will mediation cost?

After the initial interview takes place and the mediator is found to be acceptable, he or she will arrange the time and place for each conference with the parties. At the first conference, the parties will be expected to produce all information reasonably required for the mediator to understand the issues presented. The mediator may require either party to supplement the information. At that first meeting, the mediator explains exactly what the parties should expect. Good mediators explain that the process is entirely voluntary, that they are not judges and have no power to dictate solutions, and that the parties are free to terminate the mediation process at any time.

A mediator does not have authority to impose a settlement on the parties but will attempt to help them reach a satisfactory resolution of their dispute. Although usually trained in law, the mediator is not supposed to give legal advice or psychological counseling. Although parties are not typically represented by counsel at the mediation sessions (with the exception of complicated business and commercial disputes), they are encouraged to seek independent legal advice about the process or about any legal issues that may arise.

Conferences are private. The mediator may sometimes meet with both parties, sometimes with one of them privately. Other persons such as witnesses may attend only with the permission of the parties and at the invitation of the mediator. In a custody matter, for example, the mediator may want to interview the child privately, to determine the child's attitude toward the custodial arrangement or visitation rights. In conducting the interview, the mediator should not encourage the child to choose between the parents. With the approval of both parties, the mediator may obtain an opinion of a professional, such as a child psychologist, as to the best interest of a child. The opinion should be shared with the parties.

In a sense, the mediator is hired as a consultant, jointly retained, to help the parties work their way through their problems to resolution. At some point the mediator may make a recommendation or proposal. Both parties can agree or disagree or come to a compromise of their own. The mediator will draft a report confirming the agreement. The report is then presented to the parties for eventual submission to their attorneys for incorporation in a formal document, such as a settlement agreement.

If the parties fail to agree, or do not agree with the mediator's recommendation, they can break off the mediation, consult another mediator, give up, settle their dispute without a mediator, or go to court. The following is a typical mediation scenario from start to finish:

1. The mediator and parties meet at the initial conference. The mediator's role is explained, and the responsibilities and rights of the parties are set forth.
2. The mediator designs a schedule for the sessions.
3. The parties sign a formal retainer agreement with the mediator.
4. A method is adopted for obtaining whatever information is required to understand the parties' problems.
5. The mediator identifies the various areas of agreement, defines the issues that must be resolved, and assists the parties in their negotiations.
6. A final settlement is formulated.
7. The mediator arranges for the terms of the settlement to be transmitted to the attorneys of the parties for filing in court, if necessary.

FINAL WORDS ON MEDIATION

Mediation is not for everyone. Some mediators do not possess sufficient skills or training to be effective. Others have been criticized for not ending the process when the interests of each party are not receiving balanced treatment. If the mediator is a lawyer, he often has to make an adjustment in attitude. For unlike the lawyer, who tells the client what to do, a mediator must allow the parties enough freedom to structure their own unique solutions to problems. Mediation by attorneys has raised the concern of whether one lawyer can adequately advise two parties with opposing interests and whether a mediator can invoke the attorney-client privilege in any future litigation. For example, if lawyers representing the parties attend the mediation sessions and incriminating or damaging statements are made by one party, his or her lawyer may seek to prevent a judge or jury from hearing these statements in court if the mediation fails and a lawsuit ensues. A judge may or may not allow such oral testimony to be admitted in court depending on a number of factors, such as whether the parties formally agreed beforehand that statements made during the mediation were confidential and could not be introduced in subsequent court hearings.

People have experienced difficulties in finding qualified mediators. Unlike lawyers, mediators do not advertise. Probably the best way to avoid problems from the start is for both parties to interview the mediator carefully. Then, to avoid any misunderstanding about the mediator's role and compensation, be sure to hire the mediator only on the basis of a written retainer agreement. If you believe the process is not working or do not feel comfortable with the person hired, terminate the relationship immediately and discuss further options with your attorney or other professional adviser.

Understand that mediation will not work unless both parties are willing to cooperate and recognize the savings and other benefits to be achieved by resolving the dispute not through litigation, such as:

- ▸ eliminating the anxiety of preparing a case before going to court
- ▸ avoiding potential poor publicity
- ▸ maintaining privacy
- ▸ obtaining a speedier resolution
- ▸ avoiding the uncertainty of outcome when the case is tried in court
- ▸ preserving good business or personal relationships

But some people have a great need to even the score; in that event, mediation will probably fail.

Speak to your professional adviser to determine if mediation is a proper avenue for resolving any dispute you are experiencing. You may learn that its benefits exceed potential disadvantages.

MEDICAID AND MEDICARE   *Also see: Insurance*

Medicaid and Medicare are federal health benefits programs offered primarily to legal U.S. residents and citizens age sixty-five and over and to those living on low incomes. Unlike Medicaid benefits, which can vary throughout the fifty states, Medicare coverage is consistently applied throughout the United States. Some people are able to receive both forms of benefits as well as private "medi-gap" insurance to supplement medical coverage.

MEDICAID
Medicaid is designed primarily for disabled persons under sixty-five, the elderly poor sixty-five and older, and visually impaired people under sixty-five. Long-

term nursing care and home care are included and are administered by the states according to their budgets and preferences. Medicaid benefits will be paid only when all else fails, such as when you have no private health insurance and are not covered under Medicare programs. To qualify, you must be able to prove that you lived in a state for a minimum period of time (i.e., are a resident). Each state has its own rules governing how much money a person must be making to be denied Medicaid benefits. In some states with "Surplus Income Programs," if you make more than a certain minimum amount but your monthly medical expenses exceed your excess income, you can still qualify. However, if you have high rent or other nonmedical expenses, this cannot be used to offset monthly income to qualify for Medicaid benefits.

The tricky part about qualifying for Medicaid benefits for long-term institutional services, such as hospital or nursing home care, is that you must have virtually no assets or income. Unless you transfer your assets to a spouse or other selected individuals, you will not be paid for such care, and there is a length of time, which varies from state to state, after such transfers in which you will be deemed ineligible. Some people have attempted to place their money in a trust to get around this requirement. Never do so before speaking to an attorney who specializes in elderly or Medicaid law for advice and guidance.

This is especially important in light of federal legislation making it a crime in certain circumstances for the elderly to give away their money to qualify for Medicaid. The law authorizes criminal penalties of up to a year in jail and a $10,000 fine and makes lawyers, financial planners, and accountants who help in the transfer also potentially liable.

To qualify for Medicaid, a person generally cannot have more than $2,000 in assets. The spouse of someone in a nursing home can have up to $77,000, not including a house, household goods, and cars. Although transferring assets to support a sick spouse or dependent child is permitted, gifts and other nonessential transfers are not, and you must wait at least three years (five years if a trust is involved) before applying for Medicaid if you give money to a child. Historically, people gave away part of their money and reserved the rest to cover nursing home bills until they were eligible for Medicaid. That approach is probably illegal under current statutes.

A few states have enacted laws establishing insurance plans enabling older individuals to receive nursing care without first being required to dissipate their estate and/or permit individuals to prepay funeral expenses, buy a burial plot, pay debts, pay off a mortgage, repair a home, or purchase medical-related items that Medicaid doesn't cover. Inquire whether such laws exist in your state if applicable.

Nursing homes are generally prohibited under federal law from receiving a kickback (private payment) from families to get preferential treatment or admission priority. It is also illegal to require patients or their families to waive and/or relinquish their Medicaid and Medicare rights in order to be admitted or receive special care. If such pressure is being exerted on a relative, contact your state attorney general's office or Department of Insurance for advice.

Contact your local Medicaid, Agency for Aging, or Social Security Administration office to determine what benefits are available under your state's Medicaid program. Additionally, be aware that possible changes in Medicaid and Medicare requirements and benefits may occur as a result of congressional action. Procedural rules for filing, dealing with providers, and appealing an adverse decision vary, and each state has its own requirements, which should be explained to you in detail. Other groups, such as the American Association of Retired Persons (AARP) and local legal services programs, can also advise you about your rights in this area.

MEDICARE

Medicare provides health services for people sixty-five or older and disabled individuals collecting social security benefits for an extended period of time. It consists of two parts: Part A, for hospital and limited skilled nursing home and hospice care, and Part B, for medical costs such as doctor's fees, medical tests, outpatient services, and certain types of medical equipment. Most of the fees are funded from social security payments and the small monthly premiums some people are required to pay. Because Medicare does not typically pay for preventive care, prescription drugs, hearing aids, and eye care, many people are required to carry supplemental medical insurance to be reimbursed for these items.

If you are receiving social security checks when you turn sixty-five or have been receiving social security disability benefits for twenty-four months, you may automatically qualify for Medicare benefits. However, it is necessary to file for such benefits if you reach sixty-five and are still working. To avoid a lapse in coverage, apply several months before your sixty-fifth birthday. As with most social security benefits, you are not entitled to receive retroactive payments, so always file in advance of an eligibility date to receive everything that is coming to you. Speak with someone at your employer's benefit office or your local Social Security Administration office to maximize your receipt of all retirement, social security–related, and Medicare benefits.

Most hospitals either receive financial assistance under the federal Hill-Burton Act, which obligates them to admit a certain number of indigent patients, or have adopted Medicare and Medicaid programs. As a result, it is illegal for hospitals (except for a few private institutions that do not accept such funds) to disallow entry on the basis of a person's inability to pay, nor may Medicare participants be required to pay a deposit before admittance. Although doctors are not legally required to treat Medicare patients or accept the fees set by Medicare, federal law prohibits them from charging Medicare patients more than 15 percent above the approved charge. Some states have even stricter limits.

MEDIGAP INSURANCE

Not all medical and related costs you incur are reimbursable under Medicare. The exact coverage rules and limitations are often confusing. Insurance companies are frequently hired under Medicare to administer payments to health providers. You also have the option of joining a health maintenance organization (HMO). If you belong to an HMO, you may not be required to make huge additional co-payments out of your own pocket (with the exception of the additional monthly premium you may be required to pay for such coverage). But if you want to visit a doctor who is not affiliated with a particular HMO, or if the HMO does not cover important expenses, it may be necessary to purchase additional "medigap" insurance from a private insurance company.

Always read the policy carefully and question ambiguous terms before purchasing a supplemental medical policy. Know for certain what additional benefits you will receive once the policy is in effect and the extra costs, if any, involved. For example, many medigap policies do not cover catastrophic and long-term care. Be aware of this and read the fine print. Understand potential limitations and exclusions of coverage. Be certain that the policy cannot be canceled because of a preexisting medical condition that is not adequately revealed at the time you sign the application. How long did the condition have to exist before you cannot qualify? Is there a waiting period before benefits begin? Is this period too long? Is the policy renewable? Under what terms? Does the policy pay benefits for all levels of care in a nursing home, including custodial care? What about home care? Is it necessary to purchase several policies for maximum protection?

These and other items should be made clear so that you understand your duties, rights, and options. Speak to a reputable insurance broker or agent, attorney, estate planner, or other professional adviser for more information if applicable.

MINORS *See Children*

MISDEMEANORS *See Crimes and Criminal Law*

MISREPRESENTATION *See Fraud*

MORTGAGES *See Real Estate*

MOVING COMPANIES *See Consumer Transactions*

NANNIES *See Domestic Help*

NEGLIGENCE *Also see: Accidents; Automobiles*

Negligence is one party's legal failure to exercise a sufficient degree of care owed to another. If you are injured as a result of the careless or reckless conduct of another person or because someone failed to act with the degree of care that he or she had a duty to provide (e.g., a public bus driver who failed to operate a bus safely), liability (legal wrongdoing) against that party or his employer may exist.

After a negligence lawsuit is filed, a judge or sometimes a jury ultimately decides whether liability exists. If it does, the next decision is whether to award money damages and other relief to the injured party (and if so, how much). To prevail in a negligence case, the plaintiff must prove that a duty of care was imposed on the defendant which the defendant failed to exercise, and that the failure to exercise this duty was the natural and foreseeable (proximate) cause of the injury, causing damages. The standard of care necessary to establish negligence is typically measured against the actions of a reasonable, prudent person and takes into account the circumstances and age of both parties. If a professional is being sued, such as an architect who is accused of being responsible when a building collapses because of his faulty design, a higher standard of care common to other similarly situated professionals may be imposed.

Speak to a competent lawyer immediately for advice and guidance whenever you are injured. Proving negligence can be difficult, especially if it is not clear that your injuries were foreseeable or that a duty of care was owed to you by the person or persons you are trying to sue. It may also be necessary to sue many parties, such as the manufacturer, wholesaler, and retailer of an alleged faulty product that causes you harm. If two or more defendants act wrongfully, each may be deemed to be jointly and/or severally liable, which means that each alone could be liable for a plaintiff's entire damages.

Determining whom to sue in negligence actions, proving the case in court, confronting the various defenses asserted by the defendants (e.g., demonstrating there was no notice of a dangerous condition in a slip-and-fall case), proving that you were not entirely responsible (called contributory negligence) or partially responsible (called comparative negligence) for causing your own injuries or that you did not assume the risk by your conduct, and the best method of collecting money judgments in the event of a victory can all be complicated decisions that typically require a skilled attorney's assistance.

Finally, recognize that some companies attempt to disclaim liability for negligent acts by placing "release" language on tickets, contracts, and other documents. For example, if you are injured on a ride at an amusement park and the ticket you purchased states that the company is not responsible for any injuries caused by the ride, can you sue the amusement park and win? The answer depends on whether or not the release language was conspicuous (in bold typeface) and whether you were notified of this before going on the ride (i.e., by a posted sign that warned all riders of potential risks). In most cases, the law does not allow establishments to exculpate themselves from negligence lawsuits (especially for deliberate acts), but always speak to a lawyer for advice and guidance.

NO-FAULT DIVORCE   *See Divorce*

NOTARY

A notary (also called a notary public) is a person licensed by each state to witness the signature of a person signing an important legal document, such as a will or codicil, power of attorney form, deed, or sworn affidavit. Each state has its own requirements and license fees for granting notary status to individuals.

Notaries may not place a stamp or seal on a signed legal document unless they have witnessed the person sign the document and can verify his or her identity. This is required to prevent forgery or fraud.

NURSING HOME CARE   *See Medicare and Medicaid*

OBSCENITY   *See Civil Rights*

ORAL CONTRACTS   *See Contracts*

ORDERS OF PROTECTION   *See Abuse*

OUTPLACEMENT GUIDANCE   *See Employment*

OVERTIME PAY   *See Employment*

PALIMONY   *See Living Together*

PARENTAL RIGHTS   *See Abuse; Child Custody*

PARTNERSHIPS   *Also see: Contracts; Corporations*

A partnership is a voluntary association entered into between two or more competent persons engaged in a business as co-owners for profit. Partnerships are a common form of business ownership. They differ from corporations in that no stock is issued. Generally, a partnership is best suited when only a few owners exist and they do not want to follow the many formal requirements imposed on corporations (e.g., obtaining a certificate of incorporation; paying yearly federal, state, and local taxes; and filing annual corporate tax returns) to conduct business. Upon the death or withdrawal of one of the partners, the partnership may be automatically deemed by state law to have ended, while a corporation continues. Losses and distributions of the partnership are passed along to the individual partners, who must pay income tax on their share of the profits. This differs from a corporation, where profits and losses are reported directly by the corporation itself and not the stockholders.

THIS AGREEMENT OF PARTNERSHIP entered into this (specify date), by and between (specify partners).

1. Name and Purpose. The Partnership shall be carried on under the name of (specify). The purpose of the Partnership shall be (specify). Notwithstanding the foregoing, the parties may conduct business as partners in any other related or unrelated business activities to which they shall mutually agree.

2. Place of Business. The principal office of the Partnership shall be located at (specify).

3. Partners. The name and address of each of the partners is as follows: (specify).

4. Term. The Partnership has commenced business on or about (specify) and shall continue until terminated as provided for in this Agreement.

5. Capital Contribution. Each of the partners have made equal capital contributions to the Partnership. Upon the dissolution of the Partnership, each partner will (specify method of distribution).

6. Net Profits and Losses. Subject to such adjustments as may be required pursuant to this Agreement, the net profits and losses of the Partnership shall be shared by the partners as follows: (specify). The amount of annual "net profits" and "net losses" shall be determined by the accountant servicing the Partnership account and computed according to: (specify, such as by regular accounting practices).

7. Salaries and Cash Flow. (Specify the amount of salaries and/or cash flow to be distributed to each partner).

8. Management Duties: The day-to-day affairs of the Partnership shall be handled equally by both partners, who agree to devote their full time and attention to the business of the Partnership and who shall have equal rights and say in the management of Partnership business.

No partner shall be permitted to own an interest in, operate, control, or participate in any other business without the express written consent of the others, which consent shall not be unreasonably withheld. All partners shall provide services to the business of the Partnership and each other as proper and necessary, including keeping all partners informed of any letters, accounts, contracts, and other information which shall come to their attention concerning the business of the Partnership. All partners shall keep records of each transaction of the Partnership which they are involved in, and shall maintain such records at the Partnership's main office. Said records shall be open for inspection and examination by each of the partners or their duly authorized representative, at all reasonable times.

9. Finances. The fiscal year of the Partnership shall commence January 1 of each year and end on December 31, at which time the books of account shall be closed and balanced. The books of the Partnership shall be kept on a (specify, such as a cash basis). All partners shall cause the funds of the Partnership to be deposited in such bank account(s) as they shall designate. Checks and withdrawals shall be made upon (specify, such as by all or two or more partners).

10. Admission. No new partners may be admitted to the Partnership except upon the unanimous written consent of all partners. No loans or other business decisions may be taken or made without the unanimous consent of all partners.

11. Restrictions. No partner shall borrow money in the name of the Partnership or incur any liability without the written consent of all other partners. No partner shall pledge, cause a lien to be placed against, encumber or sell his interest in the Partnership in any way. In the event any partner violates the provisions of this paragraph or makes representations, warranties or commitments binding the Partnership without all other partners' consent, the breaching partner shall indemnify and hold all other partners harmless from any losses, damages, attorneys fees, and costs incurred by the non-breaching partners.

12. Disability. (If appropriate, define what constitutes a disability and for how long a disabled partner will be able to receive a salary or distributions of partnership profits.)

13. Sale of Partnership Interest. In the event a partner dies, retires, or becomes disabled according to the above definition, the remaining partner(s) shall have the right to continue

the business of the Partnership under the present name. However, said deceased, retired, or disabled partner shall receive the following remuneration for his or her Partnership interest: (specify how the Partnership is to be valued, such as one times annual gross receipts or some other formula). Closing shall be held no later than (specify) days after the end of the calendar month in which the offer to sell was made and shall take place at (specify, such as the offices of the accountant or attorney for the Partnership).

14. Manner of Payment. The selling partner shall receive (specify $) paid over a period of (specify). All deferred payments shall be evidenced by a series of promissory notes bearing (specify interest rate), and providing for the acceleration in the event of default continuing (specify) days after written notice of default is sent by the selling partner. Notwithstanding the foregoing, the maker shall have the right to prepay all or any of said notes in the inverse order of their maturity without premium or penalty.

15. Additional Items at Closing. All credit cards and personal items belonging to the Partnership shall be delivered at closing. The selling partner or estate of the deceased selling partner agrees to indemnify the Partnership against any unknown and/or unauthorized charges on such cards or property.

Any loans owed to the Partnership by the deceased or selling Partner shall be paid to the Partnership out of the first monies received for the sale of his interest in the Partnership; any loans owed to the selling or deceased partner shall be paid at the time of closing.

15. Dissolution. In the event the remaining partners do not elect to purchase the interest of the retiring or deceased partner, or in the event the partners mutually agree to dissolve the Partnership, the Partnership shall terminate and the partners shall proceed to liquidate the business of the Partnership. All assets of the Partnership shall be paid in the following manner: first to pay all just debts of the Partnership; second, to pay all undistributed funds (if any) in each partners' drawing account; third, to pay all surplus cash from the date of the last accounting to the date of dissolution; fourth, to pay all receivables as they are received; and fifth, the remaining assets of the Partnership shall then be divided equally among the partners.

16. Illegality. If any provision of this Agreement shall be determined by the arbitrators, or any court having competent jurisdiction, to be invalid, illegal, or unenforceable, the remainder of this Agreement shall not be affected thereby, but shall continue in full force and effect as though such invalid, illegal, or unenforceable provision were not a part hereof.

17. Notices. All notices required to be sent must be mailed by certified mail, return receipt requested, to the partners' last known address.

18. Binding Effect. This Agreement shall inure to the benefit of, and be binding upon, the parties hereto and their respective next-of-kin, administrators, executors, legal representatives, successors, and assigns.

19. Waiver. No waiver or modification of any of the provisions of this Agreement or any rights or remedies of the parties hereto shall be valid unless such change is in writing, signed by the party to be charged.

20. Arbitration. Any claim or controversy arising among or between the parties hereto pertaining to the Partnership or this Agreement, or the interpretation of this Agreement, shall be settled by arbitration in (specify location) under the then prevailing rules of the American Arbitration Association by three arbitrators, whose decision shall be final and binding.

IN WITNESS WHEREOF, the parties have executed this Agreement on the day and year first above written.

_____
Name of Partner
_____
Name of Partner

Witnessed: _____

▷ *Author's note:* This sample agreement contains many provisions that should be considered and included in a partnership agreement. Never draft such an agreement without an attorney's assistance.

A *limited partnership* is a more sophisticated form of partnership. Rules governing the treatment of limited partnerships (called LPs) are dictated by the Revised Uniform Limited Partnership Act of 1976, which has been adopted by a vast majority of states. Unlike partnerships, formal certificates of limited partnerships need to be filed with the state through the county clerk's office where the LP has a principal office and with other states where the LP conducts business.

Two types of partners typically exist in an LP. A *limited partner* invests money (capital) and is entitled to a specified percentage of the LP's profits. Limited partners do not participate in the day-to-day management of the partnership and generally are not personally liable for partnership obligations or debts beyond the amount of their individual investments.

A *general partner* in an LP runs the partnership, makes decisions, and acts like a partner in a partnership. LPs have at least one general partner, and all general partners have a legal duty to act in the best interest of the limited partnership. This means, for example, that they are forbidden from making secret profits at the LP's expense, must render all business decisions in a prudent, good faith manner, and are required to account accurately to the investor-limited partners all profits after expenses.

Speak to an attorney, accountant, or other professional adviser when considering investing in or operating a business as a limited partnership. If the general partners in an LP make inappropriate decisions, the limited partners suffer financially. Thus, always check references and the background of all general partners before investing in an LP. Additionally, it is important to ascertain what expenses and management fees are being charged by the general partners to run the LP. Limited partners can be exploited and denied a share of reasonable profits because of the imposition of excessive management fees and other charges.

There are several major legal differences between an LP and a corporation or partnership. For example, an LP is not as effective as a corporation in shielding owners from personal liability, and creditors have successfully sued limited partners, making them liable for an LP's debt when the conduct of a limited partner suggested that he or she acted like a general partner (i.e., took an active role in making decisions and running the LP). Changes in the structure of an LP require the preparation and execution of elaborate documents, more so than a corporation's articles of incorporation and bylaws. However, there are distinct tax advantages for using this business form, including enhanced tax deductions for research and development expenses. Thus, seek professional advice where applicable.

A partnership does not require a special preparation or filing of documents to be created. All that is needed is a partnership agreement that defines the rights, responsibilities, and duties of the partners. Although such an agreement can be oral, this is not recommended, especially if the partnership is to exist for more than a year or deals in real estate. A legal principle called the statute of frauds requires such agreements be in writing to be legally valid and enforceable.

A typical comprehensive written partnership agreement lists:

- The name of the partnership
- The business and nature of the partnership
- The names and addresses of all partners
- What each partner contributed to the partnership (e.g., money, equipment, or a valuable customer list)
- How partnership expenses will be reimbursed
- How partnership profit and losses are computed
- How partnership profit and losses will be distributed
- What percentage of the partnership's profits, if any, will remain in the partnership's bank account for future use and not be distributed (e.g., will all partners receive an equal split of profits on a monthly basis or will Partner A get 60 percent of all profits at the end of the year?)
- Powers and duties: what each partner can and cannot do
- That any partner is not liable for the actions of the others unless notified and consulted about all contemplated loans, contracts, and commitments before they are consummated
- How decisions will be made (e.g., by majority or unanimous decision) and who has the final say in the case of a deadlock
- Where the bank account of the partnership will be maintained and the ability and limit of each partner to sign partnership checks (e.g., for purchases over $200, at least two partners must sign all checks)
- The manner and amount of salaries and drawing accounts
- Whether each partner is required to work full-time or part-time
- Conditions on an individual's withdrawal from or addition to the partnership
- The duration of the partnership
- How the partnership will be valued for sale to an outsider or by one partner to another
- How disputes will be settled (e.g., that any controversy that cannot be informally resolved shall be submitted to binding arbitration according to the rules of the American Arbitration Association in the city where the partnership is located)
- The orderly dissolution of the partnership when it ceases to exist
- The rights of the remaining partners to prohibit a withdrawing partner from working for a competitor or establishing a competing business after the partnership is dissolved or that partner sells his or her interest in the partnership

Other issues should also be included in an agreement. For example, each partner should be able to receive a complete accounting of all partnership assets, bank deposits, and business transactions, together with copies of all pertinent records and information on all aspects of the partnership's business. In the event a dispute arises and the parties failed to enumerate how disputes are to be resolved in a formal partnership agreement, the Uniform Partnership Act (UPA) furnishes guidance on partnership issues. This law has been adopted in all states with the exception of Louisiana. It specifies, for example, what happens if existing partners cannot decide on whether to admit new partners or change the essential nature of the partnership's business. (The sample partnership agreement on pages 230–231 illustrates many of these points.)

Unlike a corporation, in which the shareholders are generally not liable for each other's actions, each partner is deemed to be an agent for other partners and has the legal power to bind other partners and the partnership as a result of his or her acts. The ability of one partner to act as an agent and fiduciary on behalf of another partner is an inherent danger of doing business as a partnership. Many partners have been forced into bankruptcy, have had their assets exposed when lawsuits were brought against the partnership (and themselves personally), and have faced serious financial and tax losses and audits in this area. To avoid problems that typically arise, a business lawyer should prepare a partnership agreement that specifically states that each partner must disclose all potentially harmful activities to the other partners before they occur. More important, the agreement should state that in the event of a problem, the "guilty" partner will indemnify (pay back) and hold all other partners and the partnership harmless from all losses, damages, and costs (such as attorney fees) incurred as a result of that partner's negligent and improper acts.

A partnership may dissolve automatically on the occurrence of any number of events, including the death or involuntary withdrawal of one of the partners, admitting a new partner into the partnership, the bankruptcy of the partnership or one of the partners, by court decree, or when the agreed-upon term of the partnership expires. However, a written partnership agreement may allow for the partnership to continue notwithstanding the occurrence of certain conditions. When a partnership is dissolved, its assets are collected, distributed, and sold. Partnership debts are generally first paid off to third-party creditors and then to the partners. After partnership loans are repaid, each partner may receive his or her agreed-upon share of remaining assets if any money exists. This process is called a liquidation, and each partner is given an accounting of the value of his or her partnership interest.

PATENTS *See Inventions*

PATERNITY LEAVE *See Employment*

PATIENTS' RIGHTS   *Also see: Malpractice; Medicaid and Medicare; Right-to-Die Laws; Social Security Benefits*

Your rights as a patient begin when you enter a hospital (or an emergency room), doctor's office, or health maintenance organization (HMO). All patients have the right of informed consent from a doctor, which consists of the following:

- ▶ A description of the recommended treatment procedures
- ▶ A description of the risks and benefits of the procedure, with emphasis on risks of death or serious disability
- ▶ A description of the alternatives, including other treatments or procedures, together with their risks and benefits
- ▶ The likely results of no treatment
- ▶ The probability of success and what the physician means by success
- ▶ The major problems anticipated in recuperation, and the time it will take before you can resume normal activities
- ▶ The identity of all physicians involved in your care and whether you are getting an invasive diagnostic test, such as a bone marrow aspiration or biopsy

Consent must be voluntary. For example, if you are threatened or drugged, there is no legal consent. If you are incompetent (i.e., you cannot understand the consent), or have been declared incompetent by a court of law, consent is obtainable from family members or from an appointed guardian in the event the family is acting in your best interest. You can give your doctor your living will, in which you have designated a person to make treatment decisions for you in the event you are incapacitated. The doctor of a terminally ill patient may be legally obligated to honor the patient's wishes if he or she has signed a living will (e.g., the doctor must allow the patient to refuse extreme or life-sustaining treatment). Even though the necessity of ensuring informed consent is important in crisis-oriented situations, it is even more critical in elective procedures, especially when there is a possibility that the treatment may worsen a person's condition.

You can sue for malpractice if you sustain an injury due to an undisclosed material risk or an undisclosed safer alternative. Some informed-consent forms contain provisions that attempt to have the patient waive the right to sue a doctor and/or a hospital for malpractice. A typical release or waiver reads: "The hospital is a nonprofit, charitable institution. In consideration of the hospital and allied services to be rendered and the rate charged therefor, the patient or his legal representatives agree to and hereby release the hospital from any and all liability for the negligent or wrongful acts or omissions of its employees, if the hospital used care in selecting its employees." Such waivers, however, are generally not legally binding.

If you are a competent adult, you can legally refuse treatment. Proper refusal obligates your doctor and/or hospital to abide by it. However, you will have to sign a release, holding the doctor and/or hospital harmless for any results of stopping treatment. A doctor can engage in further surgery in the event of an emergency. However, if you specifically forbid further surgery, this is malpractice and/or battery. Malpractice statutes may give you a longer time to sue (usually two years) than battery actions (often only one year). You can also limit your consent to surgery by a particular physician or request to have a particular second physician present. If these wishes are not adhered to, this may also be malpractice or battery.

Doctors. If you believe you have been victimized by an incompetent doctor or have complaints regarding professional misconduct (e.g., sexual abuse, gross incompetence, or alcoholism), you can sue the physician for malpractice in a private lawsuit or file a written complaint with your state department of health, which typically maintains an office of professional medical conduct. If your complaint is viable, it will be investigated (the process may take months). An investigation committee will decide whether the case should be given a hearing or referred to the appropriate peer group or local medical society. After an investigation, the board may make recommendations for disciplinary action, including a formal reprimand, suspension from practice, or revocation of the doctor's license in that state (rare). Recently, data banks have been established to advise people about doctors who have been banned from practice in one state (but allowed to practice in another state).

Fees. Before choosing a doctor, ask about fees. Inquire whether fees are usually paid by your insurance carrier, or do they exceed "usual and customary" costs in the doctor's area of specialty? Will the insurance company be billed first, or must payments be received up front and the patient reimbursed later? Review your insurance company's rules before nonemergency surgery. Does the plan require a second opinion before services are rendered?

By law, insurance companies must pay the bills that your policy covers. However, if you do not receive reimbursement, call the insurer immediately and speak to a representative. Document the sum and substance of the conversation, the identity of the person you spoke with, and all other pertinent facts, such as the date and time of the call. This may help establish that you tried to follow the company's rules. Clarify the amount of your deductible. Ask if you or the doctor submitted an inadequate or incorrect claim form. Inquire the precise reasons why a claim was rejected. Speak to your doctor to determine if another form can be submitted. *Learn about the procedures to appeal a negative decision and follow those rules.* For example, if a letter from your doctor must be sent by certified mail, return receipt requested, within two weeks from an adverse decision, be sure this is done. Save all letters sent or received to prove a claim. If you still get turned down, write a final "warning letter" (and send it certified mail, return receipt requested) that states you will file a complaint with the state insurance department if the matter is not amicably resolved. You may also want to consult an attorney, especially if the insurer refuses to pay because your treatment was deemed "experimental" or you were taken to another hospital for treatment not covered by your HMO.

Health-maintenance organizations. Do your homework before joining an HMO. Most people don't ask questions until they're sick and often discover their benefits are not as good as they thought. Experts suggest that people should select an HMO that pays out more than 90 percent of collected premiums to medical care because some HMOs have been accused of not spending the money collected properly. Does the contract between the HMO and your doctor prohibit either party from revealing the reimbursement arrangement or not allow doctors to recommend treatments or specialists outside the plan? Get answers as to whether the HMO treats people with chronic illnesses in terms of referrals and continuing care, and the polled level of satisfaction of the members. Answers to these questions may help you select an HMO that is responsive to your needs and provides adequate, comprehensive coverage.

Nursing homes. A nursing home admission has significant legal and financial implications, although family members and the person entering a facility typically are more interested in securing quality care than in the legal implications of the move. A nursing home admission has broad implications for estate planning, Medicaid eligibility, directives for health care decisions, potential third-party liability as a guarantor for the costs of care, extra charges not covered by Medicaid, deposits, transfer and discharge rules, and other issues. Always seek the counsel of an experienced attorney who specializes in elder law for more information where applicable.

Hospital emergency rooms. Under federal law, a hospital may not refuse you in an emergency even if you cannot pay, nor may treatment be refused on the basis of race, ethnicity, or religion. AIDS patients may not be refused available treatment.

Additionally, all hospitals must (1) provide patients with a medical screening examination to determine if an emergency medical condition exists, and (2) provide stabilizing treatment to any individual with an emergency medical condition or woman in active labor prior to transfer. If the hospital cannot stabilize the patient, the patient may be transferred to another hospital if the responsible physician certifies in writing that the benefits of the transfer outweigh the risk, the receiving hospital has space and personnel to treat the patient and has agreed to accept the patient, the transferring hospital sends medical records with the patient, and the transfer is made in appropriate transportation equipment with life support if necessary.

If a hospital knowingly and willfully, or negligently, violates any of these provisions, it can be terminated or suspended from the Medicare program. It can also be held liable for failure to take action against the attending physician. You can institute a malpractice action against a hospital in the event of a violation.

Discharge. Assuming you are a competent adult, you can decide to leave a hospital at any time. Failure to sign a release form is not grounds to detain you. Conversely, your discharge is effected by written order of your doctor. If you think that your discharge is premature, discuss it with your physician. If this is to no avail, you have the right to a consultation with another physician. If both doctors agree that you are well and you still refuse to leave, the hospital can physically remove you as a trespasser. However, it may use only reasonable force to do so. On discharge you are entitled to be informed about follow-up care. The failure to provide such instructions is a breach of care by the hospital and may be grounds for liability in the event injury results.

Federal law now requires hospitals to provide a 48-hour stay for new mothers. Additionally, government restrictions have been enacted to curtail "drive-through" surgeries, which all hospitals are required to follow.

Privacy. Your physician or health-care provider may not disclose any information about you to a third person not involved with your care and treatment, excluding the following:

> ▶ birth and death certificates (if a crime is suspected)
> ▶ contagious diseases must be reported, including AIDS but not infection with the HIV virus
> ▶ child abuse
> ▶ injuries inflicted by guns, knives, or other objects
> ▶ medical records and testimony routinely used in personal injury or malpractice cases
> ▶ use of records by agencies for survey purposes, accreditation, detection of fraud, and licensing
> ▶ if a patient threatens the life of another and the doctor has a reasonable belief that the patient will carry out this threat

Speak to a lawyer immediately to protect your rights if you believe your confidential, private medical information has been disseminated to nonessential third parties.

PENSION AND PROFIT-SHARING PLANS
Also see: Employment

Pension and profit-sharing plans are essentially money-saving vehicles established primarily by employers for the benefit of employees. The law does not obligate employers to establish such plans, but if you are a participant in any employer's or union's plan, you are entitled to certain rights and protection under the Employee Retirement Income Security Act of 1974 (ERISA) unless you are a federal, state, or local public employee.

KINDS OF PLANS

There are many different kinds of pension and profit-sharing plans, including the following:

Defined contribution plans. Examples of defined contribution plans include regular profit-sharing plans, thrift plans, money purchase pension plans, and cash or deferred profit-sharing plans. All these plans are characterized by the fact that each participant has an individual bookkeeping account under the plan that records the participant's total interest in the plan assets. Monies are contributed or credited in accordance with the rules of the plan established by the employer and contained in the plan document. In defined contribution plans, the ultimate amount of funds available on retirement depends on how much the employer and employee have contributed, and how much the money earned when it was invested (which often depends on how wisely the money was invested by the pension trustee), after applying a predetermined formula that takes into account the retiree's age, number of years of service, and amount of compensation earned during employment. In some plans, for example, in order to be 100 percent vested (as opposed to receiving only 60 or 80 percent of the ultimate funds available), you must work more than ten years for a particular company and be more than fifty-five years of age to qualify.

Defined benefit plans. These are pension plans that base the benefits payable to participants on a formula contained in the plan guaranteeing a specified sum per month on retirement. These plans are not funded individually as are defined contribution plans. Rather, they are typically funded on a company-wide basis with equal benefits for all similarly situated employees (e.g., X dollars per month for every employee reaching the age of sixty-five with twenty or more years of service with the employer).

Employee welfare benefit plans. These are often funded through insurance and typically provide participants with medical, health, accident, disability, death, unemployment, or vacation benefits.

ERISA-enforced plans. If an employer represents that certain benefits are available, who the intended beneficiaries are, and how the plan is funded, the employer may be liable for making such promises and paying the promised benefits under the federal ERISA law even in the absence of a formal written plan.

HOW TO PROTECT YOUR PENSION RIGHTS

The following strategies are recommended to help protect your pension and profit-sharing plan rights.

1. **Ask for details regarding the nature of your benefits whenever you are hired by an employer.** The employer decides what type of benefits are available, so carefully read all literature and documents furnished to you by the employer.

2. **Understand what happens to your benefits if you resign or are fired from the job.** When do your benefits vest? Can you take early retirement to receive

anticipated benefits? If so, how much will your monthly retirement benefits be reduced? How will your money be invested? Who is the plan administrator? These and many other questions should be answered by a representative from your company or by explanations in the documents you are furnished.

3. **Speak to a financial adviser to explore your rights and options if several plans are available.** For example, a matching 401(k) plan (in which the employer puts aside the same amount of money you save from your paycheck) may be more advantageous than other plans offered by an employer. It is also important to understand what options are available regarding payment. For example, in a joint and survivor annuity, a specified sum is paid to the working spouse on retirement; when that person dies, his or her spouse will then receive a smaller amount (typically between 50 and 75 percent of the regular benefit) for the rest of the spouse's life. The alternative is that by signing a waiver it may be possible to receive a greater amount during retirement, but your spouse would receive no benefit upon your death.

4. **Know your rights.** Under ERISA law, you are entitled to an accurate, written description of all benefits, including a copy of the summary description of the plan, within 90 days after becoming a plan participant or 120 days after the actual plan begins. ERISA provides that the administrators and trustees of the plan invest your money prudently and account to you your benefits on a regular basis. Plan participants are entitled to examine without charge all plan documents, such as insurance contracts and copies of all documents filed by the plan with the U.S. Department of Labor, including detailed annual reports and plan descriptions.

An investigation by the U.S. Department of Labor discovered that hundreds of companies have been misusing and diverting 401(k) employee pension programs. When the plans are operated correctly, workers determine how much they contribute to automatic savings programs, the employer withholds the stipulated amount from employee paychecks, and the company forwards the money to a plan administrator, who invests the money in a manner preselected by the worker. The Department of Labor learned that many small and midsize companies violated plan rules and federal law by delaying payment to plan administrators, diverted funds to pay other corporate expenses, or stole the money outright and never reported the contributions. For more information, call 202-219-9247 to get a copy of the free publication "Protect Your Pension" published by the Labor Department.

5. **Enforce your rights.** Under ERISA, if you request materials from a plan (including summaries of each plan's annual financial report) and do not receive them within thirty days, you may file suit in federal court. In such a case, the court may require the plan administrators to provide the materials and pay up to $100 a day until you receive them, unless they were not sent for reasons beyond the control of the administrator.

ERISA and IRS rules prohibit companies from discriminating against employees by not offering benefits to all employees. Specific rules also govern when credit toward qualifying for a pension or profit-sharing plan commences. If you are denied benefits or do not receive an accounting of your benefits, contact the plan administrator immediately in writing, sent certified mail, return receipt requested, to protect your rights. Under federal law, every employee, participant, or beneficiary covered under a benefit plan covered by ERISA has the right to receive written notification stating specific reasons for the denial of a claim. Additionally, you have the right to a full and fair review by the plan administrator if you are denied benefits.

6. **Speak to a lawyer immediately to protect your rights.** If you have claimed benefits and had your claim denied or ignored in whole or in part, you can file suit in a state or federal court. A competent labor attorney can advise you about your rights and options. If it should happen that plan fiduciaries misuse a plan's money, if you are discriminated against for asserting your rights, or if you believe the company incorrectly failed to give you credit for previous years of service after a lapse in coverage (which might occur if you worked for an employer, had a break in service, and then worked for the employer again), you can also seek assistance from the U.S. Department of Labor, as well as file a lawsuit in federal court with the help of your lawyer. The court will decide who should pay court costs and legal fees. If you are successful, the court may order the person or company you have sued to pay costs and fees. If you lose or it finds your claim to be frivolous, the court may order you to pay costs and fees.

You may also want to consult a benefits or labor lawyer with questions about your pension and profit-sharing rights in the event that:

- ▸ You hear rumors that the employer plans to file for bankruptcy or is about to be sold or merge with another company
- ▸ You believe the employer made a major mistake in the computation of your benefits (or when they vest)
- ▸ You are fired or forced to quit shortly before your benefits are to vest or become due
- ▸ Your returns show constant losses and you believe that plan officials may not be investing your money properly
- ▸ Your statements are coming late or at odd intervals
- ▸ Your friends who retired from the company say they can't get the pension plan to pay them what's due
- ▸ You are considering resigning or changing jobs and do not understand how the move will affect your benefits
- ▸ You think that you were discriminatorily excluded from an employer's plan
- ▸ You are unsure of how best to roll over or distribute your benefits on retirement

- You want to learn the effect of a divorce on your pension benefits
- You want to learn the effect, if any, social security benefits will have on your pension benefits

PERSONAL INJURY LAWS *See Accidents; Negligence*

POLYGRAPH TESTS *See Employment*

PRENUPTIAL AGREEMENTS
Also see: Divorce; Living Together; Marriage

Prenuptial agreements (also called antenuptial agreements) are commonly used, especially by persons entering second marriages. Many older couples who have accumulated money and property desire to leave it to children and grandchildren upon death rather than to a future spouse. Others have businesses or professional practices they want to protect. Still others, traumatized by a "messy" divorce the first time around, seek to define their rights and responsibilities toward the other partner on paper. While the use of these agreements before marriage is hardly romantic, it does allow parties to express their intentions for dividing property, altering inheritance rights, limiting spousal support, and gaining an equitable share in a business if and when the marriage ends. This reduces costly and messy litigation, because potential problems are anticipated and discussed by a couple before they occur.

The decision to sign a prenuptial agreement with a future spouse should be well reasoned and carefully considered. Important financial and legal ramifications flow from the execution of a valid prenuptial agreement. Couples sometimes include personal preferences in these agreements as well. For example, it is possible to include topics such as who will do the dishes and how the children will be educated. This is valid provided the topics are not illegal or contrary to public policy.

Advantages of a Prenuptial Agreement
- Reduces costly and messy divorce litigation
- Invites candor and openness between the parties before marriage
- Protects assets and property acquired by a spouse before marriage
- Reflects the parties' intentions as to the disposition of marital and non-marital (separate) property acquired during the marriage

Disadvantages of a Prenuptial Agreement
- Diminishes romantic feelings
- Strips a spouse of potentially valuable marital rights (e.g., a share of an inheritance or a pension)
- May be hard to enforce from a practical standpoint on certain issues (e.g., the number of times each week a wife is required to cook dinners for her spouse)

- May not be legally valid
- May contribute to the failure of some marriages over the emotional issue of trust

WHAT CAN BE INCLUDED IN A PRENUPTIAL AGREEMENT?

Almost anything can be included in a prenuptial contract. Matters involving support, maintenance, education of children, providing of a home, release of rights in each other's estate and assets, and all manner of property arrangements can be agreed on in contemplation of marriage. The following areas are often covered.

1. **Inheritance rights.** Parties can agree to waive, modify, or enlarge inheritance rights that the law ordinarily gives to a surviving spouse. For example, a prenuptial agreement can specify that vested pension funds or proceeds from a family business pass to the children of a prior marriage rather than to a surviving spouse.

2. **Insurance benefits.** A surviving spouse may agree to be removed as a beneficiary under a life insurance policy.

3. **Manner and amount of assets distributed from family-controlled businesses and professional partnerships.**

4. **Modification and/or elimination of spousal support.** However, certain states prohibit the concept of eliminating support, so speak with a competent lawyer on this point if applicable.

5. **Release of rights in each other's assets and estate.**

6. **Distribution of property, including real estate and personal property, on divorce.**

7. **Provisions with respect to caring for children and the expenses of maintaining a home (e.g., who will pay what bills).** Note, however, that judges will not generally agree to enforce provisions regarding support, education, and care of children if such provisions are not in the best interest of the children. This means the court is free to fashion its own policy with respect to the children, regardless of the couple's preference as stated in the prenuptial agreement.

8. **Adoption of children.**

9. **Commitments to divide household and child-care chores.**

10. **Mediation or the manner of resolving potential disputes (e.g., through arbitration).**

The sample document on pages 244–245 illustrates the kinds of points that are often addressed.

INCREASING THE CHANCES AN AGREEMENT WILL BE UPHELD

Most prenuptial agreements are enforced by the courts when they are reasonable and when both parties honestly and fully disclosed their assets and net

FORM 117. **Sample Prenuptial Agreement**

AGREEMENT, made this (specify) day of _____, by and between (state parties and addresses).

WITNESSETH:

A. The parties intend to marry in the near future.

B. Annexed hereto as Schedule A is a statement fully disclosing (specify name, such as Bob's) assets, income, property rights, and debts of every kind and nature, including copies of his prior three years of filed tax returns.

C. Annexed hereto as Schedule B is a statement fully disclosing (specify name, such as Jane's) assets, income, property rights, and debts of every kind and nature, including her prior three years of filed tax returns.

D. Each of the parties states that he or she has studied schedules A and B carefully and is fully aware of the rights he or she may be surrendering pursuant to this Agreement.

E. Bob's social security number is (specify), he has (specify) prior children from a previous marriage, is in good health, has no lawsuits or judgments presently filed against him, and supports himself as a (specify).

F. Jane's social security number is (specify), she has (specify) prior children from a previous marriage, is in good health, has no lawsuits or judgments presently filed against her, and supports herself as a (specify).

G. In anticipation of their marriage, the parties mutually desire to fix and determine the rights and claims that will accrue to each of them in the property and estate of the other by reason of such marriage and to accept this Agreement in full discharge and satisfaction of such rights.

NOW, THEREFORE, in consideration of the foregoing premises and of the mutual agreements herein below set forth, the parties hereby agree to the following provisions which shall become effective upon the occurrence of the parties' marriage:

1. Each of the parties acknowledges and agrees that he or she is contemplating entering into such marriage out of love and affection for the other party without any desire or intention to demand or receive any benefits in the other's property or estate other than those enumerated in this Agreement.

2. Each of the parties warrants and represents that the statement of such party's assets, income and property rights and expectations is true and correct to the best of each party's knowledge.

3. Each party understands the rights and obligations of the other that they are waiving pursuant to this Agreement and state that they are entering into this Agreement freely and voluntarily, without coercion or duress.

4. Each party agrees to waive, release, relinquish, and forego, any and all right, title, claims, or interest of every kind and description of the other's estate as a result of the subsequent death of either of them after the marriage, including the right to act as an executor or administrator of the other's estate. Without in any way limiting the foregoing, this provision is intended to and shall serve as a waiver and release of each party's right of election in accordance with the requirements of (specify state law) and any law of any other jurisdiction.

5. Each of the parties agrees that all respective assets set forth in Schedules A and B, the appreciation of any such assets, and anything that either of them may inherit hereafter, shall be treated as separate property under (specify state law) and each expressly agrees never to assert a claim of any kind to the assets or income derived from the respective businesses, occupations, and any appreciated value thereof.

6. The marital residence to be purchased primarily from (specify, such as Bob's) funds shall be owned jointly with right of survivorship. (Specify what will happen to the marital residence in the event of a divorce, for example, Jane being able to live in the house for a year with Bob paying all the bills, and then a sale with the proceeds going to Jane.)

7. So long as the parties shall remain married and living together, Bob shall obtain and keep in full force and effect, and pay for at his sole cost and expense, all annual premiums for a whole life insurance policy on his life, which premiums are to be paid over a period of (specify) years, each annual premium being in an amount sufficient to maintain said policy in the face amount of (specify $). The policy shall be owned by, and shall name Jane as sole irrevocable beneficiary.

8. By mutual consent of the parties upon the commencement of a divorce by either party, (specify what each party will receive in property and support, such as Jane will receive a lump sum of $25,000 for every year or part thereof the parties were married paid immediately upon the filing of a divorce action).

9. Each of the parties agrees, upon reasonable request of the other, to execute all such releases and documents necessary to carry out the purpose and intention of this Agreement.

10. This Agreement contains the entire understanding of the parties hereto, and neither has made any representations, promises, or warranties to the other to induce the execution of this Agreement, except as set forth herein. This Agreement cannot be modified except by mutual agreement signed in writing by both parties.

11. The parties agree that this Agreement and its validity and interpretation shall be governed by and construed according to the laws of the state of (specify), and shall be binding in all respects even if the parties shall become residents of another state or country.

12. This Agreement shall be binding upon, and inure to the benefit of, the parties hereto and their respective executors, administrators, heirs, next of kin, legatees, and devisees.

13. In the event that any provision of this Agreement shall be held invalid or unenforceable, it shall not in any way invalidate, impair, or affect the remaining provisions of this Agreement, it being the intention of the parties that this Agreement shall be binding upon, and enforced against, both parties to the fullest extent permitted by law.

14. Both parties represent that they have consulted attorneys of their choosing, who have counseled them concerning all aspects of this Agreement. Bob has been represented by (specify name and address of his lawyer). Jane has been represented by (specify name and address of her lawyer). Neither party will be responsible to pay for the attorney fees and costs of the other in the preparation and negotiation of this Agreement. Both parties reaffirm that they have consulted with counsel, understand their rights hereunder, and are executing this Agreement freely and voluntarily.

15. In the event any party commences a lawsuit to interpret or enforce the terms of this Agreement, the losing party shall be responsible to pay for all of the prevailing party's reasonable attorney fees and costs.

IN WITNESS WHEREOF, the parties hereto set their hands and seals on the day and year first above written.

Signature of Attorney Representing Bob

Signature of Attorney Representing Jane

Signature of Bob

Signature of Jane

Notary:

▷ *Author's note:* This sample agreement contains many provisions that should be considered and included in a prenuptial agreement. Never draft such an agreement without the advice and assistance of an attorney.

worth to each other before the agreement was signed. The following strategies should be considered and followed:

1. **Be sure the agreement is in writing and is clearly drafted.** In most states, oral prenuptial agreements are not valid.

2. **Use separate lawyers to draft and review the agreement.** It is difficult to claim that the contract is not enforceable because it was signed under fraud, duress, or mistake when each party is represented by counsel. Ethical problems can also be avoided because it is difficult for one lawyer to represent the competing interests of both parties. Because of this, a prenuptial agreement not negotiated by two lawyers may *not* hold up in court.

3. **Exchange complete information on all your assets and net worth.** Include a description of all property and assets owned by each party in the agreement. This description is usually attached as an addendum to the agreement and should include tax returns for the past three to five years, copies of deeds and other descriptions of real property, bank account balances and the numbers of the accounts, and so forth. The failure to spell out all assets and property may be a valid reason to overturn the agreement if its legitimacy is in dispute, particularly if one person got a much better deal (unless all material facts relating to the amount, character, and value of property were disclosed so the accepting party had sufficient knowledge on which to base a decision to accept an inferior deal).

4. **Attach a separate document called a waiver for additional protection.** A separate signed waiver that states that one of the parties renounces claims and ownership to certain property can help support the argument that the prenuptial agreement was not signed under ignorance or duress. The waiver, as well as the actual agreement, should be read aloud before execution and signed in front of other witnesses and a notary.

5. **Include a provision for modifications in the event of changed circumstances.** One problem with prenuptial agreements is that a judge may decide that the agreement is not presently fair (although it may have been fair when signed) because of changed circumstances. Including a clause that permits a spouse to stop support in certain instances, such as when the other dies, remarries, or wins a million dollars, or to accelerate or increase payments (e.g., if the spouse sells a business for a large profit) may minimize this problem. Discuss this with your lawyer if it seems applicable in your case.

6. **Be aware that clauses pertaining to lifestyles (e.g., the frequency of sexual acts) may not be legally enforceable.**

7. **Try to limit the agreement to a certain number of years if possible rather than leave it open-ended.**

8. **Be aware that signing a prenuptial agreement carries a certain degree of risk.** You won't actually know if the agreement is enforceable unless it is

tested in court. Prenuptial agreements are governed by state law and are subject to judicial modification and legal attack. Do not rely on the agreement as a fool-proof method to protect your assets on divorce.

9. **Examine the agreement periodically to see if both parties are living up to its terms.** Consult a lawyer to have the agreement modified to reflect your present intentions if circumstances have markedly changed. This may reduce the chances that the agreement will be invalidated on divorce or death.

10. **Contact an experienced matrimonial attorney to discuss, draft, and negotiate the document with opposing counsel. Do not draft the agreement yourself.**

PRIVACY RIGHTS   *See Civil Rights*

PROBATE   *See Trusts; Wills*

PRODUCT LIABILITY   *See Accidents*

PROPERTY   *Also see: Bailments; Contracts; Real Estate*

The many forms of property include tangible personal property such as goods (e.g., automobiles, boats, and similar items referred to as "chattels"); intangible property such as contracts, stocks, bonds, and money in bank accounts; intellectual property without a permanent location such as copyrights, trademarks, and patents; real property such as real estate and other forms of land, and the rights associated with ownership and use of land, including eminent domain and condemnation; and fixtures (personal property that is attached to real estate and becomes part of the real estate, like a fireplace built onto a house).

Property can be freely transferred by gift, deed, or sale by contract. Laws governing property bought and sold pursuant to a contract are regulated by the Uniform Commercial Code. The UCC is a series of laws adopted in virtually all states that regulates conduct between merchants and defines what remedies are available in the event an agreement relating to property is broken (breached).

A gift is a voluntary transfer of property from its owner (the donor) to another (the donee) without any compensation for the donor. When the donee is a minor and the property is held in trust, the Uniform Gifts to Minors Act defines the custodian's duties and minor's rights with respect to the property transferred. For a transfer of property to be deemed a gift, it is generally necessary that the owner's conduct (proved by language or actions) indicated the making of the gift, that the property was delivered to the donee, and that the donee accepted the gift. Gifts made during the donor's lifetime are called inter vivos gifts. Gifts conveyed when the donor is facing impending death are called causa mortis gifts. A gift given pursuant to instructions contained in a donor's valid will are called testamentary gifts.

Real property and personal property can be owned by two or more persons or entities. In a joint tenancy arrangement, each party owns real or personal property equally. On the death of one of the parties, that person's share is automatically transferred to the other equal owner(s). In a tenancy in common arrangement, the heirs of the owner receive that person's share on his or her death since the property does not revert to the other owner(s). In a tenancy by the entirety, a husband and wife acquire property and this arrangement terminates only on divorce, death of one of the parties, or mutual agreement. In the event of death, that party's share automatically reverts to the surviving spouse.

Whenever you are buying or acquiring property with others, it is important to understand the form in which the property is held. Examine any deed or other document such as a bill of sale for evidence in this regard. A deed is a document that evidences the voluntary transfer of title to real estate either by sale or by gift. A bill of sale evidences the purchase of personal property between parties. (Consult the Appendix to review a typical Contract for Purchase of Personal Property and a sample Bill of Sale [pages 423–425] for any form of personal property.) Where applicable, speak to a lawyer or other professional to discuss the legal ramifications of the various forms of ownership. These distinctions are important for business purposes and proper estate planning, such as transferring property before or on death.

It is often necessary to assert your rights via a lawsuit when you sell and deliver goods to a person, business, or company and those goods are returned for no valid reason or are accepted and used but not paid for. The following information is helpful in a "goods sold and delivered" lawsuit:

WHAT YOU MUST PROVE	HOW TO PROVE IT
1. Date, time, and person to whom you agreed to sell and deliver goods	1. Contract of sale, memorandum of agreement, your testimony, witnesses
2. The agreement to sell and deliver was made at the request and acceptance of defendant	2. Your testimony, witnesses, agreement, contract of sale, partial payment via canceled check, receipt
3. Date, place, quantity, and description of goods delivered	3. Your testimony, witnesses, delivery receipt

(continued on page 249)

(continued from page 248)

WHAT YOU MUST PROVE	HOW TO PROVE IT
4. Demand for payment	4. Your testimony, witnesses, demand letters
5. Damages	5. Contract price (contract of sale, memorandum letter of agreement), amount of money you lost on resale (canceled check, receipt)

Typical Defenses Asserted in Goods Sold and Delivered Cases:
1. Goods were not of ordered quality.
2. Goods were defective.
3. Goods were shipped late.
4. Goods were never received.
5. Goods were not ordered.
6. Payment was made.

The purchase of goods from an individual, store, or business that are defective, do not function or perform as promised, or are not what you ordered is called breach of a consumer product purchase. The following information is helpful in a lawsuit arising from such circumstances:

WHAT YOU MUST PROVE	HOW TO PROVE IT
1. Date and place of purchase	1. Contract of sale, receipt, your testimony
2. What you bought	2. Contract of sale, receipt, canceled check
3. That you paid for it	3. Same as #2 above
4. (a) The product is defective	4. (a) Your testimony, witnesses, estimates of repair
(b) The product did not perform as promised	(b) Warranties in your contract, written advertisements, statements made to you
(c) The product was not what you ordered	(c) Contract of sale, receipt, your testimony, witnesses

Typical Defenses Asserted in Goods Sold and Delivered Cases:
1. The product was used recklessly, carelessly, or in an abnormal manner.
2. Specific promises about the capabilities of the product were never given.
3. The warranties do not apply.
4. There is a disclaimer in the sales contract.
5. Store or business was never notified of the problem or given a chance to correct it.

PROSECUTORS *See Crimes and Criminal Law*

RACE DISCRIMINATION *See Civil Rights; Employment*

RAPE *See Abuse; Crimes and Criminal Law*

REAL ESTATE

The law of real estate covers the many issues of ownership, use, and possession of real property. Buying and selling a house, condominium, or cooperative are the most common situations people face with respect to real estate. Common related problems often arise involving real estate brokers, purchasing unimproved land, and landlord-tenant relationships.

WHAT IS A DEED?

Title to real estate is accomplished by delivery of a deed from the grantor (the seller) to the grantee (the buyer or person acquiring the property by gift, will, or inheritance). A deed is a document that describes the parties involved and the property transferred; it also states the amount of money, if any, paid for the property and whether the property is subject to any exceptions, special conditions, or warranties. Deeds have many forms. For example, a *general warranty deed* permits transfer of title to the property free and clear with no legal claims (referred to as encumbrances or liens on the property. Note: A person filing a lien [i.e., a lien holder] does not claim title to the property but asserts a financial claim for a debt to be repaid from the proceeds of its sale. After a valid lien is filed, the property may not be conveyed until the lien holder is paid off). A *quitclaim deed,* on the other hand, is less desirable because it contains no warranty of "clean" title but merely transfers the grantor's rights to the property subject to claims by third parties. After a deed is recorded at the county clerk's office in the county where the property is located, it provides notice to others that title to the property has passed to the buyer.

BUYING OR SELLING A HOUSE

The first step in buying or selling a house occurs when the property is listed for sale by the seller, usually through a real estate broker. The real estate broker pays the costs of advertising the property and negotiates a deal between the buyer and the seller. In many states, once the parties agree on a price, they may sign a one-page binder and the buyer will tender a small refundable deposit. Shortly thereafter, if the parties have agreed on all the key terms in a comprehensive signed written contract (typically prepared by the seller's attorney), the buyer will pay a sizable deposit (typically 10 percent of the purchase price) to be held in escrow by one of the lawyers representing the buyer or the seller. Over the next few months, the buyer will attempt to obtain financing, usually through a mortgage, and have the property inspected for termites, radon, asbestos, and building irregularities. A title insurance company will research the property to make sure that the seller owns it free and clear, that no one else has an interest in the property (e.g., an easement giving another party the right to go on or use the property), and that there are no judgments or liens filed against the property. See pages 426–430 in the Appendix to review a sample seller–real estate broker agreement, a contract for the purchase of a residence or other real estate, and an option or extension of an option to purchase real estate. These agreements are provided for illustrative purposes only; always seek the advice of a competent lawyer before entering into any real estate transaction.

Once all of this is done, a date is set for title to the real estate to pass at a "closing," which all the involved parties attend. At the closing, the title insurance company issues insurance to the buyer, the buyer shows the bank issuing the mortgage proof that the house is insured, the bank lends the buyer the money, the buyer pays the seller the balance of the purchase price, the lawyers for the buyer and the seller adjust any outstanding monies due, such as unpaid real estate, water, and other taxes, or give a credit to the seller if money was already paid for these items for a period of time (typically no more than several months), and the seller turns over the deed to the buyer together with the keys to the premises. The buyer now owns the house and is ready to take possession.

This series of events can take months to complete and never seems to occur as easily as the above narrative suggests. The following strategies outline key points you should remember during all phases of the sale or purchase of a house.

Dealing with real estate brokers. It is not necessary to attempt to sell property by using a broker. If you do, the seller typically pays the real estate broker's commission, which generally is a percentage of the sale price. If you use a broker, select an experienced broker with a good reputation such as one who belongs to the National Association of Realtors (NAR). This is important because local chapters of the NAR police their members and conduct formal hearings on complaints. Realtors who misappropriate money or engage in illegal practices such as misrepresentation (advertising a bedroom that is really a walk-in closet) or discrimination (steering minority buyers away from certain communities) are subject to disciplinary sanctions, including removal from access to multiple-listing services, fines, and suspension from the association. Some states have licensing boards that oversee and police activity. Research the law in your state for more information. If you have a problem with a real estate broker or salesperson that cannot be resolved, contact the regional Board of Realtors in your state and the local chapter of the NAR. (The letter on page 252 is an example of such a complaint.) These boards may investigate your written complaint and conduct a formal hearing on your behalf. You may also want to speak to a lawyer for advice and guidance.

FORM 120. **Sample Letter of Protest Concerning Broker**

Your Address
Telephone Number
Date

Regional Office of the National Association of Realtors
Address

Dear (Name of Directors),

Please treat this letter as a formal complaint against (realtor, address of firm).

(Describe dates and incidents in detail. For example:) I am an African-American. On (specify date), (name of broker) showed my wife and me several houses for purchase. Despite our repeated requests, we were not shown any houses in (specify neighborhood). I believe we have been discriminated against, since the houses in the neighborhoods in which we desire to live are owned by nonminorities but we can afford them.

(State what you desire—e.g., commencement of an investigation, apology, action, etc. For example:) I would appreciate a formal letter of apology from (name of realtor), together with the name of another realtor who can help me locate a suitable house in my desired neighborhood for my family. Additionally, please conduct a formal investigation against (name of broker), advise me of the progress and disposition, and notify me of the outcome of your investigation. I also request that you make this letter a permanent part of (name of broker's) file. Feel free to contact me for further information or my participation at a formal hearing, if necessary.

If you do not conduct an investigation immediately, I shall consider filing a charge with the Equal Employment Opportunity Commission and taking other action as deemed appropriate. I hope that this shall not be necessary, and I thank you for your prompt attention and assistance in this matter.

Very truly yours,
(Signature)

cc: Regional Board of Realtors
Board of Consumer Affairs

▷ Send certified mail, return receipt requested.

Negotiate the broker's commission and length of representation in advance. Many independent brokers will reduce their fees (say, from six to five percent of the sale price of the property), so insist on a reduction of the commission before agreeing to representation. Confirm the terms of your arrangement in a written listing agreement to prevent future misunderstandings. If you do not receive an agreement from the broker, prepare one yourself (as the sample Broker-Seller Agreement on page 253 illustrates). Read the agreement carefully. Avoid agreeing to pay a commission just because the broker produces a willing, able, and ready purchaser, because many deals fail to go through. Insert language that no commission shall be considered earned until the full purchase price is paid to the seller and the deed is delivered to the buyer. Specify in the listing agreement under what conditions a commission does not have to be paid (e.g., if you sell the house to a friend with no help from the broker).

Deal with real estate brokers rather than salespeople if possible, particularly for complicated transactions. In order to qualify as a broker, an individual must have a certain amount of classroom instruction and actual selling experience and must pass a state exam. Salespeople usually must pass a less rigorous exam and are restricted to working under a broker's supervision.

Understand that realtors often promote their exclusive listings, which maximize their sales commissions, even if these listings are not in your best interest. In an open or multiple listing, all the agents in an area have access to the

---

FORM 121. **Sample Broker-Seller Agreement**

Your Address
Telephone Number
Date

Name of Broker
ABC Brokerage Agency
Address

Dear (Name):
　　This will confirm that I agree to appoint you as my exclusive real estate broker effective (date) through (date).
　　You agree to use your best efforts to locate a willing, able, and ready purchaser for my home, located at (address).
　　It is agreed that the minimum acceptable price for my house will be $XXX. However, I have the right to withdraw my house from sale at any time, or to change the acceptable terms of sale.
　　For your services, you will be paid a commission of XX percent of the purchase price. However, you undertake your responsibilities with the understanding that your commission will not be earned until the full purchase price is paid to me. If this is not accomplished for any reason whatsoever, you will have no claim for commission or compensation in connection with this transaction.
　　As notice of your acceptance of this agreement, please countersign one copy of this letter and return it to me.
　　I look forward to working with you.

Sincerely,
(Signature)

Accepted and agreed to:
ABC Brokerage Agency

By:

▷ Send two copies certified mail, return receipt requested.

property and the commission goes to the agency that produces the buyer. In some cases, the original listing agency splits the commission with the agency that produces the buyer. In an exclusive listing, one agency is the sole marketer of the property for an agreed-upon period of time. If you are the seller, consider a multiple-listing service immediately. Offering an agency an exclusive can limit prospects. *But try to retain the right to show and sell the property yourself and not be obligated to pay a commission to the agency if you directly bring about the sale.*

Sometimes a buyer finds the house through one of the cooperating brokers in a multiple listing. The original listing agency and the cooperating broker then share the commission. Generally, cooperating brokers act as agents for the seller. They do not have the buyer's best interest in mind at all times, so be aware of this. For example, when initially considering buying a house, do not agree to look at properties consistently above your maximum price range or not in your preferred location. Do not let the broker argue with you about an offer you want to make. It is the broker's responsibility to communicate all offers to the seller. If you are unhappy with a broker, switch to another broker or another agency. Be wary if a broker offers you legal or tax advice. Carefully inspect the property before making an offer. Be certain you understand the asking price and what is included in the sale. How much are the yearly property taxes? How long has the house been on the market? Has the broker conducted a thorough inspection of the house for defects before attempting to sell it? Are there any hidden defects or problems (e.g., a basement that leaks or poor electrical wiring) that the broker is required by state law to reveal? If so, how much will it cost to repair the defects? Who will pay for this? Is the property owned with no liens or encumbrances? If the house is to be built, what is the builder's reputation and financial stability?

The binder. A binder is a simple written document that is typically prepared by the seller. It lists the names and addresses of the buyer and seller, the address of the property being sold, and the purchase price. Sometimes it also contains the amount of the broker's commission, the proposed closing date, and what happens if the buyer cannot obtain suitable financing. In most states, the binder is not considered a legally enforceable contract and the parties are free to back out of the deal up until the purchase and sale agreement is signed. *For protection, if you are the buyer, pay as small a deposit as possible and include a sentence that states that if the complete contract is not prepared and signed by X date your deposit will be immediately returned in full at your request.* Although some buyers do not like signing anything until the complete sales contract is negotiated and prepared, you run the risk of the seller selling the house to someone else; the advantage of a binder is that it provides the parties the exclusive right and a certain amount of time (typically a week to ten days) to go forward with the transaction and reach the point where the purchase and sale agreement can be signed.

The purchase and sale agreement. This contract is a comprehensive document that contains all the key issues of the sale. Besides routine information such as the exact description of the property being conveyed, the purchase price, the names and addresses of the parties, and the tentative closing date, the contract also includes provisions concerning financing, inspections for repairs, what comes with the house, and the condition of the house to be delivered.

The following checklists give the key points that the seller and the buyer should always try to include in the contract.

If You Are the Seller

- You will collect damages (e.g., all or a portion of the escrow deposit) if the deal does not go through for any reason.
- The buyer will pay you a penalty (e.g., $500 a day) for every day the closing is delayed beyond a specified date through no fault of yours.
- You have minimal or no liability if the condition of the house is not as the buyer expected.
- The buyer is obligated to exercise best efforts to obtain a mortgage and keep your lawyer informed of the progress of obtaining the mortgage.
- All the terms of the loan are stated if you are financing any part of the purchase price.
- You list the objects (e.g., appliances) that you are including in the price; try to get extra money for these items.
- You will be reimbursed at the closing for any expenses such as taxes and insurance that you have already paid.

If You Are the Buyer

- The seller will pay any broker's fee.
- You can back out of the deal without liability or penalty and receive the full escrow deposit, with interest, in the event you are unable to obtain suitable financing at prevailing rates or the inspection reveals termite or structural damage or environmental hazards that could not have been discovered before the contract was signed.
- Your deposit, to be held in escrow in an interest-bearing bank account by a lawyer or a reputable escrow company (never directly by the seller), should be as small as possible.
- Negotiate as much personal property and "extras" as possible to be included in the purchase price.
- The seller will repair at his cost any minor defects discovered before you move in or give an appropriate reduction of the purchase price.
- The seller will deliver the house empty and clean immediately after the closing; if this is not done, you will receive damages (e.g., storage fees and money to live in a hotel). You will also receive damages if the house is not in perfect working order when you move in.

- The contract will be null and void if the house is destroyed (e.g., by fire) before the closing.
- The sale is contingent on your receipt of marketable title and there are no encumbrances, liens, or other restrictions affecting the property.

These are just some of the many considerations to be negotiated by both parties and included in the sales contract. *Never sign the sales document before an experienced lawyer has reviewed it and negotiated any issues that arise.* Read this document carefully and question all ambiguous language. The language in the agreement governs the relationship and rights of the parties. What you may have been told by the broker doesn't matter; all promises must be included in the contract for your protection.

The contract should include a detailed list of situations in which either party may break the deal with no financial consequences. Be sure to notify the other party in writing within the time frame specified in the contract if you want to break the deal. Your lawyer should advise you if you have sufficient cause to do so. Contracts typically cannot be rescinded for minor violations. If the seller changes his mind and wants to back out, the buyer can sue the seller for "specific performance" of the contract in court and make him transfer the title in exchange for the purchase price plus incidental damages. Your lawyer should explain your rights and options whenever problems concerning the contract develop after its execution.

The closing. After the buyer arranges the necessary financing, completes inspection of the property, obtains house insurance, and receives the results of the title search assuring that the property is free from liens or other claims by third parties, the closing takes place at a convenient location, often at one of the lawyer's offices or at the bank issuing the mortgage. At the closing, many documents are prepared and executed. The buyer pays the seller for all miscellaneous expenses (e.g., the remaining oil in an oil tank), previously agreed-upon purchases (e.g., furniture), and other expenses, such as school and property taxes, that the seller previously paid. If all is in order, the seller will transfer the deed and keys to the buyer. Whether you are a buyer or a seller, you need to have a lawyer present at the closing to review and inspect all documents you are required to sign by the title insurance company, bank, broker, and any other representative. Do not attend the closing if your lawyer cannot appear.

BUYING OR SELLING A CONDO OR CO-OP

Many of the points discussed above also apply when a condominium or cooperative is bought or sold. A condominium differs from a private house in that it typically is one particular unit in a multiple-unit complex. Owners of condominiums own only their unit. The condominium homeowners' association owns the building, hallways, elevators, and recreational facilities (called common areas) in and around an individual's property. The association has written rules (bylaws) that set forth how the condominium is to be run. These bylaws impose fees and assessments that all condominium owners must pay to maintain the common areas in good condition.

Townhouse developments are like condominiums with one exception: typically, the owner and not the association owns the land under the townhouse.

A cooperative differs greatly from a private house and a condominium. The owner of a co-op owns a share of the land and the apartment building in the form of stock, because a corporation owns the entire building and the land on which the building sits. Each co-op owner signs a proprietary lease that sets forth the rules and regulations for occupying a particular unit. Before a co-op can be bought or sold, approval (which is sometimes difficult to acquire) must be obtained from the corporation's board of directors, who typically live in the building. The directors are elected by all the co-op owners in the same fashion as shareholders appoint directors in a business corporation. The directors set policies and implement rules governing how the building and each co-op is to be run (e.g., the rules for interior renovations, subletting, and the proposed use of a co-op). These rules are often quite restrictive.

Speak to a lawyer to determine all the hidden charges and extra fees to be incurred if you are considering buying a co-op or condo. How much are your monthly maintenance fees? What portion of the maintenance and related fees is tax deductible? Can special assessments be imposed without your consent? Carefully examine the bylaws and proprietary lease to understand all your rights and obligations. Recognize that it may be more difficult to obtain financing from a bank because of stringent requirements imposed by the co-op's board. Consider all the ramifications of the form of your real estate purchase before deciding to buy a unit.

PURCHASING UNDEVELOPED LAND

Vast acreage of unimproved land throughout the United States is being subdivided and offered for sale as home sites and retirement spots. Despite the advantages of purchasing such real estate, abuses frequently occur. In many cases, developers abandon projects before completing elaborate facilities. *When buying undeveloped land out of state, ask for written documentation to support advertising and promotional claims.* This can help you recognize if you are dealing with a legitimate land developer. Request copies of all documents that are required to be filed by law. Review these documents before you initially travel to the development site or sign the sales contract. The following documents must be filed with appropriate agencies under many state and federal laws:

- purchase agreement embodied in the sale program
- county engineer's report that describes the physical characteristics of the land proposed for development

- title insurance policy
- certificate of registration
- deed and opinion of title
- reports by licensed engineers regarding drainage, accessibility to roads, and availability of drinkable water
- schedule and timetable of all improvements to be made by the developer
- report from the county stating that the streets and other public places in the subdivided plot will be maintained
- proposed offering statement

According to the federal Interstate Land Sales Full Disclosure Act, developers must file a statement of record and property report with the Secretary of Housing and Urban Development (HUD) in Washington before large subdivided plots can be sold to the public. In order to be approved by HUD, all statements contained in these documents must be substantiated by supporting affidavits and exhibits. Once approval is obtained, a copy of the property report must be given to each prospective purchaser. If you are not given a copy of the property report before signing the contract, the law allows you to rescind the transaction or sue for damages.

Investigate the background and track record of the developer. Call the attorney general's office in the state where the land is located to find out if the developer has ever been charged with land fraud or other illegal practices. When you meet with the developer or his or her representative, get answers to the following questions before beginning serious negotiations:

Has a performance bond or other security been posted to assure the completion of facilities or improvements? With whom? Request a copy.

Who is the lawful owner of the land? If title is held by a corporation or limited partnership, who are the partners? Are there any judgments, liens, or encumbrances against the owner of record?

What is the track record of the developer? Has he or she completed other developments? (Investigate them.)

Who are the authorized sales agents? Where are they located? How long have they been in business? Have they worked with the developer in the past?

Once you are satisfied with the developer's reputation, familiarize yourself with the physical characteristics and other features of the land. For example, you should know the amount of yearly property taxes and whether there are any hidden costs. The following are important points to consider:

What is the total purchase price?

How much money is required as a deposit? Is it refundable?

What is the down payment?

What kind of deed and other assurances are you receiving from the seller?

What are the monthly payments and financing charges?

Is time of the essence? If the land is supposed to be built on or developed within a certain period of time, this should be specified in writing.

Has the land been zoned for special use?

If the property to be acquired is income producing, do existing leases comply with all federal and state regulations?

Have special assessments been imposed for local improvements?

Does the seller have legal authority (power of attorney) to sign the contract if he or she is not the real owner?

Have you as the buyer received a detailed description of the premises? Have you reviewed it to be sure it is accurate?

What is the range of selling prices within the development?

Does the community offer potential for future growth?

Are there provisions for water, drainage, electricity, gas, telephone lines, and sewage disposal?

Is there access to main roads?

Are there recreational and common facilities?

Are there municipal services such as fire and police protection, medical and dental facilities, public transportation, schools, and shopping?

Are the premises sold subject to an existing mortgage or can you obtain your own mortgage?

If you are satisfied with the developer's reputation and the land you are about to purchase, discuss the deal with a lawyer. Have the lawyer review all documents and represent you at the closing. This is essential in any significant real estate transaction.

LANDLORD-TENANT TRANSACTIONS

Landlord-tenant relationships govern both residential and commercial leases. The terms of virtually all landlord-tenant transactions are confirmed in a written lease, particularly those that last for a year or more (to satisfy the legal requirement called the statute of frauds). Some leases have a specific term of duration (i.e., one year). This differs from a periodic tenancy, which runs from month to month and can be terminated at any time with or without notice. Although both residential and commercial leases are governed by the agreement reached between the parties, most states have enacted laws that give residential tenants additional rights that may not be contained in the lease itself. For example, a landlord cannot refuse to rent an apartment to you because of your race, national origin, religion, or sex. In most states, you cannot be denied an apartment because you have children or because of your sexual orientation. However, a landlord can bar you from renting an apartment because you have a pet.

In a lease arrangement, the landlord has the legal right to expect that the rent will be paid on time, that the premises will be maintained in a clean fashion (and not be destroyed or damaged), that the tenant will not interfere with other tenants' quiet enjoyment (e.g., by throwing wild parties), that the tenant will not use the premises for illegal purposes (e.g., engage in prostitution), and that the tenant will not commit sanitary or environmental violations (e.g., by leaving garbage in the hallway).

Tenants have the legal right to live or work in premises that are safe and habitable. This means, for example, that landlords are required to repair all broken appliances and fixtures promptly, comply with building and housing codes, keep the building and all common areas such as lobbies and stairwells safe, respect tenants' privacy rights (e.g., by not eavesdropping or entering the premises without prior notification), and provide essentials such as heat, air conditioning, plumbing, hot running water, electricity, working kitchen appliances, and garbage removal.

All the terms and conditions of the arrangement should be specified in a written lease to reduce misunderstandings and conflicts. Many residential and commercial leases are provided to the tenant by the landlord on a preprinted form. Always review this document before signing it. Be sure that all promises and representations made to you by the landlord and/or broker are contained in the lease, because oral promises not embodied in the lease probably cannot be enforced. Question the meaning of all ambiguous and confusing language. A lease can be such a complicated document that you may want it to be reviewed carefully by an attorney or an accountant before you sign it. Even if you are presented with or use the standard type of form bought in stationery stores, review it carefully. These forms often contain clauses that can cause difficulty later. For example, as a tenant, avoid signing a lease with clauses that:

- ▶ do not provide the right to trial by jury
- ▶ obligate you to pay large attorney fees if the landlord commences legal proceedings
- ▶ require large increases on top of the base rent. Hidden costs in commercial leases often include tax escalation provisions, construction and alteration of the premises fees, insurance obligations, utility charges, and many other costs. Be sure you understand the total bill to be incurred before signing on the dotted line.
- ▶ give the landlord the right to evict you automatically when the rent is not received within X days of the beginning of the month. Maintain the right to be notified in writing before any legal action is commenced so you will be given additional time and the opportunity to cure any alleged violations or breaches of the lease.

If you are a prospective tenant and must sign a complicated lease immediately because you don't want the deal to fall through, here's a suggestion that the landlord may accept and initial on the lease and which is legally binding: add an "escape clause" after your signature. Such a clause essentially states that your obligations and rights under the terms of the lease are subject to your attorney's review and approval within X days. This may allow you to back out of the lease legally if it contains onerous provisions that your attorney objects to.

The following points should always be negotiated and included in any lease:

- Name and address of the landlord and the tenant(s)
- Amount of rent and the date the rent is due
- Whether any late charges are imposed if the rent is not paid on time or if a rent check is returned due to insufficient funds
- The amount of the security deposit. (Will the security deposit be earning interest? Under what conditions and when will the security deposit be returned?)
- Term of the lease. (Can it be renewed? If so, how much written notice is required for the lease to be renewed and under what new financial arrangements?)
- Fixtures and other property included with the premises. Degree of care that must be taken by the tenant to safeguard such property.
- Tenant's right to assign or sublet the premises. How much notice must be given to the landlord before approval is obtained? Can the landlord reasonably withhold his consent? In an assignment, a new tenant replaces the old tenant on the lease and assumes all rights and responsibilities. In a sublease arrangement, the previous tenant is still legally responsible under the terms of the lease. For example, if the subtenant fails to pay the tenant the rent or causes damage to the premises, the original tenant is still liable to the landlord. His only recourse would be to sue the subtenant.
- Are pets allowed?
- Who pays for utility charges? Must the tenant place utilities in his own name?
- Is the tenant responsible for carrying fire and other forms of property insurance? If so, what is the minimum amount of acceptable coverage?
- Who is responsible for making repairs?
- Will the landlord clean the carpets before the tenant moves in?
- What about parking space, use of a rooftop, additional storage room and concierge service?
- Who is responsible for injuries to invitees and guests?
- What rights does the landlord have if the tenant destroys the premises or moves out before the lease has concluded?
- What rights does the landlord have to commence eviction proceedings?

▶ What rights does the tenant have to prevent the landlord from entering the apartment or commercial premises? Can the landlord show the premises to a prospective purchaser or future tenant? If so, how much notice is required and at what hours? Does the landlord have a set of keys to the premises? What happens if the landlord enters the premises and property is missing?

▶ Who will pay for renovations and improvements? Can the tenant remove certain "improved" property after the lease expires?

▶ Provision for rental with an option to buy if applicable. For example, by treating some of the rent as a contribution toward the purchase price, an eventual reduction of the purchase price may be effectuated.

See pages 431–434 in the Appendix to review a sample residential lease agreement and a sublease agreement. These agreements are provided for illustrative purposes only; always seek the advice of a competent lawyer before entering into any real estate transaction.

Landlord-tenant relations is a specialized legal subject. Speak to a competent attorney before doing anything that could jeopardize your rights under a lease. For example, do not automatically withhold rent or engage in a rent strike with others when repairs are not promptly made or other poor conditions exist. By doing so you can risk losing the apartment. Document any problem by sending the landlord a letter by certified mail, return receipt requested. The letter should specify all the problems you are encountering and request immediate relief (with timetables for action). Send a second letter if the landlord fails to act within a reasonable time. Then, if the problem is not resolved, discuss your rights and options with an attorney.

Finally, tenants are sometimes exploited in their dealings with real estate brokers and agents. To protect yourself in this area, remember the following:

▶ Be sure the broker, if you use one, works for you, not the landlord.

▶ Deal only with a licensed broker.

▶ If you are the landlord, avoid giving the broker an exclusive right to rent the property; retain the right to rent it yourself or to allow other brokers to assist you. Carefully review any rental broker's agreement before signing.

▶ If you are a tenant, pay a broker's fee only after you rent an apartment found by that broker.

▶ Do not rent an apartment or commercial unit based only on a floor plan. Visit the premises. Inspect the apartment carefully—flush the toilet, turn on the oven, make sure the windows open, and so on—before you sign the lease.

▶ Always read the lease carefully before you sign. If you are leasing property on behalf of a business or company, avoid personal liability. Never personally guarantee payment of the lease if you can help it. For example, if applicable, always sign the lease in your official capacity (e.g., "Mary Smith, President," not "Mary Smith").

Other terms to consider include negotiating for the security deposit to be placed in a separate interest-bearing account with you getting the interest on a yearly basis and negotiating for the right to lease with an option to buy the property after a certain period of time. Have the broker negotiate for painting, upgrade, or replacement of old appliances where possible.

RELEASES *See Contracts*

RELIGIOUS DISCRIMINATION
See Civil Rights; Employment

RENTING *See Real Estate*

RESIGNATIONS *See Employment*

RESTRICTIVE COVENANTS *See Contracts; Employment*

RETAINER AGREEMENTS *See Attorneys*

RETIREMENT AND RETIREMENT BENEFITS
See Employment; Pension and ProWt-Sharing Plans; Social Security BeneWts

REVOCABLE TRUSTS *See Trusts*

RIGHT-TO-DIE LAWS

Most states have enacted laws allowing individuals the right to refuse to be placed on respiratory or other machines to preserve their life after becoming terminally ill, brain dead, or unconscious. These laws are often called right-to-die statutes, and their provisions vary from state to state. For example, some states allow individuals to sign a document called a living will before the onset of a serious illness. The living will may designate a person to make treatment decisions for you in the event you are incapacitated. When given appropriate authority (called a power of attorney), this person also has the power to execute medical and financial documents on your behalf. (See pages 436–437 in the Appendix for examples of a power of attorney form and a revocation of power of attorney form.) Living wills may also allow you to refuse extreme or life-sustaining treatment and dictate what treatment you want and do not want. In some states, however, they will not be followed when a pregnant woman refuses treatment because of concern for the life of the fetus.

FORM 127. **Sample Living Will/Health Proxy**

I, (name of individual), currently residing at (address), being of sound mind and health, hereby make known my directions to my family, friends, all physicians, hospitals, and other health-care providers and any Court or Judge:

After thoughtful consideration, I have decided to forego all life-sustaining treatment if I shall sustain substantial and irreversible loss of mental capacity and my attending physician is of the opinion that I am unable to eat and drink without medical assistance and it is highly unlikely that I will regain the ability to eat and drink without medical assistance; or my attending physician is of the opinion that I have an incurable or irreversible condition that is likely to cause my death within a relatively short time.

I shall be conclusively presumed to have sustained an irreversible loss of mental capacity upon a determination to such effect by my attending physician or when a Court determines that I have sustained such loss, whichever shall first occur.

As used herein, the term "an incurable or irreversible condition which is likely to cause my death within a relatively short time" is a condition which, without the administration of medical procedures, would serve only to prolong the process of dying and will, in my attending physician's opinion, result in my death within a relatively short period of time. The determination as to whether my death would occur in a relatively short period of time is to be made by my attending physician without considering the possibilities of extending my life with life-sustaining treatment.

I direct that this decision shall be carried into effect even if I am unable to personally reconfirm or communicate it, without seeking judicial approval or authority. Accordingly, if and when it is so determined that (1) I have sustained substantial and irreversible loss of mental capacity and (2) I am unable to eat and drink without medical assistance and it is highly unlikely that I will regain the capacity to eat and drink without medical assistance or I have an incurable or irreversible condition which is likely to cause my death within a relatively short time, all life-sustaining treatment (including without limitation, administration of nourishment and liquids intravenously or by tubes connected to my digestive tract) shall thereupon be withheld or withdrawn forthwith, whether or not I am conscious, alert, or free from pain, and no cardiopulmonary resuscitation shall thereafter be administered to me if I sustain cardiac or pulmonary arrest. In such circumstances I consent to an order not to resuscitate, as that term is defined in New York Public Health Law Section 2961, and direct that such an order thereupon be placed in my medical record. I recognize that when life-sustaining treatment is withheld or withdrawn from me, I will surely die of dehydration and malnutrition within days or weeks. All available medication for the relief of pain and for my comfort shall be administered to me after life-sustaining treatment is withheld or withdrawn, even if I am rendered unconscious and my life is shortened thereby.

I wish to die at home and not in a hospital, and I do not want to be transferred to a hospital unless my condition makes it impractical for me to be treated at home, as may be the case during severe hemorrhage, or extreme restlessness, convulsions, or unmanageable pain; in which case, then as soon as possible, I want to be sent back home.

I recognize that there may be many instances besides those described above in which the compassionate practice of good medicine dictates that life-sustaining treatment be withheld or withdrawn, and I do not intend that this instrument be construed as an exclusive enumeration of the circumstances in which I have decided to forego life-sustaining treatment. To the contrary, it is my express direction that whenever the compassionate practice of good medicine dictates that life-sustaining treatment should not be administered, such treatment shall be withheld or withdrawn from me. I similarly direct that in the event I am unable to personally communicate a decision to forego life-sustaining treatment in other circumstances than those described herein, such instructions shall be followed to the same extent as if originally included in this declaration.

This instrument and the instructions herein contained may be revoked by me at any time and in any manner. However, no physician, hospital, or other health-care provider who withholds or withdraws life-sustaining treatment in reliance upon this Living Will or upon my personally communicated instructions without actual knowledge that I have countermanded these instructions shall have any liability or responsibility to me, my estate, or any other person for having withheld such treatment.

I am in full command of my faculties. I make this Living Will declaration in order to furnish clear and convincing proof of the strength and durability of my determination to forego life-sustaining treatment in the circumstances described above. I emphasize my firm and settled conviction that I am entitled to forego such treatment in the exercise of my right to determine the course of my medical treatment. My right to forego such treatment is paramount to any responsibility of any health-care provider or the authority of any Court or Judge to attempt to force unwanted medical care upon me.

I direct that my family, friends, all physicians, hospitals, and other health-care providers and any Court or Judge honor my decision that my life not be artificially extended by mechanical means and that if there is any doubt as to whether or not life-sustaining treatment is to be administered to me after I have sustained substantial and irreversible loss of mental capacity, such doubt is to be resolved in favor of withholding or withdrawing such treatment.

I have discussed this document with (names of witnesses), and I appoint said (name of individual) as my Surrogate and Health Proxy to act for me in any and all of the within premises, and if any interpretation of this document is ever necessary, my said Surrogate and Health Proxy is authorized to interpret it.

_____
(Name)

Date and place of execution

WITNESS: _____
ADDRESS: _____

WITNESS: _____
ADDRESS: _____

WITNESS: _____
ADDRESS: _____

STATE OF X   )
COUNTY OF X   )

On this (date), before me personally appeared (person's name), to me known to be the individual described in and who executed the foregoing instrument, and she acknowledged to me that she executed the same.

_____
Notary Public

See pages 264–265 for an example of a living will document. **Speak to an attorney or a representative from a local hospital for more information before signing any such document.** The failure to follow your state's requirements precisely may allow a hospital or court to refuse to enforce your wishes. Also, it is necessary to sign such a document in front of impartial witnesses. For example, family members, heirs to your estate, and your doctor may not qualify.

After a living will is properly executed and witnessed, it should be attached to your will and stored in a safe place. A living will can be revoked at any time; however, it is necessary to prepare another document canceling the living will. You may want to provide copies to relevant persons, such as a doctor and the director of a nursing home, so there are no misunderstandings. Under federal law, hospitals, home health agencies, and nursing homes are required to ask patients on admission if a living will is available and whether they would like one to be completed.

The advantage of using a living will is that the doctor of a terminally ill patient will in all likelihood honor the wishes of a properly executed living will. Without a living will, some hospitals may honor a patient's or family's wishes, but only after meticulous discussions and planning.

S CORPORATIONS   *See Corporations*

SEARCHES   *See Automobiles; Crimes and Criminal Law*

SEPARATION
Also see: Alimony; Child Custody; Child Support; Divorce; Visitation

When a couple separate, they remain married but often cease living together. While separations are frequently the first step toward a formal dissolution of marriage, they do not always lead to divorce. Sometimes couples decide to live apart but remain legally married for religious, economic, or moral reasons. Being legally separated means that neither can remarry or disinherit the other spouse; they are still married in the eyes of the law. When a couple mutually agree to live apart on a permanent basis, they usually deal with questions of property rights, support, child custody, and other matters by (1) signing a written separation agreement or (2) obtaining a judicial decree of separation (which by its terms resolves these points). If both parties sign a valid separation agreement, it acts as a contract binding them for as long as they live apart or until they agree to change the agreement in some way.

An action for a legal separation (i.e., a separation decree) begins with a lawsuit in court. (This differs from a separation agreement, which is usually negotiated, prepared, and reviewed by the parties and their attorneys.) A separation lawsuit is often commenced for strategic purposes: for example, one party may believe that the other will negotiate more seriously after a lawsuit is filed, or one party may be forced to file a lawsuit because negotiations have been unsuccessful. Neither a separation decree nor a separation agreement dissolves the marriage; that can be done only by obtaining a divorce or an annulment. However, obtaining a separation decree or signing a separation agreement modifies marital relations and regulates the duties and obligations each spouse owes to the other. However, the parties may get back together at any time if they wish.

Some states require proof of grounds (e.g., adultery, cruel and inhuman treatment, or abandonment) in order to grant a decree of separation. Other states recognize merely living apart for a period of time (e.g., one year) as sufficient to constitute a legal separation. In other states, a legal separation can automatically ripen into a divorce under certain circumstances (e.g., the filing of a separation agreement in court and then living apart for a year from the filing date). It is important to know the law in your state where applicable.

The following lists summarize the advantages and disadvantages of obtaining a legal separation for both parties.

Advantages of Obtaining a Legal Separation

It allows the parties additional time to resolve their marital difficulties.

It prepares the parties for the emotional trauma of divorce.

Agreements with respect to child support, spouse support, custody, and other items can be more easily modified than after a divorce.

Legal obligations, including inheritance, pension rights, and death benefits, are still maintained.

It is easier to prove grounds for a separation than for a divorce in those states that still require proof.

Because of the perceived sanctity of marriage, some judges are more willing to grant a judgment of separation than a divorce.

Disadvantages of Obtaining a Legal Separation

It can be seen as merely postponing the inevitable.

As opposed to a divorce, it may leave a nonworking spouse with less means of support and no property-distribution benefits.

The parties may incur double legal expenses—once for the separation, once for the divorce.

Legal obligations, including inheritance, pension rights, and death benefits, are still maintained.

LEGAL SEPARATIONS

If both parties desire a legal separation, they should spell out their rights, duties, and obligations in a written separation agreement. Most people are unaware that separation agreements are also used prior to a divorce and that the terms of a separation agreement usually become part of the final divorce decree. Judges will not modify the parties' intentions in the separation agreement unless they are unfair, unconscionable, obtained under circumstances involving fraud or duress, or not in the best interest of their children.

The circumstances and formalities of executing separation agreements are governed by rules similar to those applying to prenuptial agreements. For example, there must be full disclosure and fair division of assets. The agreement should be prepared and reviewed by two lawyers to avoid any appearance of bias or partiality. Here, the skill and experience of both lawyers are required to ensure that the agreement is fair, just, and reasonable to both parties and their children. It is recommended that the agreement:

- ▶ be in writing and clearly drafted
- ▶ be notarized, with both parties signing an acknowledgment that states they have read the agreement, understand what it says, are signing the agreement voluntarily, and have discussed the terms with independent counsel
- ▶ represent the exchange of all information concerning the couple's assets and net worth
- ▶ contain provisions for modification in the event of changed circumstances.

All these factors will increase the chances that the agreement is deemed valid and enforceable by the courts.

NEGOTIATING STRATEGIES

Most people are unaware of the kinds of clauses that are included in well-drafted, comprehensive separation agreements. The following points summarize some of the many concerns that each party should discuss with an attorney (and include in the document where applicable) for maximum protection:

Names, current addresses, dates of birth, and social security numbers of both parties

Names, dates of birth, and social security numbers of all children of the marriage

Provision establishing separate residences

Provision that neither party will molest, talk poorly about, or disturb the other in any way

Full disclosure of all assets: If possible, the bank name and address and the numbers of all accounts should be stated in a separate document, together with all pertinent information concerning real estate ownership and other income-producing assets; this document should be attached to the separation agreement.

Provision for separate ownership of property and assets acquired after the separation and divorce

Mutual release and discharge of all general claims against each other

Mutual release and discharge of all claims of inheritance

Responsibility for debts: for example, that neither party will incur any debts on behalf of the other after the separation, plus how prior debts will be treated

Disposition of personal property: who gets what, when?

Disposition of the marital premises: When will it be sold? Can one spouse buy out the interest of the other. If so, at what price, when, and how? What happens if the parties cannot agree on a price for the house? Who pays for repairs to the house before it is sold?

Custody and visitation issues: For example, will there be joint or sole legal custody of the minor children? Enumerate a detailed visitation schedule for the children. Include a provision that neither parent will do anything to estrange the children from the other, allow anyone else to be called "Father" or "Mother," cause the children to be adopted by a third party, or cause a child's surname to be changed.

Support for the nonworking spouse: Include provisions for how long and the circumstances under which the support stops (e.g., on the death, remarriage, or living together of the spouse with another)

Support for the children: When is the money due? How much and where is it to be paid? Include provisions for college support; medical, dental, and life insurance coverage; tutoring, private school, summer camp; and special needs expenses (e.g., orthodontic work) if applicable. Clarify if support stops when the children visit the noncustodial parent for extended periods of time (e.g., during summer vacation)

Taxation: How should future returns be filed (jointly or separately)? Who pays the penalties, interest, and other costs for previously filed joint tax returns that are audited?

Legal representation: the names and addresses of the attorneys for both parties

If one spouse is waiving alimony or a marital share of the other spouse's ownership in a business, the agreement should describe in detail how much the asset is worth and the reasons why the party is waiving any rights or claims to marital property. For example, if a wife is waiving all claims to her husband's law practice in return for the transfer to her of his share in the marital premises, this should be stated in the agreement to avoid misunderstandings or confusion. *The more complete a separation agreement, the better the chance of its enforceability.*

Sometimes a couple may decide to reconcile on a temporary basis. Language can be inserted in the separation agreement that will not permit the document to be automatically rescinded until after a sufficient period has elapsed and the parties mutually consent in writing to revoke the document.

This lengthy list merely summarizes some of the important negotiating points and considerations to be contained in a properly drafted separation agreement. Always speak to an experienced lawyer to discuss all your rights and options in this area.

SEPARATION AGREEMENTS   *See Separation*

SETTLEMENTS   *See Attorneys; Litigation*

SEVERANCE PAY   *See Employment*

SEX DISCRIMINATION   *See Civil Rights; Employment*

SMALL-CLAIMS COURTS
Also see: Arbitration; Attorneys; Courts; Litigation; Mediation

Before considering filing a lawsuit in a small-claims court, attempt to resolve your dispute in a reasonable fashion. Presenting your complaint in person (rather than on the telephone) is often an effective way of resolving a dispute. In either case, always record the full name of the person you complain to, his or her title, and the date and time of the conversation. Then write a letter to that person, thanking him or her and confirming when and how the matter is to be resolved.

Whatever problem you have with a merchant, professional, contractor, consultant, or other entity, write a demand letter and send it certified mail, return receipt requested. (The letter on page 271 illustrates this principle.) The importance of sending such a letter cannot be overemphasized. In addition to documenting your claim, the letter advises your opponent that the matter must be corrected to your immediate satisfaction or you will take additional action. If there is no response to your letter, send a follow-up letter reporting that your initial letter has not been answered and stating what your next step will be if this second letter is ignored.

HOW SMALL-CLAIMS COURTS WORK
If you cannot obtain satisfaction in a financial or business dispute through personal negotiation, you may consider suing in a small-claims court. Small-claims courts, which help people collect money in an inexpensive manner without hiring a lawyer, hear over one million cases a year in the United States. They can be used in many situations. For example, you may want to sue for money damages when:
> your employer fails to pay you
> someone damages your property and refuses to pay for repairs
> a car dealer refuses to return a refundable deposit when you cancel the deal
> you purchase merchandise that is damaged during delivery and the store refuses to replace it or refund your money

FORM 130. **Sample Letter of Complaint**

Your Name
Address
Date

(Name/Address)

Dear _____,

On (specify date), I purchased a Sonic Dishwasher, style #1401B, from Bernard's Bargain Store in Tulsa, Oklahoma. It was installed by employees from Bernard's store. The following day the appliance malfunctioned, causing a small electrical fire and damage to my utility room wall. Based on written estimates, the approximate cost of repair to my home totals $972.50. In addition, I am seeking $488.89, which represents the purchase price and/or replacement value of the dishwasher. Demand for this amount was made repeatedly to Mr. Victor Tegeria, general manager of Bernard's Bargain Store, in person on (specify date), and (specify date); by telephone; and by two (2) certified letters dated (specify date), and (specify date). To date, my requests for reimbursement have been ignored.

Sincerely yours,
(Signature)

▷ Send certified mail, return receipt requested.

- ▸ you want to recover money you paid to a mechanic who does shoddy work or gives poor service
- ▸ you are a victim of misleading advertising
- ▸ a dry cleaning establishment ruins your clothing

Small-claims courts work. Many have night sessions, and matters are resolved quickly, sometimes within a month from the time an action is filed. The maximum amount of money you can recover varies from state to state. It is usually up to $3,500.

The following sections describe the procedures of a typical small-claims court. However, the rules vary in each city and state. Before you contemplate starting a lawsuit, call the clerk of the court and ask for a written explanation of the specific procedural rules to be followed.

Who can be sued? A small-claims court can be used to sue any person, business, partnership, corporation, or government body owing you money. If you sue in a small-claims court and recover a judgment, you are precluded from suing again to recover any additional money owed to you. Thus, if your claim greatly exceeds the maximum amount of money that can be awarded in small-claims court, consider hiring a lawyer and instituting suit in a higher court.

Do you have a valid claim? In order to be successful, you must have a valid claim. This means that you must:
- identify the person or business that damaged or caused you harm
- calculate the amount of damages you suffered
- show that there is some basis in law to have a court award you damages
- be sure that you were not the main cause of your own harm, that you haven't waited too long to start the action (under the statute of limitations), and that you did not sign a written release

The fact that you have been damaged physically or monetarily does not mean that you will automatically recover money damages in a small-claims court. For example, suppose that you are assaulted after you yourself struck someone or you receive a check that bounces after you failed to deliver goods as promised. Chances are you may not recover for your loss.

Where to sue. Call the local bar association, city hall, or county court-house to discover where the nearest small-claims court is located. (In some states the small-claims court is called a justice court, a district court, a municipal court, or a justice of the peace court). In most states, suit must be brought in the county in which the person or business you are suing lives or does business. Confirm this with the small-claims court clerk and ask what days and hours the court is in session. Also find out the maximum amount of money you can sue for, what documents are needed to file a complaint, the filing fee, and whether this can be paid by cash, check, or money order.

What can you sue for? You can sue only to collect money. If you purchased a defective dishwasher and seek replacement, the court does not have the power to order the store to give you another dishwasher. But if you win your case, you will be awarded money to buy another one. Thus, before you begin to sue in small-claims court, estimate the amount of money you want to collect. Sometimes you need not have spent money before starting an action. For example, you can sue in small-claims court when a car dealer refuses to honor a warranty, which will force you to spend money to have your car repaired. (Note: Obtain written estimates from local mechanics to prove your claim.)

When calculating the amount of your claim, include all incurred expenses, including gasoline bills, tolls, telephone costs, losses due to time missed from work, sales tax, and interest, if applicable. Save all your receipts for this purpose.

Starting the lawsuit. You begin the lawsuit by paying a small fee (about $5) and either going to the court in person or mailing in a complaint that states the following information:
- your name and address
- the complete name and address of the person, business, or company you are suing (the defendant)
- the amount of money you believe you are owed

- the facts of your case
- the reasons you (the plaintiff) are seeking redress

If you are filing a claim on behalf of an individually owned business, you must list the name of the owner in addition to the name of the business. If you are filing a claim on behalf of a partnership, you must list the name of the partnership as the plaintiff. (Note: Some states do not allow a corporation to sue an individual in small-claims court.)

Be sure to write the accurate and complete name and address of the defendant on the complaint. Write the corporation's formal name rather than its "doing business as" (d/b/a) name. Thus, if you are suing a corporation, contact the county clerk's office in the county where the corporation does business to obtain its formal name and correct address. Better still, call the department of corporations in your state for the information.

When you are suing more than one person—for example, a husband and a wife—sue each one separately in the complaint. Sue a woman in her legal name rather than her married name (Mary Kane, not Mrs. Mark Kane). If your problem is consumer-oriented, state how you were mistreated. For example, if you demanded satisfaction, or sent a certified letter, specify when and to whom the letter was sent. You might also write, if applicable, that the defendant failed to make you a reasonable offer of settlement after becoming aware of your problem. Some states require you to send a demand letter before suing in small-claims court. Investigate this with the clerk.

At this time, you may also be required to prepare another form called a "summons," which notifies your opponent that you are suing him or her. Sometimes the clerk will do this. Ask the clerk whether the court will mail the summons by registered or first-class mail or personally serve the defendant on your behalf, or whether you must hire a professional process server. If a professional process server is required, ask what is needed to prove that the service was accomplished. You may have to pay the process server an additional fee (between $20 and $50). However, if you win your case, you can ask the judge to include the process server's fee in the award. When the clerk gives you a hearing date, be sure that it is convenient and you have no other commitments.

The defendant's response. When the person or company you are suing receives the summons, the defendant or his attorney can:
- deny your claim by mailing a written denial to the court
- deny your claim by personally appearing in court on the day of the hearing
- contact you to settle the matter out of court
- sue you for money you supposedly owe (called a "counterclaim")

A counterclaim is a valid claim and has standing even if the plaintiff eventually drops the action. It is not simply a defense against the plaintiff's suit.

Thus, by bringing suit, you are opening the door to a potentially damaging counterclaim or making yourself vulnerable to paying additional legal fees that may amount to more than you are asking for in damages in your initial action. People who bring suit in small-claims or other courts sometimes fail to recognize this possibility with devastating consequences.

If an offer of payment is made, ask to be reimbursed for all filing and service costs. Notify the court that you are dismissing the action only after you receive payment. (If you are paid by check, wait until the check clears.) Do not postpone the case. Tell your opponent that unless you are paid before the day of the trial, you are prepared to go to court and either commence with the trial or inform the judge about the settlement offer.

If the defendant sends a written denial to the court, ask the clerk to read it to you over the phone or go to the court and read it yourself. This is your right and may help you prepare for your opponent's defense. The following is an example of a simple denial: "I deny each and every allegation in the face of the complaint." Now you must prove your allegations in court to recover your claim.

Your duties as the moving party. It is up to you to follow the progress of your case. Call the clerk and refer to the docket number to discover whether the defendant received the complaint and whether it was answered. If you discover that the defendant has not received the complaint by the day set for the trial, request that the clerk issue a new complaint to be served by a sheriff or process server. Go to court on the trial day anyway, to be sure that the case is not dismissed because of your failure to appear.

If the complaint has been personally served and your opponent does not appear at the trial, he or she will be in default and you may be awarded a judgment automatically. In some states you still have to prove your case in order to be successful. Also, defendants sometimes file motions (legal affidavits) requesting the court to remove the default judgment on the grounds that there was a valid reason for not attending the hearing. If this motion is granted, your trial will be rescheduled.

If you are unable to come to court on the day of the trial, send a certified letter, return receipt requested, to the clerk, asking for a continuance. The letter should specify the reasons you will be unable to appear and include future dates when you will be able to come to court. Send a copy of this letter to your opponent. When you receive a new date, send your opponent a certified letter, return receipt requested, informing him or her of the revised date. Requests for continuances are sometimes not honored. Call the clerk on the day of the original trial date to be sure that your continuance request has been granted. Be prepared to send a friend or relative to court to ask for a continuance on your behalf if a continuance has not been obtained by the day of the trial.

Preparing for trial. You have several weeks to prepare for trial. Use the time wisely. First, be sure that your friendly witnesses, if any, will attend the trial and testify on your behalf. Select witnesses who are believable and who will not say things that will surprise you. In some states, you can present the judge with signed affidavits or statements by witnesses who are unable to appear at the trial. A few states also permit judges to hear testimony via conference telephones.

If necessary, the clerk can issue a subpoena to ensure the attendance of important witnesses who you believe may refuse to attend and testify. A subpoena is a document that orders a person to testify or produce books, papers, and other physical objects on a specified date. If the subpoena is issued and the witness refuses to appear, a judge can direct a sheriff to bring him or her into court or can even impose a jail sentence for a willful violation of the order.

When you come to court for the trial, check to see if the clerk has received any subpoenaed documents. If records crucial to your case have not been received, you can ask for a continuance. If you have subpoenaed an individual and do not know what he or she looks like, ask the clerk to call out the name to determine if he or she is present so you can proceed with the trial.

To maximize your chances of success, organize your case before the trial. Gather and label all your evidence so that you can produce the documents easily. You may also want to speak with a lawyer or call a lawyer's referral service for legal advice. Many communities have such advisory organizations, and they are willing to inform you, without charge, about relevant cases and statutes. This may help you know to what damages you are legally entitled. You may cite these laws, if applicable, at the hearing.

The trial. Arrive early, locate the correct courtroom, find the name of your case on the court calendar, and check in with the clerk. You should be properly attired, preferably in business clothes. Come prepared with all relevant documents. Examples are:

> receipts and canceled checks
> correspondence
> contracts, leases, and bills of sale
> warranties, advertisements, written promises, and statements made to you
> estimates
> signed affidavits or statements from friends and witnesses unable to appear at the hearing
> clear photographs and other evidence to prove your case
> an employer's statement of lost wages; a doctor's letter reflecting time lost from work
> medical bills and reports
> police and accident reports
> diagrams or charts
> copies of applicable statutes, cases, and regulations
> actual exhibits if possible, such as the used part that was installed in your car instead of the new part you paid for

When your case is called, you and your opponent will be sworn. The judge or court-appointed arbitrator will conduct the hearing and ask you questions. Be relaxed. Keep your presentation brief and to the point. Tell why you are suing the defendant and what monetary damages you are seeking. Show your evidence. Bring along a short written summary of the case. You can refer to it during the trial, and if the judge does not come to an immediate decision, he or she can use your outline for reference. Talk directly to the judge and respond to his or her questions. Show respect. Always refer to him or her as "Your Honor" or "Judge." Listen to the judge's instructions and never argue. If the judge asks you a question while you are speaking, stop immediately. Then answer the question honestly and to the point. Be diplomatic rather than emotional. Also, avoid arguing with your opponent in court and never interrupt his or her presentation.

After both sides finish speaking, you will have the opportunity to refute what your opponent has told the judge. Do not be intimidated if he or she is accompanied by a lawyer. Simply inform the judge that you are not represented by counsel and are not familiar with small-claims court procedures. Ask the judge to intercede on your behalf if you feel that your opponent's attorney is treating you unfairly. Most judges will be sympathetic, since small-claims courts are specially designed for litigants to present their cases without attorneys.

If you are a defendant. Follow the same procedures as the plaintiff; prepare your testimony, contact your witnesses to be sure that they will appear at the trial and testify on your behalf; collect your exhibits and documents; arrive early on the day of the trial and check in with the clerk. If you have any doubts about your case, try to settle with the plaintiff before the judge hears the case. Request that the case be dismissed if your opponent fails to appear. Your opponent will speak first if he or she appears. Wait until he or she is finished speaking before telling your side of the story. Point out any inconsistencies or flaws in your opponent's story. Conclude your remarks by highlighting the important aspects of the case.

Strategies to help win your case. Some states require that you send a "thirty-day demand letter" before filing an action against a retail store or business. The letter should briefly describe what happened, your monetary and/or property loss, and what you want the seller or business to do to remedy the situation. Add that you are giving the business thirty days to make a good-faith response. Otherwise, you will begin legal action. Send the letter certified mail, return receipt requested, and consider sending copies to your state attorney general's office, your local consumer protection agency, and the Better Business Bureau. If the letter is answered and the business refuses to pay, you may learn what position it intends to take at the trial. If your letter is ignored, that is evidence in court.

Obtaining judgment. Some small-claims court judges render oral decisions on the spot. Others issue a decision in writing several days after the hearing. This gives them time to weigh the testimony and exhibits. If your opponent failed to attend the hearing, a judge usually renders a judgment of default immediately after your presentation.

If you win the case, make sure you know how and when payment will be made. Check to see that all your disbursements, including court costs, filing fees, service of process, and applicable witness fees, are added to the amount of your judgment. Send a copy of the decision by certified mail, return receipt requested, to your opponent, together with a letter requesting payment. Some states require that payment be made to the court; others allow payment to be made directly to you.

Do not hesitate to act if you do not receive the money. First, contact the clerk and file what is often called a Petition for Notice to Show Cause. This will be sent to the defendant, ordering him or her to come into court and explain why payment has not been made. You should also file an Order of Execution with the sheriff's, constable's, or clerk's office in the county where the defendant resides, works, or owns a business. This may enable you to discover where the defendant has assets. The sheriff or other enforcement agent has the power to go out and collect the judgment by seizing personal property, freezing the defendant's bank accounts, placing a lien on real estate, or even garnisheeing salary. The clerk of your small-claims court should tell you exactly what to do to collect your judgment.

Final procedural points. By bringing suit in small-claims court, you usually waive your right to a trial by jury. However, the defendant can surprise you. Some states allow defendants to move a small-claims court case to a higher court and/or obtain a trial by jury. If this occurs, you will need a lawyer to represent you, and legal services could cost as much as your claim in the dispute.

Some states do not allow losing plaintiffs to appeal. Also, an appeals court will overturn the decision of a small-claims court judge only if there is strong proof that the judge was biased or dishonest. This may be difficult to prove.

SOCIAL SECURITY BENEFITS   *Also see: Medicaid and Medicare; Unemployment Insurance; Workers' Compensation*

The Social Security Act is a federal law guaranteeing benefits to people who qualify because of age, disability, or hardship. Virtually all people who work, including employees, independent contractors, household workers, and federal, state, and local government employees, can participate, as well as people serving in the armed forces. Being fully insured means that you can collect disability and other benefits when you reach retirement age and that your dependents can also collect. To be fully insured for retirement benefits, the Social Security Administration keeps track of the number of calendar quarters you worked (in which you earned more than $630) before reaching age sixty-two, as well as the amount of social security contributions made by you or on your behalf by your employer. If you work more than forty accumulated quarters of coverage in your working lifetime, you will become fully insured.

Individual benefits are calculated through a formula that includes the period in which a worker contributed payments, the total amount the worker paid into the system, the worker's age, and the type of benefits being applied for. To confirm that you have received proper credit, you can apply for a statement of earnings every few years through a local district office of the Social Security Administration. When seeking social security retirement benefits, apply for them a few months before you reach the minimum retirement age (sixty-two) because there is a waiting period of several months before actual payments begin. There is no lifetime maximum amount a person can receive from social security.

Many forms of social security benefits are available to workers and their dependents and survivors. These include:

▶ Monthly old-age benefits. These commence at age sixty-two if you choose retirement from working. If you wait to start collecting old-age retirement benefits beyond this period, say when you reach age sixty-five, the monthly benefits are greater.

▶ Disability benefits. These begin for disabled workers at any age. Being disabled means you are incapable of engaging in any significant work activity. To prove this, it is necessary to submit reports from doctors and hospitals.

▶ Dependent benefits. These are available for spouses sixty-two and older, dependent, unmarried children under eighteen (nineteen if full-time students), and disabled, unmarried children eighteen and older if an adult wage earner becomes disabled. For example, a wife can receive half of a husband's retirement benefits if she is still married to him when she reaches the age of sixty-five. A divorced wife is eligible for social security retirement and an ex-husband's disability benefits provided she was married to him for ten years or longer and is not currently married. If a female spouse worked, she can receive both her worker's retirement or disability benefit plus an amount by which her husband's benefit exceeds her benefit. A child under eighteen can receive approximately half of the monthly benefit a father or mother receives because of old age or disability.

▶ Lump-sum death benefits. These are paid to the widow(er) of a deceased worker and dependent children.

▶ Supplemental security income. These benefits are often given to needy aged persons under state law. Speak to a representative from the Social Security Administration for more details if applicable.

The Social Security Administration provides dependents' benefits to all children who are dependents of a retired, disabled, or deceased worker, including natural children, legally adopted children, stepchildren, and illegitimate children with inheritance rights. When an issue arises concerning a dependent's (or any person's) eligibility for benefits and the amount of benefits to be paid, a multi-step appeals process has to be followed. Generally, the appeals process works this way:

1. You request in writing that an initial adverse decision be reviewed by someone at the Social Security Administration who was not involved in the decision. If possible, submit detailed, additional evidence to prove that the initial decision was incorrect. Always file a timely appeal in writing. Send the notice by certified mail, return receipt requested, to prove the date your protest was sent. If you fail to file an initial appeal within a specified time, your rights to an appeal will be lost in many instances.

2. If you receive an unfavorable decision to an appeal, you have the right to appear before a judge to present your case. This is a formal hearing where you will testify and submit (and can subpoena) evidence to support your claims. Many claimants retain the services of an attorney to represent them at such hearings because a lawyer skilled in cross-examination of witnesses and knowledgeable as to social security laws and regulations can be useful.

3. If an unfavorable decision is rendered, you can request a final Appeals Council review. The right to an Appeals Council review is not automatic. The council has the power to decide what cases it wants to review. If the council agrees to review the case, it usually does not request another hearing or additional evidence. Its job is to review the record of the earlier hearing to determine if the judge erred as a matter of law. Sometimes, it will reverse an adverse decision.

The appeals process pertaining to social security benefits and laws can be extremely confusing and complicated. Therefore, it is recommended that you consult a knowledgeable lawyer to discuss your rights and options and represent you at various stages of the appeals process for a fee. Although many people do represent themselves in this area, there are time limits for filing appeals and many people are unfamiliar on how best to represent themselves properly, especially at the hearing. To determine if you have a matter that requires a specialist's services, speak to a representative at your local social security office for guidance.

(Note: In an interesting case of bureaucracy catching up to science, a young girl who was conceived through artificial insemination after her father's death was recently awarded Social Security Survivor benefits. The SSA acknowledged that the case raised significant policy issues that were not contemplated when the Social Security Act was passed many years ago.)

SPOUSE ABUSE   *See Abuse*

SPOUSE SUPPORT   *See Alimony*

Most people are more interested in selecting a stockbroker and/or financial adviser to enhance profits than in knowing and enforcing their legal rights with regard to financial investments. However, common abuses exist. These include:

- churning (excessive trading to earn increased commissions)
- mutual fund switching that results in excessive expenses and up-front charges
- charging unauthorized transactions to an account
- charging excessive commissions and illegal markups
- giving illegal and unenforceable guarantees against losses
- making false sales presentations
- insider trading
- encouraging investors to participate in legal but risky trading such as in stock options

STOCKBROKERS

When hiring an individual broker, ask for references. Check the broker's disciplinary record. Has the broker passed the series of examinations required by the National Association of Securities Dealers (NASD)? The NASD maintains a file on serious disciplinary violations committed by stockbrokers. To avoid exploitation, ask for a written agreement spelling out proposed fees and conduct.

When dealing with a broker, never allow him or her to make unauthorized trades on your account. Keep meticulous written records documenting dates, times, the substance of conversations, and the actual deals authorized. Review and save all documents you sign when opening a brokerage account.

Investors have legal rights when they open an account. These include the right to be kept informed regarding all trades that are made and to receive copies of all executed trades with complete documentation confirming these transactions. They have the right not to be given fraudulent information and not to be misrepresented. Brokers are obligated to follow investors' instructions exactly and completely. If a stockbroker or financial professional commits a fraudulent act that results in monetary damage, an investor should consider taking the following steps:

1. Complain directly to the broker in writing sent certified mail, return receipt requested.

2. If you get no satisfaction, complain to the manager of the brokerage house in writing sent certified mail, return receipt requested.

3. File a formal complaint with the New York Stock Exchange (NYSE), American Stock Exchange (ASE), the National Association of Securities Dealers (NASD), and the Securities and Exchange Commission (SEC) if applicable.

If you haven't lost money but want to lodge a complaint against a broker or firm for misleading or fraudulent practices, you can register your complaint with the District Business Conduct Committee of the NASD. The committee can bring an enforcement proceeding and impose sanctions if the broker-dealer is guilty of misconduct. At any stage of the complaint you may decide to hire an attorney to protect or enforce your rights. This should always be considered, particularly if the amount in dispute or your losses exceed $10,000. However, you may be able to obtain recompense without the expense of an attorney by filing a claim with the enforcement section of the SEC, NYSE, or NASD. Small-claims arbitration for disputes involving less than $10,000 is available through the NASD.

It is often a good idea to speak to a knowledgeable lawyer who specializes in securities law to go over all your options. He or she can tell you how to prove a case of broker fraud, what damages you may be entitled to receive, which forum is the best for resolving your matter via legal recourse, and whether you are bound to litigate your matter through arbitration. Most forms and agreements that broker-dealers require their customers to sign contain a clause binding investors to arbitration. A knowledgeable securities attorney can advise if this applies to you.

FINANCIAL ADVISERS

There is presently no federal and little state regulation of financial planners. Although financial planners recommend investment strategies, they are not required to pass exams demonstrating minimum competence, as do CPAs and lawyers. Many do not even possess a master's degree in finance or business. To protect yourself legally from abuses that may occur, consider the following:

▸ Never give your money directly to a financial planner but to the company, bank, or institution whose assets you are purchasing or acquiring. This prevents the planner from taking your money and failing to turn it over to the appropriate entity.

▸ Invest only in deals where the money is insured.

▸ Insist that the financial planner send regular, accurate statements so that you can keep track of your investments.

▸ Do not allow a planner to make decisions without your written approval.

▸ Do not give a planner power of attorney to sign documents on your behalf.

▸ Insist on a written agreement disclosing what services will be rendered and how fees will be earned. Specify areas of investment that you do not want the planner to consider.

Note: These strategies similarly apply to all relationships you may have with bankers, insurance agents, accountants, and other professionals.

SUPPORT *See Alimony; Child Support*

Most tax disputes with the Internal Revenue Service (IRS) arise after a return is filed. Returns must be filed on time, and the deadline for individuals is April 15. Penalties are imposed for late returns unless a taxpayer can demonstrate a valid reason for the delay. The following are valid reasons for filing a late return:

> Death or serious illness of the taxpayer or an immediate family member
> Unavoidable absence by the taxpayer
> Destruction by fire or other casualty of the taxpayer's place of business or business records
> Circumstances that make the taxpayer's accountant unable to complete the return
> Circumstances in which a taxpayer was unable to get essential assistance despite timely efforts

Most extensions for filing late returns are limited to several months, and the IRS will not grant extensions greater than 180 days except for taxpayers who are abroad or who can justify why additional time is needed. Taxpayers can generally obtain an extension of several months for filing by submitting an appropriate document at the IRS Service Center where the tax return will be filed, *together with the payment of any tax owed for the year.* Be aware that payment of tax is not extended beyond April 15, and additional interest and penalties are imposed on taxpayers who fail to pay the appropriate tax when the extension is filed.

HOW AN AUDIT OCCURS

Tax returns are first reviewed at an IRS Regional Service Center. The return is checked for form, execution, and mathematical accuracy. Withholding statements are matched to the return and estimated tax returns are verified. Math errors are corrected and the taxpayer is sent a notice of the error. If the correction favors the IRS, additional tax is requested; if the correction favors the taxpayer, a refund is made.

A master computer and revenue agents select the most suspect returns for office and field examination audits. Be aware of the following "red flag items," which often attract special attention.

> ▸ Unreimbursed business deductions used for personal matters. These include travel and entertainment, an automobile, and business gifts.
> ▸ Tax shelter deductions.
> ▸ Unincorporated businesses. According to the IRS, many small business owners fail to report income. The computer is instructed to carefully analyze returns of small business owner taxpayers who file income tax returns with large gross incomes, but who claim large expenses.

- Married, filing separately. Many husbands and wives file separate returns before a divorce is finalized. Often each parent claims all the children as dependents to take advantage of the deduction. The computer is instructed to pick this up.
- Charitable contributions. If you contribute property in excess of $500 (e.g., a stamp collection, painting, or Bible) to charity, the IRS scrutinizes the transaction to be sure that the fair market value of the item is not overstated. Taxpayers sometimes purchase items at a low cost, obtain written appraisals with excessive fair market values, and donate them to charity to get large deductions.
- Large casualty loss deductions. Taxpayers may claim deductions for the fair market value of items lost, destroyed, or stolen, and not the actual cost of the item. Under the law, you can claim only the lesser of the two.
- Home-office deductions. Taxpayers often inflate the amount of space allocated for business purposes. Others claim home-office deductions, but aren't qualified to take them; auditors review these claims carefully.
- Mortgage interest deductions. Returns claiming mortgage interest deductions are sometimes audited for large deductions.
- Medical expenses. Some taxpayers claim deductions for medical insurance they do not have.
- Occupation. The IRS believes that certain jobs (e.g., waiters, cabdrivers, bartenders, etc.) allow taxpayers to hide income because they receive cash tips that are not reported, and some experts believe that these returns are scrutinized closely.

HOW TO PREPARE FOR AN AUDIT

There are two types of tax audits: *office examinations* and *field examinations*. Office examinations are conducted through correspondence or through an in-person interview at an IRS District Office. Some audits are conducted by correspondence only. This is typically done for the convenience of the taxpayer in minor disputes. The taxpayer sends his explanation and supporting evidence to the IRS district office by mail. If the taxpayer and the IRS fail to agree on an adjustment, an in-person interview is then required. Field examinations are conducted in person at the taxpayer's home or office and pertinent books and records are inspected on the taxpayer's premises.

Once your return is chosen for an audit, you cannot be excused even if you have never been audited before. After being notified of an office or field examination, you should take the following steps:

Check to see if the notice is correct. Read the notice carefully and notify the IRS immediately if you received an incorrect or wrong notification letter.

Be prepared. Be familiar with the actual manuals used by IRS tax staffers when they conduct an audit. As a result of the Freedom of Information Act, you may be able to review such publications. Speak to an accountant or professional adviser for more information if applicable.

Put pertinent records in order. All deductions must be substantiated. This does not mean you are automatically liable for additional taxes if records are not complete. Agents must report unsubstantiated deductions, but they have discretion in determining deficiencies. However, the more complete and accurate your records, the better.

Bring all relevant records and substantiation to the audit. Find out what records should be brought to the examination. You are not required to bring records from past returns unless requested to do so. Usually, the auditor will require personal information (i.e., your age, marital status, and number of dependents). A birth certificate, draft card, or marriage license can prove these items. To support a claim, travel, entertainment, and transportation expenses should be substantiated in an account book or diary with corresponding documentation.

Never volunteer information. You or your tax preparer may request that the IRS agent submit all questions in writing for the preparer to answer in writing. If you choose to answer questions orally, take your time and check your records. Never answer any question if you are unsure of its meaning. Instruct your accountant or tax preparer to answer or explain the question if you don't understand it. Your preparer can even stand in for you at the audit if you give him such authority (e.g., power of attorney).

Conduct yourself properly. Dress properly and stick to the issues.

Never be intimidated. Taxpayers have the following rights, which can be asserted during the audit examination: (1) the initial meeting can be conducted in private; (2) you can change the agent assigned to the case if you have valid cause; and (3) you can stop the examination to call a lawyer if you feel uncomfortable or believe the audit is being conducted to further a criminal investigation.

Know your rights. Taxpayers are now permitted to tape all interviews with IRS agents provided they notify the IRS in advance and use their own equipment. However, the IRS is not permitted to record any interview either by mechanical device or stenographic note taking.

Taxpayers have the right to the stop the interview at any time if they want to consult with an attorney, accountant, business adviser, or any other duly qualified representative. Additionally, taxpayers cannot be forced to attend such meetings with their representatives in the absence of a subpoena. Agents are now instructed not to request that meetings take place at the taxpayer's place of business in most situations.

If an IRS agent or representative gives written advice that is relied on by the taxpayer and that later proves to be erroneous, the law specifically requires the abatement of any penalty or tax paid in reliance thereto. This is very different from the past, when taxpayers relied on such advice to their peril.

All notices sent to taxpayers regarding deficiencies, penalties, and interest due are required to be clear, concise, and complete, and problem resolution officers have been designated to help taxpayers who think they are being harassed or are suffering undue hardship at the hands of the IRS. These officers have significant powers, including the right to release property subject to IRS levy or seizure, cease or refrain from taking any action pertaining to tax collection, and assist in the correcting of problems caused by computer errors.

Following the enactment of a federal law curbing potential IRS abuse called the Taxpayer Bill of Rights, IRS workers who illegally "browse" through taxpayer information will receive strong sanctions. The law also raises the cap on damages for reckless collections from $100,000 to $1 million and requires the IRS to give taxpayers thirty days' notice before modifying or terminating installment agreements.

Try to settle a claim. It is best to attempt a settlement with the revenue agent at the initial office or field examination. By settling the claim early on, you avoid the expense and anxiety of further proceedings and may reduce the possibility that IRS agents will discover other areas of tax avoidance.

RIGHTS OF APPEAL

Once you agree with an agent's findings, you sign a form and are granted time to pay the additional tax, interest, and penalties. If there is a disagreement, you can appeal the findings or schedule a meeting with the examining agent's supervisor. Agreements are often reached at these supplementary meetings. The IRS often will concede at the appeals level if a position is well prepared and defended. A well-prepared case shows that you are ready to go to court if necessary (a forum where a loss for the IRS can set a precedent for other cases). If an agreement is not reached, the IRS will send an examination report that states its position. You may then agree with the findings and pay the assessed tax, or you may file an appeal within thirty days.

The first step in the appeals process is an appeals conference. This is an informal hearing conducted by an appeals officer who has broad authority to settle most cases. You can represent yourself (which is unwise) or be represented by a certified public accountant, a tax lawyer, or a qualified former IRS agent at the hearing.

A settlement at the appeals conference is a final disposition of the case. If settlement is not reached or the conference is waived, the IRS then issues a statutory Notice of Deficiency. The notice sets forth the IRS claim for additional tax and is commonly called the "ninety-day letter." You then have these options: (1) settle the claim by paying the tax; (2) schedule an additional appeals conference to effectuate a settlement; (3) pay the tax and seek a refund by filing an action in District Court or the Court of Claims; or (4) file a petition to the Tax Court within ninety days from the date you received the deficiency note.

By paying the disputed tax, interest, and penalties, you gain the option of bringing suit to obtain a refund in either a local U.S. District Court or Claims Court. This must be done no later than two years after the claim is disallowed. If you go this route, you cannot bring suit later in Tax Court.

The advantage of the District Court is that cases can be appealed. However, practically all taxpayers prefer to contest the claim in Tax Court. The reason is that taxpayers are not required to pay the disputed tax in order to sue.

The following steps outline the procedure in Tax Court. A taxpayer:

1. Petitions the Tax Court within ninety days after receiving the deficiency notice
2. Receives the IRS response approximately sixty days thereafter
3. Answers the IRS response within forty-five days
4. Awaits scheduling of the hearing
5. Appears at the hearing. The case is heard by a Tax Court judge and a written opinion is issued.

The following strategies may aid the appeals process:

▸ Attempt to settle the dispute once it reaches the litigation stage. The IRS settles approximately 70 percent of all cases before reaching trial. By settling the case, you avoid paying interest and other penalties.
▸ When in doubt, ask for a private IRS ruling. Some taxpayers avoid litigating disputes by requesting private IRS letter rulings. The IRS sometimes offers its position on questions or actual problems raised by taxpayers or their tax practitioners. It usually takes about four months to obtain a ruling, and the IRS does not answer all requests. When in doubt, ask your professional adviser if it is wise to obtain a private IRS ruling.
▸ Avoid representing yourself.

Here are some additional points about IRS procedures:

AUDIT NOTICES: Examining officers can audit individual tax returns for up to twenty months after the filing date.

DELINQUENT ACCOUNTS: The IRS levies assets of delinquent taxpayers. Social security benefits and pensions are not exempt from levy unless it would cause severe hardship to the individual.

INSTALLMENT PAYMENTS: The IRS allows installment payments if payment in full imposes undue hardship or loss. However, the IRS will try to keep the payment period as short as possible. Also, interest and penalties continue to be charged while installment payments are being made.

PAID INFORMANTS: The IRS pays a "10 percent" bounty for information that leads to the recovery of taxes from an individual or business. However, if an individual uncovers social security fraud, he is not entitled to a finder's fee on the money recovered as a result of the fraud because the Social Security Agency does not give financial rewards as the IRS does.

SAVING PERTINENT RECORDS

Taxpayers can be asked to account for income tax deductions for up to three years after the April 15 deadline, up to six years if they accidentally fail to report 25 percent or more of gross income, and indefinitely in cases involving tax fraud.

The following is a suggested list of retention guidelines. Consult with your accountant or lawyer for further information.

Personal Documents to Hold Indefinitely

Wills; keep current wills only

Passports, military discharge certificates, birth certificates, marriage licenses, naturalization papers, etc.

Financial Records to Hold Indefinitely

Deeds, leases, mortgages

Stock certificates, bonds, and other securities

Pension and profit-sharing plans, IRA, Keogh, and other retirement plans

Insurance policies—accident and health, auto, homeowner's, life, etc. (current policies only)

Automobile, boat, and airplane titles; receipts and canceled checks for large purchases, home improvements, as long as you own them

Tax Records to Hold Indefinitely

Tax returns and canceled checks (federal, state, and local)

Important paperwork relating to any tax audit

Insurance Records

Accident reports	six years
Claims—settled	three years
Fire inspection reports	six years
Safety records—reports	six years

Corporate Records (for those who own a business)

Articles of incorporation	permanent
Bylaws	permanent
Charter	permanent
Contracts and agreements (employment, labor partnership, government, etc.)	permanent
Copyrights and trademarks— all registrations	permanent

Deeds and easements	permanent
Leases, expired	three years
Legal correspondence of any kind	permanent
Minutes and minute books	permanent
Mortgages and notes	six years
Patents	permanent
Pension and other retirement plans:	
IRS letters of approval	permanent
Plan and trust agreement(s)	permanent
Ledgers, journals, and all other accounting records	permanent
Actuarial reports	permanent
Financial statements	permanent
Individual employee account records	permanent
Anything else related to the plan	permanent
Personnel records and files	four years
Property records	permanent
Proxies	permanent
Stock and bond records—certificates transfer lists — anything relating to stock issues and corporate indebtedness	permanent
Stockholder lists	six years

Other Business Records (Particularly for Employers)

Personnel	
Contracts and agreements	permanent
Daily time reports	four years
Disability or sick benefits	four years
Time cards	four years
Withholding statements and all other payroll records	four years

TAXES   *See also: Divorce; Employment; Real Estate; Separation; Tax Audits; Trusts*

People are required to pay numerous forms of taxes in addition to federal, state, and local income taxes. The following sections highlight some important forms of taxes. Speak to an accountant or other professional to determine if any of these taxes apply to you and how much, if any, tax is due. Maintaining accurate records to substantiate all deductions and purchases is essential in any transaction.

Business taxes. Certain types of businesses, such as corporations, are required to file annual federal, state, and local tax returns and pay a tax on the company's profits. Social security tax and all other withholdings for employees (e.g., unemployment and workers' compensation taxes) must be reported (filed) quarterly. Sales and excise taxes are also due annually. Some businesses, such as sole proprietorships, may not be required to file separate business returns and pay special taxes. Speak to an accountant if you operate a business as a partnership or limited partnership because the amount of filing fees and special taxes often depends on the business's size, number of partners, and type of partnership.

Buying and selling a business. Federal and state taxes are required to be paid depending on the amount of profit realized from the sale and the kind of business you owned. The time period in which the purchase price will be paid, whether the goodwill of the business is an asset that was sold and was included in the purchase price, and whether the seller should receive a consulting fee over time are three factors to consider when structuring the transaction to minimize the payment of various taxes.

Buying and selling a house. After selling a house, you are required to pay federal tax (and sometimes state tax, depending on where you live) on the capital gain (net profit) unless you buy and occupy a more expensive house within two years after the sale. Federal law allows you to "roll over" any net profit when you reinvest the total amount you received into a new, more expensive, principal residence (not a vacation house).

To compute your capital gain, it is first necessary to arrive at the adjusted basis, which is the original purchase price, plus costs associated with the original closing (e.g., broker's commissions), plus all capital improvements, such as the cost of a finished basement after you moved in. The capital gain (profit) is the amount by which the selling price minus all costs incurred in the sale, such as attorney fees, exceeds the adjusted basis. If you lose money on a sale, you pay no tax. Also, if you or your spouse is fifty-five or older, federal law lets you exclude one time only the first $125,000 of capital gain from taxation.

Property taxes. Local governments assess (tax) homeowners based on the value of a home. This is often automatically determined by the new purchase price when the house is sold.

Home improvements, such as building a swimming pool, may cause your house to be assessed at a higher rate, resulting in higher school, water, and district taxes. Conversely, your tax assessment may be excessive. To determine if you are paying more property taxes than you should, review the tax bill carefully when you receive it. Talk to neighbors and brokers to determine if the reported value of your property is consistent with other homes in your town or if the market value for your property has dropped. Contact your local tax assessor's office to learn how to challenge the assessment and the filing deadlines. Better still, speak to a lawyer who specializes in this service, because doing it yourself can be time-consuming and requires skill. Many lawyers charge a contingency fee for the money you save in property taxes if you obtain a successful result. This means you pay nothing to the lawyer if you lose and a specified percentage of the savings (say, 40 percent over time) if you win. Negotiate the fee and request a retainer agreement that confirms the understanding. (Note: The author has had his property taxes reduced several times through the assistance of a lawyer. Although the lawyer asked to receive 50 percent of the tax savings for a period of three years, the author negotiated a fee of 40 percent of the tax saving for the first year only.)

Taxes incidental to divorce and/or separation. Generally, alimony and maintenance payments are taxable income for the receiving spouse and tax deductible for the paying spouse. Payments received or made for child support are neither taxable nor deductible. To be treated as alimony, payments (which include certain living expenses such as utility bills, life insurance premiums, and medical expenses paid on behalf of the other spouse) must be made under a judicial decree of divorce or legal separation, under a decree of support, or be contained in a written, signed separation agreement. However, the parties are free to specify in the agreement or decree whether payments will be treated as alimony for tax purposes. For example, you and your spouse can agree that otherwise-qualifying alimony payments are to be excluded from the receiving spouse's income and are nondeductible by the paying spouse, or vice versa.

Transfers of property made incidental to a divorce or separation have no tax consequences (are considered tax-free). Attorney fees paid to obtain a divorce or separation are nondeductible. The only exception is that if you are seeking or receiving alimony, you can deduct attorney fees paid to obtain taxable alimony income payments or fees paid to obtain tax advice incident to a separation or divorce. Finally, under the "Innocent-Spouse" rule, a spouse who signs a joint tax return but is unaware that the return is inaccurate as to items generated by the other spouse may be relieved of personal liability or be required to pay only a small share of the tax understated under certain circumstances.

Tax laws relating to family members have become quite complex. Issues such as dependency exemptions, child-care expenses and credits, head-of-household status, and transfers of property, among other subjects, make it imperative for your attorney and accountant to advise you properly. If you are contemplating a divorce or separation, be aware of the tax consequences in the negotiation process. Try to have your lawyer structure a settlement that makes economic sense; be sure you understand the tax decisions that are being made on your behalf. For example, it may be worthwhile to make a greater alimony payment, knowing that you will be able to get a tax deduction for it. Ask your lawyer to itemize fees according to deductible and nondeductible items. Understand the differences between alimony and child-support payments and property transfers so you can maximize your desired tax results.

Estate taxes. Various kinds of taxes may be paid upon a person's death, including federal estate tax, federal gift tax, state estate tax, and state inheritance tax. Federal estate taxes are imposed on estates valued at more than $600,000. These taxes are computed at percentages of the value of an estate (37 percent after $600,000, up to 55 percent on amounts over $3 million) before they are distributed to the beneficiaries. The section on "Trusts" in this book discusses strategies for avoiding or reducing various taxes in this area, such as giving gifts to an individual of up to $10,000 per year ($20,000 if a couple make a gift) before subjecting the donee to a gift tax.

Other taxes include sales and excise taxes, withholding taxes (e.g., social security taxes), and income taxes. Always obtain accurate advice from your accountant, attorney, or professional adviser when computing the payment of appropriate taxes. For more discussion of income taxes, see the section "Tax Audits."

TENANT LAW *See Real Estate*

TORT *Also see: Accidents; Assault and Battery; Defamation; Fraud; Litigation; Negligence*

A tort is a civil wrong against a person, business entity, or government. It differs from a crime (which is considered an offense against society and is punished by fines and imprisonment) because the plaintiff seeks money damages from the person or entity that caused the harm. It also differs from a lawsuit based on the breach of an agreement (called a contract action).

Many kinds of tort cases are litigated. Generally, a tort occurs when you are denied peaceful enjoyment of your property, the ability to travel around freely, or are injured as the result of someone's intentional or negligent acts. For example, in a personal injury lawsuit, a case is commenced by one party seeking damages for physical and mental injuries caused by someone else's negligence. Defamation cases (which include slander and libel) are commenced to obtain damages when someone injures another person's reputation. All kinds of tort lawsuits are filed when your property is misused or damaged or when your freedom or other rights are unjustifiably taken away. In each case, if the person commencing the lawsuit has a valid cause of action and can prove damages, such as for time lost from work, physical discomfort, mental pain and suffering, loss of companionship, and special damages (i.e., punitive damages if the person's conduct toward you was egregious) among other kinds of damages, a jury or judge will award money as compensation for such items.

The following list briefly describes some common causes of tort lawsuits:
1. Assault: threat of an unpermitted harmful touching of one person by another.
2. Battery: a harmful, offensive, unpermitted touching.

3. Defamation: an oral or written statement communicated to a third party that impugns a person's reputation in the community.

4. False imprisonment: the unlawful detention of a person against his or her will without authority or justification.

5. False arrest: the unlawful detention of one person by another who falsely claims to have sufficient legal authority.

6. Fraud or misrepresentation: false statements that are relied on and cause damage to the defrauded party.

7. Infliction of emotional distress: a legal cause of action where one party seeks to recover damages for mental pain and suffering caused by another.

8. Invasion of privacy: the violation of a person's constitutionally protected right to privacy.

9. Malicious prosecution: a legal cause of action where one party seeks to recover damages after another party falsely instigates or institutes a judicial proceeding (usually criminal) that is dismissed.

10. Malpractice: the failure of a professional to render work, labor, services, or skills of suitable competence, causing personal injury or monetary damages to another.

11. Misrepresentation: a legal cause of action that arises when one party makes untrue statements of fact that induce another party to act and be damaged as a result. (Also see Fraud.)

12. Negligence: a party's failure to exercise a sufficient degree of care owed by law to another, causing personal injury or property damage.

13. Product disparagement: false statements or depictions about the quality, condition, or capability of another's product.

14. Product liability: a type of lawsuit arising when a person is injured by a defective product.

15. Replevin (or conversion): a legal action brought in court to recover possession of goods unlawfully taken or detained by another.

If you believe you have been wronged, or if you are being sued in a civil tort lawsuit, discuss your rights and obligations immediately with a knowledgeable attorney. What you need to do to win each type of case or to defend yourself successfully in each kind of lawsuit varies from state to state. Proving damages at a court trial is a skill some attorneys lack. It is also sometimes difficult to recover damages from a person or business with insufficient assets after a successful award is obtained. Thus, the decision to hire a lawyer and proceed with any lawsuit based in tort should be done with care. Your primary objective should be to achieve desired results, such as putting a stop to unwanted acts or getting back your property.

If you have personal catastrophe or other insurance to defend and/or insure your interests, contact the insurance carrier immediately if you are

sued. Many policies require the insurance company to defend you at no cost and settle (pay the settlement amount) on your behalf. If you do not feel that the lawyer defending you is competent or is zealously protecting your interests, speak to a representative of the insurance company to voice your objections. Consider hiring your own lawyer at the insurance company's or your own expense if warranted.

TRADEMARKS   *See also: Copyrights; Patents and Inventions*

A trademark is any word, name, symbol, or device, or any combination thereof, used by a business to distinguish its goods or services from those offered by others. The law of trademarks and other trade symbols is meant to keep businesses from capitalizing on the goodwill and reputation of a competitor's products or services. A mark may consist of any combination of pictures and letters. Trademarks differ from trade names in that a trademark identifies only a product, while a trade name (which cannot be federally registered) may identify both the goods and the persons selling or making them.

Trademark rights are acquired by use. It is not necessary to register a trademark before using it to identify goods and services. However, trademarks should be registered with the U.S. Patent and Trademark Office for additional protection under federal law (i.e., proof of ownership and notice to the world, especially users of the product in foreign countries). Registering a trademark means that no one else can use the mark for an initial period of ten years (and on renewal for additional ten-year periods) unless the owner of the mark stops using it. By properly registering the trademark, the registered owner acquires the right to sue in federal court and to seek an injunction stopping its use and/or recover statutory triple damages, plus attorney fees, for its unlawful use. The Lanham Act is the governing federal law for trademarks.

Consult a trademark attorney for advice and guidance if you want to create, acquire, or register a trademark. Applications for a federally registered mark can be submitted based merely on the intent to use it across state lines instead of actual use, and filing an "intent-to-use" application has the effect of reserving the mark, making it unavailable to anyone else who tries to register it. (Note: The Trademark Office cannot officially register a mark until it has actually been placed in interstate commerce.)

There are many kinds of trademarks that cannot be registered. For example, a trademark cannot be registered if it consists of a deceptive or immoral symbol or identifies a living person without his or her consent. Also, the procedure for properly registering a trademark can be complicated and costly. The written application filed with the U.S. Patent and Trademark Office in Washington, D.C., must contain an accurate drawing of the mark, other information, and the payment of a filing fee. An attorney may charge several thousand dollars for the various services that are involved in filing a trademark, including conducting an extensive trademark search prior to the actual filing. Some people prefer, as a cheaper alternative, to register the mark only in the state where the product primarily will be sold or distributed. Others file an intent-to-use application after conducting a search to determine if the name is available and weigh potential business options.

Discuss this and other matters and options with a trademark attorney, such as the steps to take immediately to protect your mark if it is being infringed upon. For example, some states have enacted "anti-dilution" statutes that protect a claimant against the "whittling away" of an established mark's selling power and value caused by its unauthorized use, provided the claimant can prove that his mark is strong and distinctive.

TRADE SECRETS   *See Employment*

TRAFFIC VIOLATIONS   *See also: Arrest; Automobiles; Crimes and Criminal Law; Driving Under the Influence*

Driving rules and violations are governed by state, county, and local laws and ordinances. People generally receive two kinds of driving citations. Tickets are given for routine infractions (e.g., an expired meter or parking illegally in front of a fire hydrant) and for more serious moving violations (e.g., speeding, failing to stop at a red light or stop sign, or leaving the scene of an accident). Routine infractions typically result in small fines (e.g., up to $50) and rarely count as points against a driver's record. However, serious moving violations can be considered criminal misdemeanors and may result in suspension or revocation of a driver's license under the laws of many states. Monetary fines for reckless driving and other penalties may be imposed, such as attending driving school/rehabilitation, jail time, or a combination, for serious offenders.

Whenever you receive a ticket for a routine infraction, read it carefully. Examine all references to your vehicle designation, plate type, registration expiration date, and make, model, and body type. The ticket should also state the violation you are charged with, including a reference to the applicable provision of law; days and hours the law is in effect; the date, time, and place where the alleged violation occurred; and the meter number, where appropriate. If the ticket is incomplete or illegible, you may wish to plead not guilty and appear in traffic court to fight the ticket. In some states, tickets are now being automatically dismissed at the driver's request if key information is omitted, described incorrectly, or if writing on the ticket is illegible. However, to take advantage of improperly written tickets, never throw them away. Make a copy and send back the original in the manner and to the address specified on the ticket. This should always be done within the time frame stated on the ticket to avoid additional penalties.

When you receive a ticket from a police officer for a more serious violation, remember the following rules. To avoid committing other crimes, do not:

- ▶ Attempt to evade the police officer if you are signaled to pull over
- ▶ Argue with the police officer or use threatening or profane language
- ▶ Try to bribe the police officer
- ▶ Refuse to show your driver's license, insurance, or registration
- ▶ Drive away from the scene before the ticket is given to you
- ▶ Rip up the ticket, especially in the officer's presence
- ▶ Incriminate yourself by admitting guilt if you can help it
- ▶ Refuse to take a breathalyzer or drug test if requested (such refusal is cause for arrest in some states)
- ▶ Automatically plead guilty to a serious driving offense, especially if you have a past record of violations and will suffer a suspension or revocation of your driver's license as a result

Speak to a skilled lawyer to discuss your case and options in the event you receive tickets for a serious offense, such as driving while intoxicated or driving in a reckless manner. Many attorneys specialize in representing drivers charged with serious offenses. They know how to plea-bargain, reduce prohibitive fines, and aggressively cross-examine police officers for maximum results. Speak to such an attorney when applicable.

TRAVEL RIGHTS   *Also see: Bailment*

Travelers have legal rights that they often fail to utilize. This includes protection in the event you are denied a room at a hotel even with a confirmed reservation or are denied boarding (are "bumped" from a flight) by an airline even though you are a ticket holder with a reservation. People are sometimes deceived by tour operators and travel agents, among other abuses. The following sections advise you of your rights in common situations.

Being "bumped" by hotels or motels. Lodging establishments sometimes overbook to protect themselves from cancellations. If the hotel does not have a room available, you are entitled to get your deposit money back. But in most states, a confirmed hotel reservation guarantees you nothing and you can obtain your deposit only if you sue. In a small number of states, if the hotel intentionally overbooks, it will be liable for special damages. You will be entitled to receive your deposit money back, as well as compensation for out-of-pocket losses (e.g., money for loss of time from work and incidental travel expense to and from the hotel). In a few cases, people have received money for emotional distress and disappointment. If you were bumped by a hotel because of overbooking and were unable to find another room at the same or a lower rate in another hotel in the area, you may want to file a claim in small-claims court. Unless the hotel has an agent or representative in your home state, you may have to file the lawsuit in the state and county where the hotel is located. Unfortunately, the expenses incurred in traveling to litigate the suit may make it impractical for you to sue the lodging establishment. If a local travel agent arranges your hotel reservations and you are bumped, you may have a better chance of recovering damages if you sue the travel agent.

Being "bumped" by an airline. Airline passenger service is minimally regulated, and each airline has its own informal policies regulating tickets. When a greater number of reservation holders arrive for a flight than anticipated, the airline will deny boarding to some of the ticket holders despite their reservations. This is referred to as "bumping." In case of an overbooked flight, anyone without a preassigned seat is treated as a standby passenger. However, before bumping any passengers against their will, the airlines are required to request volunteers to relinquish their reservations in return for a payment of compensation. The volunteers are then paid a specified sum of money or other benefits such as a free ticket upgrade. If you do not volunteer and are bumped, you are entitled to even greater compensation. The airline must furnish you with a written statement explaining how denied compensation works. You are then entitled to receive the face value of your one-way ticket. If the airline cannot get you to your destination within two hours of the originally planned arrival time (four hours for an international flight), you will then be entitled to twice the face value of your one-way ticket.

Airlines must give you a check or money draft for this amount at the place and on the day when the bumping occurs. If you are placed on alternate transportation, you must be paid within twenty-four hours. Once you accept this compensation, the amount will serve as liquidated damages and is the full amount you can recover. However, you may refuse to accept this amount and sue the airline for damages.

Even if you are bumped, however, you will not be entitled to a refund if:

- ▶ You failed to comply with the airline's ticketing, check-in, and reconfirmation requirements
- ▶ There is a government requisition of seats
- ▶ Safety or operational reasons prevent the flight
- ▶ You are offered seating in a different section of the airplane
- ▶ You are bumped from a flight outside the United States or Europe

Delayed flights. Airlines are generally not legally responsible for damages caused by delayed flights. But if your flight is canceled through no fault of the airline (e.g., a replacement plane is not available after your scheduled plane has mechanical difficulties) and not an act of God (e.g., a severe snowstorm), negotiate for extra compensation (e.g., a free ticket or transportation to and lodging at a local hotel if you are forced to spend the night at the departure location until the next flight in the morning) just as if you were bumped.

Lost or damaged luggage. If your bags are lost or damaged on a domestic flight, the airline may invoke a $1,250 per passenger ceiling on the amount of money it will pay you, or a maximum of $750 per bag, whichever is less. On international flights, the maximum amount of liability is only about $640 per bag. If you want to transport valuables that exceed this amount, consider purchasing excess valuation insurance from the airline before checking in. (Many airlines, however, refuse to sell excess valuation.) Read the policy carefully before purchasing. For example, reimbursement may not be available for stolen bags, and immediate action is often required to receive compensation under the policy. Always report all missing or damaged bags to the airline immediately and complete a Property Irregularity Report at the airline's baggage-service desk in the airport. Save a copy of the report so you can later substantiate a claim.

Consider filing a claim with your insurance company if you purchased a homeowner's policy that also covers personal property off the premises. There are several advantages to doing this. For example, while most airlines will not compensate you for the replacement value (only the depreciated value) of the items lost or damaged, your regular insurance carrier may do so. Also, the amount of supporting documentation and proof needed to receive reimbursement is often less stringent with your insurance company than an airline.

Most airlines will pay for damage to suitcases and internal items unless they believe you were careless in packing fragile items or if there is no evidence of external damage. If you cannot negotiate a satisfactory settlement and believe the damage was not caused by your negligence, consider suing the airline in small-claims court. It will be necessary for you to have the luggage repaired first and introduce the costs at the trial. Also, it will be up to the judge or arbitrator to determine whether the airline's policy of not paying more than a certain amount per bag or its contents is valid; if so, you may be reimbursed only up to a small part of your losses. Finally, if your suitcase cannot be retrieved when you get off the flight (it is delayed), the airline may reimburse you for out-of-pocket losses, such as the cost of buying a day's worth of clothes and toiletries. The amount to be obtained is subject to your negotiation skills.

Charter flights. With a charter flight you enter into an agreement with a tour operator, not an airline. Charter agreements vary from operator to operator. *Never send your money until you review the proposed charter contract, especially the cancellation provisions and the refund clauses.* What specific steps has the charter operator taken to protect your money? For example, will the money be held in escrow at a bank until the flight takes off? If the charter contract differs from advertisements or brochures you have seen, it's the contract that controls what services and benefits you will receive. However, if your retail agent accepted your money before you signed the contract and you did not receive advertised benefits, you may have a cause of action for fraud and misrepresentation against the travel agent and the charter operator, but speak to an attorney before seeking to enforce your rights.

Car rentals. *When you rent a car, read the rental agreement carefully.* Question all ambiguous terms. Ask questions if you are unsure about the computation of mileage in the cost of the lease, insurance options, surcharge taxes, drop-off charges, and late returns. It is also important to know who pays for repairs and the age and eligibility requirements of companions driving the car with you.

The question of insurance coverage is probably the most significant legal aspect of renting a car. It may be necessary to purchase additional collision and casualty insurance for a rented car because some insurance companies are now starting to eliminate the automatic inclusion of collision and liability coverage for regular policyholders who travel on business. Thus, question what insurance coverage comes with the rented car and what options are available. Check your regular car insurance policy to determine what additional coverage is automatically extended when you rent a car. Be sure to have adequate accident, liability, and property collision coverage at all times, even with a rented car.

Parking lot liability. There are generally two types of parking arrangements. In the first type, the attendant takes control of your car at the entrance, gives you a claim check, places a duplicate of the check on the windshield, parks the car, and retains the keys. This creates a legal relationship known as a bailment. In the second type of arrangement, you usually receive a claim check at the entrance, park the car yourself, lock it, retain the keys, and give the claim check back when you pay the cashier at the lot exit. This is considered a leasing arrangement — you are leasing the parking space.

If you park in a lot and leave your keys with an attendant, you can generally recover compensation from the parking lot owner if your car is stolen. If you park your car and retain the keys, the parking lot owner may not be responsible if the car is stolen. However, the lot owner may be responsible if he or his attendants are negligent. For instance, if an attendant sees someone breaking into your car and fails to call the police, the lot owner may be liable for the theft. Whether the lot owner is responsible depends on the law in your particular state and the facts of your case. For example, if you leave your car in a parking lot after the lot has officially closed and are told in advance about the closing time, you may not be able to recover compensation if your car is stolen or broken into after hours.

If an attendant parks your car and keeps the keys, the parking lot owner may not be responsible if your car is broken into unless you specifically told the attendant that there were valuable items in the car which required extra vigilance by the attendant and the valuable items were plainly noticeable to anyone passing by your car. Thus, if you have valuable items in your car and you give your keys to an attendant, inform him about the valuables to increase the chances you can recover their value from the parking lot owner if they are stolen.

Ordinarily, you may recover all of the following expenses if your car is broken into or stolen from a parking lot at which you handed over the keys to an attendant:

- The total replacement cost of the stolen items, including the car
- The cost of cab and airfare to travel to your next location
- The cost of renting a car
- The cost of sending someone to retrieve the car if found
- Possible loss of earnings (if, for example, you are a commission salesperson and valuable, hard-to-replace samples were contained in the car, resulting in your inability to sell merchandise for a period of time)

For additional protection, parking lot owners frequently print disclaimers on ticket stubs or on posted signs. These state that the lot owner will not be responsible if your car is stolen or broken into. Many judges refuse to honor such clauses, and your best defense is that you did not read the disclaimer.

TRESPASS

Trespass is a legal cause of action that arises when one party comes onto or remains on the property of another without permission. In most states, the owner of real estate is not liable for unintentional harm or injury suffered by a trespasser, because no duty exists to warn uninvited strangers of perils located on your property. Just to be safe, however, if you are aware of a peril (e.g., animal traps you place around your property), it is recommended that you post signs to warn invitees and strangers of such perils.

Additionally, virtually no states allow owners of real estate to create devices (e.g., a loaded shotgun wired to a car that will go off when the door is opened by an uninvited visitor) to maim or injure trespassers. If you discover a trespasser on your property, you have the right to use reasonable force to remove him or her. You may also sue a trespasser in a lawsuit for wrongful acts (e.g., for deliberately dumping harmful garbage on your property.) However, never take the law into your own hands if you can help it; call the police immediately.

TRIAL *See Litigation*

TRUSTS *Also see: Wills*

A trust is a legal entity that holds property for the benefit of others. Once this entity is created, one or several trustees manage, control, and invest assets on behalf of another (the beneficiary). In some trusts, the same person can act as the trustee and be a beneficiary. Trusts are created in a written document, normally on a voluntary basis, but sometimes pursuant to a court order. Most trusts are created as a vehicle to save federal and state inheritance taxes that are due upon a person's death for estates larger than $600,000. They also may enable many or all of a decedent's assets not to be processed in probate court, thereby reducing fees and related costs.

Some trusts are formed to ensure that a child or other beneficiary will not spend money foolishly. These are called spendthrift trusts. Money is placed into a trust and the beneficiary is allowed to spend only the interest and dividends that the principal generates until the trust terminates (say, on the beneficiary reaching the age of thirty). Provided the terms of the spendthrift trust cannot be modified (i.e., that it is "irrevocable") and the trustee is given full power to administer the assets of the trust with the beneficiary having no say in its operation, the principal in the trust is shielded from claims by creditors and third parties, including a spouse in a divorce action.

Estate planning includes creating the proper form of trust and using it in connection with a comprehensive will. For estates valued in excess of $1 million, it is recommended that you seek advice and guidance from a lawyer who specializes in tax or trust and estate work.

The most common forms of trusts are living (inter vivos) trusts, which are created during a person's (the grantor's) lifetime, and testamentary trusts, which are created pursuant to a person's will and take effect on the grantor's death. Trusts can be either revocable or irrevocable, and significant tax rules affect different kinds of trusts. See pages 438–441 in the Appendix for a Sample Irrevocable Trust Agreement. Never prepare such a document without a lawyer's assistance.

COMMON FORMS OF TRUSTS AND THEIR ADVANTAGES

Life insurance trusts. These direct how the proceeds from your insurance policies should be distributed and managed.

Irrevocable asset trust. An irrevocable asset trust is similar to a life insurance trust that is set up to transfer assets to another party, usually children, without giving them control of the assets. Penalties are typically imposed in the instrument to dissuade the beneficiaries from tapping into the principal (such as a statement that in the event of a withdrawal no further contributions will be made).

Generation skipping trust. When you die, your children's inheritance goes into this trust, which can retain the investment income or pay it out to your children or grandchildren. The principal is ultimately passed on to your grandchildren with reduced taxes.

Accumulation trusts. These plans increase the amount of assets by adding to the trust's principal on a regular basis.

Charitable trusts. Created to oversee the distribution of assets to a charity or other purpose, charitable trusts often differ from other kinds of trusts in that they last for an indefinite period and do not terminate automatically upon certain events (e.g., the death of a child).

Charitable remainder trust. This trust gives the income to the donor or his family and the principal to charity.

Bypass trusts. No federal estate tax is due for estates valued under $600,000 upon a person's death. This is called the $600,000 exemption. For example, if a spouse has bequeathed assets worth more than $600,000 to a spouse, no tax is due upon his or her death, but the survivor's estate will be required to pay a significant amount of tax at the time of his or her death unless most of the money has been given away in gifts or spent before the survivor's death. Under certain circumstances, a bypass or marital life estate trust can shield up to $1.2 million from estate tax .

Spendthrift trusts. These trusts are designed to avoid giving full control of all or part of an estate to a beneficiary. The trustee has legal title to the property and manages the assets of the trust.

Totten trusts. Many people with small estates open "Totten trusts" at their local banks, naming themselves or their spouses as beneficiaries of the trust. These trusts may pass assets directly to a beneficiary, and the money in these plans will ordinarily avoid probate; speak to an attorney or bank officer to understand the ramifications and advantages of establishing a totten trust where applicable.

Each state has established guidelines for the amount of compensation in fees and commissions that can be charged by a trustee to administer a trust. If a trustee acts improperly, such as by converting money for his own gain, or acts in a manner not authorized by the trust, the beneficiary may sue the trustee in court, requesting that he be relieved of his duties, reimburse the trust for any money converted, and even pay damages for the money lost by imprudent actions.

Trusts are complicated documents that must be thoroughly understood and designed to suit an individual's particular needs. Federal rules and state laws vary on formal administrative requirements, duration, and permitted purposes of a trust. If you are seeking to avoid probate or estate taxes, they are not always foolproof. One problem with irrevocable trusts is that once you have set them up, they cannot be changed. You may lose control over your assets if you appoint a third party to act as a trustee. If you create a revocable living trust, which can be changed during your lifetime, assets in the trust may not be protected from creditors. Regardless of the type of trust you eventually choose, fees paid to attorneys and trustees may be significant.

There are advantages to creating trusts. As stated previously, when designed properly, trusts can help reduce estate taxes for couples with estates of over $600,000, can manage assets for minors or adults who are incapable of making prudent financial decisions, and may shield money from creditors. A competent trustee can make sound financial decisions for a minor in your absence or upon your death. Most important, the use of a trust may allow assets to be passed directly to named beneficiaries without time-consuming probate and court intervention.

Get answers to the following questions from a professional adviser:

▸ How can a trust ensure that my business will run smoothly after my death?

▸ What are the advantages and disadvantages of establishing a revocable living trust (whose terms can be changed during the grantor's life) and/or an irrevocable living trust (whose terms cannot be changed once it is established)?

▸ What assets need not be placed in a trust because they will automatically pass directly to a beneficiary without going through probate?

▸ Is it advisable to have a durable power of attorney and a will (sometimes called a pour-over will) drafted in connection with a trust? If so, what should be included in these documents?

▸ What steps must be taken immediately after a trust is formed? For example, do I have to transfer and rename assets that are being transferred into the trust?

Do not establish a trust yourself after reading a book. Speak to an experienced lawyer or financial adviser. Regardless of the kind of trust employed, the use of a trust and will together is quite complicated and must be evaluated on a case-by-case basis. Understanding if a trust or a will (or both used in combination) is suitable for your particular needs always requires sound professional guidance.

UNEMPLOYMENT BENEFITS   *Also see: Employment*

Each state imposes different eligibility requirements for collecting unemployment benefits (e.g., the maximum amount of money that may be collected weekly, the normal waiting period required before payments begin, the length of such benefits, and the maximum period you can wait before filing and collecting). States also differ on the standards of proof required to receive such benefits. You must learn all essential details before filing. Do this by contacting your nearest unemployment office for pertinent information.

The following are some of the questions to ask:

▸ How quickly can I file?

▸ When will I begin receiving payments?

▸ How long will the payments last?

▸ What must I do (i.e., must I actively look for employment?) in order to qualify and continue receiving benefits?

▸ How long did I have to work for my former employer in order to qualify?

▸ What must I prove to collect if my ex-employer contests my claim?

▸ When and where will the hearing be held?

- Will I have the opportunity to review the employer's defense and documentation submitted in opposition, which are often contained in the official file, before the hearing?
- How can I learn whether witnesses will appear on the company's behalf to testify against me?
- How can I obtain competent legal counsel to represent me?
- How much will this cost?
- Will a record be made of the hearing? If so, in what form?
- Can the hearing examiner's decision be appealed?
- Can I recover benefits if I was forced to resign?
- Is the burden on the employer to demonstrate that I was fired for a good reason (e.g., misconduct) or is the burden of proof on me to demonstrate that I did not act improperly?
- Can I subpoena witnesses if they refuse to appear voluntarily on my behalf? Will the hearing examiner assist me in this regard?
- Are formal rules of evidence followed at the hearing?

As you can see, collecting unemployment benefits is not always a simple matter, especially if your claim is contested by an ex-employer. In most states, you can collect benefits if you were fired due to a business reorganization, massive layoff, job elimination, or for other reasons that were not your fault. In many situations, you can even collect if you were fired for being unsuited or unskilled or for overall poor work performance. However, you generally cannot collect if you voluntarily resigned from a job (unless you were forced to resign for a good reason) or were fired for misconduct.

The following are common examples of acts that justify the denial of unemployment benefits based on misconduct:
- Insubordination or fighting on the job
- Habitual lateness or excessive absence
- Drug abuse on the job
- Disobedience of company work rules or policies
- Gross negligence or neglect of duty
- Dishonesty

Although these examples appear to be relatively straightforward, employers often have difficulty proving that such acts reached the level of misconduct. This is because hearing examiners typically seek to determine whether a legitimate company rule was violated and whether or not that rule was justified.

PREPARING FOR THE HEARING
Once you file for unemployment insurance benefits and learn that the employer is contesting your claim, it is your responsibility to follow the progress of the

case carefully. Consider whether you require representation by experienced counsel at the hearing (especially if you are considering suing the employer in court over other issues and do not want to lose the first battle). If you are anticipating receiving the maximum benefits allowed (which in some states can exceed $325 per week) and expect to be unable to find gainful employment for a long period of time (e.g., six months), it may be advantageous to hire a lawyer, because the amount of money being contested is significant. Often, people do not know how to act or represent themselves properly at unemployment hearings. Many claimants are told by unemployment personnel that a lawyer or other representative is not required and that prehearing preparation is unnecessary. They then attend the hearing and are surprised to learn that the employer is represented by an experienced attorney who has brought witnesses to testify against their version of the facts. Additionally, some claimants are unprepared for the grueling, possibly humiliating cross-examination lasting several hours that they can be subjected to. Other claimants lose at the hearing because they don't understand the purpose of their testimony or what they must prove to receive benefits.

Plan on being able to attend the hearing on the date in question. If you cannot be present, speak to a representative responsible for scheduling, explain your reasons, and ask for another convenient date. This should preferably be done in person. Indicate future dates when you know you can appear. Call that individual the day before the old hearing date to confirm that your request has been granted.

An unemployment hearing is often no different from a trial. Witnesses must testify under oath. Documents, including personnel information, warnings, and performance appraisals, are submitted as exhibits. The atmosphere is rarely friendly. Thus, you must prepare in advance what you will say, how you will handle tough questions from the employer, and what you will try to prove to win the case.

When preparing for the hearing, be certain that all your friendly witnesses (if any) will attend and testify on your behalf. If necessary, ask a representative from the unemployment office to issue a subpoena compelling the attendance of key disinterested witnesses (e.g., co-workers) who refuse to testify and voluntarily attend. If the unemployment representative has no power to do this, wait until the first day of the hearing. Explain to the judge or hearing examiner the necessity of compelling the appearance and testimony of key witnesses. The judge may grant your request depending on the relevance and reasonableness of the request.

Organize your case before the hearing to maximize your chances of success. If you have a lawyer, meet with him or her before the hearing date to learn the correct way to testify and what you must prove to win benefits. Collect all evidence so it can be produced easily at the hearing. Practice what you will say at the hearing. Prepare an outline of key points to be discussed and questions to ask each witness of the ex-employer.

THE HEARING

Arrive early on the hearing date and advise a scheduling clerk of your presence. Bring your evidence and come properly attired (preferably in business clothes). In some states you can review the entire contents of your employment file before the hearing; don't forget to ask for this if appropriate. When your case is called, all witnesses will be sworn in. Show the judge your evidence and never argue with the hearing examiner. Listen to your lawyer's questions before answering. Avoid being emotional and avoid arguing with your opponent at the hearing.

After the employer finishes testifying, you will have the opportunity to cross-examine the testimony and refute what was said. If the employer is represented by an attorney and you feel intimidated because you are not represented by counsel, tell the judge that you are not familiar with unemployment hearing procedures. Ask the judge to intercede on your behalf when you feel your opponent's attorney is treating you unfairly. Most judges are sympathetic, since unemployment hearings are specifically designed for people to present their cases without an attorney.

OBTAINING A DECISION

Decisions are not usually obtained immediately after the hearing. You will probably be notified by mail (sometimes two to six weeks later). Be sure to continue filing for benefits while waiting for the decision. Many people forget to do this and lose valuable benefits in the process.

SHOULD YOU APPEAL?

If you are notified that you have lost the decision, read the notice carefully. Most judges and hearing examiners give specific, lengthy reasons for their rulings. If you feel that the ruling was incorrect or you disagree with the judge's opinion, you may want to file an appeal and have the case reconsidered. However, it is best to speak with an experienced labor attorney to get an opinion before doing so. You may discover that your chances of success with the appeal are not as good as you think. Appeals are not granted automatically as a matter of right in many states. If the judges on the Appeals Board believe that the hearing judge's decision was correct factually or as a matter of law, the decision will go undisturbed.

Recognize that the odds of winning the appeal are not in your favor if you lose at the initial hearing. Often, the amount of time needed to review the transcript or tape of the proceeding(s), prepare an appeal brief, and reargue the case makes it too expensive and time-consuming. Thus, depending on the particular facts of your case, appealing the hearing may not be worth it. However, if new material facts come to light, if relevant witnesses are willing to come forward and testify at an appeal hearing, or if the success of another case (e.g., a discrimination lawsuit that was previously filed) depends on a successful outcome of the unemployment matter, this could make a difference.

Typically, you have only a specified period of time (say, thirty days) to file your appeal, so file the appeal properly and timely to avoid having it dismissed due to a technical error. Finally, speak to a skilled labor lawyer if you have already received benefits and now are being asked to return the money because you lost the hearing. In some states, the failure to return benefits is a crime and you can be prosecuted. A lawyer may be able to structure a settlement with a small payout over time (and no interest charges imposed) to diminish the burden of having to pay all the money back immediately. Often, people out of work do not have sufficient funds to do this, so speak to an attorney where appropriate.

UNIONS   *Also see: Employment*

A labor union is an organization of working people who collectively negotiate (or attempt to negotiate) benefits, better working conditions, grievances, and employment contracts for its members. The federal Taft-Hartley Act allows certain classes of workers to band together, form, and join unions. Supervisors, managers, executives, and some government employees cannot be union members because "blue-collar" (nonmanagement) working-class status is often required for membership.

If you belong to a union, much of your protection as a union member derives from the powers and actions of the National Labor Relations Board together with the U.S. Department of Labor and state law. For example, if you believe that your union is not zealously representing your interests, or has engaged in an unfair or illegal labor practice, it may be necessary to file a grievance against your union through a local office of the NLRB.

Under the federal National Labor Relations Act and state laws, employers are forbidden from penalizing workers who decide collectively to discuss common grievances and form and participate in a labor union. Workers cannot be disciplined, demoted, reassigned, fired, threatened, or treated poorly as a result of union involvement. Neither can employers offer nonunion workers more benefits or better working conditions than union workers. Speak to a labor attorney immediately to protect your rights if this is the case.

In certain situations, such as when an employer has entered into a comprehensive collective bargaining arrangement with a union permitting and recognizing the union to act as spokesperson for all workers of the company, you may be forced to belong to a union even if you do not want to participate in union activities. This means that union dues may be automatically deducted from your paycheck and there is little you can legally do about it. However, in some right-to-work states, people are permitted to work at companies without being required to participate in union activities or be affiliated with a union.

There are several advantages and disadvantages in belonging to a union. For example, many employers are bound to follow rules concerning discharge procedures in collective bargaining agreements previously negotiated and ratified by a union. In such agreements, employers are sometimes forbidden from terminating union workers except in situations involving worker misconduct or serious offenses. If a union worker is fired wrongly or under circumstances suggesting that the employer acted improperly, the union should schedule an arbitration proceeding or grievance procedure without delay so that an impartial arbitrator can hear the case and hopefully reinstate the terminated worker (and order back pay and other lost benefits in appropriate circumstances). If you are a union member and are fired unfairly from a job, speak to a lawyer hired by the union or a private lawyer immediately to discuss your options and rights.

Most collective bargaining agreements provide little or no severance pay and other post-termination benefits for terminated union workers. This differs from nonunion employees, who may be able to receive large severance packages after having worked for an employer for many years and been discharged through no fault of their own, such as for a job elimination or company reorganization.

Finally, when a union is organizing a strike, an employer may be able to keep workers off the premises legally (known as a "lockout") in an attempt to force the union to back down. Union workers may not receive any pay during a lockout, and sometimes the employer does not have to rehire workers if they were permanently replaced while on strike. Under federal law, the obligation to rehire union workers who were replaced often depends on whether the employer acted properly before the strike. For example, if the employer engaged in an unfair labor practice that caused the strike (e.g., failing to provide a safe work environment), the employer may be legally required to rehire its original union workers.

Rules concerning the circumstances permitting union workers to legally strike (e.g., to protest unsafe working conditions) are spelled out in the National Labor Relations Act and are discussed in the section "Employment."

VETERANS' RIGHTS

Being a veteran or serving in the military reserve provides many rights. These include receiving free medical care at VA hospitals for service-connected disabilities, enhanced job rights and job security, educational assistance under the GI Bill, guaranteed mortgages, home-improvement loans and repairs, and a disability pension, among other benefits.

Job rights. Several federal laws, including the Veterans' Re-employment Rights Act and the Military Selective Service Act, protect the rights of veterans and military personnel. These laws provide that employees who are in military service are regarded as being on an unpaid leave of absence from their civilian employment. For example, if you are on extended reserve duty (up to four years) or called up for short-term emergency duty merely to serve in a motor pool across town, you must be offered a job with the same pay, rank, and seniority upon your return. An employer is prohibited from forcing an employee to use vacation time for military training. Employers are obligated to assist employees who return from military service and cannot deny promotions, seniority, or other benefits because of military obligations. Thus if an employee was promoted or promised a raise right before a call-up, he or she must receive a job in line with the promotion or the promised raise upon return, together with reinstatement of all benefits, including those (e.g., additional pay) that would have been earned if the employee had continued to work.

Companies that receive job applications from military personnel and reservists after termination of active duty status and don't hire them must fully document the reasons for denial. Any employer not following the above rules is subject to investigation and action by the local U.S. Attorney's office or private lawsuits filed by claimants in the federal district court sitting in any county where the employer maintains a place of business. Charges can also be brought under the Veterans' Benefits Improvement and Health Care Authorization Act of 1986. These laws prohibit discrimination in all aspects of employment, including hiring, promotions, and discharge, on the basis of membership in the military.

Educational assistance. Military personnel who served on active duty for more than 180 days between February 1, 1955 and December 31, 1976 and who were honorably discharged, or who were discharged from the military due to a service-connected disability, may qualify to receive free tuition, a subsidy for books, and other educational benefits under the GI Bill of Rights. The amount of tuition assistance received depends on how long you served in the armed forces. Children and surviving spouses also qualify, so speak to a representative from a local Veterans Administration office for more details if applicable.

Loans for residence purchases. Qualified veterans may be entitled to receive guaranteed loans at favorable interest rates to purchase a residence (e.g., a private home, condominium, or mobile home). As a veteran you may use a "VA loan" to buy, build, or improve a home you intend to live in. Details regarding favorable interest rates and the maximum amount you may borrow for this purpose can be obtained from a representative at a local VA center.

Medical benefits and pensions. Qualified veterans are entitled to free medical care at a VA hospital or on an outpatient basis. And, depending on the disability they sustained, military pensions are available for veterans and their wives, children, and dependent parents. The rules regarding qualification and computation of benefits vary, so speak to a lawyer or representative from the Veterans Administration for advice when applicable.

Visitation issues affecting children must be resolved when a couple divorce or are in the process of obtaining a legal separation. Visitation (sometimes referred to as physical custody) differs from legal custody. A parent who has legal custody has the right to decide major issues affecting the child, such as religious training, health and medical decisions, and school matters. A parent who has physical custody acquires the right to visit with the child only during predetermined periods. He or she has no legal right without the other parent's consent to decide important matters affecting the child while the child visits.

Generally, the parent not awarded or given legal custody (i.e., the noncustodial parent) is still entitled to visit his or her child(ren) on a regular basis. A schedule of visitation is negotiated between the parties directly or by their lawyers, and there are many items to consider. The schedule should take into account what is in the best interest of the child as well as what works (in terms of time) for a working parent. During visitation it is important that the child be able to spend quality time with the noncustodial parent. By law, the custodial parent is not allowed to interfere with or discourage the visit.

Divorcing or separating parents should try to agree on visitation terms privately before a divorce. Although a judge is not bound by the parents' agreement concerning visitation and is free to modify a schedule that he considers not to be in the child's best interest, time-consuming and expensive litigation can be avoided by agreeing on a reasonable schedule of visitation privately.

A comprehensive checklist of points involved in divorce proceedings that parents should initially explore follows. Once a decision is reached on most of these points, they can then be incorporated into a written agreement.

- ▸ With whom will the child principally reside?
- ▸ What form of visitation rights will the noncustodial parent receive? How many visits per week? When? Is notice to the custodial parent required before each visit? How much notice is required (e.g., a telephone call twenty-four hours before the visit) to cancel a visit?
- ▸ Can visitation take place in the custodial parent's home or must the child be seen away from the house?
- ▸ How much extended visitation (e.g., four consecutive weeks each summer; alternating school holidays for a period of not less than three days per holiday) with the noncustodial party will be given?
- ▸ If the custodial parent does not allow unhampered visitation, what rights does the noncustodial parent have (e.g., the right to stop paying child support)?
- ▸ What happens to child support during the months when the child visits exclusively with the noncustodial parent? For example, can the noncustodial parent stop paying support for two months if the child lives with him or her every summer?

- Can the child visit with the noncustodial parent on special occasions such as his or her birthday (or part of the child's birthday), Father's or Mother's Day, special family celebrations, and matters affecting the child, such as awards ceremonies?
- Is the custodial parent permitted to relocate with the child or must the child live within a certain geographic area (e.g., within a fifty-mile radius) to allow the noncustodial parent's visitation rights to continue unimpaired? If the child relocates to a distant site with the noncustodial parent's permission, will the custodial parent reimburse the other for the additional travel fees and costs (e.g., airplane tickets and cab fares) necessary to visit the child?
- What happens in the event of an emergency while the child is in the noncustodial parent's care? Will the custodial parent leave a telephone number where he or she can be reached at all times for this purpose?
- If the child is ill, what extra visitation rights does the noncustodial parent have?

If you are a noncustodial parent, there are other rights you should insist on. These include:

- The right to have reasonable, unhampered telephone communications with the child at established times.
- The right to receive complete, detailed information from any pediatrician, general physician, dentist, consultant, or specialist attending the child for any reason and to receive, on request, copies of any reports given by them to the other parent.
- The right to receive a copy of the child's report card within one week after the child receives it.

The completed separation agreement should include a provision that clearly defines the rights the noncustodial parent has in the event the custodial parent fails to comply with any agreed-upon provisions. This could include, for example, the right to arbitrate the matter, with the losing party responsible for all reasonable legal fees and costs incurred by the prevailing party. The agreement should also include a clause providing for the alteration of agreed-upon terms due to changed circumstances.

Many people have the mistaken belief that joint legal custody involves joint physical custody (e.g., the child lives six months with the mother and then six months with the father). This is not so, as such arrangements are typically frowned upon by the courts as being disruptive to the child. Also, visitations should not be used as an excuse to argue with a spouse or check on the other parent.

Judges have traditionally ruled that the right of the noncustodial parent to visit the child is practically absolute. Simply stated, a parent may not be deprived of his or her right to reasonable and meaningful access to the children of the marriage unless exceptional circumstances have been presented to the court. This means that a judge cannot revoke visitation privileges unless the child's welfare is in danger. For example, it may be judicial error to deny visitation rights because the noncustodial parent has failed to make support payments or because the parents are unable to resolve their differences. Even unwed fathers are entitled to visitation privileges, unless it is judged not to be in the child's best interests.

Contact an attorney immediately if the custodial parent is denying you access to your child or is flouting court-ordered visitation benefits (e.g., not allowing you to visit your children on the days previously agreed to or shortening or canceling the visitation period without notice). This should be done particularly if you learn that your former spouse intends to move the children to a distant place; the law generally states that nothing should deprive the child of access to either parent (particularly where there is an agreement for joint custody, liberal visitation rights, or territorial restriction). Some noncustodial parents have even gained custody of their children as a result of such action.

Speak to a lawyer as well if you are a custodial parent who does not approve of a noncustodial parent's lifestyle. For example, although you have agreed to alternating weekend visitations where the child is picked up on Friday evening and returned by 7:00 P.M. Sunday evening, you do not have to agree that your child spend weekends in the same apartment with the noncustodial parent's lover, or if the noncustodial parent is a habitual drug user and leaves the child unattended.

Finally, in some states, the noncustodial parent, under certain circumstances, has the right to stop support payments if a minor child between the age of fourteen and eighteen refuses to visit or communicate with that parent.

WILLS   *Also see: Trusts*

Unfortunately, most people do not consider proper estate planning strategies before their death and die without a will (intestate). This creates a number of problems that are discussed below. Every adult reading this book should execute a will (also known as a Last Will and Testament) to save estate taxes, allow your family to be provided for, and protect an ongoing business, among other advantages.

A will performs the following functions:

▶ Enables you to name a guardian to care for minor children after your death and that of your spouse
▶ Enables you to appoint an executor you trust (a spouse or close relative) to manage your estate, simplify the administration of your estate, and save fees (by appointing a spouse, for example, all executor fees, often

one to four percent of the value of the estate, would go to her; the will could also waive the requirement of having an executor post a bond, which costs money)

▶ Enables you to distribute property in your estate, such as real estate (a house), personal property (cars and jewelry), and intangible property (money in the bank, bonds, profit-sharing benefits, and life insurance proceeds) to survivors of your choosing rather than your closest heirs by blood

▶ Directs how a business is to be run or sold

▶ Directs how and when certain assets are to be distributed

▶ Reduces the time before your property is transferred to your survivors

▶ Provides for burial, cremation, or special instructions

▶ Provides specific bequests of particular items of personal property

▶ Often saves probate and other expenses

▶ Can provide for the support of charitable causes

▶ Can establish a simple trust and identify the trustee(s) and their powers

▶ Directs the immediate payment of your burial expenses, debts, and taxes

▶ Allows you to disinherit certain members of your family if that is your desire

▶ Encourages you to collect and store important papers and legal documents (e.g., all deeds, life insurance policies, and copyright registrations) for easy access after your death

The probate process. When a person dies, a legal process called probate takes place. Probate involves a series of court proceedings that supervise the distribution of an estate. Depending on the size of the estate, probate is typically lengthy (often it takes a year or more for property to be distributed) and expensive. If a person dies intestate, state law governs to whom his or her estate will be distributed. For example, in some states, if you die without a spouse, your child or closest relative will receive 100 percent of your estate. Additionally, a judge will appoint a stranger as executor to oversee the administration of your estate, and that person may receive large fees for his or her work. That person may not have the interests of your family at heart. Obviously, it is better for you to choose the executor before your death, as well as have your assets distributed according to your stated wishes.

As the person named in a will to settle a decedent's affairs, the executor performs many valuable functions. He or she obtains death certificates for banks, insurers, and others; locates the will and distributes copies to beneficiaries; consults a lawyer for proper planning and tax advice; applies to probate court; evaluates survivors' immediate cash needs; and proceeds with an accounting of the estate's assets. The executor need not be a relative or a lawyer. Due to the size of statutory fees involved (e.g., often 5 percent of the first $100,000, 3 percent up to $1 million, and a smaller percentage thereafter in some states), executors' fees can be quite steep. To save money, it may be best to appoint a family member as the executor, who then in turn can hire a lawyer by the hour to handle many of these functions.

Filing the will in probate court. The executor or representative named in the will files it with the probate court (sometimes referred to as the surrogate court) located in the county where the deceased lived. Often the executor will hire a lawyer to ensure that the will is probated correctly. Over a period of months, the executor then files a statement that identifies the location, existence, and value of all the assets in the estate as well as all the liabilities. A Petition of Probate is prepared that describes the contents of the will. All beneficiaries and potential heirs are notified by mail that the will has been offered for probate. Proceedings may then ensue if anyone contests (challenges) the provisions in the will. Eventually, a judge approves the will and authorizes the executor to pay all the bills, such as taxes, administration fees, and executor's fees, and distribute the remaining assets to the named beneficiaries. After a final accounting is rendered to and approved by the probate judge, the estate is deemed "closed."

It is best to structure as many assets as possible to be transferred to your beneficiaries automatically and immediately without having to go through probate. For example, money held jointly in a bank account, real estate owned jointly (two names on a deed), and life insurance proceeds can pass directly to a named beneficiary or co-owner without involvement in the probate process. In this way you can use a will to arrange certain elements of your estate (e.g., designate the legal guardian of your minor children and your executor), while still allowing many of your assets to pass to your beneficiaries immediately.

Each state requires that certain formalities be followed in order for a will to be valid. The will must be clearly drafted, and at least two witnesses must be present when you sign (execute) the will. The witnesses' names and addresses must appear on the will. Typically, witnesses should not be interested parties (i.e., those that stand to benefit from an inheritance). The slightest mistake in the preparation or execution of a will may cause a judge to deem it to be null and void (not legally recognized). The sample will on pages 314–315 illustrates many of these points.

Some states permit video wills to be introduced into probate proceedings. In a video will, the deceased is observed reading the contents of his or her written will; the will is then signed in front of witnesses, who then execute their signatures. Even in a video will, the deceased has still signed a written document. The video will is used to demonstrate that the maker was competent (i.e., aware of the significance of her actions, what assets she was transferring, and what she was signing), was of sound mind, and did not sign the will under threats or duress. Speak to a lawyer to learn more about the use of a video will if appropriate.

To ensure the effectiveness of proper estate planning, it is necessary to

FORM 132. Last Will and Testament

-of-

Name

I, (name), residing at (address), being of sound mind and disposing memory, and well knowing the true extent of my worldly possessions, and the natural objects of my bounty, do hereby make, publish and declare this instrument to be my Last Will and Testament, hereby revoking any and all other Wills and Codicils at any time heretofore made by me.

FIRST:

I direct my Executor to pay my just debts, funeral expenses, and the expenses of my last illness as soon after my demise as practicable.

SECOND:

I hereby give, devise, and bequeath the following bequests:

A. To my beloved son (name), my jewelry consisting of my rings, watches, gold bracelets, and religious artifacts, for his use, now and forevermore.

THIRD:

I give, devise, and bequeath all the rest, residue, and remainder of my estate, real, personal, and mixed, of whatsoever kind or nature, and wheresoever situate, of which I may die seized or possessed, or to which I may be in any way entitled to have an interest, including all property over which I have the power to appoint (hereafter referred to as my residuary estate), to my beloved husband, (name), for his own use absolutely and forever.

FOURTH:

In the event my beloved husband (name) predeceases me, I give, devise, and bequeath to my beloved son (name), per stirpes, all the rest, residue, and remainder of my estate, real, personal, and mixed, of whatsoever kind or nature, and wheresoever situate, of which I may die seized or possessed, or to which I may be in any way entitled to have an interest, including all property over which I have the power to appoint (hereafter referred to as my residuary estate) for his own use absolutely and forever.

FIFTH:

A. I hereby nominate, constitute, and appoint as Executor under this my Last Will and Testament, my beloved husband, (name). In the event that he shall predecease me, fail to qualify, or become unable to serve for any reason, then I nominate, constitute, and appoint as Alternate Executor my son, (name).

B. I direct that my Executor (including my Alternate) be permitted to qualify and serve without furnishing a bond or other security for the faithful performance of his duties, in this or any jurisdiction, any laws of any state to the contrary notwithstanding.

SIXTH:

A. In the event that any Beneficiary or Beneficiaries under this Will and I should die in a common accident or disaster, or under such circumstances that it cannot be established by proof who died first, then all provisions of this Will shall take effect in like manner as if such beneficiary or beneficiaries had predeceased me as the case may be.

B. In the event that my beloved husband, (name), and I die in a common accident or disaster or under such circumstances that there is not sufficient evidence to determine who predeceased the other, I hereby declare it to be my will and intent that it shall be presumed that my husband shall have predeceased me and that this Last Will and Testament and any and all of its provisions, shall be construed on the assumption and basis that he shall have predeceased me as the case may be.

SEVENTH:

As used in this Will, wherever necessary or appropriate, the masculine gender shall be deemed to include the feminine and neuter genders and vice versa, and the singular shall be deemed to include the plural and vice versa.

IN WITNESS WHEREOF, I have hereunto set my hand and affixed my seal this _____ day of (specify).

_____
(Name)

The foregoing instrument, consisting of two (2) pages including this one, each identified by the initials of the Testatrix, (name), was signed, sealed, published, and declared by the above-named Testatrix as and for her Last Will and Testament, in the presence of us, who in her presence, at her request, and in the presence of each other, have hereunto subscribed our names as witnesses this _____ day of (specify), this attestation clause having first been read aloud.

_____ residing at _____

_____ residing at _____

_____ residing at _____

STATE OF _____)

COUNTY OF _____):

being severally sworn, depose and say that they witnessed the execution of the attached Will of (name), the within named Testatrix on the _____ day of (specify); that the said Testatrix in their presence subscribed said Will at the end thereof and at the time of making such subscription declared the instrument so subscribed by her to be her Last Will and Testament; that they at the request of the Testatrix and in her sight and presence and in the sight and presence of each other witnessed the execution of said Will and subscribed their names as such, and each, after observing the Testatrix herein, observed her and in their opinion believe her to be of sound mind, memory and understanding, not under any restraint or in any respect incompetent to make a Will; that the attached Will was so executed at (address) and that they are making this affidavit at the request of the Testatrix.

_____

_____

_____

Severally subscribed and sworn to me
this _____ day of (specify).

_____
Notary Public

▷ *Author's note:* This simple will was prepared for a wife with a surviving husband and married son. The couple had few assets except for a modest house. This simple will is included for illustrative purposes only; do not copy and try to use this simple will for yourself without speaking to a lawyer, as it may not be reliable or legal with respect to your own particular circumstances.

consult a lawyer experienced in trust and estate work, especially if you own your own business, anticipate a potential challenge to your will by a disgruntled heir, have children from more than one marriage, have varied and significant assets, or wish to design an estate plan to minimize estate and inheritance taxes. Although there are many books published on how to create your own will and avoid probate, this is not recommended unless you have a simple estate with very few assets. Writing your own will can be a big mistake. A lawyer should be hired to draft the document to be certain your will stands up legally and that property is disposed of per your instructions.

An initial, comprehensive consultation with a competent lawyer typically costs less than $250 dollars (unless you have a complicated estate). Hopefully, the preparation and execution of an accurate will and other documents will not cost more than an additional several hundred dollars. A knowledgeable and caring lawyer should also provide you with competent tax advice and estate savings tips, ensure that previous wills and codicils (amendments to wills) have been properly revoked, explain the legal consequence of certain provisions you may want to include, and help you prepare an inventory of all your assets. In short, you should have a sufficient opportunity to evaluate and create a well-thought-out estate plan that encompasses all your concerns and wishes. Hiring a competent lawyer is a small price to pay for peace of mind and the sound financial and legal estate planning advice you should receive.

You can always change your will during your lifetime when there has been a marked change of circumstances in your finances or lifestyle (e.g., after a divorce) or a significant change in the tax laws has occurred. The creation of a new will should also be considered if an executor, trustee, guardian, or witness has died and you want to name a substitute or change certain beneficiaries (e.g., add a new charity or another beneficiary like a newborn child or remove a disloyal relative). Although some people simply add a codicil to an existing will, it is better to destroy an old will in its entirety and draft and execute a new will. This can minimize an argument that a provision in an old will was not properly revoked.

Finally, original wills should be kept in a safe place where they will not be lost or destroyed. Do not place the original (only copies) in a safe deposit box because you may have difficulty retrieving the contents of the box after someone dies. Safe deposit boxes are often "sealed" by the IRS or another taxing authority within twenty-four hours of a safe deposit owner's death.

The Appendix contains a Sample Gift Made Prior to Will Bequest (page 442) for your review. Never prepare such a document without a lawyer's assistance. Additionally, it is a good idea to prepare a last will and testament checklist similar to the one on page 317. Keep a copy of this checklist in an accessible place so that your executor and trusted family members or advisers can retrieve valuable documents and information more easily at your death, thereby facilitating their administrative duties.

FORM 133. **Last Will and Testament Checklist**

1. Name and address of attorney who prepared the will.

2. Location of original will and copies of will and/or trust.

3. Name and address of funeral director.
   - Funeral requests: plot, type of service, special arrangements.
   - If applicable, specify payment for burial from: life insurance, social security, union benefits, Veterans Administration, pension benefits, burial insurance, or fraternal organizations (if any).

4. Statement and wishes of a personal nature, such as donor requests, special bequests, or other instructions.

5. Name and address of accountant.

6. Name and address of stockbroker, personal banker and/or financial advisor.

7. Location and account #s of stocks, bonds, bank accounts, security box.

8. Name and address of insurance agent.
   - Location of life insurance policies and other insurance policies.

9. Name and address of employer and pension administrator.
   - List pensions and retirement benefits.

10. Name and address of executor and alternate executor.

11. Name and address of guardian and alternate guardian (if applicable).

12. Location of birth certificate, passport, marriage license, tax returns, stock certificates, safe deposit keys, bank passbooks, and other important business and financial papers, such as title registrations to cars, boats, artwork, and other valuable personal property, deeds to real property, mortgages and promissory notes, copyright and patent registrations.

WORKERS' COMPENSATION BENEFITS

Also see: Accidents; Employment; Litigation

Each state has enacted its own particular laws with respect to workers' compensation benefits, which provide aid for employees who suffer job-related injuries. Compensation may be available for the following kinds of injuries:
- Preexisting conditions that the workplace accelerates or aggravates, such as a bad back, even if pain from the injury is delayed until a later time
- Injuries caused during breaks, lunch hours, and work-sponsored recreational activities such as a company-paid New Year's Eve party, and on-the-job injuries caused by company facilities, such as a shower located on premises

- Diseases such as lung cancer, if contracted by asbestos or other carcinogenic exposure at work as a result of the usual conditions to which the worker was exposed by his/her employment
- Injuries resulting from mental and physical strain brought on by increased work duties or the stress caused by a requirement that the employee make decisions on other employee dismissals. In some states, this includes employees who develop a disabling mental condition because they cannot keep up with the demands of the job and a supervisor's constant harassment

In all states, employers with more than several workers are obligated to maintain workers' compensation insurance through a company or be self-insured for the benefit of their employees (not independent contractors). The advantage to employers is that they cannot be sued in court for injuries sustained by workers during the course of employment even if an accident was caused by an employer's fault (negligence). Lawyers representing injured workers typically prefer that their clients not receive workers' compensation benefits because, if they don't, the potential of being awarded money for damages in a personal injury lawsuit becomes vastly greater.

Not every on-the-job injury is covered under workers' compensation. State courts seem to be divided on whether an employee can recover for an injury sustained during horseplay. Many states will not award benefits to a person who is injured while intoxicated or who deliberately inflicts injury on himself. Furthermore, an employee who is injured while traveling to or from work is not generally entitled to benefits unless the employer has agreed to provide the worker with the means of transportation, pay the employee's cost of commuting, or if travel is required while performing his/her duties. For example, if the employee regularly dictates office memos into a dictating machine within a vehicle, the car may be deemed part of the workplace.

If a worker leaves the employer's premises to do a personal errand and is injured, no compensation should be due. However, if an employee is injured while returning from company-sponsored education classes, or goes to the restroom, visits the cafeteria, has a coffee break, or steps out of a nonsmoking office to smoke a cigarette and is injured, workers' comp boards and courts typically recognize that employers benefit from these "nonbusiness" employee conveniences and often award compensation.

Alert your employer immediately if you are injured on the job. Under compensation laws in most states, each employer must promptly provide medical, surgical, optometric, or other treatment for injured employees as well as provide hospital care, crutches, eyeglasses, and other appliances necessary to repair, relieve, or support a part of the body. A company's medical team may eliminate unnecessary treatment, but an injured employee may select his or her own physician for authorized treatment, provided that physician is authorized by the state's workers' compensation board. Note: To review the medical care an injured worker is receiving, employers may engage the services of a competent physician, who may be able to determine, for example, whether less expensive home care is more appropriate than hospital care. A medical consultant can also evaluate claims from the employee's doctor to see if they are self-serving.

Do not be afraid to report an accident or file a claim in writing. Most states prohibit companies from firing, demoting, or otherwise punishing an employee for filing or pursuing a valid workers' compensation claim. Do this as quickly as possible so your case is not dismissed as being untimely. While you are receiving medical treatment, save all receipts of drug purchases, trips to the doctor (including tolls and cab fares), and all related purchases. You are generally entitled to full reimbursement for all direct out-of-pocket expenses, including payment for doctors, hospitals, rehabilitation, and related therapy. Dependents are entitled to receive death benefits in case of death, and you will be compensated for the loss of a limb or body part (e.g., an eye) based on a predetermined schedule. You are also entitled to compensation for lost wages and income. The type of disability you suffered (e.g., temporary, permanent, partial, and/or total disability) will determine the amount of money you receive each week and how long you will receive such benefits. Each state has maximum limits for weekly benefits, which typically do not exceed 75 percent of a worker's regular weekly salary.

Do not hesitate to consult a lawyer specializing in workers' compensation cases or a personal injury lawyer where applicable, particularly if your employer refuses to provide benefits. The lawyer can protect your rights in many ways. For example, if anyone other than your employer or co-worker was even partly responsible for the accident, you may be free to file your own liability insurance claim against that person or business. If for any reason your accident is not covered by workers' compensation because you are an independent contractor or because the company has no coverage, you may be able to file a lawsuit against your employer in the same way that you can sue anyone who causes you personal injury. In such a case, additional damages, such as attorney fees, money for mental pain and suffering, loss of companionship to a spouse, and even punitive damages, may be awarded.

Under certain circumstances you may also be able to collect social security benefits, retirement benefits or unemployment compensation, and health insurance payments while you are collecting disability benefits. A labor lawyer or one who specializes in workers' compensation law can advise you. A knowledgeable lawyer's services may be required to argue your case at the hearing stage before an administrative law judge, especially when the issues are not clear-cut (such as when and where the accident occurred to determine initially if workers' compensation is applicable). Lawyers handling workers' compensation matters are generally quite knowledgeable about medical conditions and dealing with doctors. Resolving the issue of whether an accident caused a partial or permanent disability can involve tens of thousands of dollars in future wages. (Note: workers' compensation lawyers typically work on a contingency fee basis.) It may also be necessary to retain the services of a lawyer if you want to pursue an unsuccessful verdict at the appeals stage. Thus, consult a specialist for advice and guidance where applicable.

ZONING LAWS   *Also see: Real Estate*

Each town, city, county, and state characterizes real estate as belonging to certain categories such as commercial, light commercial, or residential. Once designated, the property contains restrictions on the use and type of buildings that can be built. For example, you may be precluded from adding another wing to your house or building a gazebo in the backyard because of zoning laws. Zoning restrictions can also disallow using a piece of property commercially when it is located in a residential district.

Where real estate is located can affect its value. Although the zoning of a parcel may be redefined after a variance is approved, such hearings often take many months and are not always successful. It may be necessary to petition a local zoning board, give testimony at a hearing, submit plans by your architect, demonstrate that owners of adjacent parcels will not be adversely affected, and even supply results of environmental studies where applicable. Since obtaining a variance after you buy real estate may be difficult, carefully investigate this aspect before purchasing any piece of property. Consult a lawyer skilled in zoning and real estate work for advice where applicable.

APPENDIX OF FORMS

FORM 6. Sample Agreement of Open Adoption

[Adoptive mother] and [Adoptive father] agree to adopt [Child]. [Birth mother] and [Birth father] agree to consent to the adoption of [Child] by [Adoptive mother] and [Adoptive father].

It is further agreed that following finalization of the adoption it is in the best interests of [Child] that there be contact between him/her and the following members of his/her family: [Birth mother, Birth father, etc.].

Such contact will consist of (specify, such as the exchange of pictures twice yearly and three annual visits between [Child] and [Birth mother] and [Birth father]). The birth parents will send pictures of themselves to the [Adoption agency] on or about [Date] and [Date] of each year. The adoptive parents will send pictures of [Child] to the agency on or about [Date] and [Date] of each year. The agency will send the pictures of the birth parents to the adoptive parents and pictures of the child to the birth parents.

The visits will take place on or about [Date], [Date], and [Date] of each year at the offices of the agency. In the event the agency ceases to do business in [State], the parties will select another mutually agreeable agency to receive communications from the parties and to provide a site for visitation.

The parties agree that this agreement shall remain in force until [Child] reaches his/her eighteenth birthday, unless such agreement shall become contrary to [Child's] best interests. In such an event the parties agree to attempt to reach an amicable resolution of the issues presented in accordance with the best interests of the child and if unable to do so will petition a court of competent jurisdiction to assist in resolution of any unresolved issues.

The parties to the agreement understand and intend that any disagreement or litigation as to the issue of visitation or other contact between the child and his/her birth family after the adoption is final shall not affect either the validity of the adoption or the custody of [Child].

Signed: [Birth mother]
                                                           [Birth father]
                                                           [Adoptive mother]
                                                           [Adoptive father]

FORM 8. Alimony Questionnaire (To Help Determine Support)

1. Length of marriage

2. Present employment:
   ▷ # of years working at this job
   ▷ rate of pay
   ▷ specify bonuses, perks, extra compensation (e.g., commissions)
   ▷ prospects for raises, promotion, or advancement
   Specify important past employment.
   If not presently employed, state why.

3. Education and special training

4. Were you employed at the time of marriage? If so, state the job, rate of pay, and education level required.

5. State your education level, job skills, special training, and work experience at the time of your marriage.

6. State the education level, job skills, special training, and work experience you now possess.

7. Describe your health. Do you currently have special needs requirements that must be met by an employer in order for you to be gainfully employed?

8. Will you be self-supporting after the divorce? How? Do you anticipate any special circumstances or unusual expenses you will be required to incur that could impact your ability to be self-supporting after the divorce? If so, please specify.

9. Did you sacrifice any career opportunities so that your spouse could attend school and obtain a degree, license, or success in his or her occupation? If so, please describe.

10. Is there currently any prenuptial agreement or contract between the parties which specifies the amount of support you are to receive after the divorce? If so, please produce this for your lawyer's review.

11. Have you calculated your financial needs after the divorce? How much monthly income is required to maintain your current standard of living? Does this include cost-of-living adjustments and long-term tax consequences? How long do you think such support should be paid?

12. Do you feel you deserve to receive alimony? Why?

▷ *Author's note:* In order to evaluate your need for alimony (also referred to as maintenance), it is necessary to consider the above questions and discuss the answers with your lawyer. Remember that the law differs from state to state in this area and also depends on the unique facts of each case, so get experienced legal advice. Also, please refer to the Comprehensive Living Expenses Checklist on pages 149–151 to help you compute and determine financial need.

FORM 14. **American Arbitration Association Regional Offices**

ARIZONA
333 East Osborn Rd., Suite 310
Phoenix, AZ 85012-2365
(602) 234-0950/230-2151 (fax)

CALIFORNIA
2030 Main St., Suite 1650
Irvine, CA 92714-7240
(714) 474-5090/474-5087 (fax)

3055 Wilshire Blvd., Fl. 7
Los Angeles, CA 90010-1108
(213) 383-6516/386-2251 (fax)

600 B St., Suite 1450
San Diego, CA 92101-4586
(619) 239-3051/239-3807 (fax)

417 Montgomery St.
San Francisco, CA 94104-1113
(415) 981-3901/781-8426 (fax)

COLORADO
1660 Lincoln St., Suite 2150
Denver, CO 80264-2101
(303) 831-0823/832-3626 (fax)

CONNECTICUT
111 Founders Plaza, Fl. 17
East Hartford, CT 06108-3256
(860) 289-3993/282-0459 (fax)

FLORIDA
799 Brickell Plaza, Suite 600
Miami, FL 33131-2800
(305) 358-7777/358-4931 (fax)

201 East Pine St., Suite 800
Orlando, FL 32801-2742
(407) 648-1185/649-8668 (fax)

GEORGIA
1975 Century Blvd. NE, Suite 1
Atlanta, GA 30334-3203
(404) 325-0101/325-8034 (fax)

HAWAII
810 Richards St., Suite 641
Honolulu, HI 96813-4714
(808) 531-0541/533-2306 (fax)
In Guam, (671) 477-1845/477-3178 (fax)

ILLINOIS
225 North Michigan Ave., Suite 2527
Chicago, IL 60601-7601
(312) 616-6560/819-0404 (fax)

LOUISIANA
2810 Energy Centre
1100 Poydras St.
New Orleans, LA 70163-2810
(504) 522-8781/561-8041 (fax)

MARYLAND
10 Hopkins Plaza
Baltimore, MD 21201-2930
(410) 837-0087/783-2797 (fax)

MASSACHUSETTS
133 Federal St.
Boston, MA 02110-1703
(617) 451-6600/451-0763 (fax)

MICHIGAN
One Towne Square, Suite 1600
Southfield, MI 48076-3728
(810) 352-5500/352-3147 (fax)

MINNESOTA
514 Nicollet Mall, Fl. 6
Minneapolis, MN 55402-1092
(612) 332-6545/342-2334 (fax)

MISSOURI
1101 Walnut St., Suite 903
Kansas City, MO 64106-2110
(816) 221-6401/471-5264 (fax)

One Mercantile Center, Suite 2512
St. Louis, MO 63101-1614
(314) 621-7175/621-3730 (fax)

NEVADA
4425 Spring Mountain Rd., Suite 310
Las Vegas, NV 89102-8719
(702) 364-8009/364-8084 (fax)
From Reno, (702) 786-6688

NEW JERSEY
265 Davidson Ave., Suite 140
Somerset, NJ 08873-4120
(908) 560-9560/560-8850 (fax)

NEW YORK
666 Old Country Rd., Suite 603
Garden City, NY 11530-2004
(516) 222-1660/745-6447 (fax)

140 West 51st St.
New York, NY 10020-1203
(212) 484-3266/307-4387 (fax)

205 South Salina St.
Syracuse, NY 13202-1376
(315) 472-5483/472-0966 (fax)

399 Knollwood Rd., Suite 116
White Plains, NY 10603-1916
(914) 946-1119/946-2661 (fax)

NORTH CAROLINA
428 East Fourth St., Suite 300
Charlotte, NC 28202-2431
(704) 347-0200/347-2804 (fax)

OHIO
441 Vine St., Suite 3308
Cincinnati, OH 45202-2973
(513) 241-8434/241-8437 (fax)

17900 Jefferson Park, Suite 101
Cleveland, OH 44130-3490
(216) 891-4741/891-4740 (fax)

PENNSYLVANIA
230 South Broad St., Fl. 6
Philadelphia, PA 19102-4106
(215) 732-5260/732-5002 (fax)

Four Gateway Center, Rm. 419
Pittsburgh, PA 15222-1207
(412) 261-3617/261-6055 (fax)

TENNESSEE
211 Seventh Ave. North, Suite 300
Nashville, TN 37219-1823
(615) 256-5857/244-8570 (fax)

TEXAS
13455 Noel Rd., Suite 1440
Dallas, TX 75240-6620
(214) 702-8222/490-9008 (fax)

1001 Fannin St., Suite 1005
Houston, TX 77002-6708
(713) 739-1302/739-1702 (fax)

UTAH
645 South 200 East, Suite 203
Salt Lake City, UT 84111-3834
(801) 531-9748/323-9624 (fax)

VIRGINIA
707 East Main St., Suite 1610
Richmond, VA 23219-2803
(804) 649-4838/643-6340 (fax)

WASHINGTON
1325 Fourth Ave., Suite 1414
Seattle, WA 98101-2511
(206) 622-6435/343-5679 (fax)

WASHINGTON, DC
1150 Connecticut Ave. NW, Fl. 6
Washington, DC 20036-4104
(202) 296-8510/872-9574 (fax)

FORM 18. **Sample Attorney Opinion Letter**

Date

(Name of Client)
President
ABC Manufacturing, Inc.
City, State, ZIP code

Re: Opinion Letter Regarding (name of employee, e.g., fictitious Jane Doe)

Dear (Name):

After our initial meeting, I reviewed the papers you sent me regarding the Jane Doe matter. As I understand the situation, Ms. Doe signed a written employment agreement with your company. The agreement stated that in the event of termination or resignation from her job as your sales associate, Ms. Doe would not call upon or sell goods to any of your customers for a period of one year.

You have asked me to advise you about your rights, the chance of success, the amount of damages that may be recoverable, the costs involved, and my ability to represent you in this matter.

RIGHTS OF ABC AGAINST MS. DOE

When Ms. Doe signed a written contract with your company, she agreed not to call upon any of your customers for a period of one year. This is called a *restrictive covenant*. To enforce your covenant against Ms. Doe, you must bring an action against her and prove your case. You have a choice of forums in which to bring the action: federal district court or a state court. Since it is easier to obtain an *injunction* (an action to immediately stop her from selling to your customers) in a state court rather than a federal court, I would suggest the state court.

I must advise you that injunctions are largely discretionary with the court, and there are several factors here that might lead it not to grant one on your behalf. Since you waited eight months before threatening to sue Ms. Doe, my guess is that you have about a twenty percent (20%) chance of obtaining an injunction.

RIGHTS TO AND AMOUNT OF DAMAGES

Your chances of obtaining money damages against Ms. Doe are much greater than your chances for an injunction. From our discussion and the facts and evidence suggested in your papers, it appears that the amount of recoverable damages would be measured by the profits you have lost since the time Ms. Doe began selling competitive products to your customers.

It should be understood that if we win our case, however, Ms. Doe may not voluntarily pay the judgment. Thus, it may be necessary to enforce the judgment by having a sheriff or marshall seize and sell assets not exempt from execution. However, if Ms. Doe does not own assets, such as real estate, money in bank accounts, stocks, etc., but owns only personal items exempt from execution under the laws of our state, then any judgment you obtain may not be worth much.

NEGATIVES TO LAWSUIT

Besides the fact that you may lose a lawsuit against Ms. Doe or that any judgment obtained may be uncollectible, there are other negative factors you should consider before bringing a lawsuit. These include court costs and attorney fees. Court costs are recoverable, but other costs, such as travel, the time lost when you are called to testify (or required to help us develop the case), and attorney fees, are not recoverable.

MY SERVICES

I am familiar with the nature of your manufacturing business and am qualified to represent you in this matter if you choose to proceed. My fee would be based on my normal hourly charge of $250 for myself and $150 for associates. Trial time is billed at $1,000 per day. The initial services of preparing a complaint and serving same would cost approximately $300. Preparing a request for an injunction and attending a hearing on the injunction would cost approximately $2,500.

It is quite possible that Ms. Doe would not retain her own counsel and not answer the complaint. This means that a default judgment could be taken without the necessity of a trial. Here attorney fees would probably amount to no more than $1,000.

I require a $1,000 retainer to open a file and commence an action.

If you wish to proceed with this matter, I will need to know the full names and addresses of your customers to whom Ms. Doe is presently selling and the estimated sales volume which you have lost.

If you have any questions, please call me.

Very truly yours,
(Name of Attorney)

FORM 21. **Bill of Sale for an Automobile**

(Name of Seller, "Seller" located at: _____) in consideration of the sum of $X received from (Name of Buyer "Buyer", specify address), the receipt of which is acknowledged, hereby sells, transfers, and conveys the following personal automobile: (specify model, year, color, make, vehicle identification number, engine serial number) together with the following accessories: (specify).

1. The total price for the automobile is $X which does (or does not) include freight, shipping, delivery, and insurance costs. Payment shall be made as follows: (specify).

2. Seller warrants that he is the lawful owner of the automobile and is selling it free of all liens and encumbrances. The Seller will defend title of the automobile against any claim or demand except any lienholder disclosed in this Bill of Sale. The automobile sold is in good condition with the exception of (specify known defects). While the automobile was in Seller's possession, the odometer was not altered or disconnected and the odometer reading of X miles reflects the actual mileage.

3. Buyer has examined the automobile and purchases it as is.

4. Additional terms and conditions essential to this Agreement include: (specify).

Dated: _____   _____
                                Name of Buyer

Dated: _____   _____
                                Name of Seller

State of (specify)
County of (specify)

On (specify date), before me came (name of Seller), personally known to me to be the individual described hereinabove and who executed the foregoing Bill of Sale, and duly acknowledged to me that he (she) executed the same.

_____
Notary Public

FORM 22. **Property Storage Contract**

This contract for Storage Services, is made by and between (Name of Individual or business "Owner", located at: _____) and (Name of Individual or business "Bailee", located at: _____) on (specify date).

WHEREAS, the parties desire that Bailee provide storage services for Owner with respect to the following property ("Property", specify items); and

WHEREAS, Bailee accepts such responsibilities and agrees to perform such duties as specified herein;

NOW, THEREFORE, FOR VALUABLE CONSIDERATION SET FORTH HEREIN, THE PARTIES AGREE AS FOLLOWS:

1. This Agreement will commence on (specify date).

2. The Bailee agrees to render the following services: (specify in detail, including storage, maintenance of property, repairs, etc.).

3. The subject Property will be stored at (specify location). Bailee has inspected the Property prior to storing same and states that such Property is in good condition (with the exception of: specify).

4. The Bailee agrees to exercise reasonable care to protect the Property from theft or damage and shall maintain adequate insurance in the face amount of no less than $X to protect Owner from any loss or damage caused by Bailee's negligence. At all times during this Agreement shall title in the Property remain with Owner.

5. Bailee will be paid a monthly fee of $X.

6. This Agreement will have an initial term of X months. Thereafter, Owner can terminate this Agreement at any time upon X days prior written notice. Owner will make any last payment prior to retrieving said Property. Bailee agrees to return all Property in the same condition as such Property was received. In the event the Property is not received in such similar condition (state the penalty).

7. If Owner fails to pay for and/or retrieve the Property after the expiration of the original X month term, Bailee can (specify, such as store the Property and charge $X per month, deem the Property to be abandoned, sell it, and reimburse Owner for the difference of the net receipts of sale less what was due Bailee, etc.).

8. This Agreement supersedes all prior agreements and understandings and may only be modified in writing and signed by both parties. This Agreement is in force when signed below.

9. This Agreement cannot be assigned without the prior consent of Owner.

10. This Agreement shall be governed by the laws of the state of (specify).

_____
Name of Owner

Dated: _____

_____
Name of Bailee

FORM 23. **Animal Boarding Contract**

This Contract for Animal Storage Services, is made by and between (Name of Individual or business "Owner," located at: _____) and (Name of Individual or business "Bailee," located at: _____) on (specify date).

WHEREAS, the parties desire that Bailee provide storage services for Owner with respect to the following pet or animal(s) ("Animal," specify); and

WHEREAS, Bailee accepts such responsibilities and agrees to perform such duties as specified herein;

NOW, THEREFORE, FOR VALUABLE CONSIDERATION SET FORTH HEREIN, THE PARTIES AGREE AS FOLLOWS:

1. This Agreement will commence on (specify date).

2. The Bailee agrees to render the following services: (specify in detail, including manner of care, feeding, exercise and shelter, veterinary care, etc.).

3. The subject Animal will be stored at (specify location). Bailee has inspected the Animal prior to storing same and states that such Animal is in good condition (with the exception of: specify).

4. The Bailee agrees to exercise reasonable care to protect the Animal from harm or theft and shall maintain adequate insurance in the face amount of no less than $X to protect Owner from any loss or damage caused by Bailee's negligence. At all times during this Agreement shall title in the Animal remain with Owner. The parties agree that the value of Animal for insurance purposes shall be $X. Bailee agrees to store and care for the Animal in conformity with all appropriate state and local health rules and regulations.

5. Bailee will be paid a monthly fee of $X, including refundable security of $X. Additional expenses including veterinary bills may also be due upon the presentment of receipts documenting same.

6. This Agreement will have an initial term of X months. Thereafter, Owner can terminate this Agreement at any time with X days prior written notice. Owner will make any last payment prior to retrieving said Animal. Bailee agrees to return the Animal in good condition. In the event the Animal is not received in good condition (state the penalty). In the event all conditions are complied with between the parties, Bailee agrees to return Owner's security immediately at the termination of this Agreement.

7. If Owner fails to pay for and/or retrieve the Animal after the expiration of the original X month term, Bailee can (specify, such as store the Animal and charge $X per month, deem the Animal to be abandoned, sell it, and reimburse Owner for the difference of the net receipt of sale less what was due Bailee, etc.).

8. This Agreement supersedes all prior agreements and understandings and may only be modified in writing and signed by both parties. This Agreement is in force when signed below.

9. This Agreement cannot be assigned without the prior consent of Owner.

10. This Agreement shall be governed by the laws of the state of (specify).

_____
Name of Owner

Dated: _____

_____
Name of Bailee

FORM 28. **Acknowledgment of Paternity**

Name of Father, residing at (location), hereby acknowledges that he is the natural father of (Name of Child) born to (specify Name of Mother) on (state birth date).

Name of Father agrees to pay Name of Mother $X per month as reasonable support for said child (or state, agrees to be bound by the laws of this state concerning child support), as well as take all reasonable steps, including (specify, such as regular visits one evening per week with the child), so that his son/daughter will receive his love, care, and affection.

By acknowledging his paternity, Name of Father agrees that Name of Child is entitled to inheritance rights upon his death.

In the event Name of Mother marries, Name of Father will/will not allow said child to be adopted by her new husband.

Date: _____

Witness: _____

_____
Name of Father

State of X
County of X

On (specify date), before me came (Name of Father), personally known to me to be the individual described hereinabove and who executed the foregoing Acknowledgment of Paternity and duly acknowledged to me that he executed the same.

_____
Notary Public

FORM 29. **Acknowledgment of Parenthood**

Name of Father, residing at (location), and Name of Mother, residing at (location), hereby acknowledge that they are the natural parents of (Name of Child) born on (state birth date).

Both parties agree to take all reasonable steps to care, nurture, and provide support and affection for Name of Child.

Both parties agree that Name of Child is entitled to inheritance rights upon their death.

Date: _____

_____
Name of Father

_____
Name of Mother

Witness: _____

FORM 30. **Request Letter Under the Freedom of Information Act**

Your Name
Address
Telephone Number
Date

Name of Director or Official
Specify Agency
Address

Re: My File (specify)

Dear (specify name),

Please be advised that pursuant to the federal Freedom of Information Act (5 U.S.C. 552) and the Privacy Act (5 U.S.C. 552a), I hereby request a copy of (specify, such as "all documents maintained by your agency about me").

If it is determined that a portion of the file is exempt from release, I request that you release all documents that are not exempt, and inform me as to those specific records that cannot be released, and the reasons why. If I disagree with your decision, I understand that I have the right to formally appeal same.

In the event it is determined that none of the file can be released, please identify what specific documents cannot be released and the reasons why.

Finally, since the law permits you to waive or reduce fees when providing such information is primarily in the public interest, I request that you waive all fees since my case fits this exception.

Please contact me directly at (address) in writing or by calling me by phone (list your daytime phone number) if you have any questions concerning this request. Thank you for your prompt attention and assistance in this matter.

Very truly yours,

Your name

▷ Send certified mail, return receipt requested.

FORM 31. **Letter of Appeal Under the Freedom of Information Act**

Your Name
Address
Telephone Number
Date

Name of Director or Official
Specify Agency
Address

    Re: My File (specify)

Dear (specify name),

    Please be advised that on (date), I received a letter from (name) of your agency advising me that my request for documents pursuant to the federal Freedom of Information Act (5 U.S.C. 552) and the Privacy Act (5 U.S.C. 552a) was entirely denied (or denied in part).

    Enclosed please find a copy of the letter I originally sent together with your agency's response.

    Please treat this letter as a formal appeal pursuant to the Freedom of Information Act. As such, kindly reconsider your agency's decision and provide me with the information requested as soon as possible. The reasons for this request are (such as: that the information sought is not properly covered by the exemptions cited in the statute).

    In the event I do not receive these documents by (date), I intend to file a formal lawsuit immediately thereafter. Hopefully, this can be avoided and I thank you for your prompt attention and assistance. Feel free to contact me at (address) in writing or by calling me by phone (list your daytime phone number) if you require any additional information.

Very truly yours,

Your name

▷ Send certified mail, return receipt requested.

FORM 33. **Stop Payment Request**

Date
Your Name
Address
Bank Acct. #

Name of Bank
Address

Dear (Name of Officer):

As we discussed by telephone on (specify date), please treat this letter as an immediate request to stop payment on my check dated (specify), #X, in the amount of $X, made payable to (specify).

My account is in the name of (specify) and the account # is #X.

Thank you for your prompt assistance and attention to this matter.

Very truly yours,

Your name
Name of Business

▷ Send certified mail, return receipt requested.

FORM 34. **Notice of Bad Check**

Date

Name
Address

Dear (Name):

Please be advised that your check dated (specify) #X in the amount of $X and made payable to (specify) has been dishonored by your bank (specify bank name, address, and branch #). After speaking with your bank, we have learned that there are insufficient funds in account #X to honor this check (copy of letter or notice received enclosed).

Accordingly, it is hereby demanded that you immediately replace this check with cash or a certified check in the amount of $X, which includes the service charge of $X.

In the event we do not receive payment in full of said funds by (specify date), legal proceedings shall be immediately commenced to enforce our rights, and we reserve the right to take other legal steps, including contacting the District Attorney's Office (and specify, such as the Better Business Bureau). In the event a lawsuit is filed, we shall seek additional penalties, prejudgment interest, legal fees, costs, and other charges.

Hopefully this can be avoided, and we thank you for your immediate attention and assistance in this matter.

Finally, please be advised that upon receipt of the above amount, we will return the dishonored check to you.

Very truly yours,

Officer's or Your Name
Name of Business

▷ Send certified mail, return receipt requested.

FORM 35. **Notice of Lost Credit Card**

Date
Your Name
Address

Name of Person or Business
Address

Dear (Name of Person or Officer):

As we discussed by telephone on (specify date), I believe my credit card(s) have either been lost or stolen. Accordingly, please treat this letter as my immediate request for you to deny issuing credit on the following credit card(s): (specify card #, name to whom the card was issued, and the name of the credit card company).

In the event you receive charges on said card(s) after today, please notify me at once since such charges are unauthorized.

Thank you for your prompt assistance and attention to this matter. If you desire further information or wish to speak with me during weekday business hours, you may reach me at (provide telephone number).

Very truly yours,

Your Name
Name of Business

▷ Send via fax and certified mail, return receipt requested.

FORM 36. **Sample Loan Agreement**

THIS AGREEMENT, is made by and between (specify Borrower, located at: _____) and (Lender, located at: _____) on (specify date).

Borrower agrees to pay Lender the full balance of $X on or before (specify date) (or, if appropriate, in equal monthly installments of $X). This amount is computed as follows: (state amount of loan, down payment, amount financed, finance charges, and interest as an annual percentage rate.

Borrower has the right to prepay the entire amount due before (specify date) without penalty.

Any installments not paid within X days after they are due will be subject to a late fee of $X. If there are two or more consecutive late payments, the Lender may accelerate the entire unpaid amount and demand payment in full after giving X days' written notice.

In the event this Agreement is to be placed with a lawyer or collection agency to enforce same, legal fees and costs not to exceed $X shall also be due and owing upon the institution of a lawsuit.

_____
Lender

_____
Borrower

FORM 37. **Notice of Default (for payment or contract performance)**

Date
Your Name
Address

Name of Person or Business
Address

Dear (Name of Person or Officer):

Please be advised that pursuant to (specify, such as the terms of a contract, loan agreement, promissory note, or other obligation) you are in default because (specify, such as failing to make a payment by a certain date, failing to complete work or deliver goods pursuant to a contract, etc.).

As we discussed by telephone on (specify date), please treat this letter as an immediate request for you to comply with the terms of our agreement (copy of agreement or document enclosed).

In the event you (specify, such as do not complete the work by or we do not receive payment in full by [specify date]), legal proceedings shall be immediately commenced to enforce our rights and we shall seek additional penalties, damages, prejudgment interest, legal fees, costs, and other charges.

Hopefully this can be avoided, and I thank you for your prompt assistance and attention to this matter.

Very truly yours,

Your Name
Name of Business

▷ Send certified mail, return receipt requested.

FORM 40. State Consumer Protection Offices

ALABAMA
Consumer Assistance
Office of Attorney General
11 South Union St.
Montgomery, AL 36130
(205) 242-7334 (800) 392-5658

ALASKA
Office of Attorney General
P.O. Box K—State Capitol
Juneau, AK 99811-0300
(907) 465-3600

ARIZONA
Complaint Information and Complaints
Office of Attorney General
1275 West Washington St.
Phoenix, AZ 85007
(602) 542-5763 (800) 352-8431

ARKANSAS
Advocacy Division of Attorney
    General's Office
200 Tower Bldg.
323 Center St.
Little Rock, AR 72201
(501) 682-2341 (800) 482-8982

CALIFORNIA
Department of Consumer Affairs
Consumer Assistance Office
400 R St., Room 1040
Sacramento, CA 95814
(916) 445-1254 (800) 952-5210

COLORADO
Consumer Protection Unit
Office of Attorney General
1525 Sherman St.
Denver, CO 80203
(303) 866-5189 (800) 332-2071

CONNECTICUT
Department of Consumer Protection
State Office Bldg.
165 Capitol Ave.
Hartford, CT 06106
(203) 566-1170

DELAWARE
Department of Justice
Consumer Protection Unit
Delaware State Office Bldg. 4th Fl.
820 North French St.
Wilmington, DE 19801
(302) 577-3250

DISTRICT OF COLUMBIA
Department of Consumer and
    Regulatory Affairs
614 H St. NW, Rm. 106
Washington, DC 20001
(202) 727-7076

FLORIDA
Division of Consumer Services
Department of Agriculture and
    Consumer Services
218 Mayo Bldg.
Tallahassee, FL 32399
(904) 488-2226 (800) 435-7352

GEORGIA
Office of Consumer Affairs
2 Martin Luther King Jr. Dr., Suite 356
Atlanta, GA 30334
(404) 651-8600

HAWAII
Office of Consumer Protection
Department of Commerce and
    Consumer Affairs
828 Fort St., Rm. 600B
Honolulu, HI 96813
(808) 586-2630

(continued on page 340)

FORM 40. *(continued from page 339)*

IDAHO
Consumer Protection Division
Office of Attorney General
700 West Jefferson St.
Boise, ID 83720
(208) 334-2424 (800) 432-3545

ILLINOIS
Consumer Protection Division
Office of Attorney General
500 South 2nd St.
Springfield, IL 62706
(217) 782-9011 (800) 252-8666

INDIANA
Consumer Protection Division
Office of Attorney General
Indiana Government Center South, 5th Fl.
402 West Washington
Indianapolis, IN 46204
(317) 232-6330 (800) 382-5516

IOWA
Consumer Protection Division
Office of Attorney General
1300 East Walnut, 2nd Fl.
Des Moines, IA 50319
(515) 281-5926

KANSAS
Consumer Protection Division
Office of Attorney General
301 West Tenth
Topeka, KS 66612
(913) 296-3751 (800) 432-2310

KENTUCKY
Consumer Protection Division
Office of Attorney General
P.O. Box 2000
Frankfort, KY 40602
(502) 573-2200 (800) 432-9257

LOUISIANA
Consumer Protection Section
Office of Attorney General
P.O. Box 94095
Baton Rouge, LA 70804-9095
(504) 342-9638

MAINE
Bureau of Consumer Credit Protection
State House, Station 35
Augusta, ME 04333-0035
(207) 582-8718 (800) 332-8529

MARYLAND
Consumer Protection Division
Office of Attorney General
200 Saint Paul Pl.
Baltimore, MD 21202
(410) 528-8662

MASSACHUSETTS
Consumer Protection Division
Department of Attorney General
131 Tremont St.
Boston, MA 02111
(617) 727-8400

MICHIGAN
Consumer Protection Division
Office of Attorney General
P.O. Box 30213
Lansing, MI 48909
(517) 373-1140

MINNESOTA
Citizen Assistance Center
Office of Attorney General
1400 NCL Tower
445 Minnesota St.
St. Paul, MN 55101
(612) 296-3353 (800) 657-3787

MISSISSIPPI
Consumer Protection Division
Office of Attorney General
P.O. Box 22947
Jackson, MS 39225
(601) 359-4230

MISSOURI
Consumer Protection Division
Office of Attorney General
P.O. Box 899
Jefferson City, MO 65102
(314) 751-3321 (800) 392-8222

MONTANA
Consumer Affairs Unit
Department of Commerce
1424 9th Ave.
Helena, MT 59620
(406) 444-4312

NEBRASKA
Consumer Protection Division
Office of Attorney General
2115 State Capitol
P.O. Box 98920
Lincoln, NB 68509
(402) 471-2682

NEVADA
Consumer Affairs Division
State Mail Room Complex
Las Vegas, NV 89158
(702) 486-7355

NEW HAMPSHIRE
Consumer Protection Bureau
Department of Justice
33 Capitol St.
Concord, NH 03301
(603) 271-3641

NEW JERSEY
Division of Consumer Affairs
124 Halsey St.
Newark, NJ 07102
(201) 504-6200

NEW MEXICO
Consumer Protection Division
Office of Attorney General
P.O. Drawer 1508
Santa Fe, NM 87504
(505) 827-6910 (800) 678-1508

NEW YORK
Consumer Protection Board
99 Washington Ave.
Albany, NY 12210
(518) 474-8583

NORTH CAROLINA
Consumer Protection Section
Office of Attorney General
Department of Justice
P.O. Box 629
Raleigh, NC 27602
(919) 733-7741

NORTH DAKOTA
Consumer Protection Division
Office of Attorney General
600 East Blvd.
Bismarck, ND 58505
(701) 224-3404 (800) 472-2600

OHIO
Consumer Protection Division
Office of Attorney General
State Office Tower
30 East Broad St., 25th Fl.
Columbus, OH 43215-3428
(614) 466-4986 (800) 282-0515

OKLAHOMA
Consumer Affairs Division
Office of Attorney General
4545 North Lincoln, Suite 260
Oklahoma City, OK 73105
(405) 521-4274

OREGON
Financial Fraud Section
Department of Justice
1162 Court St. NE
Salem, OR 97310
(503) 378-4320

PENNSYLVANIA
Bureau of Consumer Protection
Office of Attorney General
Strawberry Square, 14th Fl.
Harrisburg, PA 17120
(717) 787-9707 (800) 441-2555

(continued on page 342)

FORM 40. *(continued from page 341)*

RHODE ISLAND
Consumer Protection Division
Department of Attorney General
72 Pine St.
Providence, RI 02903
(401) 277-2104

SOUTH CAROLINA
Department of Consumer Affairs
P.O. Box 5757
Columbia, SC 29250
(803) 734-9452 (800) 922-1594

SOUTH DAKOTA
Division of Consumer Affairs
Office of Attorney General
State Capitol Bldg.
500 East Capital
Pierre, SD 57501
(605) 773-4400

TENNESSEE
Division of Consumer Affairs
Department of Commerce and Insurance
500 James Robertson Pkwy., 5th Fl.
Nashville, TN 37243-0600
(615) 741-4737 (800) 342-8385

TEXAS
Consumer Protection Division
Office of Attorney General
P.O. Box 12548
Austin, TX 78711
(512) 463-2070

UTAH
Division of Consumer Protection
Department of Business Regulation
160 East 300 South
P.O. Box 45804
Salt Lake City, UT 84145-0802
(801) 530-6601

VERMONT
Consumer Assistance
Office of Attorney General
104 Morrill Hall
University of Vermont
Burlington, VT 05405
(802) 656-3183 (800) 649-2424

VIRGINIA
Office of Consumer Affairs
Department of Agriculture and
    Consumer Services
P.O. Box 1163
Richmond, VA 23209
(804) 786-2042

WASHINGTON
Consumer Resource Center
Office of Attorney General
900 Fourth Ave., Rm. 2000
Seattle, WA 98164
(206) 464-6684 (800) 551-4636

WEST VIRGINIA
Consumer Protection Division
Office of Attorney General
812 Quarrier St.
LNS Bldg. 6th Fl.
Charleston, WV 25301
(304) 558-8986 (800) 368-8808

WISCONSIN
Consumer Protection Agency
Department of Justice
123 West Washington Ave., Rm. 150
Madison, WI 53707
(608) 266-1852

WYOMING
Consumer Affairs Division
Office of Attorney General
123 State Capitol Bldg.
Cheyenne, WY 82002
(307) 777-7841

FORM 41. **Receipt Form**

Received on this date from (specify), the following ($X or describe in detail if property or goods) for (specify, such as for consulting services).

Payment for said item(s) was made by (specify, such as by cash, check, certified check, or credit card, including the nature of the credit card, card #, and expiration date) in the amount of $X (if applicable).

State additional items here:

_____
Name of Party Receiving Items or $X

Dated: _____

FORM 42. **Notice of Disputed Account**

Date

Name of Business
Address

Dear (Name):

As we discussed by telephone on (specify date), please be advised that your statement dated (specify) indicating that $X is owed to your firm (or you) is incorrect.

This amount is disputed because: (specify reasons). I am enclosing pertinent documentation to support this (enclosed).

Accordingly, please adjust your records (or send me a revised statement with the correct amount stated).

I am available to discuss this matter with you during working hours at (provide telephone number if you desire).

Thank you for your assistance and immediate attention to this matter.

Very truly yours,

Officer's or Your Name
Name of Business

▷ Send certified mail, return receipt requested.

FORM 43. **Notice of Defective Merchandise**

Date
Your Name
Address

Name of Person or Business
Address

Dear (Name of Person or Officer):

As we discussed on (specify), the goods (describe quantity) I purchased on (specify date) are defective (specify how).

Accordingly, demand is hereby made for (specify, such as the full return of the deposit or purchase price) which was tendered to you by check (or in cash) (state when).

We agreed that I could return the goods and receive a complete refund (or credit). Thus, kindly return my deposit (or full purchase price) to the above address by (specify date), to avoid expensive and protracted litigation, which under the laws of this state may entitle me to recover additional damages, penalties, legal fees, costs, and interest upon the successful institution of a lawsuit.

Hopefully this can be avoided and I thank you for your prompt assistance and attention to this matter. If you desire further information or wish to speak with me during weekday business hours, you may reach me at (provide telephone number).

Very truly yours,

Your Name
Name of Business

▷ Send certified mail, return receipt requested.

FORM 44. **Notice Authorizing the Return of Goods**

Date
Your Name
Address

Name of Person or Business
Address

Dear (Name of Person or Officer):

As we discussed by telephone on (specify date), this letter confirms that you agree to allow me to return the following items which I purchased by credit card (or check) on (date): (specify items and how paid, such as by credit card # in the amount of $X).

Per our discussion, you agree to issue me (state the terms, such as a full refund and payment, or full or partial credit. If payment is to be received, state when).

The goods I shall return shall be in good condition and the freight charges shall be paid by (state). If the goods are lost or damaged in transit, it is agreed that (state) will pay for same.

Thank you for your prompt assistance and attention to this matter. If you desire further information or wish to speak with me during weekday business hours, you may reach me at (provide telephone number).

Very truly yours,

Your Name
Name of Business

▷ Send certified mail, return receipt requested.

FORM 45. **Notice to Cancel Delayed or Back-Ordered Goods**

Date
Your Name
Address

Name of Person or Business
Address

Dear (Name of Person or Officer):

As we discussed on (specify date) by telephone, I still have not received the goods (describe quantity) I purchased on (specify date), and which, pursuant to the terms of our (specify, such as contract or purchase order, copy enclosed), were supposed to be delivered by (specify date).

Accordingly, due to your failure to ship the products to me in a timely fashion, demand is hereby made for (specify, such as the full return of the deposit or purchase price) which was tendered to you by check (or in cash) (state when). You are also notified that I shall refuse the goods and return them to you at your expense if they should be delivered to me after this date.

We agreed that I could return the goods I have already received from the partial shipment and receive a complete refund (or credit). Thus, kindly return my deposit (or the full purchase price) to the above address by (specify date), to avoid expensive and protracted litigation, which under the laws of this state may entitled me to recover additional damages, penalties, legal fees, costs, and interest upon the successful institution of a lawsuit.

Hopefully, this can be avoided, and I thank you for your prompt assistance and attention to this matter. If you desire further information or wish to speak with me during weekday business hours, you may reach me at (provide telephone number).

Very truly yours,

Your Name
Name of Business

▷ Send certified mail, return receipt requested.

FORM 46. **Notice of Cancellation of Home Solicitation Agreement**

Date
Your Name
Address

Name of Person or Business
Address

Dear (Name of Person or Officer):

On (specify date), I agreed to (state terms of contract, such as purchase aluminum siding for your house). However, under the laws of the state of (specify) and by the terms of your agreement (copy of contract enclosed), please treat this letter as my formal notice that I elect to cancel said contract under the Three Day Business Rescission Rule.

Accordingly, demand is hereby made for (specify, such as the full return of the deposit) which was tendered to you by check (or in cash) simultaneously upon the execution of said contract.

Kindly return my deposit to the above address by (specify date), to avoid expensive and protracted litigation, which under the laws of this state may entitle me to recover additional damages, penalties, legal fees, costs, and interest upon the successful institution of a lawsuit.

Hopefully this can be avoided, and I thank you for your prompt assistance and attention to this matter. If you desire further information or wish to speak with me during weekday business hours, you may reach me at (provide telephone number).

Very truly yours,

Your Name
Name of Business

▷Send certified mail, return receipt requested.

FORM 48. **Simple Suggested Contract**

THIS AGREEMENT, is made by and between (Name of Individual or business "Party #1", located at: _____) and (Name of Individual or business "Party #2", located at: _____) on (specify date).

WHEREAS, the parties desire to: (specify)

NOW, THEREFORE, FOR VALUABLE CONSIDERATION SET FORTH HEREIN, THE PARTIES AGREE AS FOLLOWS:

1. Set forth specific payment terms.
2. Set forth specific duties of parties.
3. Set forth other pertinent conditions, such as term of the contract and whether it can be extended after the initial term.
4. This Agreement supersedes all prior agreements and understandings and may only be modified in writing and signed by both parties. This Agreement is in force when signed below.
5. This Agreement binds and benefits both parties and any successors and assigns.
6. This Agreement shall be governed by the laws of the state of (specify).

_____
Name of Party #1

Dated: _____

_____
Name of Party #2

FORM 49. **Extension, Modification, Termination, or Assignment of Simple Contract**

THIS (add, such as Extension, Modification, Termination, or Assignment) of Contract, is made by and between (Name of Individual or business "Party #1", located at: _____) and (Name of Individual or business "Party #2", located at: _____) on (specify date).

WHEREAS, the parties desire to: (specify)

NOW, THEREFORE, FOR VALUABLE CONSIDERATION SET FORTH HEREIN, THE PARTIES AGREE AS FOLLOWS:

1. The prior Agreement dated (specify) is hereby (extended, modified, terminated, or assigned) as follows: (specify).

2.   a. If extended, state whether all other terms and conditions are the same as the original contract or are changed.

b. If modified, state which terms are changed, then state that all other terms and conditions remain in effect without modification.

c. If terminated, state when.

d. If assigned, state to whom and that the Assignee agrees to perform all of the duties and obligations of the Assignor.

3. Set forth other pertinent conditions, such as term of the contract and whether it can be extended after the initial term.

4. This Agreement supersedes all prior agreements and understandings and may only be modified in writing and signed by both parties. This Agreement is in force when signed below.

5. This Agreement binds and benefits both parties and any successors and assigns.

6. This Agreement shall be governed by the law of the state of (specify).

_____
Name of Party #1

Dated: _____

_____
Name of Party #2

FORM 50. **Checklist of Important Points Regarding Contract Execution**

1. Discuss all terms in advance.

2. Legal disputes often arise because many people accept a contract on a handshake; a handshake only confirms that you came to some kind of understanding, but it doesn't confirm what the arrangement was because the same oral words often have different meanings from both parties' perspective. Written words limit misunderstandings, so prepare a written agreement to minimize confusion and prove what was agreed upon.

3. Be aware that some employers insert restrictive covenants in written employment agreements that prohibit you from working in a geographic area or for a certain period of time; avoid this and seek legal advice before signing a contract with such clauses if possible.

4. Consider arbitration to resolve disputes and add this clause to your agreements where applicable.

5. When contracts are issued, be sure that all changes, strikeouts, and erasures are initialed by both parties.

6. Be sure that all blanks are filled in.

7. If additions are necessary, include them in a space provided and attach them to the contract itself; then note on the contract that addenda have been accepted by both parties.

8. Always review and respond in writing to any comments or proposed amendments to the contract you may have received so your lack of notice will not be viewed as an acceptance.

9. Be sure the agreement is signed by all parties.

10. Be sure the person signing the agreement has the legal authority to enter into the contract and bind the other party (i.e., that such person is an officer, such as a president or vice president).

11. Always save a copy of the final contract signed by all parties for your records. Store this in a safe place for future reference.

12. In most cases, any oral understandings reached after the written contract was signed will *not* be valid unless you execute a new written contract or written modification of the old contract to reflect such changes.

13. Oral understandings reached prior to the execution of a written contract are presumed to have been incorporated into the written contract; thus, generally, such oral agreements will *not* be valid unless they are contained in the written contract.

FORM 51. **Personal Guaranty**

I, _____ ("Guarantor") hereby guarantee to Lender, the prompt payment, when due, of each and every claim which Lender may have against Borrower. This continuing guaranty shall remain in force until revoked by the undersigned by written notice to Lender but any such revocation shall be effective only as to any claims which may arise out of transactions entered into after receipt of notice of revocation. This guaranty shall be effective as to the renewal of any claims guaranteed hereby or extensions of time of payment, and shall not be affected by the surrender or release by Lender of any other or additional security Lender may hold for any claim hereby guaranteed. The Lender shall be under no obligation to give the undersigned notice of renewals or extensions of existing loans.

In the event of default by Borrower in the making of any payment when due, the undersigned hereby agrees to pay on demand all sums then due and all losses or expenses which may be incurred by Lender, including but not limited to reasonable attorneys' fees, without Lender having first or prior thereto proceeded against Borrower.

Witness:

Name of Lender: _____

By: _____

Name of Borrower: _____

By: _____

FORM 57. **Sample Consumer Demand Letter**

Re: Claimant _____
Amount _____
Our File No. _____

The above-named claimant has retained our office to collect their claim against you. Please send the amount indicated above to our office, or contact us at the above telephone number to discuss a resolution of this matter.

* Despite this demand, you have the right to dispute their claim. However, unless you notify us within thirty days after receipt of this letter that the validity of this debt, or any portion of it, is disputed, we will assume the debt is valid. If you do not notify us of a dispute, we will obtain verification of the debt or a copy of the judgment, if any, and mail it to you.

* Also, upon your written request within thirty days, we will provide you with the name and address of the original creditor if different from the current creditor.

** THIS LETTER IS AN ATTEMPT TO COLLECT A DEBT, AND ANY INFORMATION OBTAINED WILL BE USED FOR THAT PURPOSE.

Yours truly,

* Required by 15 U.S.C. Section 1692(g)
** Required by 15 U.S.C. Section 1692(e)(11)

FORM 59. Document Checklist to Discuss with Divorce Attorney

▷ Federal, state, and local income tax returns for the past 3 to 5 years

▷ Corporate or partnership federal and state tax returns of your spouse's business (or your own) for the past three to five years

▷ Executed Agreements between the parties, such as a prenuptial or separation agreement

▷ All documents relating to income, expenses, and property, such as payroll stubs and W-2 or 1099 forms, copies of leases, statements of interest or dividend income, account statements from stockbroker or financial advisor

▷ Bank statements of all personal and business checking accounts for you and your spouse

▷ Deeds, mortgages, leases held to any real estate

▷ List of all income-producing assets, such as bank CDs and stock certificates

▷ Pension and retirement plan policies and statements and records for 401(k) plans, IRAs, Keoghs, etc.

▷ List of employer-provided benefits, pertinent employment contracts, stock option and profit-sharing plans and records, for you and your spouse

▷ List of all physical assets, such as paintings, coin collection, automobiles, boats, etc., including bills of sale or registration certificates

▷ Copies of life, health, auto, homeowner's, disability and other pertinent insurance policies

▷ Personal or business Net Worth Statements previously prepared and submitted for a loan or other purpose

▷ Appraisals of any personal or real property or business owned by the parties

▷ Location and itemized contents of any safety deposit boxes

▷ Description or records of any gifts or inheritances

▷ List outstanding debts, credit card records, and loans

▷ Copies of all wills and trust documents

▷ Your passport, birth certificate, and social security cards (also copies of the same for your spouse)

▷ Love letters or other written evidence or agreements documenting promises of support, conveyance of property, etc.

▷ Other important documents or records

FORM 60. **Property Checklist to Discuss with Divorce Attorney**

▷ Marital residence:
State:
Purchase price/date purchased
Down payment and source of funds for down payment
Original mortgage
Current mortgage amount
Current appraised value
Did you personally render services to increase the value of the house? If so, explain.
Have major improvements been made? If so, state cost, source of funds for improvements, and what contribution you made.
State the current mortgage payment, taxes, homeowner's insurance, and monthly utility expenses

▷ Other real estate, leases or income-producing real estate
State: same as above
What is the current monthly rent? Does the property produce a profit? If so, how much and where does the money go?

▷ State the existence, registration numbers, and accounts for all stocks and bonds.
How much yearly dividend income do these assets produce?
Where does the money go?

▷ State the amount of money contained in:
Personal and business checking accounts and bank CDs for you and your spouse
How much yearly interest income do these assets produce?
Where does the money go?

▷ List all separate property that is owned solely by you or your spouse.
Explain how such asset was acquired
If a yearly profit is produced, where does the money go?

▷ List all pension, profit-sharing, 401(k), stock option, and retirement accounts owned by you or your spouse.
State how much yearly interest or dividend income is produced by these assets. Where does the money go?

▷ List the value of all businesses owned by you and/or your spouse.
How much is the business worth? (Include the most recent appraisal.)
How much is your share of the business worth? Are there any prohibitions against sale? (Examine the most recent stockholder's or partnership agreement to compute this more accurately if appropriate.)

FORM 61. Separation Agreement for a Couple with No Children

AGREEMENT AND STIPULATION OF SETTLEMENT made this (date), by and between (name), residing at (address), (hereinafter referred to as the "Wife"), and (name), residing at (address), hereinafter referred to as the "Husband").

RECITALS:

WHEREAS the parties were married on (date) at (location); and

WHEREAS there are no issue of the marriage and there are no other children expected; and

WHEREAS the parties have experienced matrimonial difficulties; and

WHEREAS the parties desire that this AGREEMENT AND STIPULATION OF SETTLEMENT (hereinafter referred to as the "Agreement"), which is entered into after due and considered deliberation, shall be and constitute a settlement of all matters and issues between the parties, and an agreement of separation between them with respect to any funds, assets, or properties, both real and personal, wherever situated, now owned by the parties or either of them, or standing in their respective names, or which may hereafter be acquired by either of the parties; and

WHEREAS each party is being represented by separate and independent counsel of his or her own choosing with whom each has discussed his or her rights and obligations and the terms of this Agreement; and

WHEREAS the parties are entering into this Agreement and Stipulation of Settlement of their own free will, without force, coercion, or duress of whatever nature; and

WHEREAS each party fully understands the terms, covenants, and conditions of this Agreement and is of the belief that it is fair, just, adequate, and reasonable as to each of them, and, after due consideration, freely and voluntarily accepts and agrees to such terms, covenants, and conditions; and

WHEREAS the parties, having had explained to them the provisions of the law affecting financial and property rights of spouses, including those rights under (specify state's law), make this Agreement in full and complete satisfaction of all claims each may have against the other under any law except for claims as to the entitlement of either party to a divorce; and

WHEREAS the parties expressly represent that their respective rights and obligations shall be set forth in this Agreement rather than such as might be provided for, apply, or inure to either party under (specify state's law), and the parties desire and agree that the provisions hereof shall be binding upon them, notwithstanding anything to the contrary existing under (specify state's law); and

WHEREAS the parties have waived the exchange of sworn statements of Net Worth disclosing their assets, property holdings, and income, and they have had the opportunity to make an independent inquiry and investigation with respect to the other's past, present, and future assets, property holdings, and income; and

WHEREAS in consequence of disputes and irreconcilable differences, the parties have heretofore been living separate and apart from each other and the parties are now, at the time of execution of this Agreement living separate and apart and desire to continue to live separate and apart and shall, upon the sale of the marital premises, obtain separate residences.

(continued on page 356)

FORM 61. *(continued from page 355)*

NOW, THEREFORE, in consideration of the premises and of the mutual promises, covenants, releases, and undertakings herein contained, and for other good and valuable consideration, the parties respectively covenant and agree as follows:

ARTICLE 1
Separation

The parties may and shall continue to live separate and apart for the rest of their natural lives. Each shall be free from any restraint, interference, or control of the other and in all respects as if he and she were not and had never been married to each other. Each may reside from time to time at such place or places of residence or abode as he or she shall respectively choose.

Neither party shall directly or indirectly make statements to third parties derogatory of the other.

ARTICLE II
Employment

Each of the parties hereto may, for his or her support, use, and benefit, engage in any employment, business, or profession which he or she may deem advisable without in any way affecting any of the provisions of this agreement.

Each shall be free from any restraint, interference, or control of the other and in all respects as if he and she were not and had never been married each to the other.

ARTICLE III
Debts

With the exception of those debts enumerated below, each party hereto represents that he/she has not heretofore incurred nor will he/she at any time after the execution of this Agreement, incur or contract any debt, charge, or liability whatsoever for which the other party, his/her legal representatives, or his/her property or estate, is now or may become liable, and each party further covenants to keep the other party at all times thereafter free, harmless, and indemnified from any and all future debts, credit card charges, and liabilities hereafter contracted by him/her.

(Or): The Husband and Wife previously incurred the following (specify, such as credit card) debts, enumerated in greater detail on Exhibit A attached hereto. Each party agrees to pay for the following credit card bills and indemnify and hold the other harmless from any legal fees, expenses, judgments, or otherwise incurred as a result of the failure to pay said bills.

Both parties agree to notify the respective credit establishments of the sole obligation to pay off said debts and remove the other from any liability.

(Or): The Husband (or Wife) was previously indebted to the other in the sum of (specify $). The Wife (or Husband) agrees to forgive said indebtedness.

ARTICLE IV
Prior Distribution of Separate and Marital Property

Except as herein provided to the contrary, the parties have heretofore established and divided up their separate and marital property as said terms "separate property" and "marital property" are defined in (specify state's law), to their mutual satisfaction. Henceforth, each party shall own and enjoy, independently of any claim or the right of the other, all separate and/or marital property, whether real, personal, or mixed, of every kind whatsoever, with full power to dispose of the same as fully and effectively as if he/she were unmarried.

(Or): The Husband waives and releases to the Wife all right, title, and interest, in and to a certain parcel of land located at (address) held in the name of (specify).

ARTICLE V
Disposition and Maintenance of Real Property

The parties represent that they have weighed all their right, title, and interest with respect to their marital residence, presently held by the parties as a tenancy by the entirety, and therefore agree to the following:

1. The marital premises located at (address) is presently in the process of being sold. The parties agree to sell said marital residence on the terms and conditions mutually agreeable as outlined below, and to equally divide the net proceeds of said sale, subject to any reimbursements, credits, or adjustments due to either party as more fully enumerated herein.

a. On or about (date), both parties shall vacate the marital premises.

(▷*Author's note:* Optional, if there is a tenant involved): The marital premises shall be rented to (name of tenant) at a monthly rental of $X. The Husband shall collect all monthly rents and be responsible to pay the monthly mortgage on the premises in the amount of $X. The Husband shall apply all rents paid toward the payment of the premises' mortgage only and for no other purpose and shall provide the Wife with an accurate monthly accounting regarding the status of all rents received and mortgage paid.

b. The tenant will be responsible to pay for all other changes and has agreed to rent the marital premises for a period of One (1) year through (date). Thereafter, if the tenant declines to purchase the marital residence, but elects to continue to rent same, the parties shall allow him to inhabit the premises for an additional period of X months, at a monthly rental of $X. The parties agree to share equally in all surplus rents.

c. In the event the tenant elects to purchase the marital premises, the parties shall give him a credit of $X from previous rent paid, and shall sell him the house at a net amount of $X. The parties agree to retain the services of one attorney to represent both of them in connection with the sale, and whose fee shall be divided equally between the parties from the gross proceeds of sale.

d. All obligations, loans, and ordinary closing expenses, including but not limited to mortgage satisfaction, recording fees, brokerage commissions, state transfer taxes if any, and any mortgage shall be payable out of the gross proceeds of sale before division of the proceeds between the parties, and the parties agree to split equally the net proceeds from the sale.

e. If, prior to closing, it becomes necessary to expend any sum of money in order to fulfill the representations made in the contract of sale, the party expending said sum shall be entitled to receive reimbursement of said amount payable out of the gross proceeds of sale before division of the proceeds between the parties.

f. In connection with the current rental and potential sale to the aforesaid tenant, both parties shall remove their personal effects from the marital premises before (date).

g. In the event the tenant decides not to purchase the marital premises (▷*Author's note:* or if there is no tenant), the parties shall offer it for sale at the minimum initial price of $X. The parties shall select a licensed real estate broker to handle the sale of the marital premises and to list the house for sale, and both parties agree to act in good faith and cooperate in a reasonable manner in selecting an acceptable real estate broker.

(continued on page 358)

FORM 61. *(continued from page 357)*

In the event the real estate broker is unable to obtain a bona fide offer from a buyer to purchase the house for $X after three (3) months, the parties agree to list the house at $X for a subsequent three (3) month period. In the event the real estate broker is unable to obtain a bona fide offer from a buyer to purchase the house for $X after six (6) months, the parties agree to list the house at a price designed to obtain the highest sales price under current market conditions.

h. Upon receipt of a bona fide offer to purchase the subject premises, the parties agree to promptly enter into a contract of sale. The contract of sale shall provide, in addition to other standard representations made in contracts of the sale of real property in (location), that vacant and broom clean possession of the premises shall be delivered at closing of title, that the plumbing, heating, and electrical systems and all appliances included in the sale shall be in working order at the time of the closing, and that the roof shall be free of leaks, that the purchaser shall be afforded a mortgage contingency clause that will allow no greater than 80% financing of said purchase and no longer than sixty (60) days to obtain a mortgage commitment, and that the attorney for the parties shall act as the escrow agent with respect to the contract deposit, which shall be no less than ten percent (10%) of the total sale price. Both parties further agree to attend the closing of the title, not to delay the scheduling of same, and to execute any and all documents necessary to transfer title to the subject premises, including, but not limited to, the deed, affidavits of title, and all other documents required by the purchaser's lending institution, and to pay all taxes due from the gross proceeds of the sale. In that regard, all obligations and closing expenses, including but not limited to, mortgage pay-off, mortgage pick-up, and brokerage commissions, shall be payable out of the gross sales price before division of the proceeds between the parties. If, prior to closing of title, it becomes necessary to expend any sum of money to fulfill the representations made in the contract of sale, unless said expense is divided equally by the parties, the party expending said sum shall be entitled to a credit of said amount as against the division of the net proceeds of the sale.

ARTICLE VI
Division of Property

The parties represent that they have weighed all their right, title, and interest, be it legal, equitable, or otherwise, in and to the value of their joint and individual personal property and have divided all personal property, including wearing apparel, clothing, jewelry, and personal effects previously hereto (or as annexed on Exhibit B).

ARTICLE VII
Waiver of Maintenance for Wife and Husband

The Wife is in excellent health and is an experienced (specify, such as decorator). In view of the property settlement made before and hereunder, the ability of the Wife to be self-supporting, and other circumstances, the Wife forever waives any claim or right to support, maintenance, or alimony for herself from the Husband, now or in the future, which she ever had, now has, or may have to the maximum extent permitted by law.

The Husband is in excellent health and is an experienced (specify, such as architect). In view of the property settlement made before and hereunder, the ability of the Husband to be self-supporting, and other circumstances, the Husband forever waives any claim or right to support, maintenance, or alimony for himself from the Wife, now or in the future, which he ever had, now has, or may have to the maximum extent permitted by law.

ARTICLE VIII
Equitable Distribution

The Husband agrees to pay the Wife the sum of (specify) over a period of X years, commencing (date). On or before (date), the Husband shall pay the first installment to the Wife in the amount of $X by certified check or money order and forwarded to her at her residence or at such other place as she shall designate in writing to the Husband. Thereafter, the Husband shall pay to the Wife the sum of $X per annum on or before the first day of each (specify month) thereafter, commencing on or before (date) and terminating on or before (date), until the aforementioned amount is paid in full.

Upon the signing of this Stipulation and Agreement of Settlement, the Husband shall execute a Promissory Note evidencing the aforementioned agreement. By the terms of said Note, the payments due pursuant to this Article shall not bear interest so long as the Husband is not in default; after default, interest shall be due on the unpaid principal balance at the rate of X percent (X%) per annum. Notwithstanding the foregoing, the Husband may accelerate the above payment schedule and repay the unpaid balance at any time before (date).

Upon occurrence of any of the following events of default, the entire amount of the principal hereof, shall, at the option of the Wife, be accelerated and the aggregate amount thereof shall become immediately due and payable without further notice of default, presentation, demand, or protest by the Wife, all of which are waived by the Husband:

(1) The Husband fails to make any installment payment within X days after the same is due; or

(2) The Husband makes an assignment for the benefit of creditors, commences (as debtor) a case in Bankruptcy, or commences (as debtor) any proceeding under any other insolvency law; or

(3) A case in Bankruptcy or any proceeding under any other insolvency law is commenced against the Husband (as debtor) and a court of competent jurisdiction enters a decree or order for relief against the Husband as debtor in such case or proceeding, or such case or proceeding is consented to by the Husband, or remains undismissed for X days, or the Husband consents to or admits the material allegations against him in any such case or proceeding; or

(4) A trustee, receiver, or agent (however named) is appointed or authorized to take charge of substantially all of the property, of enforcing a lien against such property, or for the purpose of general administration of such property for the benefit of creditors.

In the event the Husband defaults on the payments hereunder and this Note is placed in the hands of an attorney for collection, the Husband shall be liable and agrees to pay all reasonable attorney's fees and court costs in collecting same.

No failure or delay on the part of the Wife in the exercise of any power or right in this Note shall operate as a waiver thereof, and no exercise or waiver of any single power or right, or the partial exercise thereof, shall affect the Wife's rights with respect to any and all other rights and powers.

The Husband waives presentment and demand for payment, notice of dishonor, protest, and notice of protest of this Note. The provisions of this Note shall inure to the benefit of and be binding upon any successor to the Husband and shall extend to any holder hereof of the Wife.

(continued on page 360)

FORM 61. *(continued from page 359)*

(Or: The parties have two (2) valid patents for a (specify) device currently on file with the United States Patent Office in the name of the Husband. The Husband agrees to pay the Wife X percent (X%) of all profits, cash distributions, royalties, licensing fees, and other monies emanating from the sale, lease, or use of said patents for any purpose whatsoever. The Husband shall pay said profit to the Wife within Ten (10) days of constructive or actual receipt thereof, and shall furnish the Wife with a proper accounting regarding same.)

The parties acknowledge that the aforesaid distribution constitutes a fair and reasonable equitable distribution and/or distributive award of the parties' marital property. Additionally, the Wife accepts these monies and the transfer by the Husband of his one-half interest in the marital residence as more fully described in Article V of this Agreement and Stipulation of Settlement, in full and final settlement and satisfaction of all claims she had, presently or may hereafter have against the Husband, with respect to an equitable distribution and/or distributive award of the parties' marital property as defined and used in (specify state's law), which specifically includes, but is not limited to the Husband's professional degree, license, and private architect practice.

Likewise, the Husband accepts the distribution of the articles and proceeds as more fully described in this Agreement and Stipulation of Settlement in full and final settlement and satisfaction of all claims that he had, presently has, or may hereafter have against the Wife, with respect to an equitable distribution and/or distributive award of the parties' marital property, as defined and used in (specify state's law).

Subject to the provisions of this Agreement and Stipulation of Settlement, the parties have heretofore divided their real and personal property to their mutual satisfaction, and each party shall hereafter have the right to possess, own, and enjoy, independently of any claim or right of the other, all property of every kind, nature, or description and wheresoever situated, title to which is now or hereafter may be in his or her name and relinquishes all claims to such marital or separate property, as such term is defined in (specify state's law), including, without limitation, to all bank deposits, Money Market Accounts, stocks, pension and/or profit-sharing plans or trusts, deferred compensation, IRA accounts, Keogh accounts and business interests, professional licenses, degrees or practices, real estate, residences, automobiles, and other personal property whether held jointly with another person or in the name of either spouse.

Notwithstanding the foregoing, the Wife hereby waives, now and in the future, any and all claims she may assert in or against the Husband's pension plan with (specify).

ARTICLE IX
Income Taxes

The parties have hereto previously filed joint federal and (specify state) personal income tax returns. If in connection with any such personal joint return there is a deficiency assessment on any of said returns, the amount ultimately determined to be due thereon, including penalties and interest, shall be borne by either or both of the parties, depending on whether the deficiency arouse out of the individual income of one or other of the parties (and if so, to what extent), individual deduction, individual deduction or out of a joint deduction.

If in connection with any such joint return there is a refund or credit, the same shall belong to that party whose miscalculation, overstatement, or overpayment occasioned such refund or credit provided that the party who made the miscalculation, overstatement, or overpayment made payment of taxes to the extent of such miscalculation.

Anything hereinbefore contained to the contrary notwithstanding, each party does hereby agree to hold the other indemnified, free, and harmless from any claim, damage, or expense arising out of the aforesaid returns attributable to him or her as the case may be and any deficiency in connection therewith as to any such tax penalty or interest attributable to him or her as the case may be.

Commencing with the filing of the (specify year) federal and state tax returns, the parties shall file separate returns.

ARTICLE X
Release of Estates Rights

1. The Wife agrees to release, and hereby does release, any and all claims of the Wife to or upon the property of the Husband, whether real or personal and whether now owned or hereafter acquired, to the end that he shall have free and unrestricted right to dispose of his property now owned or hereafter acquired, free from any claim or demand of the Wife and so that his estate and all income therefrom derived or to be derived shall go and belong to the person or persons who become entitled thereto by will or devise, bequest, intestacy, administration, or otherwise, as if the Wife had died during the lifetime of the Husband and, without in any manner limiting the foregoing, the Wife expressly relinquishes any and all rights in the estate of the Husband and any and all right of election to take any share of the estate of the Husband, as in intestacy, including, without limiting the foregoing, any right of election pursuant to the provisions of (specify state's law) or pursuant to any other law of any jurisdiction as said laws may now exist or may hereafter be amended, and any and all other right and interest in any real or personal property of which the Husband may die seized or possessed, and the Wife renounces and disclaims, and covenants to renounce and disclaim (i) all interest of the Wife under any will or trust agreement executed by the Husband prior to the execution of this Agreement and any right of the Wife to serve as executor or trustee under any such will; (ii) all interest of the Wife in the proceeds of any life insurance policy on the life of the Husband; (iii) all interest of the Wife under any pension, retirement, death benefit, stock bonus or profit-sharing plan, with respect to which the Husband was a participant or member; and (iv) any right of the Wife under the laws or practice of any jurisdiction to act as guardian, conservator, or committee of the property of the Husband in the event of the incompetency of the Husband or administrator of the estate of the Husband in the event of the death of the Husband intestate.

2. The Husband agrees to release, and hereby does release, any and all claims of the Husband to or upon the property of the Wife, whether real or personal and whether now owned or hereafter acquired, to the end that she shall have free and unrestricted right to dispose of her property now owned or hereafter acquired, free from any claim or demand of the Husband and so that her estate and all income therefrom derived or to be derived shall go and belong to the person or persons who become entitled thereto by will or devise, bequest, intestacy, administration, or otherwise, as if the Husband had died during the lifetime of the Wife and, without in any manner limiting the foregoing, the Husband expressly relinquishes any and all rights in the estate of the Wife and any and all right of election to take any share of the estate of the Wife, as in intestacy, including, without limiting the foregoing, any right of election pursuant to the provisions of (specify state's law) or pursuant to any other law of any jurisdiction as said laws now exist or may hereafter be amended, and any and all other right and interest in any real or personal property of which the Wife

(continued on page 362)

FORM 61. *(continued from page 361)*

may die seized or possessed, and the Husband renounces and disclaims, and covenants to renounce and disclaim (i) all interest of the Husband under any will or trust agreement executed by the Wife prior to the execution of this Agreement and any right of the Husband to serve as executor or trustee under any such will; (ii) all interest of the Husband in the proceeds of any life insurance policy on the life of the Wife; (iii) all interest of the Husband under any pension, retirement, death benefit, stock bonus or profit-sharing plan, with respect to which the Wife was a participant or member; and (iv) any right of the Husband under the laws or practice of any jurisdiction to act as guardian, conservator, or committee of the property of the Wife in the event of the incompetency of the Wife or administrator of the estate of the Wife in the event of the death of the Wife intestate.

3. Except for the obligations, promises, and agreements herein set forth and to be performed by the parties thereto, which are hereby expressly reserved, each of the parties hereto and hereby, for himself and herself and for his or her legal representatives, forever releases and discharges the other of them and his or her heirs and legal representatives from any and all debts, sums of money, accounts, contracts, claims, cause or causes of action, suits, dues, reckoning, bonds, bills, specialties, convenants, controversies, agreements, promises, variances, trespasses, damages, judgments, extents, executions, and demands whatsoever, in law or in equity, which each of them had, now has, or hereafter can, shall, or may have by reason of any matter from the beginning of the world to the execution of this Agreement.

ARTICLE XI
General Release

Except as herein to the contrary provided, the parties shall and do hereby mutually remise, release, and forever discharge each other from any and all actions, suits, debts, claims, demands, and obligations whatever, both in law and in equity, which either of them ever had, now has, or may hereafter have against the other, upon or by reason of any matter, cause, or thing to the date of the execution of this Agreement and Stipulation of Settlement, including, but not limited to, claims with respect to all separate and/or marital property as those terms are defined and used in (specify state's law).

ARTICLE XII
Agreement with Respect to Matrimonial Decree

Either party shall be free at any time hereafter to institute suit for absolute divorce against the other. The execution of this Agreement and Stipulation of Settlement shall not be deemed to constitute a waiver or forgiveness of any conduct on the part of either party constituting grounds for divorce. In any such action for divorce, this Agreement and Stipulation of Settlement shall not be merged into such judgment or decree, but shall be incorporated into and survive same and shall be forever binding and conclusive upon the parties.

ARTICLE XIII
Full Disclosure

Each party represents that he or she has made an independent investigation into the complete financial circumstances of the other party and represents to the other that he or she is fully informed of the income, assets, property, and financial circumstances of the other party. Each party acknowledges that he or she is aware of all the separate and/or marital property of the other party, and the valuations thereof, as those terms are used and defined in (specify state's law), and is satisfied that full disclosure has been made by the other party. Each party further represents that he or she has previously and fully consulted with his or her attorney.

The parties are acknowledging that they are entering into this Agreement and Stipulation of Settlement freely and voluntarily; that they have ascertained and weighed all the facts and circumstances likely to influence their judgment herein; that they have sought and obtained legal advice independently of each other; that they have been duly appraised of their respective legal rights; that all provisions hereof, as well as questions pertaining hereto, have been fully and satisfactorily explained to them; that they have given due consideration to such provisions and questions, and that they clearly understand and accept all the provisions hereof.

No representations or warranties have been made by either party to the other, or by anyone else, except as expressly set forth in this Agreement and Stipulation of Settlement, and this Agreement is not being executed in reliance upon any representation or warranty not expressly set forth herein. Without limiting the foregoing, no representations or warranties have been made by either party to the other, or by anyone else in their behalf, with respect to their past, present, or future income or assets.

The parties acknowledge that they have been advised by their respective attorneys of their right to compel discovery and inspection of the other's books and records, both business and personal, and of their right to have accountants, appraisers, or others investigate, appraise, and evaluate the other's business and property, and each has waived these rights and they have instructed their respective attorneys not to take any further steps themselves, or through others, in connection with discovery, inspection, investigation, appraisal, or evaluation of the other's business or property.

ARTICLE XIV
Legal Representation

The parties represent to each other that the Wife has been represented by (specify name and address). The Husband has been represented by (specify name and address). Both parties represent and warrant that they have dealt with no other attorney for which services the other is or may become liable and will indemnify and hold the other party harmless of all loss, expenses (including reasonable attorneys' fees) and damages in the event of a breach by one party of said representation and warranty.

Both parties agree to pay for their own respective counsel fees and will make no claim on the other, in whole or in part, for the payment of counsel fees.

ARTICLE XV
Notices

Notices required by this Agreement and Stipulation of Settlement to be sent by either party shall be sufficient if sent certified or registered mail, return receipt requested, to the other.

ARTICLE XVI
General Provisions

This Agreement and Stipulation of Settlement and all obligations and covenants hereunder shall bind the parties hereto, their heirs, executors, administrators, legal representatives and assigns, and shall inure to the benefit of their respective heirs, executors, administrators, legal representatives and assigns.

(continued on page 364)

FORM 61. *(continued from page 363)*

No modification, rescission, or amendment to this Agreement and Stipulation of Settlement shall be effective unless in writing signed by both parties hereto.

This Agreement and Stipulation of Settlement and its provisions merge any prior agreements, if any, of the parties, and is the complete and entire agreement of the parties.

This Agreement and Stipulation of Settlement shall at all times be governed by the laws of the State of (specify).

Each of the parties hereto, without cost to the other, shall at any time and from time to time hereinafter, execute and deliver any and all further instruments and assurances and perform any acts that the other party may reasonably request for the purpose of giving full force and effect to the provisions of the Agreement.

A R T I C L E   X V I I
Waiver

Any Waiver by either party of any provision of this Agreement and Stipulation of Settlement or any right or option hereunder shall not be deemed a continuing waiver and shall not prevent or stop such party from thereafter enforcing such provision, right, or option, and the failure of either party to insist on any one or more instances of the strict performance of any of the terms or provisions of this Agreement by the other party shall not be construed as a waiver or relinquishment in the future of any such term or provision, but the same shall continue in full force and effect.

A R T I C L E   X V I I I
Reconciliation and Matrimonial Decrees

This Agreement and Stipulation of Settlement shall not be invalidated or otherwise affected by a reconciliation between the parties hereto, or a resumption of marital relations between them unless said reconciliation or said resumption is documented by a written statement executed and acknowledged by the parties with respect to said reconciliation and resumption and, in addition, setting forth that they are canceling this Agreement, and this Agreement and Stipulation of Settlement shall not be invalidated or otherwise affected by any decree or judgment of separation or divorce made in any court in any action which may presently exist or may hereafter be instituted by either party against the other for a separation or divorce. Each party agrees that the provisions of this Agreement and Stipulation of Settlement shall be submitted to any court in which either party may seek a judgment or decree with such specificity as the court shall deem permissible and by reference as may be appropriate under law and under the rules of the court. However, notwithstanding such incorporation, the obligations and covenants of this Agreement and Stipulation of Settlement shall survive any decree or judgment of separation or divorce and shall not merge therein, and this Agreement and Stipulation of Settlement may be enforced independently of any such decree or judgment.

A R T I C L E   X I X
Implementation

The Husband and Wife shall, at any and all times, upon request by the other party or his or her legal representatives, promptly make, execute, and deliver any and all such other and future instruments as may be necessary or desirable for the purpose of giving full force and effect to the provisions of this Agreement and Stipulation of Settlement, without charge therefor.

ARTICLE XX
Entire Understanding

This Agreement and Stipulation of Settlement contains the entire understanding of the parties, who hereby acknowledge that there have been no representations, warranties, covenants, or undertakings other than those expressly set forth herein. Each of the parties has read this Agreement and Stipulation of Settlement carefully prior to signing thereof. Either party may cause this Agreement and Stipulation of Settlement or memorandum thereof to be filed in accordance with the laws of the State of (specify). All provisions of this Agreement and Stipulation of Settlement shall be binding on the respective heirs, next-of-kin, executors, administrators, and assigns of the parties hereto.

ARTICLE XXI
Default

In the event either party defaults with respect to any obligation hereunder, the defaulting party agrees to indemnify the other against or to reimburse him or her for any and all expenses, costs, and reasonable attorneys' fees resulting from or made necessary by the bringing of any suit or other proceeding to enforce any of the terms, covenants, or conditions of this Agreement and Stipulation of Settlement to be performed or complied with by the other, provided such suit or other proceeding results in a judgment, decree, or order in favor of the other.

For the purposes of this Agreement and Stipulation of Settlement, it is understood and agreed that if a party shall institute a suit or other proceeding against the other to enforce any of the terms, covenants, or conditions of this Agreement and Stipulation of Settlement and after the institution of such action or proceeding and before judgment is or can be rendered, the defaulting party shall comply with such term or condition of the Agreement and Stipulation of Settlement, then and in that event, the suit, motion, or proceeding instituted by the party shall be deemed to have resulted in a judgment, decree, or order in favor of the non-defaulting party.

IN WITNESS WHEREOF, the parties hereto have hereunto set their respective hands and seals the day and year first above written.

_____
Name of Wife
("Wife")

_____
Name of Husband
("Husband")

State of (specify)
County of (specify)

On the day of (date), before me personally came (name of Wife) to me known and known to me to be the person mentioned and described in and who executed the foregoing Agreement and Stipulation of Settlement, and she duly acknowledged to me that she executed same.

_____

(continued on page 366)

FORM 61. *(continued from page 365)*

State of (specify)
County of (specify)

   On the day of (date), before me personally came (name of Husband) to me known and known to me to be the person mentioned and described in and who executed the foregoing Agreement and Stipulation of Settlement, and he duly acknowledged to me that she executed same.

EXHIBIT A

   List the parties' debts:

EXHIBIT B

   The following items of personal property will be distributed per the parties' prior agreement no later than seven (7) days prior to the sale of the marital premises:

FORM 62. **Property Settlement Worksheet**

A. Marital residence:
    Equity (purchase price minus current mortgage):
    $X going to Spouse A
    $Y going to Spouse B
    (Note unique considerations, such as Wife will still live in house until youngest child graduates from high school and Husband will continue to pay monthly carrying charges.)

B. Personal property:
    List the current value of all personal property
    Wife keeps X worth $X
    Husband keeps Y worth $Y

C. Income-producing real estate:
    Equity: $X
    $X going to Spouse A
    $Y going to Spouse B

D. Income-producing leases:
    $X going to Spouse A
    $Y going to Spouse B

E. Income-producing stocks and bonds:
    $X going to Spouse A
    $Y going to Spouse B

F. Amount of money in personal, business checking accounts, bank CD's:
    $X going to Spouse A
    $Y going to Spouse B

G. Separate property

H. Pension, profit-sharing, 401(k), stock option, and retirement accounts:
    $X going to Spouse A
    $Y going to Spouse B

I. Businesses:
    $X going to Spouse A
    $Y going to Spouse B

J. Life Insurance:
    Cash surrender value of policies going to:
    Death benefits going to:

K. Credit card and other debts:
    Specify who will pay for same

FORM 64. **Contract for Housekeeping Services**

This Contract for Housekeeping Services, is made by and between (Name of Individual or business "Employer", located at: _____) and (Name of Individual or business "Employee", located at: _____) on (specify date).

WHEREAS, the parties desire that Employee provide housekeeping services for the following family (or individual) located at (specify name and address); and

WHEREAS, Employee accepts such responsibilities and agrees to perform such duties as specified herein;

NOW, THEREFORE, FOR VALUABLE CONSIDERATION SET FORTH HEREIN, THE PARTIES AGREE AS FOLLOWS:

1. This Agreement will commence on (specify date).

2. The Employee agrees to render the following duties: (specify in detail, such as housecleaning, ironing and laundry duties, shopping, cooking, gardening work, bathing the children, errands for the family, assisting in transportation duties, baby-sitting, tending bar at parties, special cleaning instructions, etc.).

3. Set forth other pertinent conditions, such as term of the contract, whether it can be extended after the initial term, living arrangements for the Employee, reporting hours, and what tools or supplies will be supplied by Employer or Employee. (For example, Employer will provide all housecleaning supplies and equipment, with the exception of: specify.)

4. Specify payment. This should include the hourly or weekly rate, and what taxes will be deducted from the Employee's regular paycheck. (For example: The Employee will be paid a weekly salary of $X. The following deductions will be taken to comply with appropriate law including Social Security; federal, state, and local employment taxes; workers' compensation and unemployment insurance; charges for personal telephone calls; and other deductions discussed and mutually approved by the Employee in advance. Said payment will be made each Monday by 5:00 p.m. (▷*Author's note:* Consult your local or state law regarding overtime and maximum weekly working hour requirements.)

5. The Employee will receive the following benefits: (specify, such as room and board, meals, sick leave, vacation days, personal days, holidays, health insurance, life insurance, transportation, or use of an auto).

6. Termination. The Employee is hired AT WILL. Either party can terminate this Agreement at any time with or without warning, notice, or cause.

7. Severance Pay. At the termination of this Agreement, Employee shall receive X week's severance pay plus all accrued wages and benefits earned up to the termination date.

8. This Agreement supersedes all prior agreements and understandings and may only be modified in writing and signed by both parties. This Agreement is in force when signed below.

9. This Agreement cannot be assigned without the prior consent of Employer.

10. This Agreement shall be governed by the law of the state of (specify).

_____
Name of Employer

Dated: _____

_____
Name of Employee

FORM 75. Checklist of Legal and Illegal Hiring Questions

Subject	You May Ask	You May Not Ask
IDENTITY	What is your full name? Have you ever used an alias? If so, what was the name you used? What is the name of your parent or guardian? (Ask only if the applicant is a minor.) What is your maiden name? (Permissible only for checking prior employment or education.)	Have you ever changed your name by court order or other means? What are the names of friends and relatives working for the company? What kind of work does your mother, father, wife, or husband do? (Do not ask for information about spouses, children, or relatives not employed by the company.)
RESIDENCE	What is your address? How long have you lived in this state/city? What is your phone number?	Do you rent or own your own home? How long have you lived in this country? If you live with someone, what is the nature of the relationship? Do you live in a foreign country?
RACE, NATIONAL ORIGIN	Do you speak a foreign language? If so, which one?	What is your skin color? Your ancestry? Your maiden name? Where were you born? What is your mother's native language? What is your native tongue? How did you learn to speak a foreign language? What is your spouse's nationality?
CITIZENSHIP	Are you a citizen of the United States? If not, do you intend to become one? Can you provide documents required to prove that you have a legal right to work in this country?	Of what country are you a citizen? Are you a native-born or naturalized citizen? Your parents? Your spouse? When did you/they acquire citizenship?
CHILD CARE	Do you know of any reason why you might not be able to come to work on time, every day? (Caution: permissible only if the question is put to every applicant, regardless of gender.)	Are there children at home? How many? Their ages? Who looks after them? If you plan to have children later on, who will take care of them while you work?

Source: The Equal Employment Opportunity Commission (EEOC)

(continued on page 370)

FORM 75. *(continued from page 369)*

Subject	You May Ask	You May Not Ask
DISABILITY	Would you be willing to take a company physical if offered the job?	Are you disabled or impaired? Have you ever received compensation for injury or illness? Have you ever been treated for (do not present a checklist). In your last job, how much sick time did you have?
PERSONAL HISTORY	Have you ever been convicted of a crime? Do you hold a valid driver's license? Do you belong to any groups or clubs related to this job or field?	Have you ever been arrested? Have you ever pleaded guilty to a crime? Have you ever been in trouble with the law? To what societies, associations, lodges, etc., do you belong?
AGE	Are you of legal job age? If you are younger than 18 or older than 65, what is your age?	How old are you? When were you born? What makes you want to work at your age?
RELIGION		What is your religion? What church are you a member of? What religious holidays do you observe? Can you work on the Sabbath?
MARITAL STATUS	What is your marital status?	Are you married, single, divorced, separated, widowed, or engaged? Should we call you Miss, Ms., or Mrs.? Where does your spouse work? What does your spouse do? Is your spouse covered by a medical/health insurance plan? Are you the head of your household? Are you the principal wage earner?
GENDER ISSUES		Do you plan to marry? Will you have children? Do you believe in birth control or family planning? Do you consider yourself a feminist? What do you think about the ERA?

FORM 76. **Sample Employment Agreement for Executives**

The parties to this Agreement dated (specify) are (Name of Company), a (specify State and type of company) (the "Company") and (Name of Employee) (the "Executive").

The Company wishes to employ the Executive, and the Executive wishes to accept employment with the Company, on the terms and subject to the conditions set forth in this Agreement. It is therefore agreed as follows:

1. Employment. The Company shall employ the executive, and the Executive shall serve the Company, as a (specify) of the Company, with such duties and responsibilities as may be assigned to the Executive by the President of the Company and as are normally associated with a position of that nature. The Executive shall devote her best efforts and all of her business time to the performance of her duties under this Agreement and shall perform them faithfully, diligently, and competently and in a manner consistent with the policies of the Company as determined from time to time by an officer of or President of the Company. The Executive shall report to the General Manager, (specify) Office of the Company. The Executive shall not engage in activities outside the scope of her employment if such activities would detract from or interfere with the fulfillment of her responsibilities or duties under this Agreement or require substantial time or services on the part of the Executive. The Executive shall not serve as a director (or the equivalent position) of any company or other entity and shall not receive fees or other remuneration for work performed either within or outside the scope of her employment without prior written consent of the President of the Company. This consent shall not be unreasonably withheld.

2. Term of Employment. The Executive's employment by the Company under this agreement shall commence on the date of this Agreement and, subject to earlier termination pursuant to section 5 or 7, shall terminate on (specify date). This Agreement may also be extended as needed by a written amendment as discussed in section 8.

3. Compensation. As full compensation for all services rendered by the Executive to the Company under this Agreement, the Company shall pay to the Executive the compensation set forth in Schedule A attached hereto. This schedule may be amended from time to time in writing by the Company and the Executive.

4. Fringe Benefits; Expenses
A. The Executive shall be entitled to receive all health and pension benefits, if any, provided by the Company to its employees generally and shall also be entitled to participate in all benefit plans, if any, provided by the Company to its employees generally.

B. The Company shall reimburse the Executive for all reasonable and necessary expenses incurred by her in connection with the performance of her services for the Company in accordance with the Company's policies, upon submission of appropriate expense reports and documentation in accordance with the Company's policies and procedures. The Company will reimburse the Executive for the expenses involved with her acquisition and business-related use of a portable cellular telephone.

C. The Executive shall be entitled to Three (3) weeks paid vacation annually, to be taken at times selected by her, with the prior concurrence of the General Manager to whom the Executive is to report.

(continued on page 372)

FORM 76. *(continued from page 371)*

5. Disability or Death

A. If, as the result of any physical or mental disability, the Executive shall have failed or is unable to perform her duties for a period of Sixty (60) consecutive days, the Company may, by notice to the Executive subsequent thereto, terminate her employment under this Agreement as of the date of the notice without any further payment or the furnishing of any benefit by the Company under this Agreement (other than accrued and unpaid base salary and commissions and expenses and benefits which have accrued pursuant to any plan or by law).

B. The term of the Executive's employment under this Agreement shall terminate upon her death without any further payment or the furnishing of any benefit by the Company under this Agreement (other than accrued and unpaid base salary and commissions and expenses and benefits which have accrued pursuant to any plan or by law).

6. Noncompetition; Confidential Information; Inventions

A. During the term of the Executive's employment under this agreement, the Executive shall not, directly or indirectly, engage or be interested (as a stockholder, director, officer, employee, salesperson, agent, broker, partner, individual proprietor, lender, consultant, or otherwise), either individually or in or through any person (whether a corporation, partnership, association, or other entity) which engages, anywhere in the United States, in a business which is conducted by the Company on the date of termination of her employment, except that she may be employed by an affiliate of the Company and hold not more than 2% of the outstanding securities of any class of any publicly held company which is competitive with the business of the Company.

B. The Executive shall not, directly or indirectly, either during the term of the Executive's employment under this Agreement or thereafter, disclose to anyone (except in the regular course of the Company's business or as required by law), or use in any manner, any information acquired by the Executive during her employment by the Company with respect to any clients or customers of the Company or any confidential or secret aspect of the Company's operations or affairs unless such information has become public knowledge other than by reason of actions (direct or indirect) of the Executive. Information subject to the provisions of this paragraph shall include, without limitation:

(i) procedures for computer access and passwords of the Company's clients and customers, program manuals, user manuals, or other documentation, run books, screen, file, or database layouts, systems flowcharts, and all documentation normally related to the design or implementation of any computer programs developed by the Company relating to computer programs or systems installed either for customers or for internal use;

(ii) lists of present clients and customers and the names of individuals at each client or customer location with whom the Company deals, the type of equipment or computer software they purchase or use, and information relating to those clients and customers which has been given to the Company by them or developed by the Company, relating to computer programs or systems installed;

(iii) lists of or information about personnel seeking employment with or who are employed by the Company;

(iv) prospect lists for actual or potential clients and customers of the Company and contact persons at such actual or potential clients and customers;

(v) any other information relating to the Company's research, development, inventions, purchasing, engineering, marketing, merchandising, and selling.

C. The Executive shall not, directly or indirectly, either during the term of the Executive's employment under this Agreement or for a period of One (1) year thereafter, solicit, directly or indirectly, the services of any person who was a full-time employee of the Company, its subsidiaries, divisions, or affiliates, or solicit the business of any person who was a client or customer of the Company, its subsidiaries, divisions, or affiliates, in each case at any time during the past year of the term of the Executive's employment under this Agreement. For purposes of this Agreement, the term "person" shall include natural persons, corporations, business trusts, associations, sole proprietorships, unincorporated organizations, partnerships, joint ventures, and governments, or any agencies, instrumentalities, or political subdivisions thereof.

D. All memoranda, notes, records, or other documents made or composed by the Executive, or made available to her during the term of this Agreement concerning or in any way relating to the business or affairs of the Company, its subsidiaries, divisions, affiliates, or clients shall be the Company's property and shall be delivered to the Company on the termination of this Agreement or at any other time at the request of the Company.

E.   (i) The Executive hereby assigns and agrees to assign to the Company all her rights to and title and interest to all Inventions, and to applications for United States and foreign patents and United States and foreign patents granted upon such Inventions and to all copyrightable material or other works related thereto.

(ii) The Executive agrees for herself and her heirs, personal representatives, successors, and assigns, upon request of the Company, to at all times do such acts, such as giving testimony in support of the Executive's inventorship, and to execute and deliver promptly to the Company such papers, instruments, and documents, without expense to her, as from time to time may be necessary or useful in the Company's opinion to apply for, secure, maintain, reissue, extend, or defend the Company's worldwide rights in the Inventions or in any or all United States patents and in any or all patents in any country foreign to the United States, so as to secure to the Company the full benefits of the Inventions or discoveries and otherwise to carry into full force and effect the text and the intent of the assignment set out in section 6E(i) above.

(iii) Notwithstanding any provision of this Agreement to the contrary, the Company shall have the royalty-free right to use in its business, and to make, have made, use, and sell products, processes, and services to make, have made, use, and sell products, processes, and services derived from any inventions, discoveries, concepts, and ideas, whether or not patentable, including, but not limited to, processes, methods, formulas, and techniques, as well as improvements thereof and know-how related thereto, that are not inventions as defined herein, but which are made or conceived by the Executive during her employment by the Company or with the use or assistance of the Company's facilities, materials, or personnel. If the Company determines that it has no present or future interest in any invention or discovery made by the Executive under this paragraph, the Company shall release such invention or discovery to the Executive within Sixty (60) days after the Executive's notice in writing is received by the Company requesting such release. If the Company determines that it does or may in the future have an interest in any such invention or discovery, such information will be communicated to the Executive within the 60-day period described above.

(continued on page 374)

FORM 76. *(continued from page 373)*

(iv) For purposes of this Section 6E, "Inventions" means inventions, discoveries, concepts, and ideas, whether patentable or not, including, but not limited to, processes, methods, formulas, and techniques, as well as improvements thereof or know-how related thereto, concerning any present or prospective activities of the Company with which the Executive becomes acquainted as a result of her employment by the Company.

F. The Executive acknowledges that the agreements provided in this Section 6 were an inducement to the Company entering into this Agreement and that the remedy at law for breach of her covenants under this Section 6 will be inadequate and, accordingly, in the event of any breach or threatened breach by the Executive of any provision of this Section 6, the Company shall be entitled, in addition to all other remedies, to an injunction restraining any such breach.

7. Termination. The Company shall have the right to terminate this Agreement and the Executive's employment with the Company for cause. For purposes of this Agreement, the term "cause" shall mean:

A. Any breach of the Executive's obligations under this Agreement;

B. Fraud, theft, or gross malfeasance on the part of the Executive, including, without limitation, conduct of a felonious or criminal nature, conduct involving moral turpitude, embezzlement, or misappropriation of assets;

C. The habitual use of drugs or intoxicants to an extent that it impairs the Executive's ability to properly perform her duties;

D. Violation by the Executive of her obligations to the Company, including, without limitation, conduct which is inconsistent with the Executive's position and which results or is reasonably likely to result (in the opinion of the President of the Company) in an adverse effect (financial or otherwise) on the business or reputation of the Company or any of its subsidiaries, divisions, or affiliates;

E. The Executive's failure, refusal, or neglect to perform her duties contemplated herein within a reasonable period under the circumstances after written notice from the General Manager, or the President of the Company, describing the alleged breach and offering the Executive a reasonable opportunity to cure same;

F. Repeated violation by the Executive of any of the written work rules or written policies of the Company after written notice of violation from the General Manager or the President of the Company;

G. Breach of standards adopted by the Company governing professional independence or conflicts of interest.

If the employment of the Executive is terminated for cause, the Company shall not be obligated to make any further payment to the Executive (other than accrued and unpaid base salary and commissions and expenses to the date of termination), or continue to provide any benefit (other than benefits which have accrued pursuant to any plan or by law) to the Executive under this Agreement.

8. Miscellaneous

A. This Agreement shall be governed by and construed in accordance with the laws of the State of (specify), applicable to agreements made and performed in (specify State), and shall be construed without regard to any presumption or other rule requiring construction against the party causing the Agreement to be drafted.

B. This agreement contains a complete statement of all the arrangements between the Company and the Executive with respect to its subject matter, supersedes all previous agreements, written or oral, among them relating to its subject matter, and cannot be modified, amended, or terminated orally. Amendments may be made to this Agreement at any time if mutually agreed upon in writing.

C. Any amendment, notice, or other communication under this Agreement shall be in writing and shall be considered given when received and shall be delivered personally or mailed by Certified Mail, Return Receipt Requested, to the parties at their respective addresses set forth below (or at such other address as a party may specify by notice to the other): (specify addresses)

D. The failure of a party to insist upon strict adherence to any term of this Agreement on any occasion shall not be considered a waiver or deprive that party of the right thereafter to insist upon strict adherence to that term or any other term of this Agreement. Any waiver must be in writing.

E. Each of the parties irrevocably submits to the exclusive jurisdiction of any court of the State of (specify) sitting in (specify) County or the Federal District Court of (specify State) over any action, suit, or proceeding relating to or arising out of this Agreement and the transactions contemplated hereby. EACH OF THE PARTIES IRREVOCABLY AND UNCONDITIONALLY WAIVES THE RIGHT TO A TRIAL BY JURY IN ANY SUCH ACTION, SUIT, OR PROCEEDING. Each party hereby irrevocably waives any objection, including, without limitation, any objection to the laying of venue or based on the grounds of *forum non conviens* which such party may now or hereafter have to the bringing of any such action, suit, or proceeding in any such court and irrevocably agrees that process in any such action, suit, or proceeding may be served upon that party personally or by Certified or Registered Mail, Return Receipt Requested.

F. The invalidity or unenforceability of any term or provision of this Agreement shall not affect the validity or enforceability of the remaining terms or provisions of this Agreement which shall remain in full force and effect and any such invalid or unenforceable term or provision shall be given full effect as far as possible. If any term or provision of this Agreement is invalid or unenforceable in one jurisdiction, it shall not affect the validity or enforceability of that term or provision in any other jurisdiction.

G. This Agreement is not assignable by either party except that it shall inure to the benefit of and be binding upon any successor to the Company by merger or consolidation or the acquisition of all or substantially all of the Company's assets, provided such successor assumes all of the obligations of the Company, and shall inure to the benefit of the heirs and legal representatives of the Executive.

By: By:

_____   _____
(Name and Title of Employer)   (Name of Employee)
(Name of Company)   ("Executive")
("The Company")

FORM 77. Sample Confidentiality and Noncompetition Agreement

In consideration of my employment or continued employment by (Name of Company) (the "Company"), together with its affiliates and subsidiaries, and any subsidiaries or affiliates which hereafter may be formed or acquired, and in recognition of the fact that as an employee of the Company I will have access to the Company's customers and to confidential and valuable business information of the Company and of its parent company, (specify), together with its affiliates and subsidiaries, and any subsidiaries or affiliates which hereafter may be formed or acquired, I hereby agree as follows:

1. The Company's Business. The Company is (specify, for example, a consulting firm). The Company is committed to quality and service in every aspect of its business. I understand that the Company looks to and expects from its employees a high level of competence, cooperation, loyalty, integrity, initiative, and resourcefulness. I understand that as an employee of the Company, I will have substantial contact with the Company's customers and potential customers.

I further understand that all business and fees, including insurance, bond, risk management, self insurance, insurance consulting, and other services produced or transacted through my efforts, shall be the sole property of the Company, and that I shall have no right to share in any commission or fee resulting from the conduct of such business other than as compensation referred to in paragraph 3 hereof. All checks or bank drafts received by me from any customer or account shall be made payable to the Company, and all premiums, commissions, or fees that I may collect shall be in the name of and on behalf of the Company.

2. Duties of Employee. I shall comply with all Company rules, procedures, and standards governing the conduct of employees and their access to and use of the Company's property, equipment, and facilities. I understand that the Company will make reasonable efforts to inform me of the rules, standards, and procedures which are in effect from time to time and which apply to me.

3. Compensation and Benefits. I shall receive the compensation as is mutually agreed upon, which may be adjusted from time to time, as full compensation for services performed under this Agreement. In addition, I may participate in such employee benefit plans and receive such other fringe benefits, subject to the same eligibility requirements, as are afforded other Company employees in my job classification. I understand that these employee benefit plans and fringe benefits may be amended, enlarged, or diminished by the Company from time to time, at its discretion.

4. Management of the Company. The Company may manage and direct its business affairs as it sees fit, including, without limitation, the assignment of sales territories, notwithstanding any employee's individual interest in or expectation regarding a particular business location or customer account.

5. Termination of Employment. My employment may be terminated by the Company or me at any time, with or without notice or cause. Upon termination of my employment, I shall be entitled to receive incentive payments in accordance with the provisions of the Company's Incentive Plan, as it may be modified by the Company from time to time, less any adjustments for amounts owed by me to the Company. I understand that I may also receive additional compensation at the discretion of the Company and in accordance with the published Company Personnel Policy on Termination Pay.

6. Agreement Not to Compete with the Company.

A. As long as I am employed by the Company, I shall not participate directly or indirectly, in any capacity, in any business or activity that is in competition with the Company.

B. In consideration of my employment rights under this Agreement and in recognition of the fact that I will have access to the confidential information of the Company and that the Company's relationships with its customers and potential customers constitute a substantial part of its goodwill, I agree that for One (1) year from and after termination of my employment, for any reason, unless acting with the Company's express prior written consent, I shall not, directly or indirectly, in any capacity, solicit or accept business from, provide consulting services of any kind to, or perform any of the services offered by the Company, for any of the Company's customers or prospects with whom I had business dealings in the year next preceding the termination of my employment.

7. Unauthorized Disclosure of Confidential Information. While employed by the Company and thereafter, I shall not, directly or indirectly, disclose to anyone outside of the Company any Confidential Information or use any Confidential Information (as hereinafter defined) other than pursuant to my employment by and for the benefit of the Company.

The term "Confidential Information" as used throughout this Agreement means any and all trade secrets and any and all data or information not generally known outside of the Company whether prepared or developed by or for the Company or received by the Company from any outside source. Without limiting the scope of this definition, Confidential Information includes any customer files, customer lists, any business, marketing, financial or sales record, data, plan, or survey; and any other record or information relating to the present or future business, product, or service of the Company. All Confidential Information and copies thereof are the sole property of the Company.

Notwithstanding the foregoing, the term Confidential Information shall not apply to information that the Company has voluntarily disclosed to the public without restriction, or which has otherwise lawfully entered the public domain.

8. Prior Obligations. I have informed the Company in writing of any and all continuing obligations that require me not to disclose to the Company any information or that limit my opportunity or capacity to compete with any previous employer.

9. Employee's Obligation to Cooperate. At any time upon request of the Company (and at the Company's expense) I shall execute all documents and perform all lawful acts the Company considers necessary or advisable to secure its rights hereunder and to carry out the intent of this agreement.

10. Return of Property. At any time upon request of the Company, and upon termination of my employment, I shall return promptly to the Company, including all copies of all Confidential Information or Developments, and all records, files, blanks, forms, materials, supplies, and any other materials furnished, used, or generated by me during the course of my employment, and any copies of the foregoing, all of which I recognize to be the sole property of the Company.

11. Special Remedies. I recognize that money damages alone would not adequately compensate the Company in the event of a breach by me of this Agreement, and I therefore agree that, in addition to all other remedies available to the Company at law or in

(continued on page 378)

FORM 77. *(continued from page 377)*

equity, the Company shall be entitled to injunctive relief for the enforcement hereof. Failure by the Company to insist upon strict compliance with any of the terms, covenants, or conditions hereof shall not be deemed a waiver of such terms, covenants, or conditions.

12. Miscellaneous Provisions. This Agreement contains the entire and only agreement between me and the Company respecting the subject matter hereof and supersedes all prior agreements and understandings between us as to the subject matter hereof; and no modification shall be binding upon me or the Company unless made in writing and signed by me and an authorized officer of the Company.

My obligations under this Agreement shall survive the termination of my employment with the Company regardless of the manner of or reasons for such termination, and regardless of whether such termination constitutes a breach of this Agreement or of any other agreement I may have with the Company. If any provisions of this Agreement are held or deemed unenforceable or too broad to permit enforcement of such provision to its full extent, then such provision shall be enforced to the maximum extent permitted by law. If any of the provisions of this Agreement shall be construed to be illegal or invalid, the validity of any other provision hereof shall not be affected thereby.

This Agreement shall be governed and construed according to the laws of (specify State), and shall be deemed to be effective as of the first day of my employment by the Company.

BY SIGNING THIS AGREEMENT, I ACKNOWLEDGE THAT I HAVE READ AND UNDERSTOOD ALL OF ITS PROVISIONS AND THAT I AGREE TO BE FULLY BOUND BY THE SAME.

Employee: _____ Date: _____

Accepted by: _____ Date: _____
              (Name and Title of Officer)

FORM 78. **Lie Detector Test Disclaimer and Release**

I, (name of employee), have been advised by XYZ Employer that employers are generally prohibited from requesting or causing any applicant or employee to take a lie detector test.

Nonetheless, I, (name of employee), acknowledge that in the course of my employment, I requested that such a test be given to clear my name of the following serious alleged workplace impropriety: (specify). As a prerequisite of such a test, I was given opportunity to obtain and consult with legal counsel before each phase of the test; I was provided at least 48 hours' notice of the time and place of the test; I was advised beforehand of the nature and characteristics of the test and the instruments involved; I was provided an opportunity to review all questions to be asked at the examination; and I was given a copy of the results together with a copy of the federal Polygraph Protection Act of 1988.

I authorize that the results of any polygraph test be communicated and disclosed to third parties. As a consequence of any negative result obtained from said test, I understand that I may be disciplined leading up to or including immediate discharge by XYZ Employer.

I hereby indemnify, release, and forever discharge and hold XYZ Employer and its subsidiaries and affiliated companies, agents and employees harmless from any and all claims, demands, judgments, and legal fees arising out of or in connection with such tests, the results, or any lawful use of the results.

_____
Signature of Employee

_____
Printed Name of Employee

Social Security Number: _____

Date:_____

Name of Witness: _____

FORM 79. **Sample Demand Letter Alleging Discrimination**

Your Name
Address
Telephone Number
Date

Name of Officer or Employer
Title
Name of Employer
Address

Re: My Termination

Dear (Name of Officer),

I am black (or state another factor, such as age, for alleging discrimination). On (date), I was notified by (name), my supervisor at (specify location or plant), that I was fired. I asked him to tell me why I was fired; he said it was because I called in sick three times in the past year. I know of several white (or, for example, younger) employees who called in sick more than three times in the past year and were not fired.

In that regard, I demand (state what you want, such as job reinstatement, severance pay, or other damages).

It is imperative that I receive a response to my request immediately to avoid having me take prompt legal action to enforce my rights, including filing a charge of race (or specify another form, such as age) discrimination with the Equal Employment Opportunity Commission.

Hopefully, this will not be necessary, and I thank you for your prompt attention to this matter; feel free to contact me immediately.

Very truly yours,
(your name)

▷ Send certified mail, return receipt requested.

▷ *Author's note:* Under federal and state law, individuals cannot be fired or denied a promotion due to their race, sex, age, or physical handicaps. If you are fired and believe you were discharged primarily because of a personal characteristic, send a letter similar to the one above as an initial step. The letter documents your protest and "starts the clock" for the purpose of computing damages if no adequate response is received. If you do not receive such response shortly after a firing, seek assistance from the EEOC or state discrimination agency to protect your rights. There is no charge for this assistance and the EEOC or state agency will handle the matter for you. A formal charge must be filed within 300 days under federal law to avoid having the statute of limitations expire.

FORM 80. **Sample Letter of Resignation Requesting Benefits**

Your Name
Address
Telephone Number
Date

Name of Officer
Title
Name of Employer
Address

Re: My Resignation

Dear (Name of Officer),

Please be advised that I am resigning from my job as (specify title) effective (specify date).

As of this date, I believe that (describe what salary, commissions, other benefits) are due, and I look forward to discussing my termination benefits with you.

I shall be returning all property belonging to the company (specify) by (date) and (optional: will be available to assist you in a smooth transition if requested).

I would appreciate your signing the enclosed letter of reference, which I have drafted, and discussing my cover story with me prior to being contacted by future potential employers.

Thank you for your attention to these matters.

Very truly yours,
(your name)

▷ Send certified mail, return receipt requested.

▷ *Author's note:* It is a good idea to send a letter of resignation similar to the one above when you need to clarify benefits, request prompt payment of monies previously due, or put on record that the resignation will not be effective until some later date. Keep the letter brief and avoid giving specific reasons for the resignation, because this can preclude you from offering other reasons or tipping your hand in the event of a lawsuit.

FORM 81. **Lawyer's Letter on Behalf of Terminated Employee**

Date

Name of Company Officer
Title
Company Name and Address

Re: Termination of (name of client, "Wilma Jones")

Dear (Name),

This office has been retained by Wilma Jones concerning her dismissal from employment with your company. On (specify date), Ms. Jones was summarily discharged without cause by (name of supervisor), an officer with your company. Ms. Jones, who is 61 years of age, was dismissed from employment after 12 years of exemplary service in the highly competitive and sophisticated field of publishing. She was replaced by an inexperienced, unqualified, younger man (specify name).

No articulable reason was provided to Ms. Jones at the time of her discharge other than that the company was downsizing. (Name of supervisor) told my client she was to be terminated, and Ms. Jones was given only one hour to clean out her desk and vacate the premises. Upon further inquiry Ms. Jones learned that your company has not engaged in a downsizing as stated.

My client demonstrated a wide variety of valuable skills in her work. She was never criticized or warned that her job was in jeopardy. The man who replaced her is much younger (under 40), is not technically skilled in her field, and is inexperienced. Ms. Jones always received favorable performance evaluations during her tenure.

The manner of my client's discharge was both humiliating and distressful. Ms. Jones is confused, deeply pained, and upset at what prompted her dismissal without explanation or notice. Your offer to pay only four weeks' severance is inadequate in light of my client's long-term contributions and achievements. Furthermore, I have been advised that other male executives with similar long-term service have received substantially greater severance packages.

My client's replacement by a much younger, less competent male causes me to conclude that your company terminated Ms. Jones primarily because of her age and sex. Under this state's laws and federal laws, the circumstances surrounding her discharge and replacement reflect a strong indication of sex and age discrimination. As such, I have advised my client she is entitled to be compensated for the arbitrary manner in which she was treated.

As a result of the termination, Ms. Jones also suffered the loss of the medical, dental, and profit-sharing benefits she was receiving while employed and which she relied on for her future welfare. At her age it is doubtful she will obtain gainful employment soon, and she was counting on working several more years before her retirement. The discharge is even more damaging in view of the fact that Ms. Jones is a widow with little means of support.

Finally, the manner in which she was terminated caused her additional harm and distress in that she was not notified of her continuation of medical benefits under federal COBRA law.

In light of the foregoing, I request that either you or your representative contact this office immediately in an attempt to resolve these and other issues in an amicable fashion to avoid expensive and protracted litigation.

Hopefully this can be avoided, and I thank you for your immediate attention and cooperation in this matter.

Very truly yours,
Name of Attorney

FORM 82. **Sample Demand Letter for ERISA Retirement Benefits**

Your Name
Address
Telephone Number
Date

Name of Officer or Employer
Title
Name of Employer
Address

      Re: My ERISA Retirement Benefits

Dear (Name of Officer),

      As you know, I was terminated (or resigned) on (specify date). However, I have not received a written description of all my retirement benefits under federal ERISA law. (Or, if applicable, state: I have not received the correct computation of all benefits due me. Or, I believe I was fired shortly (i.e., two months) before the vesting of a pension, in violation of my ERISA rights.)

      Your company has a legal obligation to provide me with accurate information concerning all applicable profit-sharing, pension, employee welfare, benefit, and other plans. Therefore I would like you to (specify what you want, such as to receive a copy of the employer's formal pension and/or profit-sharing plans, recompute your benefits, or offer you a pension, if applicable).

      It is imperative that I receive a response to my request immediately in writing to avoid having me take prompt legal action to enforce my rights.

      Hopefully, this will not be necessary and I thank you for your prompt attention in this matter.

      If you wish to discuss this matter with me, feel free to contact me immediately.

                               Very truly yours,
                               (your name)

▷ Send certified mail, return receipt requested.

▷ *Author's note:* Under federal ERISA law, if you request materials from a plan and do not receive them within thirty days, you may file suit in federal or state court. Contact the plan administrator for the company immediately in writing if your claim is denied or if you do not receive an adequate response shortly after a firing. If no adequate response is received, seek assistance from the U.S. Department of Labor to protect your rights.

FORM 83. **Sample Demand Letter for COBRA Medical Benefits Coverage**

Your Name
Address
Telephone Number
Date

Name of Officer or Employer
Title
Name of Employer
Address

Re: My COBRA Medical Benefits

Dear (Name of Officer),

As you know, I was terminated on (specify date) due to a job elimination (or specify, such as business reorganization). However, more than 30 days has elapsed from the date of my discharge and I have not yet received official notification from either your company or your medical carrier that my medical benefits have been maintained and/or extended under federal COBRA law.

It is imperative that I receive such notification immediately in writing, specifying my cost at the group rate for such coverage.

I trust that such information will be forthcoming immediately so that I am not required to take prompt legal action to enforce my rights.

Hopefully, such additional legal action will not be necessary and I thank you for your prompt attention to this apparent oversight.

If you wish to discuss this matter with me, feel free to contact me immediately.

Very truly yours,
(your name)

▷ Send certified mail, return receipt requested.

▷ *Author's note:* Federal COBRA law requires that most employers offer continuation of coverage for an additional eighteen months to former employees who were discharged as a result of a voluntary or involuntary termination (with the exception of gross misconduct); all terminated employees have the option to continue medical plan benefits at their cost. You must be notified within sixty days of your right to continue such coverage. Send a similar letter whenever you do not receive such a notification shortly after a firing. A well-drafted letter should spur the company into action and protect your rights.

FORM 84. **Sample Demand Letter for Earned Commissions**

Your Name
Address
Telephone Number
Date

Name of Officer or Employer
Title
Name of Employer
Address

Re: My Commissions

Dear (Name of Officer),

It has been (specify) days from the effective termination date of our agreement. Despite our discussions and your earlier promises that all commissions presently owed would be paid immediately, I still have not received my money.

Please be advised that under this state's law, unless I am provided a final, accurate accounting, together with copies of all invoices reflecting shipment of my orders (or state if you require anything else) and payment of commissions totaling (specify $X if you know), within (specify, such as five days) from your receipt of this letter, your company will be liable for additional damages, attorney fees, and costs upon my institution of a lawsuit to collect same.

Hopefully this will not be necessary and I thank you for your prompt attention to this apparent oversight.

If you wish to discuss this matter with me, feel free to contact me immediately.

Very truly yours,
(your name)

▷ Send certified mail, return receipt requested.

▷ *Author's note:* Most states require that salespeople receive earned commissions immediately after a firing. Many of these laws provide independent reps up to three times additional damages in excess of the commission owed, plus reasonable attorney fees and costs, when monies are not promptly paid. Thus always send a detailed written demand for unpaid commissions. This should always be done by certified mail, return receipt requested, to document your claim and prove delivery. Such a demand will "start the clock" for the purpose of determining the number of days that commissions remain unpaid and put the employer on notice that additional damages and penalties may be owed if money is not received immediately. A written demand is essential in enforcing your rights and typically will get the employer to contact you and resolve the matter amicably.

FORM 85. **Sample Demand Letter for Earned Bonus**

Your Name
Address
Telephone Number
Date

Name of Officer or Employer
Title
Name of Employer
Address

Re: My Bonus

Dear (Name of Officer),

Please be advised that I am currently owed a bonus of (specify $X if you know). I was fired on (specify date, such as January 15) suddenly for no valid reason and not as a result of any negative or detrimental conduct on my part. Prior to my termination, I complied with all company directives and was expecting to receive a bonus for the work I rendered in the preceding year.

This expectation was in accordance with our previous understandings and practices since I have regularly received bonuses for the past (specify) years ranging from (specify dollar amounts).

Therefore, to avoid further legal action, I request prompt payment of my earned bonus. Hopefully, additional legal action will not be necessary and I thank you for your prompt attention to this apparent oversight.

If you wish to discuss this matter with me, feel free to contact me immediately.

Very truly yours,
(your name)

▷ Send certified mail, return receipt requested.

▷ *Author's note:* Some employers fire workers right before they are scheduled to receive a bonus by requiring that workers be employed on the day bonus checks are issued as a condition of payment. If this happens to you, or you are denied a bonus for any reason, send a letter similar to the one above to protect your rights. Argue that you would have received the bonus but for the firing. And demand that you are entitled to receive a pro rata share of the bonus if you are fired close to but before the end of the year. For example, if you are fired on December 1, negotiate to receive eleven-twelfths of the bonus you were expecting.

FORM 86. Sample Demand Letter for Accrued Vacation Pay

Your Name
Address
Telephone Number
Date

Name of Officer or Employer
Title
Name of Employer
Address

Re: My Earned Vacation Pay

Dear (Name of Officer),

Please be advised that I am currently owed vacation pay totaling (specify number of days or weeks due or $X if you know). As you know, I resigned (or was fired) on (specify date). According to your company's policy specified in (state, such as a handbook or manual), I am entitled to (specify) weeks per year.

To avoid having me take legal action, including my contacting this state's Department of Labor and requesting a formal investigation, I expect to receive my earned, accrued vacation pay immediately.

Hopefully, additional legal action will not be necessary and I thank you for your prompt attention to this apparent oversight.

If you wish to discuss this matter with me, feel free to contact me immediately.

Very truly yours,
(your name)

▷ Send certified mail, return receipt requested.

▷ *Author's note:* Most states require employers to pay accrued vacation pay in all circumstances, even after resignations by employees or terminations for cause. Although each company is free to implement its own rules governing vacation pay, employers must apply such policies consistently to avoid charges of discrimination and breach of contract. To avoid problems, be sure you understand how long you must first work to qualify, whether vacation days must be taken in a given year, whether they can be carried over to the next year, or whether you can be paid in cash for unused, earned vacation days. Also, how much notice must you give before being allowed to take vacation time?

If your ex-employer fails to respond to your initial letter and even a second, final request, contact the Department of Labor for assistance.

FORM 87. **Sample Demand Letter for Accrued Overtime Pay**

Your Name
Address
Telephone Number
Date

Name of Officer or Employer
Title
Name of Employer
Address

Re: My Earned Overtime Pay

Dear (Name of Officer),

Please be advised that I am currently owed (specify hours) of overtime pay totaling (specify $X). As you know, I resigned (or was fired) on (specify date). Under federal law, since I was an hourly worker for your company, overtime at one and one half times my regular pay rate must be paid for hours worked in excess of 40 hours per work week.

I am enclosing copies of time sheets for overtime work approved by my superior from (specify date) to (specify date). To avoid having me take prompt legal action, including my contacting this state's Department of Labor and requesting a formal investigation into your company's violation of the Fair Labor Standards Act, I expect to receive my earned overtime pay immediately.

Hopefully, additional legal action will not be necessary and I thank you for your prompt attention to this matter.

If you wish to discuss this matter with me, feel free to contact me immediately.

Very truly yours,
(your name)

▷ Send certified mail, return receipt requested.
▷ *Author's note:* Overtime is not generally available for salaried workers who work in executive, administrative, or professional jobs (called "exempt employees"). But if you are a salaried worker, your company is not generally allowed to deduct a few hours off your weekly paycheck for time off for any reason, including personal time. If it does so, you may be determined to be an hourly worker, capable of receiving overtime for up to three years.

If you have kept proper records and took authorized overtime, contact a representative at your state's Department of Labor or the Wage and Hour Division of the U.S. Department of Labor for help if your ex-employer fails to respond to your initial letter or a second final written request.

FORM 88. **Sample Demand Letter to Review Contents of Personnel File**

Your Name
Address
Telephone Number
Date

Name of Officer or Employer
Title
Name of Employer
Address

      Re: My Termination

Dear (Name of Officer),

      On (date) I was fired suddenly by your company without notice, warning, or cause. All that I was told by (name of person) (state what was said).

      Under the laws of this state, I hereby demand to receive a copy of my personnel file, including any documents that refer to my discharge.

      Thank you for your prompt attention and cooperation in this matter.

Very truly yours,
(your name)

▷ Send certified mail, return receipt requested.

▷ *Author's note:* State law governs whether employees have the right to review their personnel records pertaining to employment decisions. In some states, including California, Connecticut, Delaware, Illinois, Maine, Michigan, Nevada, New Hampshire, Ohio, Oregon, Pennsylvania, Washington, and Wisconsin, you generally have this right. However, even in these states, you generally cannot inspect confidential items, such as letters of reference furnished by other employers, information about other employees, records of an investigation, or information about misconduct or crimes, that have not been used adversely against you.

If you receive a file with information that is incorrect, you have the right to prepare and send a rebuttal statement in some states.

FORM 89. **Sample Letter of Recommendation**

Date

To whom it may concern:

I am pleased to submit this letter of recommendation on behalf of (your name).

(Your name) worked for the company from (date) through (date). During this period (your name) was promoted from (specify title) to (specify title) and received salary increases and other bonuses (if applicable, or specify other awards received, etc.).

During the past (specify) years, I have had the opportunity to work closely with (your name). At all times I found (your name) to be diligent and dependable, and (your name) rendered competent and satisfactory service on the company's behalf.

I heartily recommend (your name) as a candidate for employment of his/her choosing.

Very truly yours,
(your name)

▷ *Author's note:* Savvy fired workers request that a copy of a favorable letter of recommendation be given to them. Do not rely on promises that your ex-employer will furnish prospective employers with a favorable recommendation, since many fail to do this. Thus, attempt to have such a letter in hand before you leave the premises the final time. If possible, type the letter yourself on company stationery and have it signed by your immediate supervisor or appropriate officer.

FORM 90. **Summary of Things to Consider If Your Job Is in Jeopardy**

1. It may be illegal for a company to fire you to deprive you of large commissions, vested pension rights, a year-end bonus, or other expected financial benefits.

2. It may be illegal for a company to fire you after returning from an illness, pregnancy, or jury duty.

3. It may be illegal to fire you after you have complained about a safety violation or other wrongdoing.

4. It may be illegal to fire you in a manner inconsistent with company handbooks, manuals, written contracts, and disciplinary rules.

5. It may be illegal to fire you if you are over 40, belong to a protected minority, or are a female, primarily because of such personal characteristics.

6. It may be illegal to fire a large number of workers and/or close a plant without giving *at least* 60 days' notice or 60 days' severance pay.

7. It may be illegal to fire you if you received a verbal promise of job security or other rights which the company failed to fulfill.

8. It may be illegal to fire a long-term worker when the "punishment does not fit the crime" and other workers were not similarly treated, particularly if you are over 40, belong to a protected minority, or are a female.

9. If you signed a written contract, reread it. Review what it says about termination, because if the company fails to act according to the contract, your rights may be violated.

10. Try to make copies of all pertinent documents in your personnel file while working. If you have received excellent performance reviews and appraisals and the file indicates you have received merit salary increases, you may be able to use this material to fight the firing. Or you may be able to use this information to successfully negotiate more severance than the company is offering.

11. Refuse the company's offer to resign whenever possible. This is because if you resign you may be waiving your claim to unemployment and other severance benefits.

12. Avoid accepting the company's first offer of severance. Stall for time and follow the negotiating strategies found in the Appendix to increase your chances of obtaining more severance pay and other post-termination financial benefits than the company initially offers.

Finally, since the above twelve strategies are merely suggestions and are not intended to be legal advice per se, always seek legal counsel where warranted.

FORM 91. **Negotiating Strategies to Maximize Severance Pay and Retirement Benefits**

1.   Generally, there is no *legal* obligation for a company to pay severance unless you have a written contract stating that severance will be paid, oral promises are given regarding severance pay, there is a documented policy of paying severance in a company manual or handbook, the employer voluntarily offers to pay severance, or other employees in similar positions have received severance pay in the past.

2.   If you are fired, request an additional negotiating session to discuss your severance package.

3.   Stall for time and try not to accept the company's first offer.

4.   Appeal to corporate decency and fair play; avoid threatening litigation at the initial meeting. For example, it is better to say "I am 58 years old and have to pay for two children in college right now, and your offer of just 4 weeks' severance will probably put me on the road to financial ruin since it is unlikely I can find another comparable job in 4 weeks," rather than "If you don't pay me more money, I will sue."

5.   Recognize that by asking for many additional benefits (say, 15 items), you may be able to get the company to settle for some of them.

6.   Confirm all arrangements in writing to document the final deal of severance and post-termination benefits. Do not accept the company's promise that "everything will work out."

7.   Insist on receiving more money and other benefits before signing any release or waiver of age discrimination claims.

8.   Do not rely on promises from the company that you will receive a favorable job reference. Rather, draft your own favorable letter of reference and get an officer or your supervisor to sign the letter of reference before you depart. (See page 391 in the Appendix for a sample of such a letter.)

9.   Do not be intimidated or forced into early retirement. Recognize that you may have rights, particularly if your early retirement causes you to lose large, expected financial benefits.

10.   Be cautious when the employer asks you to sign a release, because you may be waiving valuable rights and benefits in the process.

Finally, since the above ten strategies are merely suggestions and are not intended to be legal advice per se, always seek legal counsel where warranted.

FORM 92. List of Acceptable Documents for Conformance with Immigration and Control Act

LIST A Documents That Establish Both Identity and Employment Eligibility	OR	LIST B Documents That Establish Identity	AND	LIST C Documents That Establish Employment Eligibility
1. U.S. Passport (unexpired or expired) 2. Certificate of U.S. Citizenship (INS Form N-560 or N-561) 3. Certificate of Naturalization (INS Form N-550 or N-570) 4. Unexpired foreign passport with I-551 stamp or attached INS Form I-94 indicating unexpired employment authorization 5. Alien Registration Receipt Card with photograph (INS Form I-151 or I-551) 6. Unexpired Temporary Resident Card (INS Form I-688) 7. Employment Authorization Card (INS Form I-688) 8. Unexpired Reentry Permit (INS Form I-327) 9. Unexpired Refugee Travel Document (INS Form I-571) 10. Unexpired Employment Authorization Document issued by the INS which contains a photograph (INS Form I-688B)		1. Driver's license or ID card issued by a state or outlying possession of the U.S. provided it contains a photograph or information such as name, date of birth, sex, height, eye color, and address 2. ID card issued by federal, state, or local government agencies or entities provided it contains a photograph or information such as name, date of birth, sex, height, eye color, and address 3. School ID card with a photograph 4. Voter's registration card 5. U.S. Military card or draft record 6. Military dependent's ID card 7. U.S. Coast Guard Merchant Mariner Card 8. Native American tribal document 9. Driver's license issued by a Canadian government authority *For persons under age 18 who are unable to present a document listed above:* 10. School record or report card 11. Clinic, doctor, or hospital record 12. Day-care or nursery school record		1. U.S. Social Security card issued by the Social Security Administration (other than a card stating that it is not valid for employment) 2. Certification of Birth Abroad issued by the Department of State (Form FS-545 or Form DS-1350) 3. Original or certified copy of a birth certificate issued by a state, county, municipal authority, or outlying possession of the United States bearing an official seal 4. Native American tribal document 5. U.S. Citizen ID Card (INS Form I-197) 6. ID Card for use of Resident Citizen in the United States (INS Form I-179) 7. Unexpired employment authorization document issued by the INS (other than those listed in LIST A)

FORM 97. Contract for Home Maintenance or Extensive Repairs

This Contract for Home Maintenance/Repairs, is made by and between (Name of Homeowner, "Homeowner" located at:) and (Name of Contractor "Contractor", specify address or if applicable, provide: name of state and Corporation) on (specify date).

WHEREAS, the parties desire that Contractor perform home repairs (or specify, remodeling) at (specify the address of subject premises); and

WHEREAS, Contractor agrees to perform the services enumerated hereunder competently, and in a professional manner;

NOW, THEREFORE, THE PARTIES AGREE AS FOLLOWS:

1. This Agreement will commence on (specify date).

2. Contractor shall render the following services (specify).

3. Homeowner agrees to pay the following: (such as "Contractor agrees to build a backyard patio for Homeowner. The total job will cost $X including labor and materials. Homeowner agrees to pay $Y upon the signing of this Agreement, $Z when the land renovation is completed, and the final balance of $A when the bricks are satisfactorily laid").

Specify:

* Full amount to be paid for the job
* What deposit, if any, is required as a down payment
* The stages of payment; for example, upon completion of Y, a payment of $X is due; etc.
* If Contractor works by the hour, state the hourly rate; that Contractor will maintain accurate time sheets for himself and his workers and supply Homeowner with said time sheets on a daily basis; and that the job will not exceed X hours
* Who pays for materials, the maximum amount to be paid for materials, and that the Homeowner will receive copies of all receipts or invoices for the materials before payment is made
* Describe the quality of materials to be used, that all materials shall be new or of good quality in compliance with all applicable laws and codes, free of defects for a period of X years, and shall be covered by a manufacturer's warranty if practicable

4. The specified work shall begin on or before (specify date) and Contractor agrees to complete the job by (specify date). Since the parties agree it is imperative that the job be completed by said date and time is of the essence, Contractor agrees to deduct $X from the final price if the job is not completed to Homeowner's reasonable satisfaction by said date.

5. Contractor shall provide his own tools and be responsible for all state and local building licenses and permits and registration requirements. Contractor shall be responsible to procure all appropriate permits, workers' compensation, and property and personal injury insurance, and shall furnish proof of the existence of such coverage to Homeowner before starting the job. The work rendered shall comply with all applicable building codes and regulations.

6. In the event that Subcontractors are used, Contractor agrees to indemnify and hold Homeowner harmless from any claims of payment, as such payment to said

(continued on page 396)

FORM 97. *(continued from page 395)*

parties shall be Contractor's sole responsibility. Final payment of $X shall be withheld until Contractor presents Homeowner with proof that all bills for materials, work, and labor from Subcontractors have been paid in full. (Or: Contractor authorizes Homeowner to make all checks for payment directly to any Subcontractors and/or material suppliers.) Both parties agree to protect the Homeowner from any liens being filed on the premises from Subcontractors or materials suppliers by (specify what protection will be given).

   7. Any case or controversy arising among or between the parties, this Agreement, or the subject matter hereto, shall be settled by binding arbitration in (specify location) under the then prevailing rules of the American Arbitration Association. The decision of the arbitrator shall be final and binding. Both parties agree to share the costs of such arbitration equally but the Arbitrator shall be instructed to award reasonable attorney fees to the prevailing party.

   8. Additional terms and conditions essential to this Agreement include: (specify).

   9. This Agreement supersedes all prior agreements and understandings and can only be modified in a writing signed by both parties.

Dated: _____   _____
                                         Name of Homeowner

Dated: _____   _____
                                         Name of Contractor

FORM 99. **Work for Hire/Invention Agreement**

THIS AGREEMENT, is made by and between Name of individual ("Employee"), residing at (specify), and Name of Company or Individual ("Employer") (specify address).

WHEREAS, Employee has accepted employment (or Individual agrees to work to develop certain inventions), commencing on (date); and

WHEREAS, the Employee agrees to accept consideration for such work;

NOW, THEREFORE, THE PARTIES AGREE AS FOLLOWS:

1. This Agreement shall commence (specify date).

2. In the course of his/her duties, Employee may create various (specify, such as inventions, programs, works or products). The parties agree that any works created by Employee shall belong to and be the exclusive property of Employer as such works shall be deemed MADE FOR HIRE.

3. Employee agrees to waive any and all claims for compensation or benefits derived from the creation, use or sale of such works by the Employer and shall execute all documents required to evidence ownership of said property by Employer and Employer's request.

4. At Employer's request, or upon termination of this arrangement for any reason, Employee shall immediately provide Employer with all originals and copies of all samples, designs, models, data, and information pertaining to any of Employee's works in progress.

5. This Agreement supersedes and replaces all prior agreements and understandings, whether oral or in writing, and may only be modified in a separate writing signed by both parties. This Agreement is in force when signed below.

6. In the event that any one or more of the provisions contained in this Agreement shall for any reason be held to be illegal or unenforceable in any respect under the law of any state by a court of competent jurisdiction, such unenforceability shall not affect any other provision of this Agreement, and the remainder of the contract shall still be upheld.

Date: _____

Name of Employee or Individual

_____

Name of Employer or Party
Contracting for Services

_____

FORM 100. **Example of Lawyer's Business Litigation Retainer Agreement**

Date

Name of Client
Address

Re: *Name of Case*

Dear (Name of Client):

This will confirm our retainer agreement whereby you have hired the law offices of (specify) as the attorney of record and this office in an Of Counsel capacity to file a lawsuit in Federal Court, County of (specify), State of (specify) to recover damages incurred by the alleged breach of contract by (name of defendant).

Based on my extensive review of all pertinent facts, and the comprehensive meeting between (name of attorney) and myself in (location) on (date), the damages we will be seeking shall exceed $X on your company's behalf from the above, including additional potential statutory-granted damages, attorney fees, interest, and costs.

In that regard, you agree to pay a retainer of $X as a minimum fee in this matter. Said retainer shall be paid as follows: $A upon your signing of this retainer agreement; $B within 30 days from that date; and the balance of $C within 60 days from the signing hereof. All checks will be made payable to my name and will be forwarded to my law office in (specify).

Upon my receipt of the signed retainer agreement and clearance of the first $A check, I will immediately contact the defendant for the purposes of attempting to settle the matter without the necessity of formal litigation. In the event the matter can be resolved before institution of a formal lawsuit or within 30 days after the filing of a formal lawsuit, all retainers paid shall be applied against a discounted contingency fee of TWENTY FIVE PERCENT (25%) of all sums collected in settlement. (Note: As was discussed, (name of defendant) would have to offer at least $X at this stage for us to settle the matter now and it is doubtful they will do so now.)

In the event no immediate satisfactory offer is forthcoming, and we become involved in protracted litigation, the $X retainer paid will be applied against a final contingency fee of THIRTY FIVE PERCENT (35%) of all gross monies collected on your behalf (including money collected for lawyer's fees) by settlement, judgment, or otherwise.

Upon the filing of litigation papers, (name of attorney) and this office will split equally all legal fees paid and earned in connection with your matter. Both of us will handle the litigation but I am responsible for coordinating all trial strategy with respect thereto. This office will handle the actual filing of all papers and formal legal requirements in (specify state). I will attend and participate at the actual trial. Furthermore, I will travel to (specify) at my own cost to attend any depositions of important witnesses and be available at important motions, sessions, etc.

The aforesaid retainer only covers this current litigation and not any work rendered in appellate courts or other actions or proceedings and there will be no additional charges such as trial fees or otherwise, with the exception of litigation costs, expenses and disbursements. In this regard, you agree to pay for or reimburse us promptly for all out-of-pocket disbursements incurred on your behalf. Out-of-pocket disbursements include but are not limited to costs of filing papers, court fees, process servers, witness fees, expert witness fees (note: a qualified economist might charge as much as $10,000.00 for computing actual damages and testifying in court) and court reporters' stenographic fees (which could be as much as $1,000.00 per day for lengthy depositions). In that regard, and in the event formal litigation becomes necessary, you will forward an initial sum of Five Hundred Dollars ($500.00) for this purpose to be deposited into (name of attorney's) escrow account to cover initial costs and fulfill this aspect of our agreement.

All settlements will require your consent and approval before concluding same. Additionally, although (name of attorney) and I have advised that it appears that your claims are strong, you understand that despite both of our law firms working on your behalf, there is no assurance or guarantee of the success or the outcome of this matter.

Additionally, although (name of attorney) will be the attorney of record in the actual lawsuit, I shall serve as the final decision-maker in all aspects of your lawsuit when tactical decisions are involved.

As always, we look forward to serving you. If the terms of the above meet with your approval, please sign the original and FAX your approval back to me. Please forward the initial $X retainer made payable to (specify) and the $X for travel reimbursement as a result of our initial meeting.

If you have any questions or comments, feel free to call.

Very truly yours,

Name of Attorney

I, (name of client), have read and understand the above retainer letter, have received a copy, and accept all of its terms:

_____   Dated: _____
Name of Client

Accepted and Agreed To:

_____
Name of Lawyer

FORM 101. **Verified Complaint**

Name of Court
Name of County

_____x

Name,

                Plaintiff,   INDEX NO.

                                         VERIFIED COMPLAINT

                - against -

Name,

                Defendant.

_____x

       Plaintiff, Name, by her attorney, (Attorney's Name), complaining of the defendant, alleges as follows:

       1. Plaintiff is a resident of the State of (specify) residing in the County of (specify).

       2. Upon information and belief, defendant is a foreign corporation organized under the laws of the State of (specify) and is authorized to do business in the State of (specify) by virtue of the fact that said corporation transacts business and derives substantial revenue within the State by shipping merchandise to stores and accounts located in (specify) and accepting orders for its merchandise to accounts located in (specify), thereby subjecting it to the jurisdiction of this Court pursuant to (specify).

AS AND FOR A FIRST CAUSE OF ACTION

       3. Plaintiff repeats and realleges paragraphs 1–2 as though more fully stated herein.

       4. That heretofore plaintiff entered into an Agreement with defendant on (date), a copy of which is attached hereto and annexed as Exhibit A. Said exhibit is hereafter referred to as the Agreement.

       5. That pursuant to said Agreement, plaintiff agreed to act as the exclusive sales representative for sale of defendant's product lines in (specify exclusive territory) with the exception of agreed-upon house accounts and (specify) independents.

       6. That in consideration therefore, defendant agreed to pay plaintiff a draw of $X per week to be applied against a commission of Ten Percent (10%) on regular goods sold, Three Percent (3%) on closeouts and Five Percent (5%) on promotional goods sold at well below line price as agreed upon by management.

       7. That plaintiff duly performed all the conditions of said Agreement.

       8. That on or about (date), defendant unilaterally terminated said Agreement.

       9. That upon information and belief, defendant shipped plaintiff's orders from (date) to (date) to plaintiff's customers and into plaintiff's exclusive territory exceeding $X.

       10. That in accordance with the terms of said Agreement, defendant owes plaintiff commissions totaling $X, no part of which has been paid although duly demanded.

AS AND FOR A SECOND CAUSE OF ACTION

       11. Plaintiff repeats and realleges each and every allegation contained in paragraphs 1 through 10 as though more fully stated herein.

12. Upon information and belief, there have been many orders and reorders for defendant's products received directly by defendant between (date) and the present, and through the end of the Fall (date) Season resulting in a large volume of sales to plaintiff's customers within plaintiff's exclusive territory; and by reason of the aforesaid Agreement, large sums of money, the exact amount of which is not known to plaintiff, but upon information and belief is believed to be in excess of $X, resulting in a commission due plaintiff in the sum of $X.

13. Upon an accounting by defendant, there will be found due and owing from defendant a large sum of money, the amount of which is not known to plaintiff.

14. Heretofore and prior to the commencement of this action, plaintiff duly demanded that defendant account to plaintiff for commissions and unauthorized chargebacks and deductions taken under the Agreement, and to pay over to plaintiff the amount due her, but defendant has refused to do so and has never rendered an accurate complete accounting to plaintiff for shipments of defendant's products to plaintiff's customers and into plaintiff's exclusive territory from (date) through the present and through the end of the (year) Fall reorder season.

15. Plaintiff has no adequate remedy at law.

AS AND FOR A THIRD CAUSE OF ACTION

16. Plaintiff repeats and realleges each and every allegation contained in paragraphs 1 through 15 as though more fully stated herein.

17. That as a result of all orders obtained by plaintiff and reorders received directly by defendant and shipped by defendant to plaintiff's customers and into plaintiff's exclusive territory after (date) through the present and through the end of the Fall (year) reorder season, defendant benefited from plaintiff's efforts and was unjustly enriched thereby.

18. That plaintiff's efforts in soliciting and obtaining said orders and the reorders resulting thereto, was not furnished on a voluntary basis, but was rendered with the expectation of being paid.

19. That upon information and belief defendant shipped goods to plaintiff's customers and into plaintiff's exclusive territory from (date) through the present and through the end of the (year) reorder season in an amount exceeding $X.

20. That as a result of plaintiff's efforts, defendant is indebted to plaintiff and is obligated to pay plaintiff the reasonable value of plaintiff's services rendered thereto: to wit, commissions totaling $X.

AS AND FOR A FOURTH CAUSE OF ACTION

21. Plaintiff repeats and realleges each and every allegation contained in paragraphs 1 through 20 as though more fully stated herein.

22. That plaintiff commenced working for defendant as an independent manufacturer's representative on or after (date).

23. That defendant failed to pay plaintiff all commissions due her within Five (5) business days after said commissions were earned or the Agreement between the parties was terminated.

24. That pursuant to (specify State) law, defendant is obligated by its failure to pay plaintiff her commissions owed in a timely fashion, double commission damages plus reasonable attorney fees incurred by plaintiff in instituting this action.

(continued on page 402)

FORM 101. *(continued from page 401)*

WHEREFORE, plaintiff demands judgment from defendant as follows:

1. In the first cause of action, that plaintiff be awarded a money judgment in the sum of $X.

2. In the second cause of action, that defendant be required and directed to give a just and true account to the plaintiff of all sales of its products emanating from orders obtained by plaintiff and reorders shipped between (date) and the present, and through the end of the Fall (year) season, to plaintiff's customers and into plaintiff's exclusive territory and that defendant be ordered to pay plaintiff money due her as commissions, which, upon information and belief, exceeds $X.

3. In the third cause of action, that plaintiff be awarded a money judgment in the sum of $X.

4. In the fourth cause of action, that plaintiff be awarded double commission damages and reasonable attorney fees.

5. Interest, costs and disbursements in this action.

6. Such other and further relief as to the Court may deem just and proper in the premises.

Dated: _____

_____
Name
Attorney for Plaintiff
Address

VERIFICATION

STATE OF X   )
COUNTY Y   )

(Name), being duly sworn, deposes and says:

Deponent is the plaintiff in the within action. Deponent has read the foregoing Verified Complaint and knows the contents thereof; and the same is true to Deponent's own knowledge, except as to the matters therein stated to be alleged upon information and belief, and as to those matters Deponent believes it to be true.

The grounds of Deponent's belief as to all matters not stated upon Deponent's knowledge are documents in Deponent's files.

_____
Name

Sworn to before me this
_____th day of (Month), (Year)

_____
Notary Public

FORM 102. **Verified Answer**

Name of Court
Name of County

_____x

Name,

               Plaintiff,   INDEX NO.

                                              VERIFIED ANSWER

               - against -

Name,

               Defendant.

_____x

    Defendant, by its attorney, (Name of Attorney), as and for its answer to the complaint herein sets forth and alleges as follows:
    1. Denies each and every allegation contained in plaintiff's complaint.

FIRST DEFENSE

    2. This Court lacks jurisdiction over the person of the defendant.

SECOND DEFENSE

    3. This Court lacks subject matter jurisdiction against the defendant.

THIRD DEFENSE

    4. The complaint fails to state a cause of action.

    WHEREFORE, defendant demands judgment dismissing the complaint in its entirety, and requests reimbursement for the costs and disbursements of this action, together with reasonable attorney's fees.

Dated: _____

                                              _____

                                            Name
                                            Attorney for Defendant
                                            Address

(continued on page 404)

FORM 102. *(continued from page 403)*

TO: Name of Plaintiff
        Address

VERIFICATION

STATE OF X   )
COUNTY Y   )

(Name), being duly sworn, deposes and says:

Deponent is the defendant in the within action. Deponent has read the foregoing Verified Answer and knows the contents thereof; and the same is true to Deponent's own knowledge, except as to the matters therein stated to be alleged upon information and belief, and as to those matters Deponent believes it to be true.

The grounds of Deponent's belief as to all matters not stated upon Deponent's knowledge are documents in Deponent's files.

_____
Name

Sworn to before me this
_____th day of (Month), (Year)

_____
Notary Public

FORM 103. **Stipulation**

Name of Court
Name of County

_ _x

Name,

               Plaintiff,   STIPULATION

                                        VERIFIED ANSWER

               - against -

Name,

               Defendant.

_ _x

      IT IS HEREBY STIPULATED by and between the parties that the plaintiff shall extend the period of time to which an Answer is due under the CPLR and permit the defendant to file an Answer and responsive pleadings to its Verified Complaint until (date).

Dated: _____

_____   _____
Name   Name
Attorney for Plaintiff   Attorney for Defendant
Address   Address

FORM 104. **Defendant's First Set of Interrogatories**

Name of Court
Name of County

_____x

Name,

          Plaintiff,   INDEX NO.

                              DEFENDANT'S FIRST

          - against -   SET OF INTERROGATORIES

Name,

          Defendant.

_____x

S I R S :

      PLEASE TAKE NOTICE that defendant, (specify name), through its attorney, (specify name), propounds the following interrogatories to be answered by plaintiff within fifteen (15) days after service thereof.

INTERROGATORIES

1. Identify the person or persons answering these interrogatories.
2. State whether the agreement alleged in plaintiff's Complaint alleging commissions owed in the sum of $X was partly oral or all or partly in writing. For each such agreement:
    (a) If all or partly oral, state:
        (1) Who acted on behalf of plaintiff and who acted on behalf of defendant;
        (2) When, where and by what means said agreement was reached;
        (3) the identity of all other persons present at the time said agreement was reached; and
        (4) Each and every term comprising said agreement.

(b) If all or partly written, identify and annex copies of any and all documents pertaining to said agreement.

3. State the capacity and title of the person who entered into the rental agreement on behalf of plaintiff.

4. Did the plaintiff have approval of its Board of Directors to enter into the aforesaid rental agreement and if so, when was such consent given?

5. State the duration of the aforesaid rental agreement.

6. With respect to the demands for commission as alleged in the Complaint, set forth:

(a) The date and time that plaintiff duly demanded of defendant that it account to plaintiff for commissions owed;

(b) To whom those demands were made;

(c) Whether the demands were oral or in writing, and if in writing attach copies hereto.

7. With respect to the demands for rent as alleged in the Complaint, set forth:

(a) The date and time that plaintiff duly demanded of defendant that it account to plaintiff for commissions owed;

(b) To whom those demands were made;

(c) Whether the demands were oral or in writing, and if in writing, annex copies hereto.

Dated: _____

_____
Name
Attorney for Defendant
Address

TO:
Name
Attorney for Plaintiff
Address

FORM 105. **Stipulation Discontinuing Action with Prejudice**

IN THE CIRCUIT COURT OF (SPECIFY COUNTY), (SPECIFY STATE)
COUNTY DEPARTMENT, LAW DIVISION

_ _X

Name,

              Plaintiff,   INDEX NO.

                               STIPULATION

          - against -   DISCONTINUING ACTION

Name,   WITH PREJUDICE

              Defendant.

_ _X

    IT IS HEREBY STIPULATED AND AGREED, by and between the undersigned, the Attorneys of record for all the parties to the above entitled action, that whereas no party hereto is an infant or incompetent person for whom a committee has been appointed and no person not a party has an interest in the subject matter of the action, the above entitled action be, and the same hereby, is discontinued with prejudice without costs to either party as against the other. This Stipulation may be filed without further notice with the Clerk of the Court.

Dated: _____

_____   _____

Name   Name

Attorney for Defendant   Attorney for Plaintiff

Address   Address

FORM 106. **Affidavit for Judgment by Confession**

IN THE CIRCUIT COURT OF (SPECIFY COUNTY), (SPECIFY STATE)
COUNTY DEPARTMENT, LAW DIVISION

_ _x

Name,

                                  INDEX NO.

           Plaintiff,

                                  AFFIDAVIT FOR

           - against -   JUDGMENT BY

Name,   CONFESSION

           Defendant.

_ _x

STATE OF X   )
COUNTY Y   )

Name ("Y"), being duly sworn, deposes and says:

1. I ("Y") am the defendant in the within action, whose address is (specify).

UNDERLYING FACTS

2. This Affidavit for Judgment by Confession ("Affidavit") is given for a debt due to plaintiff ("X") arising out of the following facts:

X and Y entered into an oral agreement in or about (date) whereby Y agreed to become an independent sales agent for X. From time to time Y requested certain advances on her commissions from X and certain samples from X which she was obligated to repay from commission earnings. Y agreed to repay to X all overages due to the company if her commissions did not exceed such sums. To date, such overages total $X.

3. X has made claims against Y for such overages allegedly due and owing.

4. In settlement of all claims, Y delivered to counsel for X the following:
(1) an executed Settlement Agreement and Mutual Release: (2) this Affidavit; and
(3) a $X promissory note, an unsigned copy of which is attached as Exhibit A to this Affidavit ("Note").

CONFESSION OF JUDGMENT

5. If and only if (a) Y fails to make a payment required by the Note and (b) Y fails to make said payment pursuant to the ten-day Notice of Non-Payment provisions of Numbered Paragraph 2 of the Note ("Ten-Day Notice Provisions") and (c) X files a declaration under penalty of perjury with the above-entitled court after first giving a three-day Notice of intention to do so that states that Y failed to make a payment required by the Note and that Y thereafter failed to make such payment pursuant to the Ten-Day Notice Provisions, then Y authorizes X to file this Affidavit and have judgment

(continued on page 410)

FORM 106. *(continued from page 409)*

entered against Y in the total amount of $X (less any payments on the Note already received by X ("the Judgment"), in the form of the Judgment attached as Exhibit B. Such judgment may be entered in the Circuit Court of (specify) County or such other court or jurisdiction that may be necessary or convenient to the plaintiff.

     6. X's total recovery for its claims against Y shall consist of (1) the Judgment, (2) interest on the Judgment at the rate of Twelve Percent (12%) per annum or the maximum legal rate, whichever is greater, and (3) reasonable attorney fees incurred in filing, enforcing and collecting the Judgment.

     7. This Affidavit for Judgment by Confession is not for the purpose of securing X against a contingent liability and is not an installment loan.

     8. I, Y, am freely signing this Affidavit.

_____
Name

Sworn to before me this
_____th day of (Month), (Year)

_____
Notary Public

FORM 107. **Judgment Pursuant to Affidavit for Judgment by Confession**

IN THE CIRCUIT COURT OF (SPECIFY COUNTY, (SPECIFY STATE)
COUNTY DEPARTMENT, LAW DIVISION

_____x

Name,

Plaintiff,	INDEX NO.
- against -	JUDGMENT PURSUANT TO AFFIDAVIT FOR
Name,	JUDGMENT BY CONFESSION
Defendant.	

_____x

Pursuant to the Affidavit for Judgment by Confession ("Affidavit") executed by Name of Defendant ("Y") that has been filed with this Court, and the concurrently filed declaration under penalty of perjury of Name of Plaintiff ("X") that states that Y failed to make a payment required by the Note that is referenced in the Affidavit *and* that Y thereafter failed to make said payment pursuant to the Ten-day Notice of Non-Payment provisions of Numbered Paragraph 2 of the Note after first receiving a three-day Notice of intention to do so, judgment is entered in favor of X and against Y in the amount of $X less any payments already received by X from Y on the Note ("the Judgment"). The Judgment shall include additional amounts for interest, costs and reasonable attorney fees. X shall also be awarded interest on the amount of the Judgment, after Judgment is entered and until the Judgment is paid in full, at the rate of Twelve Percent (12%) per annum or the maximum legal rate, whichever is greater. Furthermore, X shall be entitled to reasonable attorney fees and costs incurred in filing, enforcing and collecting the Judgment.

Principal amount ($X less any payments already received by X from Y on the Note)	_____
Pre-judgment Interest	_____
Interest	_____
Pre-judgment Attorney Fees	_____
Attorney Fees	_____
Costs	_____
TOTAL JUDGMENT	_____

_____
Judge of the Circuit Court of the
State of (specify), County of (specify)

FORM 108. **Settlement Agreement and Mutual General Release (in a business dispute)**

     This SETTLEMENT AGREEMENT AND MUTUAL GENERAL RELEASE (hereinafter referred to as the "Settlement Agreement") is executed as of (date) by and between Party #1 and Party #2.

     WHEREAS, Party #2 has asserted a claim for (specify in detail) and other monies allegedly owing; and

     WHEREAS, in the interest of avoiding the risks and burdens of litigation, the parties now wish to settle their dispute;

     NOW, THEREFORE, it is agreed as follows:

     1. Party #1 shall pay #2 the sum of $X, in full and final settlement of all claims. The aforesaid settlement amount shall be paid by check to (specify name), attorney for Party #2, within ten (10) days from the date hereof.

     2. As consideration for this payment, Party #2 shall deliver to Party #1 a signed original of this Settlement Agreement, thereby fully and forever releasing Party #1 from any and all liability with respect to any matter arising from its association with Party #1.

     3. Party #2, on behalf of itself and its predecessors, successors, parents, subsidiaries, affiliates, heirs, beneficiaries, representatives, and assigns on the one hand and Party #1, on behalf of itself, its predecessors, successors, parents, subsidiaries, affiliates, heirs, beneficiaries, representatives, and assigns on the other hand, hereby release, discharge, and promise not to sue each other and/or their employees, officers, agents, lawyers, heirs, beneficiaries, predecessors, successors, assigns, and business entities on all rights, claims, lawsuits, charges, and actions, whether known or unknown, which all parties may have against each other from the beginning of time to the date of this Settlement Agreement.

     4. Each party represents and warrants that it is represented by separate legal counsel of its own choice in connection with this Settlement Agreement, has read this Settlement Agreement and understands the terms used herein. Each party has had the opportunity to investigate this matter, determine the advisability of entering into this Settlement Agreement and has entered into this Settlement Agreement freely and voluntarily.

5. This Settlement Agreement constitutes the entire understanding of the parties. It is intended to and does cover the parties' expenses, costs, and attorney fees incurred as of the date of this Settlement Agreement arising out of or connected with the claims hereby released, all of which shall be borne by the party who incurred such expenses, costs, and fees. Should any proceeding of any kind be instituted to enforce this Settlement Agreement, the court shall award to the prevailing party its costs, expenses and fees, including attorney fees. In the event the aforesaid settlement payment is not received in the amount or timely manner as specified in Paragraph 1 hereinabove, the terms of this Settlement Agreement shall be null and void.

6. This Settlement Agreement shall be binding upon and inure to the benefit of each of the parties hereto and their respective successors and assigns. The parties each represent and warrant to one another that they have not sold, assigned, transferred, conveyed or otherwise disposed of any claim or demand covered by this Settlement Agreement.

7. There shall be no amendment or modification of any of the terms of this Settlement Agreement unless it is reduced to writing and signed by the parties hereto.

Dated: _____

Accepted and Consented To:

Party #1

By: _____
    Name, Title

Party #2

By: _____
    Name, Title

▷ *Author's note:* This is the kind of document that may be prepared to confirm a settlement in a business dispute.

FORM 109. **Settlement Agreement and Mutual General Release (in a discrimination dispute)**

This Settlement Agreement and Mutual General Release (hereinafter referred to as the "Settlement Agreement") is executed as of (date), by and between Name of Employer ("Company"), a (specify state) limited partnership, and Name of Employee, ("Y"), a resident of (specify state).

WHEREAS, Y was terminated from her employment with Company on or about (date) and received severance and other benefits from Company; and

WHEREAS, Y alleges that she signed a letter (dated specify) under duress accepting said benefits and had no time to seek legal counsel in connection with the signing of said letter; and

WHEREAS, Y alleges that the termination and benefits offered to her were not fair and will cause her to file a charge with the Equal Employment Opportunity Commission to protect her rights; and

WHEREAS, in the interest of avoiding the risks and burdens of litigation, both parties wish to settle their dispute with prejudice;

NOW, THEREFORE, it is agreed as follows:

1. Y agrees to accept the additional sum of $X in full and final settlement of all claims. This amount shall be paid upon the expiration of the seven-day revocation period set forth in Paragraph 7 (below) and Company shall deliver to Y's attorney a check in the above amount made payable to "(name) as attorney."

2. Y on behalf of herself and her predecessors, successors, parents, subsidiaries, affiliates, heirs, beneficiaries, representatives, and assigns on the one hand and Company, on behalf of itself, its predecessors, successors, parents, subsidiaries, affiliates, heirs, beneficiaries, representatives, and assigns on the other hand, hereby release, discharge and promise not to sue each other and/or their employees, agents, lawyers, heirs, beneficiaries, predecessors, successors, assigns, and business entities (collectively "Releasees") on all rights, claims, lawsuits, charges and actions, whether known or unknown, which all parties may have against each other from the beginning of time to the date of this Settlement Agreement, including without limitation a release of any rights or claims she may have under Title VII of the Civil Rights Act of 1964, as amended, and the Civil Rights Act of 1991 (which prohibit discrimination in employment based upon race, color, sex, religion, and national origin); the Americans with Disabilities Act of 1990 and the Rehabilitation Act of 1973 (which prohibit discrimination based upon disability); the Family and Medical Leave Act of 1993 (which prohibits discrimination based on requesting or taking a family or medical leave); Section 1 of the Civil Rights Act of 1866, 42 U.S.C. S 1981 (which prohibits discrimination based upon race); Section 2 of the Civil Rights Act of 1871, 42 U.S.C. S 1985 (3) (which prohibits conspiracies to discriminate); the Employment Retirement Income Security Act of 1974 (which prohibits discrimination with regard to benefits); any state, city, or local laws against discrimination; or any other federal, state, city, or local statute, regulation or ordinance or common law relating to employment, wages, compensation, hours, or any other terms and conditions of employment or the termination of employment. This includes a release by Y of any claims for wrongful discharge, breach of contract, torts, or other wrongful conduct or any other claims in any way related to her employment with or departure from the Company. This also includes a release of any claims for age discrimination under the Age Discrimination in Employment Act ("ADEA"'). The ADEA requires that one be

advised to consult with an attorney before waiving any claim under the ADEA. In addition, the ADEA provides at least 21 days to decide whether to waive claims under the ADEA and seven days to revoke the waiver.

This release does not include a release of any claim for any vested benefits Y may be entitled to under the Company's 401(k) Profit Sharing Plan or a waiver of any rights she may have to disability insurance, unemployment insurance or workers' compensation insurance benefits. Y further agrees that she will indemnify Releasees for any and all liability, costs, and expenses (including any and all attorney fees) that Releasees incur as a result of any claim brought by her which she has hereby released.

3. Each party represents and warrants that it is represented by separate legal counsel of its own choice in connection with this Settlement Agreement, has read this Settlement Agreement and understands the terms used herein. Each party has had the opportunity to investigate this matter, determine the advisability of entering into this Settlement Agreement, and has entered into this Settlement Agreement freely and voluntarily.

4. Y's release includes, but is not limited to, claims under the Age Discrimination in Employment Act of 1967, as amended ("ADEA").

5. This Settlement Agreement constitutes the entire understanding of the parties. It is intended to and does cover the parties' expenses, costs, and attorney fees incurred as of the date of this Settlement Agreement arising out of or connected with the claims hereby released, all of which shall be borne by the party who incurred such expenses, costs, and fees. In the event the aforesaid settlement payment is not received in the amount or timely manner as specified in Paragraph 1 hereinabove, the terms of this Settlement Agreement shall be null and void and Y shall be allowed to enforce all of her rights hereunder, without prejudice.

6. This Settlement Agreement shall be binding upon and inure to the benefit of each of the parties and their respective successors and assigns.

7. Y has had at least 21 days to discuss this Release with legal counsel of her choosing before signing and realizes that it applies to all claims, demands, and causes of action against Company or Releasees or any of them, whether or not she knows or suspects them to exist at the present time. She understands that she has a period of seven (7) days from the date she signs this Release to revoke it. If she decides to revoke this Release, the revocation must be in writing signed by her and received by Company before the expiration of the seventh (7th) calendar day following the day she signs this Release. Consequently, this Release shall have no force and effect until the expiration of seven (7) calendar days following the day on which she signs it, and Company shall likewise have no obligation hereunder until after that time.

8. Y will not apply for or otherwise seek re-employment with Company at any time.

9. Nothing herein nor any payment made hereunder shall be construed as an admission of any liability on the part of anyone for any matter, all liability being denied.

10. Y has not relied on any representation, express or implied, made by Company or any of its representatives.

11. Y intends that this Release shall not be subject to any claim of fraud, duress, deception, or mistake of fact, and that it expresses a full and complete settlement of any claims she has whatsoever or may have against Company or any Releasee. By signing this Release, she agrees that she will not file any complaint, suit, claim, or charge against Company or any Releasee with any local, state, or federal agency or court and will not accept any payments in connection with same. If any agency or court assumes jurisdiction

(continued on page 416)

FORM 109. *(continued from page 415)*

of any complaint, suit, claim, or charge against Company or any Releasee on her behalf, she will request such agency or court to dismiss the matter and be responsible to pay for all reasonable legal fees incurred by Company in connection with the enforcement of this Release.

12. Both parties, intending to be legally bound, hereby apply their signature voluntarily with full understanding of the contents of this Release.

Dated: _____

_____
Name of Company

By: _____
                Title

Dated: _____

_____
Name of Employee ("Y")

STATE OF X   )
COUNTY OF X   )

On this _____ day of (Month), (Year), before me personally came _____ , to me known to be the person described in the foregoing instrument, and acknowledged that she executed the same.

_____
Notary Public

STATE OF X   )
COUNTY OF X   )

On this _____ day of (Month), (Year), before me personally came _____ , to me known as (state position) of (state name of company), known as the person described in the foregoing instrument, and acknowledged that he executed the same.

_____
Notary Public

▷ *Author's note:* This is the kind of document that may be prepared to confirm a settlement in a discrimination suit.

FORM 112. **Living Together Agreement (To Share Income, Property, and Purchase Assets Jointly)**

THIS AGREEMENT, is made by and between Name of individual ("Party #1"), and Name of individual ("Party #2").

WHEREAS, the parties plan to live together at (specify location) commencing on (date); and

WHEREAS, the parties desire to accumulate and share all real and personal property acquired hereinafter the signing of this agreement jointly:

NOW, THEREFORE, THE PARTIES AGREE AS FOLLOWS:

1. Effective (date), all property previously purchased and owned by Party #1 affixed on Schedule A shall remain the sole property of Party #1.

2. Effective (date), all property previously purchased and owned by Party #2 affixed on Schedule B shall remain the sole property of Party #2.

3. Notwithstanding Provisions 1 and 2 of this Agreement, one-half of the following separate property affixed on Schedule C shall be assigned to the other party and now constitutes joint property (specify).

4. Notwithstanding Provisions 1 and 2 of this Agreement, all profits, dividends, and interest income produced from said property shall be deposited into a joint bank account (specify name of bank and location) and considered joint property. Additionally, in the event either party desires to transfer separate ownership to joint ownership with respect to any property listed on Schedule A or B, the parties will execute a formal agreement, signed by both parties, evidencing same.

5. Although each party will continue to use his/her own separate credit cards, the other party agrees to share in the enjoyment of such purchase, and, therefore, agrees to be liable to third parties or secondarily responsible for making payment for any purchases or debts incurred by the other party.

6. (Specify the treatment of money received from inheritance or gift.)

7. Any money required to purchase real property (such as an expensive boat, house, furniture, etc.) will be contributed equally by the parties and the deed or title to said property will be issued jointly, unless a separate arrangement is agreed upon and reflected in writing.

8. This Agreement supersedes and replaces all prior agreements and understandings, whether oral or in writing, and may only be modified in a separate writing signed by both parties. This Agreement is in force when signed below.

9. In the event that any one or more of the provisions contained in this Agreement shall for any reason be held to be illegal or unenforceable in any respect under the law of any state by a court of competent jurisdiction, such unenforceability shall not affect any other provision of this Agreement, and the remainder of the contract shall still be upheld.

(continued on page 418)

FORM 112. *(continued from page 417)*

Date: _____   Party #1 _____

Date: _____   Party #2 _____

State of (specify)
County of (specify)

     On (specify date) before me came (name of Party #1 and name of Party #2), personally known to me to be the individuals described hereinabove and who executed the foregoing Living Together Agreement, and duly acknowledged to me that they executed the same.

_____
Notary Public

FORM 113. **Living Together Agreement (To Keep Property Separate)**

THIS AGREEMENT, is made by and between Name of individual ("Party #1"), and Name of individual ("Party #2").

WHEREAS, the parties plan to live together at (specify location), commencing on (date); and

WHEREAS, the parties desire to keep all real and personal property acquired heretofore by each of them separate;

NOW, THEREFORE, THE PARTIES AGREE AS FOLLOWS:

1. Effective (date), all property affixed on Schedule A, including any profits, dividends or interest income inuring from said property, shall remain the sole property of Party #1.

2. Effective (date), all property affixed on Schedule B, including any profits, dividends or interest income inuring from said property, shall remain the sole property of Party #2.

3. While the parties will establish and maintain a joint bank account at (specify name of bank and location), and each party will equally deposit the sum of $X monthly into said account to pay for all living expenses including, but not limited to (specify, such as rent, food, utilities, gas, etc.) from money deposited into said account, neither party will make a claim upon the other for any money or property traceable to his/her separate property.

4. Each party will continue to use his/her own separate credit cards and neither party will be liable to third parties or responsible for making payment for any purchases or debts incurred by the other party.

5. Any money required to purchase real property (such as a house) or a business in the future will be contributed equally by the parties and the deed or title to said property will be issued jointly, unless a separate arrangement is agreed upon and reflected in writing.

6. This Agreement supersedes and replaces all prior agreements and under-standings, whether oral or in writing, and may only be modified in a separate writing signed by both parties. This Agreement is in force when signed below.

7. In the event that any one or more of the provisions contained in this Agree-ment shall for any reason be held to be illegal or unenforceable in any respect under the law of any state by a court of competent jurisdiction, such unenforceability shall not affect any other provision of this Agreement, and the remainder of the contract shall still be upheld.

Date: _____   Party #1 _____

Date: _____   Party #2 _____

(continued on page 420)

FORM 113. *(continued from page 419)*

State of (specify)
County of (specify)

On (specify date) before me came (name of Party #1 and name of Party #2), personally known to me to be the individuals described hereinabove and who executed the foregoing Living Together Agreement, and duly acknowledged to me that they executed the same.

_____
Notary Public

FORM 114. **Living Together Agreement (For Equal Purchase of House or Apartment)**

THIS AGREEMENT, is made by and between Name of individual ("Party #1"), and Name of individual ("Party #2").

WHEREAS, the parties plan to purchase (or rent) a residence at (specify location), commencing on (date); and

WHEREAS, the parties desire to purchase said residence equally; and

WHEREAS the parties desire to set forth each party's obligations in the event they split up to avoid expensive and protracted litigation;

NOW, THEREFORE, THE PARTIES AGREE AS FOLLOWS:

1. Effective (date), the property located at (specify) shall be purchased (or rented).

2. Title in said residence will be held jointly and the deed will state same. (Or, the apartment lease will be issued to both parties named on the lease as co-tenants.)

3. Each party will contribute $X toward the deposit and down payment. Each party will equally pay for one-half of all closing costs, attorney fees, and expenses.

4. The parties will deposit $X monthly into a joint checking account located at (specify bank and address). Each party will pay for one-half of the monthly mortgage (or rent).

5. All furniture purchased for the residence will be purchased equally by both parties. Title in all of said property will be held jointly.

6. *If living in an apartment, state:* If the parties desire to separate, Party #1 agrees to move out of the apartment on X days written notice. The parties agree to divide all personal property acquired in their apartment as follows (specify), or state, in a fair and equitable manner. If the parties are unable to do so, this Agreement confirms that they agree to submit any dispute between themselves, this Agreement, or the subject matter herein to mediation or binding arbitration if mediation is unsuccessful in (specify city) under the then prevailing rules of the American Arbitration Association. The decision of the arbitrator shall be final and binding and both parties agree to share in all fees and expenses related to any such mediation or arbitration equally.

If purchasing or living in a house, state: If the parties desire to separate, Party #1 agrees to move out of the house on X days written notice. Once Party #1 vacates said residence, he/she will be no longer responsible for paying one-half of the mortgage and monthly carrying expenses, and the parties will sign all necessary documents reflecting this agreement with third parties, and between themselves so that the non-moving party agrees to indemnify and hold the moving party harmless from any claims or demands incurred by the aforesaid.

7. Party #2 agrees to pay to Party #1 prior to his/her moving (or specify by when), $X representing one-half of the equity for said house. (Or, state that the parties will sell the house for a minimum price of $Y and the proceeds will be shared equally after the closing.) Note: During the time the house is being sold, specify who will be responsible for paying the monthly mortgage, other expenses, and repairs to ready the house for sale and the consequences if that party fails to pay. There should also be a clause which

(continued on page 422)

FORM 114. *(continued from page 421)*

discusses what happens if the parties cannot agree with their real estate broker on the minimum purchase price. For example, the parties agree to have the property appraised by three separate appraisers, and the purchase price would be determined by the average price of the three; the costs of said appraisals would be paid for by the parties equally (or specify otherwise).

8. At the closing, both parties will be represented by one attorney who shall be instructed to distribute the net profit of the sale equally. The parties agree to divide all personal property and furnishings acquired in the house as follows: (specify), or Party #2 agrees to pay $X to Party #1 representing his one-half share of (specify property). If the parties are unable to divide the property in a fair and equitable manner, or if a dispute arises concerning any matter between the parties, this Agreement, or the subject matter herein, they agree to submit any such dispute to mediation or binding arbitration if mediation is unsuccessful in (specify city) under the then prevailing rules of the American Arbitration Association. The decision of the arbitrator shall be final and binding and both parties agree to share in all fees and expenses related to any such mediation or arbitration equally.

9. If either party dies while this Agreement is in effect (specify how the other party's share of the house and furniture will be divided, sold or paid for).

10. Any money required to purchase real property (such as an expensive boat, house, furniture, etc.) will be contributed equally by the parties and the deed or title to said property will be issued jointly, unless a separate arrangement is agreed upon and reflected in writing.

11. This Agreement supersedes and replaces all prior agreements and understandings, whether oral or in writing, and may only be modified in a separate writing signed by both parties. This Agreement is in force when signed below.

12. In the event that any one or more of the provisions contained in this Agreement shall for any reason be held to be illegal or unenforceable in any respect under the law of any state by a court of competent jurisdiction, such unenforceability shall not affect any other provision of this Agreement, and the remainder of the contract shall still be upheld.

Date: _____   Party #1 _____

Date: _____   Party #2 _____

State of (specify)
County of (specify)

On (specify date) before me came (name of Party #1 and name of Party #2), personally known to me to be the individuals described hereinabove and who executed the foregoing Living Together Agreement, and duly acknowledged to me that they executed the same.

_____
Notary Public

▷ *Note:* Although the two forms that follow appear similar, a Contract for Purchase of Personal Property typically is completed before any transfer takes place, and lists conditions of the conveyance of property and any penalties to take effect in the event that these conditions are not met; a Bill of Sale for Personal Property functions as a receipt, and primarily describes the nature, quantity, condition, and price of what has been transferred after the actual sale has taken place.

FORM 118. **Contract for Purchase of Personal Property**

This Contract for (specify item, such as a computer, boat, used car, etc.), is made by and between (Name of Buyer, "Buyer" located at:) and (Name of Seller, "Seller"), (specify address).

WHEREAS, the parties desire that Seller sell the following (specify item); and WHEREAS, Buyer agrees to purchase said item;

NOW, THEREFORE, THE PARTIES AGREE AS FOLLOWS:

1. This Agreement will commence on (specify date).

2. Buyer agrees to purchase (specify item(s), including Model or Serial Number, Vehicle Registration Number, and other particulars). For example, if a boat, state the make and serial number of engines, registration number of hull, standard equipment, and removable items being purchased, such as life vests, etc. If a car, state the year, make, and personal property being acquired as part of the sale (i.e., luggage rack, CB radio, etc.). If a computer, state the brand, serial number, and other equipment included in the sale, i.e., a spare printer. If purchasing jewelry, a coin collection, musical instrument, or sports equipment, describe the item(s) in detail.

3. The total price for the item is $X which does (or does not) include freight, shipping, delivery, and insurance costs. Payment shall be made as follows: (specify).

4. Seller warrants that he is the lawful owner of the items purchased and is selling the items free of all liens and encumbrances. The items sold are in good condition with the exception of (specify known defects).

5. Buyer purchases the goods as is and it is understood and agreed to by the parties that Seller does not warrant the Buyer's use of the items purchased and does not warrant to Buyer that the items are merchantable or fit for any particular purpose.

6. The goods shall be delivered to the Buyer by (specify date) and the price of delivery shall be paid by (specify). Buyer shall examine the item(s) promptly upon receipt and advise the Seller of any defects.

7. Specify:

— the full amount to be paid for the item

— what deposit, if any, is required as a down payment

— the stages of payment; for example, upon delivery, the final payment of $X is due

— describe the quality of goods sold if relative, e.g., that the item is new or in good condition in compliance with all applicable laws and codes, free of defects for a period of X years, and shall be covered by a manufacturer's warranty if practicable

(continued on page 424)

FORM 118. *(continued from page 423)*

    — If the car or boat has been examined by an independent mechanic at Buyer's expense and request, attach the report and make it a part of the sale so that if the item is delivered damaged or with a defect after the sale, the Buyer can receive reimbursement

    — If a car or boat is purchased, state what the odometer reading is or how many running hours the boat motor has, and state that the Seller is providing an accurate reading of the mileage or running time

    8. If applicable, state that time is of the essence and Seller agrees to deliver item by (specify date), or deduct $X from the final price if the item is not delivered in the contracted-for condition to Buyer by said date.

    9. Any case or controversy arising among or between the parties, this Agreement, or the subject matter hereto, shall be settled by binding arbitration in (specify location) under the then prevailing rules of the American Arbitration Association. The decision of the arbitrator shall be final and binding. Both parties agree to share the costs of such arbitration equally but the Arbitrator shall be instructed to award reasonable attorney fees to the prevailing party.

    10. Additional terms and conditions essential to this Agreement include: (specify).

    11. This Agreement supersedes all prior agreements and understandings and can only be modified in a writing signed by both parties.

Dated: _____

_____
Name of Buyer

Dated: _____

_____
Name of Seller

By: _____

FORM 119. Bill of Sale for Personal Property

(Name of Seller, "Seller," located at: _____) in consideration of the sum of $X received from (Name of Buyer, "Buyer," specify address), the receipt of which is acknowledged, hereby sells, transfers, and conveys the following personal property (specify or say attached on Schedule A).

1. The total price for the items is $X which does (or does not) include freight, shipping, delivery, and insurance costs. Payment shall be made as follows: (specify).

2. Seller warrants that he is the lawful owner of the items purchased and is selling the items free of all liens and encumbrances. The items sold are in good condition with the exception of (specify known defects).

3. Buyer has examined the property and purchases the goods as is. It is understood and agreed to by the parties that Seller does not warrant the Buyer's use of the items purchased and does not warrant to Buyer that the items are merchantable or fit for any particular purpose.

4. Additional terms and conditions essential to this Agreement include: (specify).

Dated: _____   _____
                                     Name of Buyer

Dated: _____   _____
                                     Name of Seller

                                     By: _____

FORM 122. Sample Seller–Real Estate Broker Agreement

AGREEMENT made on (specify date) by and between (name of individual residing at [specify]) ("Owner") and (name of real estate broker, [specify office address]) ("Broker").

WHEREAS, Owner is the titleholder in (specify, such as fee simple) of the property located at (specify); and

WHEREAS, Broker agrees to assist Owner in the sale of said property on a nonexclusive (or exclusive) basis;

NOW, THEREFORE, THE PARTIES AGREE AS FOLLOWS:

1. Owner agrees to sell the property to a third party procured by Broker provided it is sold at a minimum price of $X and under the following terms of sale: (specify).

2. Provided Broker obtains a bona fide purchaser for the property who concludes the transaction at the minimum terms specified in Paragraph 1 of this Agreement, Owner agrees to pay Broker a commission of X% of the purchase price, payable (specify, such as only when title actually closes and the funds are received).

3. Specify other terms here:

4. This Agreement supersedes and replaces all prior agreements and understandings, whether oral or in writing, and may only be modified in a separate writing signed by both parties.

IN WITNESS WHEREOF, the parties have signed this Agreement as of the date first above written.

Name of Broker

By:_____

Witness: _____

_____

Name of Owner

FORM 123. **Contract for Purchase of Residence or Other Real Estate**

THIS CONTRACT is made on (specify date) by and between (name of individual residing at [specify]) ("Seller") and (name of individual or business located at [specify address]) ("Buyer").

WHEREAS, Seller is the titleholder in (specify, such as fee simple) of the property located at (specify) and desires to sell said property to Buyer; and

WHEREAS, Buyer agrees to buy the property located at (specify);

NOW, THEREFORE, THE PARTIES AGREE AS FOLLOWS:

1. The Seller agrees to sell and the Buyer agrees to buy the property located at (specify), consisting of (specify, such as the land and all the buildings, other improvements, and fixtures on the land; all of the Seller's rights relating to the land; and all personal property specifically included in this Contract).

2. Purchase Price. The terms upon which this offer is made are as follows:

Purchase price:	$X
Deposit upon signing of this contract:	$X
Amount of mortgage:	$X
Balance to be paid at closing of title, or by certified, bank cashier's, or attorney trust check (subject to adjustment at closing). Third-party and endorsed checks are not acceptable.	$X
	Total: $X

3. Deposit Monies. All deposit monies will be held in a non-interest-bearing trust account by (specify Name or Name of Attorney) until closing of Title.

4. Time and Place of Closing. The Buyer and Seller agree to make (specify) the date for the closing. Said date is deemed to be "OF THE ESSENCE." The closing will be held at (specify).

5. Transfer of Ownership. At the closing, the Seller will transfer ownership of the property to the Buyer. The Seller will give the Buyer a properly executed bargain and sale deed with covenants against grantors acts and an Affidavit of Title.

6. Personal Property and Fixtures. All fixtures are INCLUDED in this sale unless they are listed below as being EXCLUDED.

(A) The following items are EXCLUDED from this sale: (specify)

7. Physical Condition of the Property. This property is being sold "as is." The Seller does not make any claims or promises about the condition or value of any of the property included in this sale. The Buyer makes this offer in full reliance upon his own independent investigation and judgment and there are no verbal agreements which modify or affect this offer. The acceptance of a deed by the Buyer shall be deemed to be the full performance of every obligation on the part of the Seller.

8. Inspection of the Property (include if applicable).

9. Termite Inspection (include if applicable).

10. Engineering Inspection (include if applicable).

11. Radon Inspection (include if applicable).

(continued on page 428)

FORM 123. *(continued from page 427)*

12. Repair Limitation. In no event will the Seller expend more than $X for repairs.

13. Condition and Use of Property. Seller makes no representation as to the condition of the property or that the premises comply with local, county, state, or federal ordinances and statues. Buyer must obtain certificates of occupancy and all other municipal certificates. Seller will not provide the buyer with a Certificate of Occupancy, Lead Paint Inspection, if applicable, or any other municipal certificate from the municipality in connection with the transfer. Buyer is advised to contact the municipality for any matters which are of concern to him prior to signing this contract. By signing this contract, Buyer has made the necessary investigation concerning the obtainment of the Certificate of Occupancy or any other municipal certificate required by the municipality in a transfer of property within this municipality.

14. Risk of Loss. The Seller is responsible for any additional damage to the property, except for normal wear and tear, until the closing of title. If there is substantial damage, the Seller reserves the right to cancel the contract and refund Buyer's deposit monies or to negotiate the terms of the repairs with the Buyer.

15. Flood Area. Buyer has X days from the receipt of this contract to determine if this property lies within a flood zone.

16. Property Lines. The Seller does not have a survey for this premises and makes no representation that all buildings, driveways, and other improvements on the property are within its boundary lines or that no improvements on adjoining properties extend across the boundary lines of this property.

17. Ownership. The Seller agrees to transfer and the Buyer agrees to accept ownership of the property free of all claims and right of others, except for: (specify, such as: the rights of utility companies to maintain pipes, poles, cables, and wires over, on, and under the street, the part of the property next to the street, or running to any house or other improvements on the property; and recorded agreements that limit the use of the property).

18. Title Insurance. Buyer and Seller agree that Seller shall order a title binder for the subject property from a title company authorized to do business in the State of (specify) in order to ensure a timely closing of subject property. It shall be the Buyer's responsibility to pay for all costs associated with these title charges except as indicated below. Seller's attorney shall provide Buyer's attorney with appropriate information regarding where title has been ordered. In the event that the subject transaction does not close, through no fault of the Buyer, Seller shall be responsible for all title charges.

19. Correcting Defects. If the property does not comply with Paragraphs 17 & 18 of this contract, the Buyer must notify the Seller and the Seller will be given an additional X days to correct. If the property still does not comply after that date, the Buyer or Seller may cancel this contract or the Seller will have more time to comply. In the event that the Seller's title is uninsurable, then the Seller's only obligation will be to refund Buyer's deposit.

20. Assessments for Municipal Improvements. All unpaid assessments against the property for work completed before the closing will be paid by the Seller. If the improvement is not completed before the closing, then the Buyer will be solely responsible.

21. Adjustments at Closing. The Buyer and Seller agree to adjust the following

expenses as of the date of closing: municipal water and sewer charges, real estate taxes, condominium dues, if applicable, and rents. If the property is fueled by fuel oil, the Buyer will be responsible to pay the Seller for any fuel that remains in the burner on the day of closing. The Buyer and Seller may require that any person with a claim or right affecting the property be paid off prior to closing.

22. Possession. Buyer shall receive possession at the closing of title.

23. Damages. If this offer is accepted by the Seller, and the Seller's title is insurable and Buyer neglects or refuses to complete the purchase of this property, and to execute and deliver all documents required, then the Buyer will be held liable for any and all actual damages caused to the Seller by such breach.

24. Completed Agreement. This contract is the entire and only agreement between the Buyer and the Seller. This contract replaces and cancels any previous agreements between the Buyer and Seller. This contract can only be changed by an agreement in writing signed by both Buyer and Seller.

25. Parties Liable. This contract is binding upon all parties who sign it and all who succeed to their rights and responsibilities.

26. Notices. All notices under this contract must be in writing. The notices must be delivered personally or by certified mail, return receipt requested, or by facsimile, to the other party at the address written in this contract. Service of any notices to the attorney for the buyer shall be deemed as service upon the buyer.

27. Broker's Commission. The Seller agrees to pay a commission fee, as per the listing agreement. This commission is not earned or to be paid until the title has been transferred and the purchase price has been paid. This commission will be paid at the closing, and taken out of the Seller's proceeds. Buyer represents that he has not used the services of any other broker than those set forth below.

List names of broker(s):

28. Assignability. This agreement shall not be assignable by the Buyer without the Seller's written consent.

29. Offer to Purchase. The within contract constitutes the Buyer's offer to purchase the subject property. Acceptance of the Buyer's offer is subject to Seller's review of the aforesaid document and shall be evidenced by Seller's execution of same.

30. Legal Representation. Buyer acknowledges that Buyer has the right to hire a lawyer to represent Buyer's interests in this transaction.

SIGNED AND AGREED TO BY: _____

WITNESSED OR ATTESTED BY: _____

DATE SIGNED BY BUYER(S) _____
BUYER

_____   _____
AS TO BUYER(S)   BUYER

_____
DATE SIGNED BY SELLER

FORM 124. **Option or Extension of Option to Purchase Real Estate**

AGREEMENT made on (specify date) by and between (name of individual residing at (specify) ("Owner/Optionor") and (name of individual or business located at (specify address) ("Optionee").

WHEREAS, Owner/Optionor is the titleholder in (specify, such as fee simple) of the property located at (specify) and desires to offer (or extend) Optionee the option of purchasing said property; and

WHEREAS, Optionee desires to purchase from Owner/Optionor the option of purchasing said property;

NOW, THEREFORE, THE PARTIES AGREE AS FOLLOWS:

1. Owner/Optionor agrees to offer Optionee the option of purchasing the property for $X and under the following terms of sale: (specify).

2. This Option shall expire automatically on (specify date) unless (state the conditions, if any, under which the option will be renewed). If Optionee fails to exercise this Option in strict accord with the terms and conditions herein or within the time provided herein, the consideration paid to Owner/Optionor shall be retained by him and neither party shall have any further rights or claims against the other by reason of this Option.

3. For the option to be effective, Optionee agrees to notify Owner/Optionor in writing, sent certified mail, return receipt requested, to (specify address).

4. Neither party has dealt with any Broker concerning this Option and neither party shall be liable for any Broker's fees due pursuant to this Agreement (or, if a Broker's fee is due, state who will pay for same).

5. This Agreement supersedes and replaces all prior agreements and understandings, whether oral or in writing, and may only be modified in a separate writing signed by both parties.

IN WITNESS WHEREOF, the parties have signed this Agreement as of the date first above written.

Witness: _____

_____
Name of Owner/Optionor

_____
Name of Optionee

FORM 125. Residential Lease Agreement

THIS RESIDENTIAL LEASE AGREEMENT is made on (specify date) by and between (name of individual or business residing at (specify) ("Landlord") and (name of individual or business located at (specify address) ("Tenant").

WHEREAS, Landlord agrees to lease the premises located at (specify); and WHEREAS, Tenant agrees to lease the premises located at (specify);

NOW, THEREFORE, THE PARTIES AGREE AS FOLLOWS:

1. The Landlord agrees to lease and the Tenant agrees to rent the property located at (specify), consisting of (specify, such as the apartment, fixtures, and personal property specifically included in this Contract).

2. Term. The term of this Lease is for X years, starting on (specify) and ending on (specify). The Landlord is not responsible if the Landlord cannot give the Tenant possession of the Apartment at the start of this Lease. However, rent will only be charged from the date on which possession of the Apartment is made available to the Tenant. If the Landlord cannot give possession within 30 days after the starting date, the Tenant may cancel this Lease.

3. Rent. The Tenant agrees to pay $X as rent, to be paid as follows: $X per month, due on the (specify, such as the 1st) day of each month. The first payment of rent and any security deposit is due upon the signing of this Lease by the Tenant. The Tenant must pay a late charge of $X for each payment that is more than 10 days late. This late charge is due with the monthly rent payment.

4. Security Deposit. The Tenant has deposited $X with the Landlord as security that the Tenant will comply with all the terms of this Lease. If the Tenant complies with the terms of this Lease, the Landlord will return this deposit within X days after the end of the Lease, including any extension. The Landlord may use as much of the deposit as necessary to pay for damages resulting from the Tenant's occupancy. If this occurs prior to the Lease termination, the Landlord may demand that the Tenant replace the amount of the security deposit used by the Landlord. If the Landlord sells the property, the Landlord may transfer the deposit to the new owners for the Tenant's benefit. The Landlord will notify the Tenant of any sale and transfer of the deposit. The Landlord will then be released of all liability to return the security deposit. The Landlord will fully comply with any applicable Rent Security Laws. This includes depositing the security deposit in an interest-bearing account and notifying the Tenant, in writing, of the name and address of the banking institution and the account number. Interest due the Tenant will be credited as rent on each renewal date of this Lease.

5. Landlord's Agent. The Landlord authorizes the following person(s) to manage the property on behalf of the Landlord (name[s] and address[es]): (specify)

6. Use of Property. The Tenant may use the Apartment only as a private residence for the following persons: X AND NO MORE THAN TWO OTHER PERSONS referred to as "household members."

(continued on page 432)

FORM 125. *(continued from page 431)*

7. Utilities. The Landlord will pay for the following utilities (check where applicable):
( ) cold water   ( ) hot water   ( ) electricity
( ) heat   ( ) air conditioning ( ) gas
The Tenant will pay for the following utilities:
( ) cold water   ( ) hot water   ( ) electricity
( ) heat   ( ) air conditioning ( ) gas

8. Eviction. If the Tenant does not pay the rent within X days after it is due, the Tenant may be evicted. The Landlord may also evict the Tenant if the Tenant does not comply with all of the terms of this Lease and for all other causes allowed by law. If evicted, the Tenant must continue to pay the rent for the rest of the term. The Tenant must also pay all costs, including reasonable attorney fees, related to the eviction and the collection of any monies owed the Landlord, along with the cost of re-entering, re-renting, cleaning, and repairing the Apartment. Rent received from any new tenant will reduce the amount owed the Landlord.

9. Payments by Landlord. If the Tenant fails to comply with the terms of this Lease, the Landlord may take any required action and charge the cost, including reasonable attorney fees, to the Tenant as additional rent. Failure to pay such additional rent upon demand is a violation of this Lease.

10. Care of the Apartment. The Tenant has examined the Apartment, including the living quarters, all facilities, furniture and appliances, and is satisfied with its present physical condition. The Tenant agrees to maintain the property in as good condition as it is at the start of this Lease except for ordinary wear and tear. The Tenant must pay for all repairs, replacements, and damages caused by the act or neglect of the Tenant, the Tenant's household members or their visitors. The Tenant will remove all of the Tenant's property at the end of this Lease. Any property that is left becomes the property of the Landlord and may be thrown out.

11. Repairs by Landlord. If the Apartment is damaged or in need of repair, the Tenant must promptly notify the Landlord. The Landlord will have a reasonable amount of time to make repairs. If the Tenant must leave the Apartment because of damage not resulting from the Tenant's act or neglect, the Tenant will not have to pay rent until the Apartment is repaired. If the Apartment is totally destroyed, this Lease will end and the Tenant will pay rent up to the date of destruction.

12. Interruption of Services. The Landlord is not responsible for any inconvenience or interruption of services due to repairs, improvements, or for any reason beyond the Landlord's control.

13. Alterations. The Tenant must get the Landlord's prior written consent to alter, improve, paint, or wallpaper the Apartment. Alterations, additions, and improvements become the Landlord's property.

14. Compliance with Laws. The Tenant must comply with laws, orders, rules, and requirements of governmental authorities and insurance companies which have issued or are about to issue policies covering this Apartment and/or its contents.

15. No Waiver by Landlord. The Landlord does not give up any rights by accepting rent or by failing to enforce any terms of this Lease.

16. No Assignment or Sublease. The Tenant may not sublease the Apartment or assign this Lease without the Landlord's prior written consent.

17. Entry by Landlord. Upon reasonable notice, the Landlord may enter the Apartment to provide services, inspect, repair, improve, or show it. The Tenant must notify the Landlord if the Tenant will be away for 10 days or more. In case of emergency or the Tenant's absence, the Landlord may enter the Apartment without the Tenant's consent.

18. Quiet Enjoyment. The Tenant may live in and use the Apartment without interference subject to the terms of this Lease.

19. Subordination. This Lease and the Tenant's rights are subject and subordinate to present and future mortgages on the premises which include the Apartment. The Landlord may execute any papers on the Tenant's behalf as the Tenant's attorney in fact to accomplish this.

20. Hazardous Use. The Tenant will not keep anything in the Apartment which is dangerous, flammable, explosive, or might increase the danger of fire or any other hazard.

21. Injury or Damage. The Tenant will be responsible for any injury or damage caused by the act or neglect of the Tenant, the Tenant's household members, or their visitors. The Landlord is not responsible for any injury or damage unless due to the negligence or improper conduct of the Landlord.

22. Renewals and Changes in Lease. The Landlord may offer the Tenant a new lease to take effect at the end of this Lease. The new lease may include reasonable changes. The Tenant will be notified of any proposed new lease at least X days before the end of the present Lease. If no changes are made, the Tenant may continue to rent the Apartment on a month to month basis (with the rest of the Lease remaining the same). In either case the Tenant must notify the Landlord of the Tenant's decision to stay or to leave at least X days before the end of the term. Otherwise, the Tenant will be responsible under the terms of the new lease.

23. Pets. No dogs, cats, or other animals are allowed in this Apartment without the Landlord's prior written consent.

24. Notices. All notices provided by this Lease must be written and delivered personally or by certified mail, return receipt requested. Notices to the Landlord may be sent to the Landlord's Agent.

25. Signs. The Tenant may not put any sign or projection (such as a TV or radio antenna) in or out of the windows or exteriors of the Apartment without the Landlord's prior written consent.

26. Tenant's Social Security number is 000-00-0000.

27. Tenant acknowledges that the apartment being rented herein does not come with parking space.

28. Landlord agrees that if Tenant performs all of its obligations pursuant to the terms of this Lease, it shall have the right to extend the term of this Lease for an additional year at a rent not to exceed X. If tenant wishes to exercise this option, it must do so by advising Landlord by Certified Mail Return Receipt Requested not less that X days prior to the presently scheduled expiration of the Lease. Notice will be deemed to occur upon Landlord's receipt of the letter.

29. Landlord agrees to perform the following repairs not later than (specify date) (specify repairs, such as):

1. Sand and polyurethane the hardwood floors.
2. Repair or replace the bathroom cabinet.
3. Repair the kitchen cabinets.

(continued on page 434)

FORM 125. *(continued from page 433)*

4. Install a refrigerator.
5. Repair plaster and/or sheetrock in living room and bathroom ceilings.
6. Install a microwave oven.

30. Validity of Lease. If a clause or provision of this Lease is legally invalid, the rest of this Lease remains in effect.

31. Parties. The Landlord and each of the Tenants is bound by this Lease. All parties who lawfully succeed to their rights and responsibilities are also bound.

32. Entire Lease. All promises the Landlord has made are contained in this written Lease. This Lease can only be changed by an agreement in writing by both the Tenant and the Landlord.

33. Signatures. The Landlord and Tenant agree to the terms of this Lease. If this Lease is made by a corporation, its proper corporate officers sign and its corporate seal is affixed.

Witnessed or Attested by:

_____
Landlord

_____   _____
                                  Tenant

                                  _____
                                  Tenant

FORM 126. **Sublease Agreement**

THIS SUBLEASE AGREEMENT is made on (specify date) by and between (name of tenant) ("Tenant") residing at (specify address) and name of subtenant ("Subtenant") residing at (specify address).

For valuable consideration, the parties agree to the following terms and conditions.

1. The Tenant subleases the premises located at (specify address) to Subtenant under the following terms and conditions: (specify length of sublease, amount of monthly payments, when due, etc.)

2. In all other respects the Lease entered into (date) between Landlord and Tenant, a complete copy which is attached hereto and made a part of this Sublease, will remain in full force and effect and the Tenant warrants that the consent of the Landlord enabling Tenant to make this Sublease has been obtained. In the event Tenant does not have said authority, he/she agrees to indemnify and hold Subtenant harmless from any claims which may result from the Tenant's failure to perform under this Lease prior to the date of this Sublease.

3. Subtenant agrees to perform all of the obligations of the Tenant under the original Lease and receive all of the benefits of the Tenant under said Lease. Notwithstanding the foregoing, Tenant shall remain primarily liable to the Landlord for the obligations under the Lease.

4. The parties agree to the following additional terms: (specify)

5. Subtenant may not assign or further sublet the premises without the express written consent of Tenant and the Landlord.

6. This Sublease supersedes and replaces all prior agreements and understandings, whether oral or in writing, and may only be modified in a separate writing signed by both parties.

IN WITNESS WHEREOF, the parties have set their hand and seal this (specify date).

_____
Name of Tenant

_____
Name of Subtenant

Consented to: _____
Name of Landlord

FORM 128. **Power of Attorney Form**

I, (name of individual), residing at (specify address) hereby grant this Power of Attorney to (name of individual) located at (specify address) ("attorney-in-fact").

My attorney-in-fact shall have full powers and authority to do and undertake the following on my behalf (specify, such as):

▷ making health care and medical treatment decisions, including decisions to withhold or withdraw life-support

▷ sell, deed, buy, rent, or dispose of my current or future real or personal property

▷ borrow, lend, invest, or reinvest my funds

▷ initiate, defend, commence, or settle legal actions on my behalf

▷ deposit or withdraw my bank account funds

▷ hire accountants, physicians, attorneys, or advisors to protect my interests

Any powers not specifically mentioned herein shall not be given. My attorney-in-fact hereby accepts this appointment and agrees to perform said fiduciary duties (specify with or without pay) in a competent fashion, with my best interests always in mind.

State if and how the power-of-attorney can be revoked (for example, "This power of attorney can be revoked at any time for any reason upon written notice").

This formal power of attorney supersedes and replaces all prior agreements and understandings, whether oral or in writing, and may only be modified in a separate writing signed by both parties.

IN WITNESS WHEREOF, I sign this Power of Attorney on the date below written.

_____
Name of Person Granting Power of Attorney

Witness: _____

Dated: _____

State of (specify)
County of (specify)

On (date) before me personally appeared (name of person), to me known to be the individual described in and who executed the foregoing Power of Attorney, and duly acknowledged to me that he/she executed the same.

_____
Notary Public

FORM 129. **Revocation of Power of Attorney**

I, (name of individual), residing at (specify address), hereby revoke the Power of Attorney (dated) previously given to (name of individual) located at (specify address).

All rights, power, and authority previously granted to (name of individual) pursuant to said instrument are hereby revoked, effective immediately.

IN WITNESS WHEREOF, I sign this Revocation of Power of Attorney on the date below written.

_____
Name of Person Revoking Power of Attorney

Witness: _____

Dated: _____

State of (specify)
County of (specify)

On (date) before me personally appeared (name of person), to me known to be the individual described in and who executed the foregoing Revocation of Power of Attorney, and duly acknowledged to me that he/she executed the same.

_____
Notary Public

FORM 131. Sample Irrevocable Trust Agreement

AGREEMENT made this _____ day of _____, _____, by and between (Name), residing at (specify), (hereinafter called the "Grantor") and (Name), residing at (specify), (hereinafter referred to as "Trustee") for the benefit of Grantor's grandchild (Name).

WITNESSETH:

WHEREAS, the Grantor desires to provide a trust fund to be used primarily for the education and benefit of (Name).

NOW, THEREFORE, and in consideration of the covenants contained herein, Trustee agrees to hold the assets received by the Trustee hereunder IN TRUST for the following uses and purposes and subject to the terms and conditions hereinafter set forth.

FIRST: Grantor hereby transfers and delivers to the Trustee the sum of $X, receipt of which is hereby acknowledged by the Trustee upon the express terms and conditions and with the powers and limitations set forth. Additional cash or property may from time to time be transferred by Grantor, or by any person or persons to the Trustee with his consent and such property shall thereupon become a part of the trust estate and shall be held, managed, invested, and reinvested and disposed of on the same terms and conditions as the property originally transferred.

SECOND: The Trustee shall hold, manage, invest, and reinvest the trust estate and shall collect and receive any interest income and profits for the benefit of (Name), the grandchild of both Grantor and Trustee, upon the following terms:

A. So long as (Name) is under the age of twenty-one (21) years, the Trustee shall pay or apply so much of the income of this trust fund as the Trustee in his sole discretion deems necessary for the education and support of such beneficiary and shall accumulate the balance of such income and pay same over to (Name) when she shall attain the age of twenty-one (21) years.

B. When (Name) attains the age of twenty-one (21) years, the Trustee shall pay over to (Name) the net income from this trust fund not less often than quarter-annually for so long as this trust fund shall continue and shall, thereafter, distribute to, or expend for the education and benefit of (Name) so much of the principal of this trust fund in such amounts and manner as the Trustee, in his sole discretion, may determine.

C. When (Name) attains the age of thirty-five (35) years, the Trustee shall pay over to (Name) one-third of the principal balance of this trust fund. When (Name) attains the age of forty (40) years, the Trustee shall pay over to (Name) one-half of the principal balance of this trust fund, and when (Name) attains the age of forty-five (45) years, the Trustee shall pay over to (Name) the entire principal balance plus all accumulated income.

D. Upon the death of (Name) prior to the distribution of the entire balance of this trust fund, the Trustee shall pay over the then principal of the trust fund, together with any undistributed or accrued net income therefrom, to all sisters and brothers of (Name) then living, in equal shares, and, in default thereof, to (specify) presently located at (specify).

THIRD: The following provisions, in addition to all others, shall apply to the Trustee to the extent permitted by law:

A. The Trustee shall not be responsible for the use made by any person of any payment of income or principal which may be made to that person hereunder, and he shall not be obliged to see to the proper use or application thereof by such person.

B. In the exercise of any discretionary powers over the payment or application of income or principal under this Agreement, the judgment of the Trustee as to the amount of any payment or disbursement and as to the advisability thereof shall be final and conclusive upon all persons beneficially interested in any trust hereunder.

C. In determining the amounts of income and principal, if any, which shall be paid or disbursed pursuant to any discretionary powers given hereby, the Trustee shall not be required to take into consideration any other sources of income available to, or assets owned by or held for the benefit of, the person for whose benefit such power might be exercised, but neither shall he be barred from making any inquiries in connection therewith.

D. No person dealing with the Trustee shall be bound to see to the application or disposition of cash or other property transferred to the Trustee or to inquire into the authority for or propriety of any action by the Trustee.

E. Neither Trustee nor any Successor Trustee, whether herein named or otherwise designated or appointed, shall be required to give any bond or security in any Court or jurisdiction.

FOURTH: The Trustee may, at any time, resign as Trustee. In the event of such resignation, or in the event the Trustee dies or shall otherwise cease to act in such capacity, Grantor hereby appoints the following three persons as Successor Trustees: (Name), (Name), and (Name) or the survivors of them. The Successor Trustees shall have all of the rights, powers, privileges, and immunities granted to the Trustee hereunder.

FIFTH: The Grantor confers upon the Trustee and the alternate Trustees with respect to the management and administration of any property, real and personal, at any time forming a part of the Trust estate or any trust created hereunder, the following discretionary powers without limitation, by reason of specification and in addition to powers conferred by Section (specify) of the Estate's Powers and Trusts Law and of the State of (specify) and any successor to said Section, and by other laws:

1. To retain such property for any period and to invest and reinvest in any securities or mutual funds or in accounts or certificates of deposit in banks or savings and loan associations which are insured by the United States Government.

2. To sell, transfer, exchange, convert or otherwise dispose of, or grant options with respect to any property forming a part of the trust created hereunder, at public or private sale, with or without security in such manner, at such time or times, for such purposes, for such prices and upon such terms, credits and conditions as the Trustee may deem advisable.

3. To join in or become a party to, or to oppose any reorganization, readjustment, recapitalization, foreclosure, merger, voting trust, dissolution, consolidation or exchange, and to deposit any securities with any committee, depository or trustee, and to pay any and all fees, expenses, and assessments incurred in connection therewith.

4. To vote in person at meetings of stock or security holders or any adjournment of such meeting or to vote by general or limited proxy with respect to any such shares of stock or other securities held by the Trustees.

5. To hold securities in the name of a nominee without indicating the trust character of such holding, or unregistered or in such form as will pass by delivery.

6. To pay, compromise, compound, adjust, submit to arbitration, sell, or release any claims or demands of the trust estate or of any trust created hereunder against others or of others against the same as the Trustee may deem advisable, including the acceptance

(continued on page 440)

FORM 131. *(continued from page 439)*

of deeds of real property in satisfaction of bonds and mortgages, and to make any payments in connection therewith which the Trustee may deem advisable.

7. To possess, manage, insure against loss by fire or other casualties, develop, subdivide, control, partition, mortgage, lease or otherwise deal with any and all real property; to satisfy and discharge or extend the term of any mortgage thereon; to execute the necessary instruments and covenants to effectuate the foregoing powers, including the giving or granting of options in connection therewith; to make improvements, structural and otherwise, or abandon the same if deemed to be worthless or not of sufficient value to warrant keeping or protecting, to abstain from the payment of taxes, water, rents, assessments, repairs, maintenance, and upkeep of the same; to permit to be lost by tax sale or other proceeding or to convey the same for a nominal consideration or without consideration; to set up appropriate reserves out of income for repairs, modernization, and upkeep of buildings, including reserves for depreciation and obsolescence, and to add such reserves to principal, and if the income from the property itself should not suffice for such purpose, to advance out of other income any sums needed therefor, and to advance any income of the trust for the amortization of any mortgage on property held in trust.

8. To execute and deliver any and all instruments in writing which he may deem advisable to carry out any of the foregoing powers. No party to any such instrument in writing signed by the Trustee shall be obliged to inquire into its validity.

9. To make distribution of the trust estate or of the principal of any trust created hereunder in kind and to cause any share to be composed of cash, property, or undivided fractional shares in property different in kind from any other share.

10. To delegate discretionary powers to agents, remunerate them, and pay their expenses; employ and pay the compensation of accountants, custodians, legal and investment counsel at the expense of the trust estate or any trust created hereunder.

11. To hold separate parts or shares of any trust wholly or partially for the convenience of investment and administration.

SIXTH: As used in this Agreement, any gender shall be construed as including all other genders and the singular shall be construed as including the plural and the plural the singular, as the sense requires.

SEVENTH: The Trustee may settle his account of this trust fund by agreement or judicially. An agreement made with those beneficiaries who are subject to no legal disability and who at the time would be entitled to the principal if the same were then distributable, shall bind all persons whether or not then in being or of legal capacity, then or thereafter entitled to any principal or income of the trust accounted for, and shall release and discharge the Trustees for their acts and proceedings embraced in the account as effectively as a judicial settlement.

EIGHTH: The Trustee is authorized and empowered but not required, at any time and from time to time during the Grantor's lifetime or after her death, to accept by way of addition to the trust estate, any property which the Grantor or any other person may wish to transfer and deliver to the Trustee or which he or any other person may devise and bequeath by his Last Will and Testament to the Trustee and any property so added may be commingled with other property in such trust and shall be held, administered, and disposed of as part of such trust.

NINTH: The Grantor hereby declares this Agreement to be irrevocable and reserves no right to alter or amend the same in any respect or particular.

TENTH: The Grantor declares that this Agreement and each trust created hereunder shall be construed under and regulated by the laws of the State of (specify), and that the validity and effect of this Agreement shall be determined in accordance with the laws of that State.

IN WITNESS WHEREOF, the parties hereto have executed this Agreement as of the day and year first above written.

_____
Name of Grantor

_____
Name of Trustee

STATE OF)
COUNTY OF)

On this (specify date), before me personally came (Name), to me known to be the individual described in and who executed the foregoing instrument, and acknowledged that he executed the same.

_____
Notary Public

STATE OF)
COUNTY OF)

On this (specify date), before me personally came (Name), to me known to be the individual described in and who executed the foregoing instrument, and acknowledged that she executed the same.

_____
Notary Public

FORM 134. **Sample Gift Made Prior to Will Bequest**

I, (name of individual), residing at (specify address), hereby give, transfer and convey the following gift(s) (specify) valued at $X to (name of individual) located at (specify address).

I am making this gift in advance of any provision I may make in my will and/or trust to said individual and instruct my Executor to deduct its value from any future testamentary bequest I may make to said individual.

IN WITNESS WHEREOF, I sign this document on the date below written.

_____
Name of Person Giving Gift

Witness: _____

Dated: _____

State of (specify)
County of (specify)

On (date) before me personally appeared (name of person), to me known to be the individual described in and who executed the foregoing document, and duly acknowledged to me that he/she executed the same.

_____
Notary Public

GLOSSARY OF TERMS

ABUSE OF PROCESS A cause of action that arises when one party misuses the legal process to injure another.

ACCORD AND SATISFACTION An agreement between two parties, such as the employee and his or her company, to compromise disputes concerning outstanding debts, compensation, or terms of employment. Satisfaction occurs when the terms of the compromise are fully performed.

ACTION IN ACCOUNTING A cause of action in which one party seeks a determination of the amount of money owed by another.

ADMISSIBLE Capable of being introduced in court as evidence.

ADVANCE Sometimes referred to as "draw," it is a sum of money that is applied against money to be earned.

AFFIDAVIT A written statement signed under oath.

ALLEGATIONS Written statements of a party to a lawsuit that charge the other party with wrongdoing. In order to be successful, allegations must be proven.

ANSWER The defendant's reply to the plaintiff's allegations in a complaint.

ANTICIPATORY BREACH A breach of contract that occurs when one party, i.e., the employee, states in advance of performance that he or she will definitely not perform under the terms of his or her contract.

APPEAL A proceeding whereby the losing party to a lawsuit requests that a higher court determine the correctness of the decision.

ARBITRATION A proceeding whereby both sides to a lawsuit agree to submit their dispute to arbitrators, rather than judges. The arbitration proceeding is expeditious and is legally binding on all parties.

ARRAIGNMENT A proceeding whereby an accused person is brought before a judge to plead to charges filed against him or her.

ASSIGNMENT The transfer of a right or interest by one party to another.

ATTORNEY IN FACT A person appointed by another to transact business on his or her behalf; the person does not have to be a lawyer.

AT-WILL EMPLOYMENT See Employment at will.

AWARD A decision made by a judicial body to compensate the winning party in a lawsuit.

BILL OF PARTICULARS A document used in a lawsuit that specifically details the loss alleged by the plaintiff.

BREACH OF CONTRACT A legal cause of action for the unjustified failure to perform a duty or obligation specified in an agreement.

BRIEF A concise statement of the main contents of a lawsuit.

BURDEN OF PROOF The responsibility of a party to a lawsuit to provide sufficient evidence to prove or disprove a claim.

BUSINESS DEDUCTION A legitimate expense that can be used to decrease the amount of income subject to tax.

BUSINESS SLANDER A legal wrong committed when a party orally makes false statements that impugn the business reputation of another (e.g., imply that the person is dishonest, incompetent, or financially unreliable).

CALENDAR A list of cases to be heard each day in court.

CAUSE OF ACTION The legal theory on which a plaintiff seeks to recover damages.

CAVEAT EMPTOR A Latin expression frequently applied to consumer transactions; translated as "Let the buyer beware."

CEASE-AND-DESIST LETTER A letter, usually sent by a lawyer, that notifies an individual to stop engaging in a particular type of activity, behavior, or conduct that infringes on the rights of another.

CERTIFICATE OF INCORPORATION A document that creates a corporation.

CHECK A negotiable instrument; the depositor's written order requesting his or her bank to pay a definite sum of money to a named individual, entity, or to the bearer.

CIVIL COURT Generally, any court that presides over noncriminal matters.

CLAIMS COURT A particular court that hears tax disputes.

CLERK OF THE COURT A person who determines whether court papers are properly filed and court procedures followed.

CLOSELY HELD BUSINESS A business typically owned by a small number of owners.

COLLATERAL ESTOPPEL *See* **ESTOPPEL**. Collateral estoppel happens when a prior but different legal action is conclusive in a way to bring about estoppel in a current legal action.

COMMON LAW Law that evolves from reported case decisions that are relied on for their precedential value.

COMPENSATORY DAMAGES A sum of money, awarded to a party, that represents the actual harm suffered or loss incurred.

COMPLAINT A legal document that commences a lawsuit; it alleges facts and causes of action that a plaintiff relies on to collect damages.

CONFLICT OF INTEREST The ethical inability of a lawyer to represent a client because of competing loyalties, e.g., representing both employer and employee in a labor dispute.

CONSIDERATION An essential element of an enforceable contract; something of value given or promised by one party in exchange for an act or promise of another.

CONTEMPT A legal sanction imposed when a rule or order of a judicial body is disobeyed.

CONTINGENCY FEE A type of fee arrangement whereby a lawyer is paid a percentage of the money recovered. If unsuccessful, the client is responsible only for costs already paid by the lawyer.

CONTINUANCE The postponement of a legal proceeding to another date.

CONTRACT An enforceable agreement, either written, oral, or implied by the actions or intentions of the parties.

CONTRACT MODIFICATION The alteration of contract terms.

COUNTERCLAIM A claim asserted by a defendant in a lawsuit.

COVENANT A promise.

CREDIBILITY The believability of a witness as perceived by a judge or jury.

CREDITOR The party to whom money is owed.

CROSS-EXAMINATION The questioning of a witness by the opposing lawyer.

DAMAGE An award, usually money, given to the winning party in a lawsuit as compensation for the wrongful acts of another.

DEBTOR The party who owes money.

DECISION The determination of a case of matter by a judicial body.

DEDUCTIBLE The unrecoverable portion of insurance proceeds.

DEFAMATION An oral or written statement communicated to a third party that impugns a person's reputation in the community.

DEFAULT JUDGMENT An award rendered after one party fails to appear in a lawsuit.

DEFENDANT The person or entity who is sued in a lawsuit.

DEFENSE The defendant's justification for relieving himself or herself of fault.

DEFINITE TERM OF EMPLOYMENT Employment of a fixed period of time.

DEPOSITION A pretrial proceeding in which one party is questioned, usually under oath, by the opposing party's lawyer.

DISCLAIMER A clause in a sales, service, or other contract that attempts to limit or exonerate one party from liability in the event of a lawsuit.

DISCOVERY A general term used to describe several pretrial devices (e.g., depositions and interrogatories) that enable lawyers to elicit information from the opposing side.

DUAL CAPACITY A legal theory, used to circumvent workers' compensation laws, that allows an injured employee to sue his or her employer directly in court.

DUE PROCESS Constitutional protections that guarantee that a person's life, liberty, or property cannot be taken away without the opportunity to be heard in a judicial proceeding.

DURESS Unlawful threats, pressure, or force that induces a person to act contrary to his or her intentions; if proved, it allows a party to disavow a contract.

EMPLOYEE A person who works and is subject to an employer's scope, direction, and control.

EMPLOYMENT AT WILL Employment by which an employee has no job security.

EMPLOYMENT DISCRIMINATION Conduct directed at employees and job applicants that is prohibited by law.

EQUITY Fairness; usually applied when a judicial body awards a suitable remedy other than money to a party (e.g., an injunction).

ESCROW ACCOUNT A separate fund where lawyers or others are obligated to deposit money received from or on behalf of a client.

ESTOPPEL Estoppel is a legal bar to prevent a party from asserting a fact or claim inconsistent with that party's prior position that has been relied on or acted on by another party.

EVIDENCE Information in the form of oral testimony, exhibits, affidavits, etc., used to prove a party's claim.

EXAMINATION BEFORE TRIAL A pretrial legal device; also called a "deposition."

EXHIBIT Tangible evidence used to prove a party's claim.

EXIT AGREEMENTS Agreements sometimes signed between employers and employees on resignation or termination of an employee's services.

EXPRESS CONTRACT An agreement whose terms are manifested by clear and definite language, as distinguished from agreements inferred from conduct.

FALSE IMPRISONMENT The unlawful detention of a person who is held against his or her will without authority or justification.

FILING FEE Money paid to start a lawsuit.

FINAL DECREE A court order or directive of a permanent nature.

FINANCIAL STATEMENT A document, usually prepared by an accountant, that reflects a business's (or individual's) assets, liabilities, and financial condition.

FLAT FEE A sum of money paid to a lawyer as compensation for services.

FLAT FEE PLUS TIME A form of payment in which a lawyer receives one sum for services and also receives additional money calculated on an hourly basis.

FRAUD A false statement that is relied on and causes damages to the defrauded party.

GENERAL DENIAL A reply contained in the defendant's answer.

GROUND The basis for an action or an argument.

GUARANTY A contract in which one party agrees to answer for or satisfy the debt of another.

HEARSAY EVIDENCE Unsubstantiated evidence that is often excluded by a court.

HOURLY FEE Money paid to a lawyer for services, computed on an hourly basis.

IMPLIED CONTRACT An agreement that is tacit rather than expressed in clear and definite language; an agreement inferred from the conduct of the parties.

INDEMNIFICATION Protection or reimbursement against damage or loss. The indemnified party is protected against liabilities or penalties from that party's actions; the indemnifying party provides the protection or reimbursement.

INFLICTION OF EMOTIONAL DISTRESS A legal cause of action in which one party seeks to recover damages for mental pain and suffering caused by another.

INJUNCTION A court order restraining one party from doing or refusing to do an act.

INTEGRATION The act of making a contract whole by integrating its elements into a coherent single entity. An agreement is considered integrated when the parties involved accept the final version as a complete expression of their agreement.

INTERROGATORIES A pretrial device used to elicit information; written questions are sent to an opponent to be answered under oath.

INVASION OF PRIVACY The violation of a person's constitutionally protected right to privacy.

JUDGMENT A verdict rendered by a judicial body; if money is awarded, the winning party is the "judgment creditor" and the losing party is the "judgment debtor."

JURISDICTION The authority of a court to hear a particular matter.

LEGAL DUTY The responsibility of a party to perform a certain act.

LETTER OF AGREEMENT An enforceable contract in the form of a letter.

LETTER OF PROTEST A letter sent to document a party's dissatisfaction.

LIABLE Legally in the wrong or legally responsible for.

LIEN A claim made against the property of another in order to satisfy a judgment.

LIFETIME CONTRACT An employment agreement of infinite duration that is often unenforceable.

LIQUIDATED DAMAGES An amount of money agreed on in advance by parties to a contract to be paid in the event of a breach or dispute.

MALICIOUS INTERFERENCE WITH CONTRACTUAL RIGHTS A legal cause of action in which one party seeks to recover damages against an individual who has induced or caused another party to terminate a valid contract.

MALICIOUS PROSECUTION A legal cause of action in which one party seeks to recover damages after another party instigates or institutes a frivolous judicial proceeding (usually criminal) that is dismissed.

MEDIATION A voluntary dispute-resolution process in which both sides attempt to settle their differences without resorting to formal litigation.

MISAPPROPRIATION A legal cause of action that arises when one party makes untrue statements of fact that induce another party to act and be damaged as a result.

MITIGATION OF DAMAGES A legal principle that requires a party seeking damages to make reasonable efforts to reduce damages as much as possible; for example, to seek new employment after being unfairly discharged.

MOTION A written request made to a court by one party during a lawsuit.

NEGLIGENCE A party's failure to exercise a sufficient degree of care owed to another by law.

NOMINAL DAMAGES A small sum of money awarded by a court.

NONCOMPETITION CLAUSE A restrictive provision in a contract that limits an employee's right to work in that particular industry after he or she ceases to be associated with his or her present employer.

NOTARY PUBLIC A person authorized under state law to administer an oath or verify a signature.

NOTICE TO SHOW CAUSE A written document in a lawsuit asking a court to expeditiously rule on a matter.

OBJECTION A formal protest made by a lawyer in a lawsuit.

OFFER The presentment of terms, which, if accepted, may lead to the formation of a contract.

OPINION LETTER A written analysis of a client's case, prepared by a lawyer.

OPTION An agreement giving one party the right to choose a certain course of action.

ORAL CONTRACT An enforceable verbal agreement.

PAROL EVIDENCE Oral evidence introduced at a trial to alter or explain the terms of a written agreement.

PARTNERSHIP A voluntary association between two or more competent persons engaged in a business as co-owners for profit.

PARTY A plaintiff or defendant in a lawsuit.

PERJURY Committing false testimony while under oath.

PETITION A request filed in court by one party.

PLAINTIFF The party who commences a lawsuit.

PLEADING A written document that states the facts or arguments put forth by a party in a lawsuit.

POWER OF ATTORNEY A document executed by one party allowing another to act on his or her behalf in specified situations.

PRETRIAL DISCOVERY A legal procedure used to gather information from an opponent before the trial.

PROCESS SERVER An individual who delivers the summons and/or complaint to the defendant.

PROMISSORY NOTE A written acknowledgment of a debt whereby one party agrees to pay a specified sum on a specified date.

PROOF Evidence presented at a trial and used by a judge or jury to fashion an award.

PUNITIVE DAMAGES Money awarded as punishment for a party's wrongful acts.

QUANTUM MERUIT A legal principle whereby a court awards reasonable compensation to a party who performs work, labor, or services at another party's request.

REBUTTAL The opportunity for a lawyer at a trial to ask a client or witness additional questions to clarify points elicited by the opposing lawyer during cross-examination.

RELEASE A written document that, when signed, relinquishes a party's rights to enforce a claim against another.

REMEDY The means by which a right is enforced or protected.

REPLY A written document in a lawsuit conveying the contentions of a party in response to a motion.

RESTRICTIVE COVENANT A provision in a contract that forbids one party from doing a certain act, e.g., working for another, soliciting customers, etc.

RETAINER A sum of money paid to a lawyer for services to be rendered.

SERVICE LETTER STATUTES Laws in some states that require an employer to furnish an employee with written reasons for his or her discharge.

SEXUAL HARASSMENT Prohibited conduct of a sexual nature that occurs in the workplace.

SHOP RIGHTS The rights of an employer to use within the employer's facility a device or method developed by an employee.

SLANDER Oral defamation of a party's reputation.

SMALL-CLAIMS COURT A particular court that presides over small disputes (e.g., those involving sums of less than $2,500).

SOLE PROPRIETORSHIP An unincorporated business.

STATEMENT OF FACT Remarks or comments of a specific nature that have a legal effect.

STATUTE A law created by a legislative body.

STATUTE OF FRAUDS A legal principle requiring that certain contracts be in writing in order to be enforceable.

STATUTE OF LIMITATIONS A legal principle requiring a party to commence a lawsuit within a certain period of time.

STIPULATION An agreement between the parties.

SUBMISSION AGREEMENT A signed agreement whereby both parties agree to submit a present dispute to binding arbitration.

SUBPOENA A written order requiring a party or witness to appear at a legal proceeding; a subpoena duces tecum is a written order requiring a party to bring books and records to the legal proceeding.

SUMMATION The last part of the trial wherein both lawyers recap the respective positions of their clients.

SUMMONS A written document served on a defendant giving notification of a lawsuit.

TEMPORARY DECREE A court order or directive of a temporary nature, capable of being modified or changed.

TESTIMONY Oral evidence presented by a witness under oath.

"TIME IS OF THE ESSENCE" A legal expression often included in agreements to specify the requirement of timeliness.

TORT A civil wrong.

UNFAIR AND DECEPTIVE PRACTICE Illegal business and trade acts prohibited by various federal and state laws.

UNFAIR DISCHARGE An employee's termination without legal justification.

VERDICT The decision of a judge or jury.

VERIFICATION A written statement signed under oath.

WAIVER A written document that, when signed, relinquishes a party's rights.

WHISTLE-BLOWING Protected conduct where one party complains about the illegal acts of another.

WITNESS A person who testifies at a judicial proceeding.

WORKERS' COMPENSATION A process in which an employee receives compensation for injuries sustained in the course of employment.